P9-DNW-706

**THIS IS THE STORY
OF AN IOWA FARM FAMILY'S
HEARTBREAKING EXPERIENCE
DURING THE VIETNAM WAR.
WHAT HAPPENED TO THIS
FAMILY, HAPPENED TO AMERICA.**

FRIENDLY FIRE

**"Not since Truman Capote's IN COLD BLOOD
. . . has there been as powerful, as emotional
a piece of nonfiction."**

—Washington Star

"Writing so fine, so brilliantly done, that . . . it sometimes seems as if Eugene O'Neill were alive and well and practicing journalism."
—Boston Globe

"As close to elemental tragedy as any non-fiction account to come out of the war. Bryan conveys Peg Mullen's grief and rage with such purity and tact that at times she seems like a Middle Western Antigone."
—Time

"A triumph . . . Bryan has entered an elusive realm of universal truths related to war . . . He engages us—in a way that no Vietnam polemic or slogan or documentary or drama yet has."
—Chicago Sun-Times Book Week

"Powerfully affecting . . . A dramatic comment on what the war did to America."
—Saturday Review

"The Mullens' dogged probing of the 'why' of Mike's death peels back layer after layer . . . finally laying bare to them and the reader the larger conceptual failure of the cause in which he died."
—Newsweek

... an epic drama of a nation at war with itself

"Records the entire spectrum of attitudes and emotions, moral issues and political viewpoints which embroiled America over Vietnam . . . Bryan has documented a situation which details the paradox of war."
—Christian Science Monitor

"Great visceral power and emotional impact."
—Publishers Weekly

"An engrossing and quietly powerful, heartbreaking account of the Mullens' struggle—with themselves, their neighbors, their country—a portrait-in-microcosm of how the war tore us apart."
—Village Voice

"To read this book is to weep, to despair and ultimately to cheer ... It is a work of passionate energy."
—Washington Post Book World

"The great war stories do not deal solely with the death of soldiers but with the death of idealism, and Bryan's handling of that theme is certainly the finest that has come out of the Vietnam war."
—New York Times Book Review

FRIENDLY FIRE

C.D.B. BRYAN

BANTAM BOOKS · TORONTO · NEW YORK · LONDON

*This low-priced Bantam Book
has been completely reset in a type face
designed for easy reading, and was printed
from new plates. It contains the complete
text of the original hard-cover edition.*
NOT ONE WORD HAS BEEN OMITTED.

RLI: $\dfrac{\text{VLM 8 (VLR 6–9)}}{\text{IL 8+}}$

FRIENDLY FIRE

*A Bantam Book | published by arrangement with
G. P. Putnam's Sons*

PRINTING HISTORY

*Putnam's edition published May 1976
2nd printing .... August 1976*

Portions of this book have previously appeared in NEW YORKER
Magazine.

Book club editions have also been published by Book-of-the-
Month Club, Quality Paperback Book Service and Newsweek
Books.

*Bantam edition | May 1977
2nd printing
3rd printing
4th printing
5th printing*

*All rights reserved.
Copyright © 1976 by Courtlandt Dixon Barnes Bryan.
This book may not be reproduced in whole or in part, by
mimeograph or any other means, without permission.
For information address: G. P. Putnam's Sons,
200 Madison Avenue, New York, N.Y. 10016.*

ISBN 0-553-10858-1

Published simultaneously in the United States and Canada

*Bantam Books are published by Bantam Books, Inc. Its trade-
mark, consisting of the words "Bantam Books" and the por-
trayal of a bantam, is registered in the United States Patent
Office and in other countries. Marca Registrada. Bantam
Books, Inc., 666 Fifth Avenue, New York, New York 10019.*

PRINTED IN THE UNITED STATES OF AMERICA

To
Michael Eugene Mullen,
his family
and the men of Charlie Company,
1st Battalion, 6th Infantry,
198th Infantry Brigade, Americal Division,
who were with Michael on the night that he died

Author's Note

All the material in this book not derived from my own firsthand observation of the events is taken from historical texts, public or official records, original correspondence, journals kept by a participant or extended interviews with those persons directly involved. All interviews with the major participants were tape recorded. Transcripts of these interviews were then submitted to those individuals to provide them an opportunity to make corrections. In those few instances of disparate recollections or failing memory, I have had to rely upon the majority opinion and my own judgment in determining what actually took place.

In reconstructing those conversations which I was not present at, I have assumed that if an individual recalled what was said and this recollection was confirmed by a second individual and there was no obvious advantage to be gained from a depiction of the conversation as recalled, then a reconstruction using the dialogue as remembered might be accepted as true. In most instances with the Mullens it was possible to reconstruct their conversations through corroboration by a third party, notes taken by Peg Mullen at the time of the event and the consistency of details as recalled.

The reconstructed "Mission" chapter at the end of the book was achieved through separate interviews with Lieutenant Colonel H. Norman Schwarzkopf, Captain Tom Owen Cameron, Abraham Aikins, Martin L. Culpepper, Gary Samuels and Willard Polk, each of whom had either taken part in the planning of the operation or been present on the hilltop when Michael Mullen died. Each man received a transcript of his interview and subsequent reconstructed version of the mission for review and correction. Although Willard Polk's court-martial transcript was valuable for details of subsequent events, I naturally had to rely on the men's memories of that night. I am most grateful to them for their cooperation and the dedication with which they assisted me in getting the story right.

This is also as good a place as any to express my gratitude to certain other individuals who have been instrumental in this book: Carl D. Brandt, Harvey Ginsberg, William Shawn, Martin J. Baron and Sam.

I have taken the liberty of changing the names of some of the minor participants in this book.

I suppose one can never be satisfied that one has asked all the questions one might have asked, double-checked all the details one might have double-checked, seen all the people one might have seen. But because all the major people in this story have read the finished manuscript and have expressed their agreement with the incidents as described, I am confident that what I have written is true and that the events, scenes and conversations took place as depicted.

C. D. B. B.

Chapter One

✝

September 3, 1969, his last night of leave, Michael Eugene Mullen worked until ten o'clock on his family's 120-acre farm five miles west of La Porte City in Black Hawk County, Iowa. He remained down in the lower 80 acres upon his father's old plum-red Farmall H-series tractor ripping out brush and dead trees, bulldozing the trash into the dry streambed of Miller's Creek, clearing and filling in the land so it could be used as pasture again.

By midnight, when his father, Gene Mullen, had returned from working the late shift at the huge John Deere tractor plant in Waterloo, Michael had completed his packing and was still awake talking to his younger brother, John, behind the closed door of the bedroom they shared. Peg Mullen, Michael's mother, and Mary and Patricia, his two younger sisters, were asleep, so Gene made himself a cup of instant coffee and sat alone at the kitchen table. From where he sat Gene could see Michael's Vietnam orders resting on the same little corner table in the living room where they had stayed during his older son's entire twenty-three-day advance leave. One morning, when Michael had picked up the thick sheaf of duplicate orders and riffled through them absently, Gene had said, "Mikey?"

Michael put the orders down. "Yes, Dad?"

"Mikey, what are you going to *do?*"

Michael met his father's look with a thin, uneasy smile. "I guess, Dad," he said, "I guess I'm going to do what they taught me to do."

Gene started to ask, "How?" Michael, as a boy, could not bear to be present when livestock were slaughtered. Gene wondered how the Army had been

1

able to teach Michael to kill. He had started to tell his son that he believed the force that makes people kill is the greatest evil on earth. But Gene hadn't said anything, and Michael did not speak either.

And so that last night of Michael's leave, Gene sat cradling the mug of coffee in his hands, listening to the muted voices of his sons. Then he stood up and knocked on their bedroom door. Michael opened it. Gene could see beyond his son the closed barracks bags, the Army uniform and shined black shoes set out for the morning.

"Would you like anything from the kitchen, Michael? A beer?"

Michael finished locking up his metal tackle box. It held his arrowhead collection, special letters, snapshots, the corporal stripes he'd earned at Fort Benning, addresses, insurance papers.

"No, no thanks, Dad," Michael said. He carefully taped the key to the lid and slid the tackle box onto the top shelf of his closet.

Gene, still standing in the doorway, could not look away from Michael's uniform hanging on the back of the open closet door.

"Mikey?"

"Yes?"

"Be careful?"

Michael smiled at his father. "I will, Dad. I will."

The next morning was warm and sunny. John got up early and caught the bus to school. Michael was all packed and in his uniform. Breakfast was over, the dishes done. Gene kept looking at the electric clock over the oven. "What time did you say your plane left?" he asked.

"Ten," Michael said. "I have to check in by nine thirty."

Michael looked at his watch, and Gene glanced again at the electric clock over the wall oven door.

Peg was moving back and forth across the kitchen, dabbing at counters with a sponge. "Would anyone like some more coffee?"

"No thanks," Gene said.

2

"You, Michael?"

"No thanks, Mom."

"What time is it?" Patricia asked him.

And before Michael could tell her, he had to look at his wristwatch once more.

Gene stood up, tucked in his shirt and walked over to the kitchen window. He bumped into Peg turning around and apologized.

The Mullens decided to leave for the Waterloo Airport early. Gene drove with Michael sitting up front next to him. Peg, Patricia and Mary sat in the back. The family hardly spoke.

The center of Waterloo is about fifteen miles northwest of the Mullens' farm, and the airport is another few miles beyond that on the other side of town. They drove past the big new shopping center on Route 218 with the Hy-Vee Market, the Sears and J.C. Penney stores. Gene said something about how fast all that area was changing, and Michael agreed.

They passed the Robo-Wash and Burger King, Donutland and the Cadillac Bowling Lanes, and soon they were caught up in Waterloo traffic. They cleared the city, and beyond were the flatlands and railroad tracks they had to cross before reaching the airport.

Michael wouldn't let his father help him with the barracks bags, insisting it would be easier for him to carry them both himself. The Mullens entered the terminal building a little after nine. They took seats in the small, near-empty waiting room and stared out the large window at the vacant airfield.

Michael kept wiping his palms on his knees.

"Do you need a magazine?" Peg asked. "Something to read?"

Michael stood up abruptly. "Maybe I can check in anyway," he said.

"It's still early yet," his father said.

"I know. But maybe I can check in."

"I'll go with you," Mary said.

"No, don't." Michael smiled at her. "I'll be right back."

Peg worriedly followed her son with her eyes.

3

"He looks scared," Patricia said.

"He's fine!" Gene said gruffly.

A few minutes later Michael returned waving his tickets. He sat back down next to his mother. "I'm all checked in."

"Did you get a magazine?" she asked.

"I'll read something on the plane."

"Do you have everything?"

"I'm fine, Mom. *Really*."

Peg looked away from her son and out the window.

When Michael's plane landed, he stood up and his family rose with him.

"Look," Michael told them, "don't stick around for the plane to leave. You don't have to wait."

"We'll wait," his mother announced firmly.

"No, please," Michael insisted, "I'll be all right." He went to Mary and Patricia and told them goodbye, that they shouldn't wait around, that they should tell John there'd be a lot more work now that he was going. And Patricia and Mary each had a moment to themselves with Michael, a chance to tell him to take care of himself, to be careful, that they would pray for him, miss him, that they loved him and would write letters all the time and would send him things, anything, all he had to do was tell them what he needed. Michael kissed them each, and they moved away because it was their parents' turn.

Gene fingered a small bronze medallion the size of a twenty-five-cent piece that hung from a chain around his neck. The medal, depicting the Virgin Mary, had been struck in commemoration of the first Catholic missionaries who went into China. The inscription around it was in Chinese. The medallion had been given Gene thirty-five years earlier by a Chinese student he had befriended when they were undergraduates together at Marquette University in Milwaukee. Gene had worn it ever since. He lifted its chain from around his neck and handed it to his son, saying, "Mikey, I've tried to give you everything. . . ." Gene's voice broke, and he took a deep breath and

4

began again: "Tried to do everything that a father could do. . . ."

Michael was looking down at the medallion now chestnut-colored with age.

"I wore this medal through the Second World War," Gene was saying. "It protected me, and so I give you this . . . I give you. . . ." He could say no more. Gene looked at his son, half in pride, half in agony, his throat too tight to speak.

"I'll wear it," Michael said. He loosened his black Army tie and unbuttoned the collar button of his khaki shirt. He draped the medal and chain around his neck, carefully centered it with the dog tags on his chest and buttoned his shirt back over it. Michael then turned to his mother and hugged her.

It was an awkward embrace, shorter in duration than either of them wished. When Michael stepped back, he was startled to see his mother's eyes were damp. He could not remember ever having seen her cry before. Michael put his hand out to comfort his mother, and she took it. When Peg looked up at her son, she, too, was unable to speak.

"Mom?" Michael said. "Don't worry yourself now, okay?" He squeezed her hand lightly and repeated, "Okay?"

His mother just looked at him, shaking her head sadly.

"Come on now, Mom, please?" Michael pleaded. "It'll . . . it will all be over March first, okay?"

He gently pulled his hand from hers, picked up his barracks bags and turned away. Peg unconsciously pressed the hand he'd been holding to her lips. She watched her son walk past the cafeteria toward the doors that would lead to his plane. Michael stopped in the narrow passageway, dropped his barracks bags and turned back for one last look at his family. But as they started toward him, he quickly lifted his bags and hurried out the door.

Michael's family moved closer to the big picture window and stood silently staring at the airplane. They saw Michael again when he took a seat at a window on the near side just behind the wing. He did not wave.

5

He did not move. He simply sat there framed by the silver airplane's window, looking out at them as they looked back in at him.

Mary and Patricia cried quietly on the drive back to the farm. Peg could see that Gene was gripping the steering wheel so tightly his knuckles were white. When they were once again on the other side of Waterloo, back on Route 218 past the Robo-Wash and Burger King heading toward their farm, Peg resolved to cheer everybody up by telling them what Michael had said just before boarding the plane.

"Why March first?" Gene asked her.

"I don't know," Peg said. "He just told me not to worry. That it would all be over then."

On March 1, 1970, Michael Eugene Mullen, age twenty-five, was returned to the Waterloo Airport in a U.S. Army issue twenty-gauge silver-gray casket.

And one year after that, his mother was under surveillance by the FBI.

Chapter Two

++

Long before the sacrifice of their oldest son the Mullens had earned their place upon that prairie land. Michael was to have been the fifth generation of his family to work their same Iowa fields and the most recent link in an unbroken family chain reaching back through more than two-thirds of our history as a nation to John Dobshire, his paternal great-great-grandfather, who, seeking a better life in the new land, emigrated from Ireland in 1833, leaving behind his wife, Ellen, and their then nine-month-old daughter, Mary Ann.

The America John Dobshire arrived in, the America of the 1830s, was still a nation of rural people living for the most part on farms or in country villages. And even though at the start of that decade the number of persons living west of the Allegheny Mountains —west, in other words, of central Pennsylvania —was beginning to approach the population to their east, vast tracts of land across the Mississippi River did not belong to the United States, and still greater areas, though they "belonged," had not yet been explored.

Iowa had not become a part of the United States until the Louisiana Purchase in 1803. Although the state was named after the Iowa (also, Ioway) Indians who were part of the Winnebago people originally living north by the Great Lakes, in 1804, when the explorers Lewis and Clark first came upon the Iowa, the tribe had been so decimated by smallpox that there were fewer than 800 left. They were living not in "Iowa" but where the Platte River joins the Missouri in what is now Nebraska.

The Indians who dominated Iowa at the start of the nineteenth century were the Sioux in the west and north, the Potawatami (also, Pottawatami) in the north-central part of the state, and the Sauk (also, Sac) and Fox, (in their language, the Mesquakie), whose vast domain centered on the Mississippi River and extended north to the Wisconsin River, east to the Illinois River, south into what is now Missouri and west across the gently rolling plains of east-central Iowa into what would become the Mullens' land. Saukenuk, the chief Sauk village, lay just north of where the Rock River flows into the Mississippi at what is now Rock Island—one of the "Quad Cities" of Rock Island, Davenport and East Moline. At the time of the Louisiana Purchase the Sauk and Fox had already been planting their corn at Saukenuk for more than 100 years. Black Hawk, the Sauk warrior chief after whom the Mullens' Black Hawk County in Iowa is named, was born in Saukenuk in 1767. He was forty-five years old in 1812 when the British and Americans returned to war. Black Hawk stood about five feet four inches, had a high, sloping forehead, ruddy, angular features and shaved his head clean except for the scalp lock to which eagle feathers, the mark of his warrior status, were tied. With very little urging, British agents won Black Hawk and others of the Sauk-Fox Confederation over to their side; Black Hawk was given the rank of colonel and fought next to Tecumseh and the British against the Americans, wearing a British "red coat" and war paint.

For the next twenty years Black Hawk defiantly resisted every attempt by the whites to expand into his lands. Not until 1832 was Black Hawk subdued. Abraham Lincoln, then a twenty-three-year-old captain in the Illinois Militia, rode off to take part in this "Black Hawk War" on a borrowed horse. Jefferson Davis, then a young lieutenant, escorted Black Hawk to Jefferson Barracks, where the now sixty-five-year-old warrior spent his winter shackled and chained.

Black Hawk's imprisonment removed the last formidable barrier to westward expansion into the unorganized territory of Iowa; and on June 1, 1833, the Iowa lands were officially opened. Previous to that

8

date only a small trickle of whites had crossed the Mississippi; the Army had been ordered to turn back anyone who attempted to settle on the other side. Of course, some white men had gone among the Indians, had established trading posts, hunted, mined and prospected, intermarried. Explorers had traced the Mississippi and Missouri river valleys. But the "Iowa" that existed when John Dobshire landed in America was still considered the "Far West," a dark wasteland on the Indian frontier beyond which lay the Great American Desert. Iowa's vast prairie fields were then considered "almost unwholly fit for cultivation."

On June 1, 1838, Iowa achieved formal territorial status and included in addition to what is now the present state of Iowa, lands which would become Minnesota, and North and South Dakota as well. One of the initial problems, however, was resolving where to build the territorial capital. It was finally agreed that the proper site should be along the banks of the Iowa River, but because the location selected was still so remote and unsettled that no trail went to it, it was doubtful whether any pioneer or new territorial legislator would even be able to find the spot. A Mr. Lyman Dillard was therefore hired to plow a guide furrow 100 miles west across the prairie from the Mississippi River to the site chosen for the territorial capital to be called Iowa City.

On the Fourth of July, 1838, in celebration of Iowa's formal territorial status and the nation's sixty-second year of independence, the citizens of Fort Madison at Iowa's southeastern tip invited Black Hawk to be their Independence Day guest of honor. Black Hawk had been released from prison only four years before and placed with his family on the reservation near Fort Des Moines. A banquet table was set up on a bluff overlooking the Mississippi River, and the old warrior chief, now seventy-one years old, his skin parched and wrinkled, his legs needing a cane for support, sat at the table beneath the shade trees and listened to their words of friendship and unity, progress and prosperity, strength and peace. And when they

9

called on him to speak, Black Hawk pushed himself to his feet, steadied himself and talked to them of the past.

"Rock River was a beautiful country," he told them. "I loved my villages . . . my cornfields . . . the home of my people. I *fought* for them!" He glared at the white men seated around him, and then, looking beyond the banquet table to the broad Mississippi below, Black Hawk paused lost in memories. The citizens of Fort Madison waited patiently for him again to speak.

"I was once a great warrior . . . a great warrior . . . now," Black Hawk said in almost a whisper, "now I am poor. . . . Now I am . . . old."

Three months later, on October 3, 1838, Black Hawk died and was buried sitting erect within a small log mausoleum near his home. The following year an Illinois doctor dug up Black Hawk's remains and attempted to exhibit them for profit. When Black Hawk's bones were finally recovered, they were placed on display in the Geographical & Historical Building in Burlington, Iowa.

The Mullens do not know when John Dobshire first set foot in Iowa; in fact, they aren't really sure what he did for the thirteen years following his arrival in America in 1833. They *believe* he came out to Iowa in 1846, looked the land over, then left to serve as a driver of supply wagons for Zachary Taylor during the Mexican War. Taylor was known to like Irishmen, and during that period of "No Mick Hired" prejudice, a teamster job with the Army meant not only an income, but the promise of a presidential land grant after the war. John Dobshire had nothing against the Mexicans; he saw military service simply as his only opportunity to help his wife and daughter escape Ireland.

John Dobshire returned to Ireland in 1850 after an absence of seventeen years. During the potato famines of 1845 and 1846 more than 1,000,000 Irish died of malnutrition and disease. Coffins were openly offered for sale at county fairs, and fallen bodies were

10

being devoured by packs of starving dogs. Nearly one out of every eight Irish man, woman and child between 1841 and 1851 had succumbed to cholera, typhus, starvation or a famine-related epidemic disease. Out of those who had survived, more than one out of eight decided to emigrate—predominantly to the United States. Among these, of course, were John and Ellen Dobshire and their now eighteen-year-old daughter, Mary Ann. The Dobshires must have been fully aware of the ocean crossing's risks. During the years 1847–1853 fifty-nine ships carrying Irish and British emigrants to North America were lost at sea. In 1847 alone, it has been estimated that one out of every two emigrants died. One of those who died that year was Peg Mullens' great-grandfather, whose twelve-year-old daughter, Peg's Grandmother Wolfe, was left to continue the crossing to New York alone.

After landing in America, the Dobshires journeyed directly to New Orleans, where they boarded a paddle-wheel steamboat for the trip up the Mississippi River to Dubuque. The river might have seemed tame after the ocean, but the Dobshires must have been alarmed by the shriek of the steamboat's whistle, the steady rain of curses from the pilothouse—glassed in and gingerbreaded like some fantasy mansion's gazebo, and the thick black smoke and shower of sparks pouring out those elegantly towering rose-petaled stacks. Consider also the Dobshires' concern at the sudden, shocking thump as the steamboat hit an underwater log or a raft that had broken loose, the ragged, shifting rhythm of the engine, the clamor of bells, whistles and orders screamed back and forth as their steamboat maneuvered over the shoals. Still, there was that vast soothing panorama of land passing by: the great plantations set back from the levees, the cotton fields worked by hundreds of slaves, and farther north, as the languorous sweep of the paddle blades walked their boat up the river, the small, drowsing riverbank towns. The Dobshires, leaning out over the carved and ornamental railings, could not help having sensed the excitement of the young country, seen the energy of the farmers, observed the pride the set-

11

tlers took in their little houses and marked the groups of Indians restlessly edging along the shore.

In Dubuque John Dobshire purchased a prairie schooner, a flatbed lumber wagon with a canvas top which could be drawn in for shelter at each end. Unlike the more famous Conestoga wagon, the prairie schooner was light enough to be pulled by two horses or a yoke of oxen even on virgin prairie trails. Two German immigrants, Isaac and Jacob Walker, made friends with the Dobshires and decided to accompany them to the new lands.

Gene Mullen likes to think of their two wagons crossing the prairie together, the tall grasses higher than their wagons' wheels. He pictures his great-grandfather's prairie schooner with its barrel of water strapped to its side, the bucket of grease for its axles, an iron skillet, perhaps, gently banging back and forth. He wonders what goods they might have brought with them from Ireland. Only a darkened tin tea canister with an elaborate raised floral relief has survived. It sits now on the bureau in what had been Michael's side of the boys' room.

John Dobshire chose to homestead the site upon which the Mullens' modern ranch-style farmhouse now stands because there was a plentiful water supply—he was within two miles of the Cedar River and within a short walk of Miller's Creek. There were springs on the top of his hill—a hill so slight one is hardly aware of it as such. About a half mile east of his homestead stood two very tall trees, one a black walnut, the other an oak. "They were the monarchs of the forest," recalled A. J. Peck, who homesteaded in Black Hawk County ten years after the Dobshires arrived. "They were, I suppose, the survival of the fittest, for all that growth had been blown down by a terrible tornado perhaps a century before as their prostrate forms were in evidence all through the woods. The tall oak was called 'The Old Eagle Tree' for every year a pair of eagles built their nest there." (*1910 Atlas of Black Hawk County*)

And just to the west of the Dobshires was another landmark: a huge, lone boulder that must have been left behind by the glaciers. It lies atop the next slight hill like the fallen plinth of some vanished Stonehenge or the brow of some half-buried monolithic Easter Island head. Hubbard Frost, who came to Black Hawk County after the Civil War and homesteaded the land on which the boulder rests, would drive his wagon into La Porte City—then but an infant town—and if he were unable to return before nightfall, his wife would light a fire atop the rock as a beacon to guide him home.

It is difficult to comprehend the terrible isolation the Dobshires must have felt. One can only try to imagine that most awful, poignant, physical loneliness endured by the young daughter, Mary Ann, whose entire life centered on her mother, this strange father she barely knew and an occasional encounter with the two German-speaking Walker boys. For those living on that unbroken prairie sea, the simple act of getting from one place to another required a major effort of planning and preparations and, in Mary Ann's case above all, a liberty she was doubtless denied. Even had she been free to travel and wished to, there was no place for her to go. In 1852 La Porte did not exist. There were no settlements larger than a few cabins and a sawmill anywhere within miles. Dubuque, the closest "city," was more than a week's travel away.

The land alone sustained the Dobshires; they depended on it to survive. What they could grow, they ate. They chopped through the thick matted roots of the prairie grass to reach the soil, planted their corn, their wheat, cleared more and more of the prairie so they could plant more crops. The abundance harvested then had to be measured out and put away to carry them through the harsh winters. There were wildfowl and game, and they ate what meat John Dobshire could kill. Dobshire's gun was not for taking life, but for maintaining it; his ability to provide for his family was dependent upon his ability to shoot. And if there were no meat from Dobshire's winter hunts, and if his women had failed properly to preserve the produce harvested before, the family could expect only a cold and unforgiving death. But even if the land supported

13

them, they had still to contend with Iowa's brutal weather.

Winter brought gale-force Arctic winds, blizzards, weeks of twenty-below-zero cold. Monstrous snowdrifts crushed in roofs, buried wagons, livestock, woodpiles. Settlers sickened in the iciness and could not survive the fifteen-mile lung-searing journey to the nearest doctor. Hailstorms killed hogs, chickens; cabins caught fire, and their inhabitants froze to death going for help.

In the spring torrential rains washed the earth from the hillsides, gullied the ditches into streams that overflowed the homesteads, drowned the freshly seeded fields, flooded the rivers which fed the Mississippi and swept the topsoil out to sea. Oxen and wagons mired down in the mud, and John Deere's newly invented sodbuster iron plows had to be abandoned in midfield.

Then suddenly it would be summer and thunderstorms would savage the air; wind-whipped prairie fires would race across the shoulder-high grasses with frightening speed. Thick, gargantuan, kettle-black clouds would explode with lightning, and tornadoes would visit Armageddon upon tiny, unsuspecting religious settlements. The Dobshires learned to sense a tornado's coming, smell it, feel its heavy breath on the darkening air. And always there would be that heat, that incandescent whiteness that bubbled the pitch in raw wood or left the air so webbed and close the birds would not even bother to fly. Then the evening sky flashed and flickered with summer lightning; moths beat themselves to ashes against the kerosene lamps. The moon would rise huge and full, and the prairie wolves would howl with summer madness beneath the canopy of stars.

In the fall the winds would come and cool the cornstalks. The months of jarring and preserving, of grinding flour and tanning hides would be upon them. John Dobshire, out gathering wood along the banks of the Cedar River, would look up at the great skeins of duck and geese, watch them form their august Vs and beat their way south. The corn would be harvested, the wheat gathered and threshed. The grouse would

14

call, the incredible swarms of passenger pigeons (whose numbers then could be measured only by square miles) would whirl and scatter like an old lady's handwriting, gather again, then flash away. The buffalo would pass, fewer and fewer with each succeeding year. The first snow would fall, and at night, looking out their cabin window, the Dobshires might see the lantern of a far-off wagon glowing as brightly as a distant boat across a glaze of frozen water, like some ephemeral voyager upon a tideless sea.

Since John Dobshire could neither read nor write, no record exists of what homesteading meant to him. The Mullens do know that the Dobshires spent their first winter, the winter of 1852, in their prairie schooner and three times fled their homestead when Indians, coming up the Cedar River from Tama to hunt and fish, scared the family away. John Dobshire took his wife and daughter for refuge to Sturgis Falls, where there was a sawmill and a gristmill and a couple of cabins. (Sturgis Falls would later grow into the City of Cedar Falls.) There was a closer settlement at Waterloo—called Prairie Rapids then—containing six cabins and a post office. But Dobshire chose Sturgis Falls because of the sawmill, and when he built his house the following spring, it was made of cut boards, not logs like those of the Black Hawk County homesteaders around him. John Dobshire's small house, completed in 1853, sheltered his descendants off and on for the next 100 years. It was the house to which Peg and Gene Mullen returned with their infant son, Michael, following Gene's service in the Second World War.

In 1855 Dobshire had occupied his homestead for three years and was qualified to receive his forty-acre site free for his service during the Mexican War. The land grant is "for the North West quarter of the North West quarter of Section Nine, in Township Eighty-Seven, North of Range Twelve, West," and the document states:

the UNITED STATES OF AMERICA, in consideration of the premises, and in conformity with the several acts of Congress in such case,

15

made and provided, HAVE GIVEN AND GRANTED, and by these premises DO GIVE AND GRANT unto the said JOHN DOBSHIRE and to his heirs, the said tract above described, TO HAVE AND TO HOLD the same, together with all the rights and appurtenances of whatsoever nature belonging unto the said JOHN DOBSHIRE and to his heirs and assigns forever.

There is a special quality to that document's language, a self-portrait of America at that time: a slight swagger, an unconscious arrogance, a need to impose man's orderly straight-lined numerical boundaries upon nature's abundant chaos, a sense that all that open space must be filled. But most of all, there must have seemed to John Dobshire, when the land grant was read to him, a boundlessly optimistic promise, an absolute certainty in all that goodness to be his family's . . . *forever!*

The year Dobshire received his land grant, the Geographical & Historical Society Building in Burlington, Iowa, was consumed by fire. Among those display cases totally destroyed was the one containing Black Hawk's bones.

That same year also the Illinois Central Railroad reached the east bank of the Mississippi opposite Dubuque. Among the section hands laying track was young Patrick J. Mullen, Michael's paternal great-grandfather-to-be. Patrick, who had emigrated from Ireland five years before, was then twenty-one, stood about five feet eight inches, was thin but hard and broad-shouldered. He had thick black hair, a narrow face with prominent cheekbones and dark eyes that appeared deepset and somewhat close together because of his nose, which projected out from above his wide, straight mouth like a hatchet blade. Patrick Mullen quit the railroad at its river terminus and crossed the Mississippi to Dubuque.

Dubuque, by then, had already become a thriving river port, a lumber and milling center and a major supply and jumping-off place for settlers heading west. Patrick probably stayed in one of the two-story brick-front and wood-sidinged hotels—they were more like

16

boardinghouses, really, with gaslit parlors and kerosene lamps in the rooms. He might have shared the front parlor with the ebullient salesmen, the dour merchants, grizzled soldiers, adventurers and small-time gamblers looking for a stake. He would certainly have shared a meal with other young settlers and discussed their hopes in the future or seen in their faces their despair at what the past had failed to provide. Patrick J. Mullen, like all the others, must have suffered the disorientation and anxiety of waiting. They were all alike in these frontier towns, stalled on their journeys from some *place* to some *where*. And so they sat around those gaslit parlors, eagerly scanning the newest issue of the Du Buque *Visitor* with its advertisements for land, the latest business opportunities, the most recent settlers' reports, searching for some sign, some indication, some hint of what to expect when next they moved on.

Late in 1855 Patrick continued west and met John and Ellen Dobshires' daughter, Mary Ann. He courted her through the harsh winter, and she consented to be his bride that spring. They were wed by a French missionary priest in a little log cabin church across the Cedar River at Gilbertville. About this time John Dobshire bought out the two German Walker boys and took title to their eighty acres northwest of his land grant forty, the same eighty-acre piece that Michael Mullen worked his last night of leave. After their marriage Patrick and Mary Ann moved to Waterloo.

That summer Calvin W. Eighmey built a small log house about two miles west of John Dobshire's homestead site. Eighmey's younger brother recalled:

> One day Calvin and his wife were afforded a peculiar spectacle. A wagon pulled by a yoke of oxen, driven by a man and woman, was seen approaching in the distance. And it was a sight so unusual to see anyone passing over the prairie that they watched them with interest. When within a short distance of the house, the man stood up in the wagon, took off his hat, waved it about, and gave some lusty whoops that might have done credit to an Apache. Calvin had never be-

fore seen the people, and their unusual actions were explained by the man to be only expressions of joy at seeing someone else living on the wild prairie. The couple proved to be settlers who lived farther east and the two families became very intimate friends. *(1910 Atlas of Black Hawk County)*

The man in the wagon who had whooped with such joy might have been John Dobshire. He and his wife had already been living to the east for five years, and with the departure of their only child and the Walker brothers, they must have felt awesomely alone.

Two years later, on August 5, 1858, the last great meeting of Indian tribes in Black Hawk County took place. The Sauk had long since been moved to their reservation outside Des Moines, the new state capital, but the Potawatami, the Winnebago, the Musquakie and the Omaha still drifted back and forth across the land. However, despite rumors of trouble caused by occasional marauding bands, no serious incidents since the settlement of that part of Iowa had occurred. The meeting, between the Winnebago and Potawatami, was held just north of Waterloo.

The meeting was called by Little Priest, a Winnebago chief, who with his band had arrived at the Fork of the Cedar near Newell's in Washington and Union townships. The Pottawattami braves had been invited to meet them there.

The Pottawattami arrived opposite Janesville and ferried over, the river being very high. They formed in battle array a mile north of Newell's house, and marched to the Winnebago tents in columns twelve deep, breaking into a circle and firing their guns and beating their drums every hundred yards. When they reached the Winnebago tents, they dismounted and fired a salute, the squaws taking care of the horses.

A great feast was served and at night they had a dance witnessed by many white settlers. The next morning a Council was held, speeches made, followed by smoking "the pipe of peace" at which each Indian took a puff, the Pottawattami chief lighting it and passing it to Little Priest.

The whites tried to induce the Indians to repeat the dance of the night before, but to no purpose. The Indians packed up at once and were all gone at the time announced.

(Mrs. Julian W. Richards,
History of Black Hawk County)

C. A. Rownd of nearby Cedar Township witnessed that meeting, too, and his impression in its succinctness is even sadder: "The last Indian Council between the Winnebagoes and Pottawattamies was smoked at Turkey Ford Forks. Then they drifted west to die or become 'cabin indians.' " (*1910 Black Hawk County Atlas*)

In 1860 Patrick and Mary Ann Mullen left Waterloo and bought a parcel of land in the northwest corner of Section 18, two miles west of John Dobshire's farm. There Patrick Mullen opened a creamery route and quarry—many of the stone buildings in nearby communities were built of Patrick Mullen's stone. But his primary reason for moving was that the Dubuque and Sioux City Railroad reached Waterloo that year and Patrick knew it was time to farm.

It would be difficult to overestimate the impact the railroad made on that area. The years of isolation, loneliness, the estrangement born of living separated physically and emotionally from the rest of the country were ended. The solitary homesteader adrift in his acres of wheat and corn could hear, in the steam engine's slamming, shrieking passage across the plains, the boisterous, welcoming call of a nation which not only wanted but needed all he could produce. Patrick quit his job as a laborer in Waterloo because now that distant markets had become accessible the demand for farm products created a financial opportunity he could not ignore.

Patrick J. Mullen and Mary Ann Dobshire Mullen had seven sons and five daughters; two of the sons, however, died in infancy. Patrick put every piece of

19

money he could spare into purchasing more land. As soon as he had a son old enough to drive a team of horses, he would buy more acres for that son to work. Gene Mullen's father, Oscar L. Mullen, was born on July 29, 1880. John Dobshire died when Gene's father was six years old.

At his death Dobshire left his 120-acre homestead to his wife, Ellen, who in turn deeded it over to their daughter, Mary Ann, on the condition that she "agree to support and maintain said Ellen Dobshire during her natural life and furnish her with proper food, suitable clothing, proper attention and medical care during sickness, and pay all funeral expenses after her death." If Mary Ann should prove willing, then "this land shall stand as security for the faithful performance of said contract."

John Dobshire was buried in the small Catholic cemetery at Eagle Center on Section 15, about five miles southwest of his farm. Andrew Jackson, himself the son of Irish immigrants, had been President of the United States when John Dobshire emigrated to America; Grover Cleveland was President when Dobshire died. While John Dobshire had gone about his daily chores, the first oil wells at Titusville were dug. Mrs. O'Leary's cow set fire to Chicago's heart. General Custer was massacred at the Little Bighorn. Thomas Edison invented the electric light, Alexander Graham Bell the telephone. Four major railroads now crossed the Iowa prairies; New York to San Francisco was but a seven-day trip. John Dobshire lived long enough to see the "Far West" he had helped settle become but a passing glance out the window of a transcontinental train. After the funeral Ellen Dobshire moved into her daughter and son-in-law's new house.

Patrick J. Mullen had become one of the most successful farmers in Black Hawk County, land-rich enough to provide each of his five sons with his own driving team. The new two-story frame house, built to shelter his growing family, was on a slight hill about a mile south of his original quarry homestead near one of the loops of Miller's Creek. By 1910 Patrick J. Mullen owned more than 1,000 acres in Black Hawk

20

County and an additional 640 acres in Palo Alto County 180 miles to the northwest.

Northwest Iowa was still open range, and during the summers some of Patrick's sons would load their father's purebred Herefords onto the railroad cars at Waterloo and travel with them to Fort Dodge. There the boys would unload the cattle and drive them north to Emmetsburg, where the livestock would remain all summer fattening up on Patrick Mullen's grazing land. Patrick's other sons would meanwhile be tending the Black Hawk County farmlands, one-third of which would be in row corn, one-third in wheat and the remaining third resting up as pastureland. The quarry continued in operation, and in addition to the Herefords, Patrick raised Percheron horses for sale to the Chicago breweries and never had fewer than seventy draft and driving horses in his huge new L-shaped barn.

Oscar L. Mullen and Margaret McDermott, Gene's mother and father, were married at Blessing, Iowa, on February 12, 1908. By 1910 Gene's father was listed as the manager of his father's Grand Hereford Stock Farm, and Gene's mother, had already become involved in local Democratic politics—an activity which would remain the consuming interest of her life. Oscar's older brother, L. G. Mullen, managed their father's Miller Creek Stock Farm which adjoined the Grand Hereford farm in Section 18's northwest corner. Patrick's oldest son had become a lawyer; the two youngest still worked in the fields.

Although Patrick Mullen had retired at the turn of the century, he retained titular control of his lands. On the 1910 maps of Cedar, Eagle and Big Creek townships in Black Hawk County a total of 1186.64 acres, valued at between $80 and $125 an acre, is listed in the Mullen name. In addition, the 640 acres of northwest rangeland was worth about $50 an acre at that time. So Patrick and Mary Ann Mullen had reason to be pleased with themselves, and evidence exists that they were.

Patrick paid to have a photograph of his austere two-story frame house included in the *1910 Atlas of*

Black Hawk County. The house was painted gray with contrasting white trim edging the corners and the eaves beneath the roof. There were ornate carved lintels over the windows and doors, neat white shutters for every downstairs window and the two windows on the second floor beneath the peak of the roof. The house had two chimneys and a tidy front walk of crushed quarry gravel leading directly to the larger of the two porches. With his proper farmer's sense of perspective, however, Patrick paid to have two other photographs placed in the *Atlas,* too. They depicted his Percheron and Hereford breeding stock posed in front of his barns.

The photographs are small, no more than 2½ by 2 inches, but one can recognize Patrick and Mary Ann Mullen seated stiffly on their porch above their sons and daughters gathered on the porch steps and lawn below. Their faces are no larger than the head of a pin, but with the help of a magnifying glass it is possible to make out five young men and five young women, one of whom appears to be holding a child. The Mullen sons are wearing dark suits and soft derbies; the daughters are in long skirts and high-collared puffed-sleeved blouses, their faces shaded by elaborately fashionable hats. Patrick and Mary Ann, alone, are bareheaded. They are seated on almost opposite sides of the porch from each other, she with her white hair pulled severely back, one hand covering the other in her lap. Patrick is sitting ramrod straight, his feet planted squarely in front of him. Their posture— rigid, proud, formal, all sharp horizontals and verticals —curiously resembles the house.

Gene Mullen tells of his Grandmother Mullen developing a "felon," an extremely painful pus-producing infection at the end of her little finger beneath the nail. To rid herself of the agony it caused her, she simply chopped the end of that finger off. It could not have seemed to her a particularly significant act compared to what she had already been through. After all, she had survived the potato famine and pestilence in Ireland, the absence of her father for seventeen years. She had braved the ocean crossing, made the physical and perhaps more difficult emotional adjustment to the new land. She had overcome the terrible isolation of those early years, the loss of two sons in infancy, and had had the strength to rear ten children more. She had helped her young Irish husband "bust" through the thick prairie sod, survive the fierce winters, the prairie fires, tornadoes, floods, blistering heat. She had buried her father and unhesitatingly taken her mother in, and when her mother's time had come, Mary Ann buried her, too, next to her father in the Eagle Center plot. She had placed her trust in God and seen her faith and devotion rewarded. There is then a strange Biblical sensibility to her act: if thy fingertip offend thee, cast it off.

Even La Porte City was booming. What did it matter if Main Street was dust-blown in the summer, a mud bog in the spring and icebound in winter? It was wide enough to accommodate the wagon trains that continued to pass through with their loads of lumber, wheat, corn and hogs. The sidewalks were wooden planks placed upon the dirt with boardwalks laid to cross to the corners. Patrick could ride his old black mare, Dolly, into town to purchase his Dan Patch chewing tobacco, fill himself with whiskey and sell his eggs. His youngest boys could get a Coca-Cola at the brick-fronted Norris Drug Company where there existed even a fair selection of cigars. It was possible to buy Paine's Celery Compound which was 21 percent alcohol or, for sore muscles, Barker's Liniment, whose slogan was "Joy to the World, Relief has Come!" La Porte's population had reached 1,400, and "As a business location and place of residence," crowed the *1910 Black Hawk County Atlas,* "La Porte City cannot be excelled in Iowa."

Unfortunately, neither La Porte nor the Mullens would have it quite so good again.

Chapter Three

+++

Mary Ann Dobshire Mullen died in 1914; she was seventy-six. Patrick J. Mullen died eleven years later on March 26, 1925, just nine days after his ninety-first birthday. Gene Mullen was nine years old at the time.

By then "The Old Eagle Tree" had fallen, and there were no eagles in Black Hawk County anymore. There were no wild turkey, no prairie wolves, no buffalo and few—if any—deer. The last passenger pigeon had died in captivity eleven years before. The rich prairie earth once held fast by the thick roots of the vast fields of shoulder-high grass now lay exposed by the plow. And the chill winter winds were stripping the topsoil. Miller's Creek was slowly silting in.

There is a photograph of Gene Mullen and his sister, Mary Lois, sitting with their grandfather before a little grove of cottonwood trees. Patrick is wearing thick black woolen pants and a vest over a white shirt and tie. A wide, pleated, broad-visored tweed cap shades his stern face, and although his thin, straight mouth is unsmiling, there is considerable humor in his eyes. Gene and his sister—Gene must have been about five years old here—are seated in the grass on either side of Patrick Mullen. This is no photograph of a maudlin old man hugging his grandchildren; it is a photograph of a *pioneer*. And the grandchildren, as if aware of the legend, seemed too cowed to sit close.

Patrick J. Mullen died while the rural Midwest was suffering from an agricultural depression. Almost his entire estate was locked up in land and each of his children demanded an equal share. None of the daughters wanted to farm and by the time the estate was settled Gene's father's share was reduced to the original

24

Dobshire holdings: the land grant 40 acres and the 80 acres purchased from the Walker brothers. Gene's Uncle Edward was the only other Mullen to want to hold onto the land. The other brothers, the bank, taxes, lawyers' fees, insurance and sisters liquidated all the rest. Although the quarry remains in operation, its current owners have blasted through the stone upon which Patrick's original homestead stood. However, the austere two-story frame house he later built remains, but it, too, has passed out of the family's hands.

Still, even though John Dobshire's house was torn down in 1960 when Gene and Peg built their modern ranch-style house, an indelible mark of that old man's spirit too exists: almost the only break in the regular checkerboard pattern of Black Hawk County's section line boundary roads is the dirt road passing Gene Mullen's farm. Dobshire, instead of following the boundary, wore down his own road about a quarter mile south of the section line. He did it for no better reason than that was the direction his house faced, and the path provided him the most direct route to Forbes' post office by the Cedar River and, later, the main La Porte to Waterloo road.

Although Gene's father, Oscar, liked the land, he never really wanted to work it. Whenever he had a chance he would escape to play baseball. During the Depression, while Gene was working his way through Marquette University in Milwaukee, his father was managing the semiprofessional Waterloo Cardinals. Between 1929 and 1931, under his management, the Cardinals lost but four games those entire three years. Gene's mother, Margaret McDermott Mullen, had continued to work hard for local and state Democratic organizations, but she was sick for most of their married life.

One winter when Gene was still very young, his mother, pregnant with a second child, was stricken with appendicitis. A severe blizzard had rendered the roads impassable, and Margaret Mullen had to be pulled into Waterloo by sled. Although she recovered from the appendicitis, she miscarried from the rough journey and was confined to the hospital for six months.

Oscar Mullen took a job in Waterloo selling farm implements. In 1941 it was discovered that Margaret Mullen had cancer and again had to be confined to a hospital in Waterloo. Oscar Mullen never returned to the farm. He supported himself by being groundkeeper for the old Waterloo baseball park and by designing and laying out ballfields in a number of nearby towns. His baseball diamonds had a reputation for such excellence that in 1955 he was offered the job of park custodian for the then newly franchised Kansas City Athletics of the American League. Oscar Mullen was tempted enough to go to Kansas City to look the ball park over, but he couldn't find any place to live that he liked. So when Waterloo offered him a raise, he happily returned home.

Everyone in Waterloo knew Oscar Mullen; he was an affable, gregarious man. If he had any failing, it was that he wasn't especially ambitious. He just loved baseball more than anything else in the world. Oscar Mullen died in 1960 a few months short of his eightieth birthday and three weeks before he was to have been given the honor of throwing out the first baseball of the season when the Waterloo Hawks opened their Midwest League games.

Gene Mullen, now in his late fifties, has the powerful sloping shoulders and strong forearms of a man who has worked all his life with his hands. He has a round face—more a Dobshire shape than the long, thin face of Patrick Mullen—and an Irish-pink complexion set off by a full head of silver-white hair as fine as a child's. He wears plain black half-frame glasses, the bottom halves of the lenses held in place by simple metal rims. And a thin wire curls up to the hearing aid in his right ear. Gene's voice is low, deep, surprisingly gentle. When he speaks of his land, his voice grows hushed, almost reverent. He will talk of turning that first spring furrow of rich black soil, a dirt far darker than any in the East, and of kneeling down to smell it, cupping the sweet earth to inhale its fragrance in his hands. "There's an odor in that ground," Gene will say, "that's not in any catalogue of

26

smells." He is an unabashedly sentimental man who describes farmers as "just a breed. It's a love of the land, the soil, the grade."

In late November, 1941, Gene Mullen married Margaret "Peg" Goodyear of Pocahontas County northwest of Fort Dodge. It was the tail end of the Depression, and Gene was working for the Census Department because the only jobs that existed at this time were government jobs. Peg was working for the government, too. Her office with the Work Projects Administration (WPA) was in the same Waterloo office building as Gene's.

Peg had been working for the government since 1936. She was graduated from high school in 1935, and although she had been awarded scholarships to Buena Vista College at Storm Lake, Iowa, and Briar Cliff in Sioux City, she was unable to attend because she didn't have enough money for train fare. So Peg took a Civil Service examination to achieve a stenographic eligibility rating instead. She passed, and armed with her eligibility certificate, Peg went with her mother to see Senator Guy Gillette at his home office in Cherokee, Iowa, about getting a job.

Peg's mother, Jo Goodyear, had been chairman of the Pocahontas County Democratic Party for years. Peg had been attending political meetings with her mother from the time she was six. Therefore neither Peg nor her mother was a stranger to Senator Gillette. Because of her mother's intervention and influence, Peg received a Civil Service appointment to the Department of Labor in Des Moines. That winter her immediate boss, G. D. Miller, was responsible for conducting a survey of Iowa coal mines. Miller's superior, the administrator of the Bureau of Labor Statistics Office, was a hot-tempered red-haired Irishman named Joyce. One afternoon Joyce called the then nineteen-year-old secretary Peg Goodyear into his office and told her he wanted to read every piece of correspondence originating in the office before it was placed in the mail. Further, Joyce told Peg, he didn't want her boss, Miller, to know about it. Peg refused, saying she could not show him her boss' letters without her boss' consent. If Mr. Joyce wanted to read Mr. Miller's mail, he would have to ask Mr. Miller himself. Joyce persisted, and Peg continued adamantly to refuse. "All right then, Miss Goodyear," Joyce told Peg, "you're fired!"

"You can't fire me," Peg answered. "You're not the man who gave me my job."

Joyce was so furious that he picked up a paperweight and threatened to throw it at her. Peg fled his office and got on the telephone. She called both Iowa Senators Guy Gillette and Clyde Harring in Washington and told them she was losing her job. They each called Joyce the next morning, and as a result, both Peg's employment and the privacy of her boss' mail were sustained. In 1939 Peg shifted to the WPA office in Waterloo. She was working in the Women's Division, which handled women's programs such as sewing rooms and school lunches, when she and Gene Mullen met. Sixteen days after their marriage the Japanese bombed Pearl Harbor, and Gene Mullen left Black Hawk County to serve in the war. Because of his hearing defect, he was not able to go overseas. He was sent to Camp Dodge, and Peg was able to continue working when she was hired by the Civil Service commissioner in nearby Des Moines. Gene and Peg Mullen's son, Michael Eugene Mullen, was born on September 11, 1944.

By then Gene was a U.S. Army master sergeant. He was stationed now at Fort Carson, Colorado, and was in charge of feeding German prisoners of war. For ten years afterward Gene continued to exchange Christmas cards and correspondence with some of his former POWs.

While Gene was in the Army, the Mullen farmland was rented out. Each year for the five years Gene was away, a different tenant farmer would come in, do spring plowing, fall harvesting, and depart. When Gene returned in 1946, the land had been left in such poor shape he was unable to earn a living off it. Only $875 remained out of his discharge pay, rationing was still in effect, jobs were scarce, and in addition to his wife

28

and infant son, Gene had his ailing mother and father to help support.

Gene, Peg and Michael had moved back into John Dobshire's old house and borrowed $3,500 from a local bank to buy enough equipment to start the farm again. During that first fall harvest he spent two weeks helping his neighbor Cecil Joens pick his corn, but Joens needed to spend only four *hours* helping Gene pick his. The following year Gene tried raising cattle and lost all his pastureland in the spring flood. In debt for his cattle, Gene was forced to take an outside job. In the meantime, Peg had given birth to a second son, Daniel, who died only twenty-two hours after his birth of the same respiratory defect that took the life of President John F. Kennedy's infant. Gene found work at the Rath Packing Company in Waterloo and remained with them until 1955, when he took a different job with John Deere.

Gene felt he was never close enough to Michael. It wasn't because Gene, gentle and good father that he is, didn't want to be or didn't try to be. He simply couldn't be because he wasn't at home. Gene farmed in the morning and left for the second shift of the huge tractor plant in Waterloo at two thirty each afternoon. He would not return to the farm before midnight five days a week. As the years passed and his daughters, Patricia and Mary, then his son John were born and grew up and, like Michael, went off to the local parochial school, they, too, would be asleep when their father returned from work and in school by the time Gene awoke. So, seeing his children only on weekends and vacations, Gene came to feel he was watching them grow up from a distance.

Michael, however, had the same love for the land that his father did. When Gene Mullen walks his fields, he will sometimes pause and wonder whether his great-grandfather might have walked that same section, or his grandfather. And he will recall his father speaking about a childhood when there were no fences, no roads. "I have feelings for this land," Gene explains. "My great-grandfather lived here. My grandfather. My mother and father. Peg and me. We've all lived right here!" and it was that sense of continuity which was, perhaps, the strongest link between Gene, as father, and Michael, his son. Gene never felt Michael was to fall heir to acres only. He was to inherit all those generations of Mullens and Dobshires who would walk beside him each time he turned the soil.

Michael was always the one to have received the farm. Mary and Patricia would presumably marry young men met in school or college and move away with them. John, younger than Michael by seven years, never seemed to have the same feeling for the land that Michael did. So there was never any question about which of the children would succeed to the farm. There certainly wasn't any question in Michael's mind; he spent his life preparing for it.

Michael realized early on that it was his responsibility to take care of the farm when his father was at John Deere. Gene could leave a note, "Mikey, fill the hog water. . . . Mikey, take care of the cattle. . . . Mikey, clean out the hog house and get the corners." And Gene would know that whatever he asked would be done, that *more* would be done because Michael worked hard, drove himself and never excused himself if a job was not done right.

In 1944, the year of Michael's birth, 55 bushels an acre were considered a high yield for an Iowa cornfield. Twenty-five years later it was necessary to harvest 100 bushels an acre just to break even. And, as Michael knew, even higher yields would be required were there to be any profit when it became time for him to inherit the land. Therefore, Michael was determined to educate himself, to learn as much about the land and farming as he could.

He showed his first 4-H project, a Berkshire sow, when he was ten. At fourteen he had his first winner, a Hereford steer that became Black Hawk County Reserve Champion. A photograph of Michael at twelve shows a wiry, fiercely determined black-haired boy, perhaps a bit small for his age, with one cowboy-booted foot braced against the side of a box stall; he is grimly tugging at a balky steer's halter, pitting all his weight

30

and strength against his steer's unwillingness to move. The photograph taken by a passing Associated Press photographer at a county 4-H show appeared in wire service newspapers across the country captioned "Something's Got to Give." It is unlikely that Michael was amused. He took his farming seriously—but, then, it had never occurred to him not to.

Everybody liked Michael, especially older people. At times, however, he was so *straight* he made people his own age feel a bit uneasy. He didn't smoke. He didn't swear. He rarely drank anything stronger than an occasional beer. He never learned how to dance. He served as an altar boy at La Porte City's Sacred Heart Catholic Church. He kept his grades near the top of his class at Don Bosco, the local parochial school. He worked his way through Rockhurst, a small, quiet, conservative Jesuit college in Kansas City, Missouri.

In 1964, when Michael was twenty and in his Rockhurst sophomore year, he urged his parents to pay attention to Goldwater in the upcoming presidential election because Goldwater was telling the truth. To entertain them, he took his parents to concerts. Michael stood about five feet eight inches then and weighed 145 pounds. He had a dark complexion and the long face of his grandfather Patrick J. Mullen. Even though Michael was handsome in a somber sort of way, he had no serious girlfriends. Perhaps with his solemn, steady gray eyes, his black hair already prematurely flecked with white and his earnest, brisk demeanor, he seemed far older than his years. His maturity certainly inspired confidence: the summer following his sophomore year, Michael worked for the Iowa State Highway Commission and proved himself so trustworthy and responsible that his employers gave him practically unrestricted use of a state-owned car.

On the fourth day of August, while Michael was out with his highway survey crew, the U. S. Navy destroyers *Maddox* and *C. Turner Joy* were supposedly attacked by North Vietnamese patrol boats in the Gulf of Tonkin off Vietnam. Less than twelve hours later U.S. Navy carrier-based planes carried out reprisal raids, intruding for the first time into North Vietnam.

This "important threshold of the war," as it was referred to in a then-secret Defense Department study, was crossed with virtually no domestic criticism. Two days later, on August 7, 1964, Congress passed the Gulf of Tonkin Resolution, empowering President Lyndon Baines Johnson "to take all necessary measures to repel any armed attack against the forces of the United States and to prevent further aggression."

Michael Mullen, like his family, had no reason to believe that the previous President, John Fitzgerald Kennedy, had committed advisers and Special Forces troops to Vietnam for any more sinister reason than that Americans wanted the Vietnamese to have what the Vietnamese were supposed to want for themselves: the freedom to resist Communist aggression, to survive as a nation, to *become like us*. The Mullens believed we were in Vietnam to defend it. They believed Vietnam was a moral war, that if Vietnam fell, all Southeast Asia would fall to Communism with it. They believed it possible to equate our presence in Vietnam with our presence in Korea and our participation in the Second World War. The Mullens believed, in other words, what they were being told.

In February, 1965, President Johnson commenced Operation Rolling Thunder, the sustained air bombardment of North Vietnam. Michael called his mother from Rockhurst, "You remember kidding me about Barry Goldwater?" he asked. "Well, who's 'trigger-happy' now?"

That June U.S. military commanders were authorized to send American troops into combat. One month later President Johnson sanctioned the increase of U.S. forces in Vietnam from 75,000 to 125,000 men. The Mullens were concerned by the growing war and the escalating troop commitment, but they did not protest. They simply hoped the war would end.

La Porte City had by this time grown into a predominantly Protestant, Republican town with a population of a little over 2,000. It had more churches than taverns, and the proud brick fronts of its turn-of-the-century stores had darkened and become grimy with age. The town was clearly losing business to the newer, bigger shopping centers on the road to Waterloo. There was little new construction in La Porte, no more than two or three houses a year. The signboard on the outskirts of town listing the churches and the Rotary and Chamber of Commerce meetings had begun losing its paint. One didn't see many young people lounging about the streets, and La Porte City's only non-Caucasian was an Indian woman on welfare.

The citizens of La Porte thought well of the Mullens, spoke of them as "hard workers." They appreciated how difficult life had been for Peg having to take care of Gene's sick parents and four young kids. They saw, too, that she did not give herself any rest when Gene's parents died in 1960. Instead, to help pay for the hospital and funeral expenses, Peg returned to work. She became an executive secretary for an advertising specialty business in Waterloo. Peg had always been politically active in the local Democratic Party; she attended every state convention and always took time off to meet each candidate who came into town. But she continued active in volunteer work as well and remained teaching catechism classes at the Sacred Heart Catholic Church. By this time Gene had worked his way up to becoming a quality control inspector at John Deere.

The Mullen children, too, were well liked. They stayed out of trouble, got good grades, were popular with their classmates. Peg and Gene Mullen are innately generous, decent people, and they brought up their children to believe in the same basic values with which they themselves had been brought up. When the Mullens spoke of themselves, they described themselves as being "average" or "typical" or "good, solid citizens" in no way different from others in their neighboring communities. They would explain their behavior and responses as that of the "working class," as "farmers," and if they identified themselves as representative of any groups, it was as "Catholics," as "Democrats," "Irish-Americans," or "Iowans" and as being from a background typical of the "Silent Majority."

The Mullens did not avoid controversy; it is just that in a community like La Porte City controversial

33

situations rarely arose. When the Mullens did discover something wrong, however, they tried their best to stop it.

In 1965 Peg Mullen campaigned for election to the local school board. Peg is a very handsome woman with high, prominent cheekbones, a firm jaw and slightly upturned nose. She wears her gray-streaked hair short. Her face reflects enormous strength and determination, and yet, when she smiles, which is often, all that toughness shatters, and her blue eyes glisten and her cheeks dimple like a child's. There is none of Gene's Irish softness in Peg's voice. She has a hard, abrasive accent, thin, but not flat, an accent which comes down heavily on the *R*s. When she is angry, her voice rises sharply and her consonants rip the air about her.

Peg is a far more impatient, outspoken person than Gene, and when her aggressiveness and tenacity are directed toward local issues, she can precipitate the sort of small-town antagonisms that endure. Peg ran for the school board because she opposed the rising busing budget, because she discovered irregularities in the school-lunch program and because La Porte's taxes were the highest in the state. Out of the $30-an-acre tax rate, $25 went to the local nonparochial schools. Since a school board generally reflects the politics and mood of its community, and since La Porte is Republican and conservative, Protestant and traditional, the sort of small town in which it is considered "imprudent to make waves," Peg Mullen lost.

The Mullens next became involved with the local telephone company. A neighbor complained to Gene that some board members of the telephone company were calling up some of the older people in town and offering them $50 a share for their stock. The bylaws prevented any person from owning more than one share of stock. The board members would then place their new stock, worth actually six to eight times that much, in their grandchildren's or children's or relatives' names. Gene Mullen went into La Porte City and told them that if they didn't stop, he would go to the state attorney's office. As a result of Gene's intervention, Peg says with a sigh, "We don't have a lot of

34

friendship with the telephone company." Still, they were the only persons in town willing to do anything about it.

In 1967 Michael received a grant allowing him to go on from Rockhurst to the University of Missouri's Agriculture School. When Michael returned to the farm for his first summer vacation, he brought Caroline Roby, a diminutive, pretty, happy auburn-haired girl with him. Caroline, four years Michael's junior, was a student in one of the undergraduate biochemistry sections he taught. Michael was clearly in love with her. Caroline stayed a week, then went south to spend the rest of the summer with her divorced mother. Michael mooned about a bit, but he didn't let his dejection interfere with his work. And during the evenings he would sit for hours with his mother and brother and sisters discussing the presidential campaign. All the family, with the exception of Gene, hoped Senator Eugene McCarthy would be the Democratic Party's nominee. Gene Mullen thought McCarthy "lived in a cloud." Still, like the Mullens, McCarthy was a Democrat, an Irish-Catholic, and, more important, his peace candidacy reflected the Mullens' own growing concern over the war. That fall Michael would swallow his disappointment with McCarthy and vote for Humphrey over Nixon, pulling the straight Democratic Party lever in doing so. It was a party loyalty perhaps inherited from his grandmother.

One morning, shortly before Michael was due to return for the University of Missouri's summer session, he came in from the fields, sat down opposite his father at the round kitchen table and said, "Dad, you're going to see the day when you won't be able to afford to feed the grain we raise here to livestock!"

"Oh-h-h?" his father asked. "And why not?"

"Those cereal grains will be needed to feed people."

Gene looked over his breakfast mug of coffee at his son with a chiding smile. "Well, Mikey, what are you going to do about that?"

Without a moment's hesitation Michael replied, "I'm going to learn how to take roughage—normal

35

roughage—and make food from it that can be fed live-stock and it'll make them grow more meat to feed more people."

"I believe you will," his father said.

Michael was then working toward a combined MA-PhD degree in animal nutrition. His specific project was an experiment to develop a high-lysine corn which would eliminate the need to add supplementary proteins to livestock feed. If Michael said he would learn how to boost the protein content of corn from 8 percent to 12, his father believed there was no reason why he shouldn't do it.

"Mike's so much more intelligent than I," Gene would tell his friends at John Deere. "If I try to give him a little static, he'll just cut me off in one sentence. He'll say, 'Now here's your argument, and here's where's it's wrong.' But," Gene would be quick to add, "he won't be trying to hurt me. He's never talked back to me—he might not like what I say for him to do, but Mike's never, ever talked back to me."

Michael never talked back, and he always did what he was told. That is why, when shortly after he returned to the University of Missouri that summer and received his draft notice ordering him to report in September for induction into the United States Army, he dutifully gave up graduate school and reported to the Des Moines draft headquarters.

After his induction he was to have been placed on a military flight to Fort Polk, Louisiana, to begin infantry basic training, but no military flights left that day. To keep busy, Michael was given a job in the draft headquarters office filing case histories of young men who opposed the war, rejected the draft, who had found ways of having their induction orders changed, revoked or ignored. Michael Mullen spent the day reading about young men who had had themselves certified physically or psychologically unfit for the military, who had fled the country rather than serve. He read about young men who did not for one instant believe it was their patriotic duty—or any of their country's business—to fight a war halfway around the world in Vietnam, who had burned their draft cards, been ar-

36

rested in campus demonstrations, who had gone to jail, done everything in their power to escape the draft and show their opposition to the war. He filed paper after paper on young men who had not been pulled away from their studies, who had never even attended college, much less a graduate school, but who had still found ways to beat the draft. All day long Michael Mullen read about young men unlike himself.

At first he was angry and resentful of them, then furious with himself, and finally, inevitably, depressed. That night Michael telephoned his mother back at the farm and told her, "The whole setup is corrupt! I don't need to *be* here!" Over and over again, as if in disbelief, he repeated, "I don't need to *be* here! I don't need to *be* here! I simply didn't *need* to be drafted!"

The next morning Michael was flown to Fort Polk and began basic training. On December 3, 1968, he was ordered to "forfcit $26.00 a month for the period of one month" because, "having knowledge of a lawful order issued by Captain Joseph P. Holles, Jr., your Commanding Officer, to keep all personal valuables secured, an order which it was your duty to obey, you did fail to obey same." Michael had left his wallet on his bunk.

Michael spent his Christmas pass with Caroline and her mother, then returned to Fort Polk to complete his basic training. While there he applied for Noncommissioned Officers School. By so doing, he hoped to forestall being immediately sent to Vietnam. His application was accepted, and Michael received orders to attend the NCO school at Fort Benning, Georgia. He made sergeant (E-5) at Benning and was sent next to Fort McClellan, Alabama, for advanced infantry training (AIT). Michael had been able to delay his Vietnam orders for six additional months, but when he completed AIT, his time ran out. His gamble that the war would wind down before his additional training would end had failed. The Army now needed noncommissioned officers in Vietnam more than ever. At McClellan, Michael again was ordered to Vietnam.

Michael applied for and was granted twenty-three days' advance leave prior to reporting to Fort Lewis,

Washington, for transshipment overseas. He decided to spent his entire leave at home in Iowa and arrived at the farm on August 10, 1969.

Peg Mullen had expected Caroline to visit for at least part of Michael's leave. She had written the girl over Christmas, inviting her to the farm. A letter addressed to Caroline, in care of the Mullens, had been waiting on the kitchen table, but Michael wasn't saying whether she was coming or not. Finally, after four days of not knowing, Peg could not remain silent any longer and asked Michael, "Isn't Caroline coming?"

"No," he said. "She's in the West this summer with her father."

And that's all he would say. He did not mention Caroline again. However, Peg could not help noticing that Michael spent two whole afternoons writing Caroline and that he never received an answer.

There were then 534,000 U.S. troops in Vietnam fighting a war which had dragged on for almost nine years and which had already cost the lives of more than 38,000 American men. During that first week of leave, while Michael was out fixing fences, clearing brush, painting, and doing general cleanup work around the family farm, 244 U.S. soldiers were killed and 1,409 were wounded.

On his last day of leave Michael planted two small evergreens next to the house, sprayed the lawn for dandelions, visited his friend and neighbor Cecil Joens, then climbed up on the old plum-red Farmall tractor to clean up the lower field.

By ten o'clock that night Michael had ripped out the last stump, the remains of a cottonwood tree. He stepped down from the tractor to unhook the chain, and as he knelt by the stump, his eye was caught by the faint flinty gleam of an arrowhead caught in the cottonwood's bole. Michael picked at it until the point came free, then wiped the arrowhead clean on his blue-jeaned thigh. It was a beauty, side-notched, about an inch and a half long and three-quarters of an inch across, the sort used for deer and smaller game. The tip was white, but unlike the other quartzite arrow-

38

heads he had found, this one darkened to orange and black at its base. The point was still sharp, the notch and base unchipped by any plow; the cottonwood tree must have grown up around it. The arrowhead may even have been old enough to have been fired by Black Hawk himself. Michael dropped the arrowhead into his breast pocket, climbed back up on the tractor and just sat for a moment listening to the deep drumming of the Farmall's motor in the moonlight. He rested his elbows on the steering wheel and looked out over the land; then, reluctantly, he double-clutched the tractor into gear, advanced the ignition and slowly drove back up to the farm. Michael backed the Farmall into the shed, carefully aligned its wheels with the newer Farmall and shut the motor off. The sudden silence was broken only by the crackling sounds of the engine cooling, the distant chuckle of a cock pheasant and moments later another pheasant's answering call. Michael climbed down from the tractor and walked into the house.

The next morning, September 4, 1969, Michael's family watched his airplane lift off from the Waterloo Airport, saw it climb northwest over the Cedar River and Turkey Ford Forks where the last Indian council had been held, and then he was gone.

Chapter Four

When the telephone rang in the parish office of the Sacred Heart Catholic Church off Poplar Street in La Porte City a little after nine o'clock on Saturday morning, February 21, 1970, the thin, stooped late-middle-aged country priest assumed it was just another mother whose child, sick with a midwinter cold, would be unable to attend catechism classes that day. He unhurriedly walked to his desk and, lifting the receiver, was surprised to hear an entirely unfamiliar male voice ask for him by name.

"Father Otto Shimon?"

"Yes-s-s?"

"Father Shimon, this is Master Sergeant Fitzgerald. I'm with Fifth Army Headquarters. . . . Do you have an O. E. Mullen in your parish?"

" 'O. E. Mullen'?" Father Shimon repeated, giving himself time enough to move to the chair behind his desk and ease himself down.

"That's right," Fitzgerald said. "I was just talking to the priest at the Carmel parish and—"

"That would be Father Rahe at St. Mary's," Father Shimon interrupted, then added, "Sergeant," because he had been a captain in the Army during World War II and served now as chaplain for the local American Legion chapter in La Porte.

"Yes, sir, that's the one," Sergeant Fitzgerald said. "Well, the Father, Father Rahe, thinks he has a *Ralph* Mullen in his parish, but I'm trying to locate an *O. E.* Mullen and I thought perhaps you—"

"That would be Oscar Eu*gene* Mullen," the priest said. "He's listed in the phone book, however, as *Gene* Mullen, hence"—Father Shimon chuckled—"your, ah, confusion."

40

"Then this O. E. Mullen *is* in your parish, sir?"

"Yes-s-s, Gene Mullen's in my parish." The priest did not like this sergeant's tone; he was being altogether too businesslike. "As a matter of fact, Sergeant, the Mullens have always been very good members of th—"

"May I see you this morning, sir?"

"Me? This morning, Sergeant? . . . Fitzgerald, you said it was?"

"Fitzgerald, that's right."

"A fine old Irish-Catholic name," Father Shimon said still trying to be congenial, still fighting down the apprehension rising within him. "You are, I presume, Catholic?"

"No, sir, Episcopalian," Fitzgerald said. "Please, Father Shimon, it's important I see you this morning. As soon as possible."

"About Gene Mullen?" Father Shimon asked, his lips suddenly dry. "Is there something, ah-h-h, wrong?"

That morning the sun had finally broken through the flat pearl-gray overcast that had been brooding over the Mullens' farm. Although the temperature hovered near freezing, the week-long Arctic winds had ceased, and at last it again felt warm enough to be outside.

Gene Mullen walked back from the mailbox to the house. As he climbed the stairs into the kitchen, he called out, "Letter from Mikey." He dropped the bills, the Des Moines *Register* and the second-class mail on the kitchen table and tore open the envelope. Peg wiped her hands on a dish towel and put a kettle of water on to boil.

"What's he say?" she asked. "When did he write it?"

Gene glanced at the top of the letter. "Dated the thirteenth," he said. "Let's see now 'Dear Mom and Dad: Went down off the hill to get a haircut and clean up, but ended up hitching a ride to Chu Lai. Went to the MARS station by chance—they were open and not busy—so got a chance to call. Suppose it was midnight at home and guess you were surprised—' "

"Oh," Peg said, "he must have written this the same day he called." Gene had not been home when

41

Michael had telephoned from Vietnam eight days earlier. Peg had written "Mike called" on an envelope and left it on the kitchen table for Gene to read following the late shift at John Deere. It was twelve thirty by the time Gene returned to the farm, and after reading the note, he woke Peg up. She told him that she had spoken with Michael for only about a minute and a half and that before hanging up, Michael had said, "Good-bye, Mom, it's so bad here. . . ." Peg had been so depressed that she hadn't felt like waiting up to tell Gene when he came home and had simply left him a note. She mixed Gene a mug of instant coffee, brought it to him at the kitchen table and sat down. "What else does he say?"

"He says, '. . . guess you were surprised,' . . . now, here: 'Will be on the bunker line about two more days, then back out into the field.'"

"Ugh!" Peg groaned. "That means more search and destroy."

"No, it doesn't," Gene said. "He's been doing company sweeps like he wrote in the other letter."

"Same thing," Peg said.

"No, it isn't," Gene insisted. "A company sweep is—"

Peg waved her hand impatiently. "Go on with the letter."

"All right, all right. He says, 'Glad that all is well—weather here been rather good. Have decided not to take R&R if I can get a drop. So 'til later, hang loose.'" Gene looked at the letter more closely. "Hang loose'?"

"Hang loose, you know," Peg said, "take it easy."

Gene shrugged. "'So 'til later, hang loose, Love Michael.'"

"That's it?"

"That's it," Gene said. He passed the letter across the table to his wife.

Peg read through it quickly, "Oh, see," she said, "he's decided for sure to ask for an early drop. You remember the letter before last Michael said he was writing the University of Missouri to get the necessary papers."

Michael hoped to be released early from Vietnam so that he could be readmitted to the Agriculture School. Peg and Gene discussed for a moment what they thought his chances were; Michael himself had written that he felt they were very good. The only part of his letter that bothered them was that he would again be going into the field, that he wouldn't be in the relative safety of the fire base bunker line anymore. Still, in one of his first letters, Michael had written that he was in "probably one of the better places over here," a comparatively quiet part of Vietnam.

"So he might be coming home in June," Gene said.

"Looks that way," Peg said, "knock wood."

Gene finished his coffee and stood up "Well, Mother," he said, "I guess I might as well try to fix the television antenna for you."

"What's it like outside?"

"Fine," Gene said. "Cold, but it's fine. The wind's stopped."

He buttoned up his heavy woolen red and black plaid lumber jacket, turned off his hearing aid, put the earplug into his pocket and went outside.

The windblown television antenna was attached to a post near the east side of the farmhouse. Gene was just coming around that east corner, blowing hot breath on his fingertips and trying to remember where he had last put the light wrench he would need, when, out of the corner of his eye, he noticed two automobiles turning into his driveway. Without his hearing aid he had not heard them approach and he fumbled beneath his lumber jacket for the earpiece, inserted it and thumbed the volume up.

Gene thought he recognized the first car, believed the parish priest, Father Shimon, had one like it, but that second car. . . . Gene read the black letters painted on the Chevrolet's olive-drab door: U.S. ARMY —FOR OFFICIAL USE ONLY. Gene's chest tightened, and he stood still while the priest and the Army sergeant stepped out of their cars and slammed shut the doors.

Gene watched them walking toward him as if in slow motion, their footsteps thundering across the metallic crust of the drifted snow. He tried to see beyond the country priest's black metal-framed glasses to what might show in his eyes. But Father Shimon's downcast lenses reflected only the snow. Not until the priest forced himself to look up did Gene recognize the fright, the despair, the agony within them, then very quietly Gene asked, "Is my boy dead?"

Father Shimon halted so abruptly that the Army sergeant, who was following, bumped into him from behind. "Gene," the priest said, "this is Sergeant Fitzgerald. He's from Fifth Army Headquarters. He. . . ." Shimon was silent.

Gene looked beyond Father Shimon to the sergeant and asked again, "Is . . . my . . . boy . . . *dead?*"

"Let's go into the house, Gene," Father Shimon said. "I want to talk to you there."

"No!" Gene said, not moving. "I want to *know!* Tell me, *is . . . my . . . boy . . . dead?*"

"I can't tell you here," Father Shimon said, his hand fluttering up toward Gene's shoulder. "Come into the house with us . . . please?"

Gene spun away before the priest's pale fingers could touch him.

Peg Mullen heard the back door open, heard Gene rushing up the stairs into the kitchen, heard him shouting, *"It's Mikey! It's Mikey!"* His voice half a sob, half a scream.

She hurried out of the sewing room in time to glimpse the Army uniform entering the kitchen. Peg found Gene standing with his back to the sink, clutching the counter behind him, the Army sergeant halted just to the side of the doorway. Father Shimon, between them, had removed his glasses to wipe away the steam. Peg started to move toward her husband but had to turn away. Never had she seen such terrible devastation in his face, so raw a wound. She looked next at the sergeant, who avoided her eyes by glancing at the priest whose job it was to tell them. But Father Shimon would not stop wiping his glasses, and Peg, feeling herself wanting to scream, to kick over a chair, to thrash about,

44

to do *anything* rather than listen to this awful silence a moment longer, saw her husband's lips move as if to say, "It's Mikey," but no sound would come out.

Peg scowled at the Army sergeant and said, "Michael died on Thursday."

Thursday morning, upon waking up, Peg had burst into tears for no apparent reason. Off and on that entire day she had cried, and so that Gene wouldn't know, she had spent the morning by herself down in the sewing room. She decided to make new curtains for the boys' room, and she sewed and sewed but would have to stop because she would begin crying again and couldn't see the material through her tears. She would wait for the tears to pass, pull herself together and sew some more until finally, a little after two o'clock, when she heard Gene leave for the John Deere plant in Waterloo, she stopped sewing altogether.

The following day, yesterday, Friday, Peg had awakened not sad, just angry. No matter what Gene said to her she snapped back, contradicting him, defying him. And seeing the hurt and confusion in his face, she wanted to apologize but instead became angrier still for feeling that need. At noon Peg felt she simply had to get out of the house. She drove off to spend the day with friends who shared her feelings about the war, with whom she could talk about how worried she was, how frustrated she felt trying to find something meaningful to do.

Before Michael had been drafted, the war had appeared so far away, so purposeless and distant. But when Michael was sent to Vietnam, the war no longer seemed remote. A month after Michael was assigned to the Americal Division, Peg wore a black armband on October 15, Moratorium Day, to indicate her opposition to the war. The same day, in La Porte City, an American Legionnaire backed her up against the post office wall, told her she was a disgrace to the country and ordered her to take the armband off. Peg brushed his arm aside and told him, "You better get with it, you sonuvabitch!"

45

Still, Peg realized, she had never actively campaigned against the war. She had written letters to Jack Miller, Iowa's hawkish Republican Senator to express her opposition. Each time the Des Moines *Register* carried an account of an Iowa boy's death in Vietnam, Peg would forward the clipping to the Senator's office in Washington with the note: "Put another notch in your gun, Jack." She had written several letters to President Nixon, pleading with him to end the war. She joined Another Mother for Peace, but really, Peg had to concede, her opposition so far had been limited and ineffective.

Yesterday she had not returned to the farm until dusk and, to keep busy, had begun to clean house. For the next six hours she scrubbed and dusted, waxed and polished, pausing only at ten o'clock for the late evening news on television, There was an account of an accidental shelling at Bien Hoa by South Vietnamese artillery resulting in the deaths of about a dozen American men. The story stuck in Peg's mind when she went back to cleaning, and at midnight she called one of the friends she had seen that afternoon to ask if she had watched the news. They talked about how the accidental shelling seemed to epitomize the stupidity and wastefulness of the Vietnam War. Peg told her friend how busy she had been cleaning, that she had felt this compulsion to polish the house from top to bottom. The friend asked Peg if she were expecting visitors.

"No, none that I know of," Peg had said. "I don't know what's going on with me—I really don't. But whatever it is," she added, "I'm ready."

The Army sergeant did not answer her, so Peg spoke again, "Did Michael die on Thursday?"

"Why do you ask me when he died?" Sergeant Fitzgerald said. "I haven't told you your son is dead."

Peg glared at him with such utter contempt that the sergeant flinched. "You *know* the Army doesn't come to tell parents that their sons are wounded!" Peg said. "You know the Army comes only when they're *dead!*"

46

The sergeant again turned to the priest, waiting for Father Shimon to break the news, to speak. But the priest was incapable of talking.

Very slowly, deliberately, almost threateningly, Gene Mullen pushed himself away from the sink and moved toward the two men. "Now I want to know the truth!" he told them. "Is . . . my . . . boy . . . dead?"

Sergeant Fitzgerald looked at the priest, then back at Gene and said, "Yes."

And, "Yes-s-s-s," Father Shimon said, too, as if he had been holding his breath all this time. "Yes, Gene, yes, Peg, I'm sorry, yes-s-s-s."

Gene sagged as if hit. He looked at Peg and she at him. Gene stumbled backward until he was again against the sink. He shook his head to and fro like a groggy fighter trying to clear his brain. He began to cry gentle tears that welled up hot in his eyes, overflowed and traced down his cheeks. "Why?" he said to no one in particular. "Why?"

Peg had moved to the kitchen table and stood now gripping the wooden rung of a chairback until she felt herself under enough control to speak. Then she asked the sergeant how Michael had been killed.

Sergeant Fitzgerald sorted through some papers and pulled one out. "I only know the official casualty message given me by Fifth Army Headquarters this morning over the phone."

"Read it," Peg said.

The sergeant lifted the paper to the light. "It states that 'Sergeant (E-5) Michael Eugene Mullen, US 54 93—' so on, 'died while at a night defensive position when artillery fire from friendly forces landed in the area.'" Sergeant Fitzgerald's hand dropped. "I'm sorry . . . I really am very sorry, Mr. and Mrs. Mullen. . . ." He put the paper away and began buttoning up his trench coat as if to leave. "Generally, at this time," he said, "families of casualties prefer to be alone with their priests—"

"Sit down," Peg said quietly.

"Perhaps," Sergeant Fitzgerald was saying, "tomorrow would be a better time to—"

"Sit down!" Peg repeated firmly. "We're going to talk about this message, this, this official casualty report."

Gene watched the sergeant leaf back through his papers, start to say, "Mrs. Mullen, I only—"

"Sergeant," Gene ordered, "read that thing again."

Fitzgerald cleared his throat. " 'Sergeant (E-5) Michael Eugene Mullen, US 54 93 22 54, died while at a night defensive position when artillery fire from friendly forces landed in the area.' " He looked up from the paper. "That's all it says . . . really."

"Listen," Gene said, "I was a master sergeant in the United States Army, myself, during World War Two, and I . . . and I. . . ." He stopped, no longer certain what the point was that he had wished to make.

"We're going to talk about this message," Peg said. "I want you to explain it to me. This word, what do you mean by 'friendly'?"

"It merely means that it wasn't enemy artillery," the sergeant said. "Your son was killed by friendly fire."

"Friendly fire? *Friendly fire?*" Peg repeated incredulously.

Sergeant Fitzgerald shrugged lamely. "It means any artillery from forces not the enemy."

"Not the enemy! *Goddamn you!"* Peg cried, beating the chairback with her fists in frustration. "You couldn't even give him the . . . the decency of being killed by the enemy!" She glared at the sergeant. "These, these 'friendly forces not the enemy,' how come the word 'American' isn't used?"

The back door opened, and Michael's younger brother, John, finished with his chores came up the stairs and into the kitchen. He peered curiously at the Army sergeant first and next at the priest, then at his mother and father before quietly taking a place by the door.

"Why wasn't the word 'American' used?" Peg repeated.

"Because it wasn't 'American,' " the sergeant said.

"And why wasn't the word 'accidental' there?"

"Because, Mrs. Mullen, it wasn't an accident."

"Wait a minute," Peg warned ominously.

Sergeant Fitzgerald began talking about the accidental shelling at Bien Hoa.

"We know all about Bien Hoa," Peg snapped.

"Well," Sergeant Fitzgerald said, "this is how and where your son was killed."

There was a sudden moan, and before Peg could reach John, his knees buckled and he collapsed onto the floor. Gene rushed over and, with Peg, eased their son into a chair. "Oh, poor John," Peg said, "are you all right?"

"Take it easy, son," Gene said.

"Michael's dead?" John asked.

"What were you thinking?" Peg asked him. "I thought you knew. I thought seeing the Army car. . . ."

"No, I never, I never thought of Michael," John said. "I thought they were after me! That I'd done something wrong!"

John had registered for the draft only five days before.

"What happened to Michael?" he asked.

"This sergeant is telling us," Peg said.

"But is he . . . ? Is Michael . . . ?"

"Yes, son," Gene said. "Mikey's gone."

"And now," Peg said, whirling on the sergeant, "we want to know how, and we want to know why!"

"You said you heard about Bien Hoa. . . ."

"*Bien Hoa?*" Peg said. "You don't know very much! Michael wasn't anywhere near Bien Hoa. My son was three, four hundred miles from there!"

"Good God," Sergeant Fitzgerald said, "it must have happened all over Vietnam that night." He sat down at the kitchen table. "You understand, how it could have happened," he said. "The Vietcong infiltrated these South Vietnamese artillery units, got onto their radio channels and called in the wrong artillery coordinates so that when the ARVN artillery fired, they hit Americans." Sergeant Fitzgerald apologized for not having any more information than was contained in the official casualty message and added he did not want to say positively that this was what had happened to

Michael, but the Vietcong had infiltrated ARVN radio channels in the past, and this is what might have happened to their son's unit.

Sergeant Fitzgerald next explained that the Mullens had the right to request a special escort to accompany Michael's body back from Vietnam. If they had some special friend of Michael's in mind, someone whom they would like to have return with Michael's remains, they should let him know.

"Well, it's so soon, so sudden . . ." Peg said. "Michael had so many friends, I really don't know. . . ."

"There's no need to decide now," Sergeant Fitzgerald said, "Either myself or another survivors' assistance officer will call you tomorrow. Now," the sergeant said, "What funeral home do you want your son's body delivered to?"

Peg and Gene looked at each other speechlessly.

"Well, we don't know," Peg said. . . . "We really don't know yet."

"How long will it be before Michael . . . Michael's body returns?" Gene asked.

"Just as soon as they have a plane full," Sergeant Fitzgerald said.

Peg said, "I know it won't be long then."

"One more thing, Sergeant," Gene asked. "When will Michael's death be announced on the news?"

"After I notify Fort Leonard Wood that I've seen you, they'll release it. That should be about two hours from now."

"Two hours!" Peg protested. "You can't! You've got to give us time to tell our other children. Our daughters are away at college, and we can't let them hear about it on the radio. You've got to tell them to hold back the news."

"Can't you call them?" Sergeant Fitzgerald asked. "You'll have at least two hours."

"They'll be in classes," Peg said. "I won't be able to reach them until tonight. Can't you wait?"

"I'm sorry, Mrs. Mullen, I'm only a sergeant. I can't tell the Army what to do."

"I can!" Peg said angrily. "I'm not afraid of the Army or the Pentagon. If you won't do anything about

50

it, then I'll . . . I'll call Senator Hughes in Washington. He'll help."

"Look, Mrs. Mullen," Sergeant Fitzgerald said, "you don't have to do that. I'll tell Fifth Army you want them to wait. They won't release the news until you give them the go-ahead."

"Gene, I can't just tell Mary and Patricia over the phone. They'd. . . ." She shook her head helplessly.

"What about your sister?" Gene asked.

"Louise?" Peg thought for a moment. "She could maybe drive to Kansas City and pick up Mary. . . ."

"If there's nothing else . . ." Sergeant Fitzgerald said. He was standing by the door, ready to leave.

"I'll walk you out," Gene said.

"That's not necessary," Sergeant Fitzgerald said. "Oh, and, Father Shimon? You'll stay a little longer, won't you?"

"Of course, Sergeant, of course," the priest said.

Peg looked at Father Shimon and shrugged. Back in November, after a Sunday service, she had stopped on the way out of church to ask Father Shimon to say some special prayers for Michael. "You've got to pray for him, Father," she had said. "He hasn't got a chance!"

"Oh, I know, I know," Shimon replied, taking Peg by the arm to move her out of the path of his other parishioners. "I do pray for him, I'm praying for him every day. We pray for all our servicemen."

Peg telephoned her friend in La Porte to tell her that Michael was dead and to ask if she would be good enough to drive the seventy-five miles to Iowa City to inform Patricia, who was a senior at the University of Iowa there. Peg next called her sister, Louise Petersen, and asked her to pick up Mary, who was a freshman at Rockhurst College, Michael's alma mater, in Kansas City. Then she telephoned her brothers, Bill Goodyear in Omaha and Howard Goodyear in Pittsburgh. She did not cry. She kept the calls short; she remained strong and in control of herself. She informed them only of what she knew so far, that Michael had been killed by South Vietnamese artillery. Her brothers told her they would arrive at the farm as soon as possible. When she

51

finished, she saw that Sergeant Fitzgerald had left and Gene was waiting to use the phone.

Gene telephoned the local newspapers and television stations and gave them what little details he knew and begged them not to release the news until they had been able to inform their daughters. While Gene was doing that, Peg began drawing up a list of those persons they would need to contact.

"Now, Peg," Father Shimon said, joining Peg at the table, "ah-h, I didn't know Michael very well and I'm sure you'll want, ah-h, someone else to say the mass. . . ."

"Well, yes," Peg said. "As a matter of fact, we'll want Father Hemesath to say the mass." Father Gregory Hemesath of New Haven, a small town in Mitchell County, northern Iowa, was an old friend of the Mullens'.

"That's just fine," Father Shimon said. "You write down whoever you want and I'll ask them. I'll bow out and won't have any part in the, ah-h, funeral mass."

"We'll want music, too," Gene said, pausing in mid-phone call. "Michael always liked good music."

"Whenever we went to Kansas City," Peg said, "if there was any good music being played, Michael would take us to hear it."

"As you know," Father Shimon said, licking his lips, "our church doesn't have an organ. . . ."

"So it'll be Sister Richard and the Don Bosco High School Chorus," Peg said.

"Oh, all right," Father Shimon said, "that's fine. That's just fine."

"And I'd like Father Hirsch to say a few words," Peg said. Father Robert Hirsch was the principal of the Don Bosco High School in Gilbertville where all the Mullen children had gone. "And I want a White Funeral. . . ."

"I can't, Peg," the priest said, shaking his head. "I can't have one."

"Why not?"

"Because when the permission order came to change the service, each parish had to request the permission from the archdiocese. . . ." In the Black Funeral, the then-traditional Catholic mass, the priests wore black vestments. The mass mourned the departed, and its prayers were directed toward the salvation of the sinner's soul. In the White Funeral, which had only recently been introduced, the priests wore white vestments. The funeral service marked the deceased's entrance into eternal life. It was a celebration of the resurrection rather than a mass of mourning. "I didn't want the change," Father Shimon told Peg, "so I ignored it."

"That doesn't matter," Peg said, "All you've got to do is have it now. We had one only two months ago when that La Porte boy from the Jesup parish died in Vietnam."

"Nope. Nope. Nope," Father Shimon said, "I can't do it."

Peg regarded him coldly, then lowered her head and went back to work on her list.

After a moment, Father Shimon stood up. "Well," he said, "I, ah-h, probably, ah-h, should be going."

"Fine, Father," Peg said.

A few minutes later they heard the priest's car driving away. Gene, off the telephone, came over to the kitchen table, too. There was nothing that they could do while waiting for the rest of the family to arrive but make a list of those friends who would want and need to know that which they themselves were still scarcely willing to accept: their son Michael was dead.

Chapter Five

The Mullens' friends and neighbors, stunned by word of Michael's death, began arriving at the farm shortly after Father Shimon left. They were stricken, outraged, bewildered that this distant war in Vietnam, a war so wearying, so incomprehensibly foreign, so enduring, could somehow have taken Michael's life as it had claimed the life of that Jesup parish boy only two months before. The men wearing faded bib overalls, ankle-high work boots, day-glo orange earflapped vinyl caps, their mellow, weathered faces creased with sorrow, approached Gene shyly, hesitantly. Gently they touched him on the shoulder, laid their calloused hands almost tenderly across his back. Their wives, in woolen slacks and heavy hand-knit cardigans, brought baskets of food, stews and casseroles, pots of coffee which they set to simmer at the rear of the Mullens' stove. And then they moved back to take Peg's hands in their own, hugged her, kissed her lightly upon her cheek, begged her to give them something to do, wanting to help, and could barely contain the grief in their eyes.

The women gathered around the kitchen table with Peg, and the men sat in the living room with John and Gene. They talked in low voices about Michael, what a wonderful young man he had been, how they felt he had been—in many ways—like a son of their own, how hard he had worked, the many little kindnesses he had shown. They retold stories about Michael, about his 4-H activities, how much he had wanted to be good at basketball, about the time back in 1960—or was it '61?—the time Michael wouldn't let any of his family into their newly completed house until the lawn had been seeded and dragged and rolled. Michael had been fourteen then, and his family hadn't finished the lawn until at least eleven at night. Or how about the time that neighbor, the one whose young wife had died of the aneurysm, had driven off the dead end, dragged himself out of his demolished car, his face smashed by the windshield, and crawled all the way to the Mullens' back door, where Michael discovered him, brought him inside, wrapped him in blankets and placed crushed ice on his shattered face until the ambulance and doctor could arrive. Over and over again the men tried to express their sorrow, tried to make some sense out of the war, to say something comforting about Michael's service to his country. And suddenly, astonishingly, one of the men, and then another, would begin to cry, would hide his face, wipe at the tears with the back of his hand and blow his nose into a great billowing pocket bandanna.

These men were part of "the great Silent Majority" President Nixon had referred to, and they wept as much out of confusion and frustration and rage as they did out of grief for the Mullens' loss. From kindergarten through the twelfth grade in their Iowa schools they had pledged their allegiance to the flag, been taught to love their country, respect their government. To them, America's history was of Genesisic simplicity, its early Presidents Old Testament prophets whose lives were parables of selflessness and virtue. Standing there by the Mullens' big picture window, looking out across John Dobshire's road to the rolling snow-swept hills beyond, they were simple, decent people who saw their silence as a form of stoicism, not acquiescence, who interpreted silence as a strength and virtue and whose lonely lives on isolated farms were testimony to the little stock they placed in talk.

Of course, they thought themselves patriotic. Of course, they believed that a man has a duty to serve his country. Many of them, a majority, had fought in the Second World War, a war which had had front lines and battlefields and winners and losers, where success could be measured, enemy territory absorbed behind ribbons and pins and flags on the carefully kept maps back at home. These men had been young then, thinner and tougher, and they remembered how, mov-

55

ing up through the liberated cities and villages, they had been greeted as heroes, how the grateful citizens had gifted them with flowers and wine, how the pretty young dark-haired girls had climbed up the armor-plated sides of their half-tracks and Sherman tanks to be kissed. It was a war which had confirmed the image they carried both of America and of themselves: strong and generous, invincible and humane. And of course, they had been scared. There was no shame in admitting that—but they had gone, hadn't they? In some jewelry box, or sock drawer, or half forgotten in the bottom of some desk somewhere, they still had their dog tags, their combat infantryman's badges, maybe even the medal or two awarded them because against their better judgment, on some occasion and in spite of it all, they had volunteered for something especially dangerous, something that they hadn't even needed to do. But they had done it. Why scarcely mattered; the point, to them, was that they had risked their lives and survived. They had survived and come home to Poyner and Cedar and Big Creek townships, to Eagle Center and La Porte, proud of their participation in that war. Later they joined the local American Legion chapter or the VFW and with the passing years found themselves looking back on their experiences with a strange and paradoxical longing that disturbed them.

They had returned as young lions, brave warriors, to be celebrated and praised . . . and absorbed and confused . . . and frustrated and forgotten as their war became American history, shuffled farther and farther back into chapters superseded by the new crises Americans responded to in Korea and Hungary and Berlin and Czechoslovakia and the Suez and Lebanon and Cuba and now in Vietnam. The irony was not lost on them that the two Axis powers which they as young men had warred against, which they had helped reduce to rubble and had subsequently helped to rebuild with tax money taken out of their own pockets, had re-emerged as the two most powerful nations in Europe and Asia. That is why that afternoon at the Mullens' farm these men remained mute. The death of

Michael reminded them how powerless they had become. These sudden crises, which in retrospect seemed so inevitable and abundant, unnerved them because they no longer felt they had access to the facts—whatever they might be—facts which they were no longer sure they would want to know even if there were someone around who was willing to tell them.

Gene would be explaining to the latest arrival that the family knew only that Michael had been killed by the South Vietnamese artillery, that the Vietcong had somehow made the artillery fire on Michael's platoon's position and that Michael had been killed two days ago. On Thursday.

"But, Gene," the man would say, "I didn't see nothing in the paper about it. Where'd it say anything about American boys being killed by South *Veet-*namese artillery?"

"You heard about the shelling at Bien Hoa?" Gene asked. "How a lot of American boys got killed and wounded at Bien Hoa? Well, see, it happened all over Vietnam that night."

"I sure am sorry, Gene. It seems the whole world is coming apart. It gets so a man just doesn't want to read or know about anything anymore."

"You got to care," Gene said. "You got to keep caring."

"Yup, well, I do, I guess," the man would say, "I do, but it doesn't seem to make sense."

What so confused these men was that no one really seemed to believe that America stood to gain anything from the Vietnam War, that all the reasons given to justify an American presence in Vietnam—to prevent outside invaders from taking over the country, to provide the people of South Vietnam with a chance to choose their own leaders—were myths dispelled nightly on the television news. Every returning GI felt that *he* had been the outside invader, that the government he had been sent to defend was incorrigibly corrupt, its elections rigged, its political opposition tortured and jailed. Most appalling of all was the fact that the South Vietnamese not only were unwilling to fight

57

for themselves but fired upon, booby-trapped and ambushed the American boys who had come halfway around the world to defend them.

So the men wrung their hands and wept with rage and frustration and confusion because what could any of them say to the Mullens except how terribly sorry they were?

And how were the Mullens supposed to respond?

When a young man is killed in a war, his parents console themselves that he gave his life for some higher ideal, that he died in the service of his country and that his awful sacrifice is recognized and appreciated by a grateful government and citizenry. But how could Gene and Peg Mullen comfort themselves over their son's death in Vietnam? Didn't anyone understand that Michael had been their hope? Their way back up? That Michael would have returned the Mullen name to the stature it had enjoyed when his great-grandfather Patrick J. had owned that 1,000-acre farm?

What could the Mullens say to these friends, these neighbors, these well-meaning townspeople who had driven out to see them? Peg and Gene could not help thinking how none of these people's sons had had to go. How Michael was the only boy from any of the farms around who had put himself through graduate school, who showed the most potential for making a success out of farming. What's more, the Mullens sensed that the general attitude among their son's contemporaries was not that Michael had been a patriot, but rather that he had been a poor, unfortunate scapegoat who hadn't had enough sense or enough pull not to get caught. "I don't need to be here! I don't need to be here!" Michael had protested that night he telephoned from Des Moines. "I simply didn't *need* to be drafted!"

Patricia Mullen, then twenty-one years old, had been met by Peg's friend in Iowa City and reached the farm late that afternoon. Like her mother's, Patricia's reaction to Michael's death was a cold and bitter rage. Only three days before she had written their Senator, Harold Hughes, pleading with him to get her brother out of combat, that it was such a waste to let "Michael's

58

mind to be destroyed." Senator Hughes had replied the same day to explain the process by which Michael could request an out-of-combat assignment. Patricia had received the Senator's letter that morning.

Peg's sister, Isabel Strathman, and her husband, Gerald Strathman, arrived at the farm next. Gerald Strathman, an Army Air Corps bombardier during World War II, had taken part in the raids on the Ploesti oilfields.

Peg's brother, Bill Goodyear, arrived early that evening. He had driven to the farm directly from Omaha. Bill Goodyear had served in the Army during World War II and had taken part in the construction of the Burma Road.

Mary Mullen, then nineteen years old and a freshman at Rockhurst, had been picked up in Kansas City by Peg's other sister, Louise Petersen, and Mike Kitt, the Petersens' son-in-law. Herman Petersen, Peg's brother-in-law, had fought through the Battle of the Bulge. Mary and the Petersens would not arrive until late that night.

Howard Goodyear, Peg's older brother, was driving in from Pittsburgh and could not reach the farm before Sunday afternoon. Now an executive with Alcoa, Howard had been the radio operator-medic on the weather plane which had preceded the *Enola Gay* to Hiroshima. As part of its mission Howard Goodyear's B-29 had to fly over Hiroshima to report the effects of the first atomic bomb.

Peg does not remember her brothers and brothers-in-law ever swapping war stories or even wanting to talk about the war.

By midnight Saturday night the Mullens' friends and neighbors had left. Peg's brothers and sisters had gone to their motel rooms; Patricia was asleep. John was in his bedroom awake and staring at the ceiling. Peg and Gene were seated across the kitchen table from each other, isolated by grief, each tentatively prodding and testing the barriers that would protect them from the anguish of their loss.

"The thing is when you have a boy in combat," Gene said, "the thing you always keep foremost in your mind is that . . . is that"—he took a deep breath—"is that *it can't happen to him*—" BLAM! He slammed the flat of his hand down on the table so hard that the spoon skipped out of his coffee mug. "It can't happen to him!"

Peg nodded, watching him sadly.

"It can't happen to him," Gene repeated and slumped in the chair.

A few minutes later Peg sighed. "Gene, I knew . . . I think I knew after Michael called on the thirteenth. When he said, 'Good-bye, Mom, it's so bad here . . .' I think I kind of started to know he'd be killed. . . ."

"What are we going to do-o-o?" Gene cried.

"Whatever needs to be done," she announced firmly. Peg pushed herself up from the table. "First of all, I'm going to open up Michael's tackle box."

"That's right." Gene nodded. "Michael said, 'Don't open it. Only if I don't come back.' "

"O-h-h, Gene." Peg stopped at the bedroom door. "He didn't say that. Michael never thought for a minute he wouldn't be coming back. He didn't think that way at all. He was a positive thinker." She continued on into the bedroom, past John, who was still lying there, and took the tackle box from the top of Michael's closet to the kitchen table. She untaped the key, unlocked the box and lifted out the tray with his arrowheads, the stripes and infantry school insignia from Fort Benning. Beneath the tray was a carefully folded piece of tablet paper. Peg opened the paper and saw that Michael had meticulously copied out the names and addresses of all the people who were important to him. Peg sat there holding the list in her hands.

"What is it?" Gene asked.

"Names," Peg said. "Everybody in Michael's life. . . ."

There were Michael's roommates at Rockhurst and the University of Missouri, the eighty-five-year-old La Porte couple whose grocery shopping he did when he was home, the close friend whose wife he had always liked so much, Caroline Roby and her mother, his sisters' college addresses. There were maybe twenty names on the list, some of which Peg didn't recognize.

She passed the paper over to Gene, who didn't know them either but felt they were important enough to call. Peg next came to Michael's insurance papers.

There was a $10,000 policy with the Knights of Columbus, a $1,000 policy with Federal Life and another $10,000 policy with the U.S. Army. Michael had indicated that he wanted the Army policy split four ways: $2,500 each to Gene and Peg, $2,500 to the Don Bosco High School "for the purchase of new science equipment" and the last $2,500 to "a dear friend so that she might study medicine." The "dear friend," obviously, was Caroline Roby, but Peg didn't know how to go about getting in touch with her.

"Call John Stagg," Gene suggested.

John Stagg had been Michael's roommate at the University of Missouri, and Stagg knew Caroline through Michael. Gene felt Stagg would be the best one to tell her. "She'll have to know that Michael is dead, that he left her that money."

"I know, I know," Peg said, "it's just that. . . ." Her voice trailed off.

"What?"

"I get the feeling that the thing between Michael and Caroline had, well, tapered off."

"We still got to tell her," Gene said.

At two thirty in the morning, while the Mullens were waiting for their daughter Mary and Peg's sister, Louise Petersen, to arrive from Kansas City, Peg started writing down all the information she had learned from her conversation with Sergeant Fitzgerald. She wasn't sure yet why she was doing it, but she felt a need to commit the details to paper. Gene got up from the kitchen table to check on John, who was awake, lying with his arms folded behind his head, staring up at the ceiling.

"Johnny," Gene asked quietly, "are you all right?"

"I'm okay, Dad. . . ." John turned to his father standing in the doorway. "You know, Dad? Mikey's got it made."

"What do you mean?"

"I mean he's in heaven now. He doesn't have to be afrai—to worry about what's going to happen to him next."

Gene stood looking down at Michael's empty bed, then back at John, and because he knew he was going to cry, Gene hurried out through the kitchen past Peg and on into the darkened living room, where he sank into a chair and buried his face in his hands.

"Gene?"

There was only the sound of Gene crying.

"Gene?" Peg called across the room. "Are you all right?"

He struggled to bring himself under control. "I was thinking about Johnny," he said, "I was thinking here's this boy, just eighteen years old, with this mind of . . . of purity and love for his fellowman"—he shook his head sorrowfully—"and here you have these, these people, these vicious people in the world who want to take him away from us, who want him in their army so that he can . . . can fight in their war. . . . *Who wants war?*" He glanced up at Peg sitting beneath the glare of the kitchen lights and answered his question himself: "I don't."

Peg did not speak.

"I don't want war," Gene said again.

Chapter Six

There is no telegraph office in La Porte City. Telegrams are transmitted by teletype from the Waterloo Western Union office to the office of the mayor of La Porte, and it is old Peter Dobkin's job to deliver the telegrams in person. Dobkin, a tall, thin, grandfatherly-looking World War I veteran in his mid-seventies, knocked on the Mullens' door on Sunday morning, Washington's Birthday.

Gene Mullen ushered Dobkin up the stairs and into the kitchen, which was already crowded again with the Mullen family and friends.

"Hello, Peter," Peg said, "would you care for a cup of coffee?"

"No, no, thank you, Mrs. Mullen," he said, "I've come on official business. I've got a telegram for you."

"Oh?" Peg started to reach for the telegram, but Dobkin didn't pass it to her.

"I'm supposed to read it to you," he said. He looked at his wristwatch and, as the voices hushed about him, began to read: "Time: Eleven Seventeen A-Yem. To: 'Mr. and Mrs. Oscar E. Mullen, Rural Route Three, La Porte City, Iowa, Report. Deliver. Don't Phone. . . .'" Dobkin paused to clear his throat, then continued. " 'The Secretary of the Army has asked me to express his deep regret that your son, Sergeant Michael E. Mullen, died in Vietnam on 18 February 1970. He was at a night defensive position when artillery fire from friendly forces landed in the area. Please accept my deepest sympathy. This confirms personal notification made by a representative of the Secretary of the Army.' . . . It is signed, 'Kenneth G. Wickham,'" Dobkin read, " 'Major General, United States Army, C-dash-Zero-Five-Two-dash-One-Eight

63

Nine, The Adjutant General, Department of the Army, Washington, D.C.' ' "

There was an awkward moment of silence while Dobkin stood in a pose somewhat suggesting the position of attention, and Peg said, "Well, thank you, Peter. . . ."

Dobkin nodded perfunctorily, handed her the telegram and left.

Peg dropped the telegram onto the growing stack of papers on the kitchen table. "It doesn't tell us anything we don't already know," she said.

Sunday afternoon Peter Dobkin returned with a second telegram. "Time: Three Oh Five, P-Yem. To: 'Mr. and Mrs. Oscar E. Mullen, Rural Route Three, La Porte City, Iowa. Report. Deliver. Don't Phone. . . .' "

The telegram contained information on the return of Michael's body, how much money would be allowed for the burial and cautioned the Mullens not to make formal arrangements until contacted by the Army again. It also listed Michael's rank as private first class, not sergeant.

The error was routine administrative carelessness. But as an indication of the bureaucratic impersonality with which the Army considered the death of their son, it infuriated the Mullens.

Dobkin handed the telegram to Peg, and because he was also a representative of the local Veterans of Foreign Wars chapter, he began talking about the military funeral he expected the Mullens to hold. "We will provide both an American flag and a VFW flag at the funeral home," Dobkin was saying, "and at the grave we can have an honor guard and a bugler—oh, the honor guard will be in uniform, caps and ties, with polished rifles. We can fire a salute if you wish—"

"I don't wish!" Peg said.

"Pardon?"

"We don't want a military funeral, Peter," Peg said. "Michael was a biochemistry student."

"Well, yes," Dobkin said, "but he's entitled. . . ."

"I don't care," Peg said.

"Okay, but if you should change your mind. . . ."

64

"We won't!" Gene said with such certainty that Peg looked at him with surprise.

"You don't want one either?" she asked.

Gene Mullen had been on one of the first honor guard firing squads in Iowa during World War II. The body of a young Army private killed on Wake Island had been brought back to Des Moines for a military funeral, and his grave was no more than twenty-five feet from one of the main roads into Des Moines. As Gene and the rest of the honor guard had stood at attention with their rifles at present arms, car after car had passed by. Not one driver had slowed or paid the least bit of attention. Gene had never forgotten the sham their lack of respect had made of the young soldier's sacrifice. He didn't want that to happen to his boy. And, too, Gene had been angered by Dobkin's obvious eagerness to hold a military funeral, an eagerness that suggested Michael's death meant no more to him than an opportunity for all the local American Legionnaires and VFW members to dress up in their uniforms so that they could play soldier again. Gene knew who would make up Dobkin's honor guard firing squad, and later, when Peg asked Gene why he hadn't wanted a military funeral, he answered, "I don't want those Legion types firing over our son's grave."

Several of the Mullens' friends called that afternoon to ask them to release the news of Michael's death since there were still many people in La Porte who thought it was only a rumor. Peg hadn't realized that the Army, as the Mullens had requested, had not sent out the news to the press. She called the local radio and television stations and newspapers and confirmed what Gene had told them the day before, that Michael had been killed by ARVN artillery and that the story could now be released.

Father Shimon, who had declined the Mullens' invitation for dinner Sunday night, did stop by later for some coffee. At first, conversation around the kitchen table was casual and light. Gene discovered that he and Father Shimon had been together at Camp Dodge for about a year just after the start of the Second World War. They talked about life in the Army until, over second cups of coffee, Gene asked the priest what he thought of the Vietnam War.

"Do you consider this war an immoral war?" Gene asked.

"*Im*-moral?" Father Shimon repeated, licking his lips.

"Yes or no?" Gene asked.

"Peg knows I'm, ah-h, against the war."

"Then you do consider the war immoral?"

"Yes-s-s."

"And how long have you felt this way about the war?" Gene asked.

"I've been, ah, thinking it for about a year. . . . I have my own private feelings about it."

"Only 'private' feelings?" Gene asked.

"I've never taken a public stand on the war."

"Why not?"

"Because I don't think that's my place. I don't make public statements," Father Shimon said. "I have private feelings, my own, ah, personal feelings. I go to veterans hospitals. I say prayers. Peg knows how I feel."

"Peg knows! *Peg knows*," Gene said angrily. "But nobody else does. What kind of man of God are you? Why don't you stand up like a man and speak out instead of whisper against the war!"

Father Shimon sat in embarrassed silence.

"Do you plan to take any public stand?" Gene asked him.

"No-o-o, Gene, I don't think so. . . ."

"Why not? Because you're chaplain for the American Legion?"

"Gene," Peg said, laying her hand on his arm, "wasn't Sergeant Fitzgerald supposed to get back in touch with us today?"

"That's right," Gene said, "he never did call about the escort, did he?"

Father Shimon, grateful for the change of subject, finished his coffee and hurried home.

66

"What was the matter with you?" Peg asked Gene later. "I thought you were going to hit him!"

A little after ten o'clock the next morning Army Captain Ralph T. Pringle introduced himself as the senior survivors' assistance officer. He had come to the farm to pick up their request for the special escort and alternate special escort. The Mullens provided the names, ranks, serial numbers and APO addresses of two boys who had been in college with Michael, both of whom were now in Vietnam. Captain Pringle said he would send their request to the Pentagon immediately since time was short, and the Mullens naturally wondered why, if time was so short, hadn't Captain Pringle or Sergeant Fitzgerald got in touch with them yesterday?

"Now, Mr. and Mrs. Mullen," Captain Pringle was saying, "you can plan on a delay of about ten days between the time of your son's death and his body's arrival. That would mean he should arrive in Waterloo on or about the . . . let's see, the twenty-eighth."

"He'll be here Saturday?" Gene asked.

"We can't state that for certain," Captain Pringle said. "The time of his arrival depends entirely upon the number of deaths in Vietnam during the week he died."

"We know that," Peg said. "Sergeant Fitzgerald told us the body is returned when they have enough to make a planeful. I also know Michael will be home soon. I'm sure the losses are greater than we're being told. I'm positive of that."

Unknown to Captain Pringle and the Mullens, Michael's body was to arrive in Oakland that very day.

Late that afternoon an Iowa couple whose son had been killed in Vietnam the year before came to the Mullens' farm to lend sympathy and support.

"The thing that sticks most in my mind," the father told them, "was the night before our boy left for Vietnam, he was lying on his bed in his room and I went in to see him. I walked in and he turned over and looked at me and he said, 'Dad?' he said, 'Dad, I'm scared.' He was lying there shivering, shaking in his bed. He said, 'I'm so *scared,* Dad.' "

"You see," the mother said, "our son told us he'd never come back. He died only a month after he got there. I knew he would. I knew it! The day he left for Vietnam I *knew* I would never see him again."

Peter Dobkin arrived back at the Mullens' farm a little after nine thirty on Tuesday morning with a third telegram. Dobkin stood at the door, looked at his watch, cleared his throat and announced, "Time Zero Nine Thirty-seven Hours. To: 'Oscar E. Mullen, Rural Route Thr—' "

"I can read," Peg interrupted impatiently. "Just give me the telegram."

"I got to," Dobkin said. "It's my job." He read them the telegram, which stated that Michael's remains would be consigned to the funeral home of the Mullens' choice in Waterloo, and again he suggested they consider a military funeral, but when he saw the look on Peg and Gene's faces, he decided not to press the matter and left.

Gene immediately telephoned William Wagner, a La Porte lawyer and former mayor, who was then vice-commander of the local American Legion chapter. "Now look," Gene told him, "this Dobkin is plain bothering us about having a military funeral, and we're not going to have one. So you better not send him out here again!"

That morning's mail brought the first letters from others whose sons had been killed in Vietnam. The majority were short, not more than three or four lines each:

> May it help comfort you to know that the loss you bear is shared by many others. Our son is still missing in Vietnam.
> (s) The Family of Staff Sergeant Michael T_____.

> We read in the paper of your son's death. We know you don't know us, but we wanted to extend to you our deepest sympathy. We know only too well the depth of your loss. We, too,

have lost our son. Is there anything we can do to
help you?
(s) Mr. and Mrs. Leroy P————.

We're so sorry that you, too, have lost a pre-
cious son.
(s) Parents of Michael B————.
Born Feb. 20th, 1947, Killed Dec. 20th, 1970,
Vietnam

That same mail brought a letter from the former
neighbor whose young wife had died of the aneurysm,
the man who had smashed up his car at the dead
end. Peg read it silently, then called her husband
over.

"Gene, listen to this." Peg told him who the letter
was from. "It says, 'Dear Peg and Gene: It isn't that I
couldn't afford a card, but I couldn't find one that
would express my feelings. I'm deeply sorry about
Mike. He is probably the only one of your kids that I
got to know. I know it is a shock to get a telegram
like that. I heard the news Sunday. You people went
through so much with my family and even me, that I
don't know where to thank you. . . .' See!" Peg said
holding up the letter. "Look at the blanks."

She showed Gene the open space on the stationery
about the size of an eight-line paragraph.

"See?" she asked. "He says, 'I'm leaving it out to
express my belief or maybe the reason. . . .'" Peg
looked up at Gene again, "'The blank space is for what
he can't say. Can't express." And then she read on:
"'For no one knows for sure what is beyond. But we
are certain that it isn't worse than a lot of things we
have to live with here. You were always the best neighbors we had and I don't intend to forget it.

"'My paragraphing, my spelling, and my language is bad. But I think you will be able to read it.
I don't know how to spell the words.

"'Gene, if you need a pallbearer, I would be available if you call on me. . . .'" Peg refolded the letter
and carefully slid it back into its envelope. "Isn't that
nice, Gene?" she asked. "That's just so nice of him."

At five minutes to four the Mullens received a telephone call from an employee of the Loomis Funeral Home in Waterloo, who said he had received notification that Michael's body would arrive at 7:45 P.M. the following evening, February 25, "escorted by Sergeant First Class Ronald Fallon."

"*Fallon?* Who?" Peg asked, "We didn't ask for any Sergeant Fallon! Hold on a minute, will you?" She cupped the mouthpiece and called for Gene. "It's the funeral home. They say Michael's body will be here tomorrow night, escorted by a Sergeant Ronald Fallon."

"Who's he?" Gene asked.

"Hello?" Peg said back into the telephone. "We don't know any Sergeant Fallon. We've never heard of him. He isn't the escort we asked for."

Peg called Captain Pringle immediately. The survivors' assistance officer explained that he had telegraphed their request for the special escort to the Pentagon, but that it had either arrived too late in the day for anyone to act on it or been ignored because Monday had been an official holiday since Washington's Birthday had fallen on a Sunday.

"Captain Pringle," Peg said—and she began to come down hard on her R's—"Captain Pringle, may I remind you that our son tramped through the mud and jungles of Vietnam for six months regardless of holidays, and we still want the escort we chose, not this Sergeant Fallon, who nobody's heard of. We were told that to have a deceased soldier's body returned accompanied by a special escort chosen by the next of kin was our right! A right accorded the families of *all* war victims. Isn't that so?"

"Yes, but—"

"Then that's what we'll have," Peg said. "That's who we want. We don't want this Fallon, who Michael never met. We want either Tom Hurley or John Salvato; those are the boys we want. Now don't you tell me that the Pentagon can't even honor the dead by providing the services they need simply because it's a holiday."

70

"All right, Mrs. Mullen," Pringle said, "I'll call the Pentagon and see what I can do."

"You do that," she said, and hung up.

About twenty minutes later Captain Pringle called back. "Mrs. Mullen," he said, "I'll give it to you straight. The man in the Pentagon in charge of special escorts, a Mr. McClain, when I told him you still wanted your escort, he said, 'Tell that lady in La Porte City that she can have her escort in—take it or leave it—ten to fifteen more days.' "

"Fifteen more days!" Peg stormed. "Captain Pringle, you can tell that sonuvabitch in the Pentagon that I'll wait fifteen years for my son to come back! My son's dead! We could put off having him come back in a casket forever! We don't care when he gets back. He's dead!"

Captain Pringle tried to explain why there would be such a long delay: that it would take a couple of days to cut the orders in Washington, another couple of days to get them to Vietnam, another couple of days to locate their escort, another day to get him on a plane and so on. Peg listened impatiently, then said, "I don't believe you! My boy was killed in the jungles of Vietnam, airlifted out of there, rammed through a mortuary in Saigon, put on a plane and was in Oakland in less than five days! So don't you tell me that you can't get a *live* boy out of there in less than two days!"

Captain Pringle thought for a moment. "I'll tell you what, Mrs. Mullen. I think you'd be better off if you called the Pentagon yourself and told them that. The man's name is McClain, and he's the one to talk to." He gave her the telephone number.

"Well, I don't see why we have to make that call," Peg said. "You're the man who's supposed to assist us."

"I'm trying to, Mrs. Mullen," Captain Pringle said, "but I think you should be aware that your insistence on the special escort will definitely be a delaying factor. A great many people prefer to cancel the special escort requests so that they can more quickly complete their funeral plans, but if you insist. . . . I feel

71

certain you'll have more success if you call Mr. Mc-
Clain at the Pentagon yourself."

As soon as Captain Pringle hung up, Peg called
Senator Harold Hughes' office in Washington. Peg had
met Hughes, then governor of Iowa, through her activities with the Democratic Party.

Hughes had just received Patricia's letter telling
him of Michael's death, and he told Peg how terribly
sorry he was, especially since he knew his letter suggesting how Michael might get out of combat must
have arrived after Michael died. Peg relayed Captain
Pringle's remarks about Mr. McClain at the Pentagon,
and said she felt the Senator was the only one she could
turn to for help.

Senator Hughes hesitated. "Peg, I can't cure all
the ills in the world. . . ."

"But can't you do something?" Peg pleaded. "My
family is so upset. . . ."

"All right, Peg, we'll try. Look, let me get you to
talk to Pat. He's my liaison man, with the Pentagon.
Hold on a minute, okay?"

Peg told the same story to the Senator's liaison
man, who asked, "Are you sure you really want to insist that we bring Hurley or this Salvato out of Vietnam? I mean, has it occurred to you what might happen to your escort when he went back? He might have
a good assignment now, see, but I'm wondering whether
the Army mightn't put him in combat when he returns
just because of our interference."

"I'm not afraid of the Pentagon," Peg answered.
"And I still have enough faith in the Good Lord and
my dead son that whoever it is, Tom Hurley or John
Salvato, they'll be taken care of."

"I don't agree with you," the aide said. "They
may put him directly into combat."

"You won't do it?"

"No, we'll do it. We'll do it," the aide told her.
"Give us about twelve hours. We'll call you back tomorrow morning."

Between seven and eight that evening Peter Dobkin read the Mullens their fourth telegram. He did not

72

come out to the farm; he relayed its contents over the telephone. The telegram from the Oakland Army Terminal Mortuary instructed them to disregard all previous messages. Michael's body would be held pending arrival of his special escort.

An hour later the Mullens received a telephone call from the Memorial Division duty officer at the Pentagon advising them that their special request for the escort would be honored after all.

And then Father Shimon called.

"Peg," he said, "I've been thinking about what you want. . . . this White Funeral, this Don Bosco Chorus, Father this and Father that, and, ah, I think it's time to call a halt to the production you're talking about for Michael's funeral. I can't go along with you, Peg. We're not going to have a production."

"Well, Father Shimon," Peg replied, "if you consider 'perfection' a production, that's what we'll have. Because Michael's life was sort of perfect. He did things well. He didn't leave many jobs undone. If doing things right for him means having a production, we'll just have a production."

Father Shimon said, "Nope. Nope. Nope."

Peg hung up on him.

Peter Dobkin telephoned the Mullens early Wednesday morning with the fifth telegram. It was sent by the Memorial Division and confirmed that either Tom Hurley or John Salvato would be located in Vietnam and returned as their special escort.

The morning mail contained a 9-by-12-inch brown manila envelope from the White House. Inside, on a piece of note paper with a half-size White House letterhead, was a message signed by some minor aide stating that, because of the correspondence Peg had addressed to the White House, President Nixon wished her to know that he was truly sorry that her son had died. The note was paper-clipped to a Xeroxed collection of President Nixon's various Vietnamization speeches. Peg was so offended that she resealed the envelope immediately, showed its contents to no one and mailed it back to the White House with the notation printed in large red letters in the upper-left-hand corner: RETURN TO SENDER. NOT INTERESTED.

The mail also contained more letters from friends and the parents of other young men killed in Vietnam. Gene and Peg sat at the kitchen table sifting through the correspondence, selecting parts to read aloud.

"Now, who's this?" Peg asked. She turned the letter over to see the signature. "Oh! This is someone else who lost their son. 'You don't know us,' they write, 'but we are truly sorry and know just how you feel. We lost our own dear boy, September 15, 1968. He was a wonderful son. . . .' " Peg picked up another and read it silently to herself. "Oh, now, Gene, here, listen to this. . . ."

It was a woman from a neighboring township whose son had been killed the year before. The mother wrote that although her boy had suffered a terrible head wound, she was grateful she had been able to recognize that it was her son. "She says, 'We didn't care to let anybody else see but the family; it was terrible to take.' She then goes on to say that there are some mothers who are never certain it is their son they bury. The people in L_____ weren't. They still doubt it, you know. . . ."

Added to their anguish over the continuing wait was the Mullens' uncertainty over what condition Michael's body would be in. A close friend had told them that her sister-in-law's brother, a mortician in Oakland, had called to tell her he had worked on Michael's body. He said that three planeloads of bodies had arrived in Oakland—one on Monday of "viewable" bodies and two on Tuesday of "nonviewable" bodies. Michael, the Mullens believed, had arrived in Oakland on Monday, but they could not be certain. Peg and Gene were unable to believe that Michael could be "viewable." If Michael had been killed by ARVN artillery, should he not have been "blown to pieces"?

Gene put his letters aside, but Peg could not leave hers. She would pick up one after another, turn

74

it over, read it, put it down and search through the stack for a new one. "Oh, Gene, this is from A_____," an Ozark girl who had baby-sat for the Mullen children years before. "Listen, she says, 'Dear Peg and Gene: We heard about Mike. I can't tell you how sorry I am. Peg, I was just sick when I heard it. It seems like such a waste. . . .'" Peg looked up at Gene for a moment, then reached for another letter and skimmed through it silently. "Here, Gene, another: 'Your family has our sympathy. What a tragedy, yes. Our Mike came home Friday night. He was killed at _____.'" Peg put the letter down and brushed her hand through the stack. "All these letters. . . ."

"Who would have thought . . ." Gene said.

"They mean so much, you know?"

"I know," Gene said.

"This one's from those two women we met when we went on the bus trip east last October. . . . And this is from another girl who baby-sat for us. . . . And this, let's see . . . 'Just to let you know our thoughts and prayers are with you constantly in these trying days and nights. We wonder if the saying, "These are the days that try men's souls," was ever more applicable to we Americans and those back of us, the ones coming up. We truly wish there was something we could say. . . .'"

"Who's that?" Gene asked.

It was from an elderly lady on a neighboring farm. Peg fanned through a batch of small cards. "'Remembering you, Parents of Sgt. Jay K _____,' . . . 'Our Michael was killed at . . .' . . . 'The Parents of the Late Thomas W _____,' . . . 'My Michael died at _____' —all these *Michaels!*" Peg exclaimed. "It seems that everybody twenty-five years ago named their sons Michael!" She gathered the letters together in her lap. "It's like a fraternity, you know? I mean these people all over the state who have lost their sons. I never would have thought they'd write like this, but they do. . . . Here, this one says, 'I'm simply no good at expressing myself, but I had to tell you that your grief is shared. It is so difficult to understand why. . . .'" Peg rubbed her brow. "'To understand why,'" she repeated. "These letters, they all write and try to explain, to understand why their sons died and you guess there's a reason, but I don't see it. I really don't see it. Do you, Gene?"

"What?" Gene asked, lost in thought.

"Out of the—what? How many now, thirty-five thousand? Forty thousand? Out of all those thousands who have lost their sons, I bet all but a few feel the way we do. . . ."

Peg would not leave the letters alone. " 'In memory of Thomas C _____, August 12, 1969,' " she read. "And here, 'Parents of Lance Corporal James P _____, December 19: We want you to know that you have our sympathy. We truly understand your heartache. These things are so hard to understand and not something you will ever get over. But with God's help . . .' and so on—no, here: 'Our sons are all fine men and we can be proud of them.' . . . Did you know that two Waterloo fathers who lost their sons died within a year after their boys were killed? There's that, too," Peg said, glancing over at Gene. "Fathers grieve worse than mothers, I think. They can't handle it. Can't express their grief."

Gene did not move.

Peg looked at him worriedly. She passed him a letter. "Here, Gene, read this."

The letter was from a family who had moved away. Gene read it slowly, softly, with obvious effort. "We grieve with you. I told our girls, what can friends do? Really nothing. Only God can console you. Our Carmelite sister, Mary, keeps reminding us parents that God gave us our children and so they really belong to Him. We can pray for Mike and we are having a mass said for him. I'm beginning to become a Conscientious Objector myself when our finest young men are being taken from us in this crazy war. But accept our humble condolences and our far away presence. I wish we were closer. I simply hate to tell our Patricia, she—' "

"Remember her?" Peg interrupted. "Her Patricia and our Patricia worked in the post office together one summer?"

Gene nodded and continued to read: "'hate to tell our Patricia, she feels things so deeply, and is so antiwar now. . . .' " Gene could not read any more.

"That girl was in everything there was at the University of Michigan," Peg said. "Then she got tied up and dropped out completely. She didn't even finish school. She's out in—oh, I don't even know where. California somewhere?"

Gene dropped the letter back in the pile.

"This, too, Gene. Listen, 'From the Parents of Specialist Dean B _____, January 23, 1970. Only ones—' Oh, now *listen,* Gene. 'Only ones who have lost a son in Vietnam.' " Peg paused and reread the line again with great deliberateness: "'Only-ones-who-have-lost-a-son-in-Vietnam-know-the-*heartache*-and-*anguish*-it-brings. We lost our son a month ago at the age of twenty-one.' " Peg looked up at her husband. "Oh-h-h, Gene. . . ."

He was sitting across from her quietly, not moving, tears flowing down his cheeks.

"Gene? Don't, please?"

He shook his head and wiped at the tears with his hands. Peg walked over to him and laid her hand on his shoulder. "Gene?"

"I can't help it," he said. "I can't help it."

"It's all right," Peg said. "It's all right."

For the six days since the Mullens had learned of their son's death, their farmhouse had been filled with family and friends waiting for Michael's body to arrive. The people in town knew only that for some reason or other the Mullens had refused to permit the corpse to be returned. There was one rumor in La Porte that the Mullens had taken a shotgun after the survivors' assistance officer who had brought them word of Michael's death. A great many La Porte people couldn't understand the Mullens' behavior, thought it vaguely un-American, somehow unpatriotic.

Cecil Joens, a bachelor neighbor whom Michael had gone to see his last afternoon on the farm, had reportedly got into several scrapes defending the Mullens in town, and yet he had not stopped by to see Gene or

Peg at the farm. Cecil had always been the Mullens' closest friend and neighbor, a man whose understanding and generosity they could always count on, and it bothered them that he had not been by. It was unlike Cecil to ignore them. When the farmer who lived down at the corner of John Dobshire's road took his tractor out onto Route 218, the two-lane hardtop between La Porte City and Waterloo, and was run down by the speeding tractor trailer truck, it was Cecil who brought in that farmer's harvest, stored his grain until the price was right and took care of the widow's needs. But Cecil had suffered a heart attack. Although not a major one, the attack was still brutal enough to make Cecil know that that was how he was going to die, and it scared him. It touched him deep in the very pit of his being, and he was never quite the same. No more would he subject his heart to a strain—physical or emotional. He had loved Michael like a son. They had gone to basketball games, football games, 4-H meetings together. In a sense, Cecil was Michael's second father, the man who came when the hogs escaped and Gene was off at John Deere. Cecil had stayed home rather than visit the Mullens because his grief was already so great that he dared not put the extra strain on his heart. Nevertheless, he was the first to defend the Mullens against the Legionnaires outraged by Gene's comment about not wanting those "USO soldiers" firing over his son's grave. And Father Shimon quashed a rumor about the Mullens going after Sergeant Fitzgerald with a shotgun.

Thursday morning Father Shimon telephoned to ask Peg if she knew yet when the funeral would be held.

"I hope to know by noon, Father," Peg said. "If Michael comes today, we'll hold the funeral on Saturday."

"Saturday?" the priest said. "You know we can't have the funeral on Saturday!"

"Why not?" Peg asked. "Why can't we?"

"We have catechism on Saturday, Peg. . . . And I'm, ah, I'm not going to interrupt my catechism program."

"Okay, Father," Peg said. "We'll have our funeral service on our front yard if we have to. But we'll have it Saturday if this is what we want."

She hung up the telephone and looked first at her husband and next at her houseful of family and friends, the classmates of their children, neighbors who had come to their farmhouse. She told Gene she thought it might be nice to get out of the house for a while.

Four more area boys had died in Vietnam that week, and one was missing in action. Sergeant Fitzgerald had confided to the Mullens that it was only a matter of time before he would have to tell the missing boy's mother her son was dead, that he had been killed in his tank. She was a widow, and he had been her only son. Peg thought they should visit her to see whether there was anything they might do.

The boy's mother lived in a little tenant farmhouse outside Waverly, the county seat of Bremer County, about fourteen miles north of Waterloo. The Mullens found her farm and were surprised that no other cars were there. Peg was particularly shocked because they were surrounded by people at their own home. She and Gene got out of their car, walked up to the small porch and knocked. After a long wait a middle-aged woman opened the front door, but remained behind the locked storm door looking through the window at Peg and Gene.

"May I see Mrs. F_____?" Peg asked.

"I'm Mrs. F_____," she said.

"Are you alone here?" Peg asked.

"Yes. What do you want?"

"I'm Peg Mullen," she said. "This is my husband Gene. Our son was killed last week in Vietnam and . . . well, we know your son is missing, that he's missing in action and we thought maybe we could help you. . . ."

The woman remained behind the locked door.

"Really," Peg said, "can't we come in?"

The woman did not answer.

"We've had so many people, friends come to see us, and they've been such a help to us. . . . I can't believe you're here all alone. Can't we come in?"

The woman finally nodded yes and unlocked the

storm door. Peg and Gene followed her inside, where two little girls stood watching wide-eyed and frightened, knuckles pressed to their lips. The woman brushed some books and papers off the old sofa and gestured that that was where the Mullens were to sit. She lowered herself onto a worn upholstered chair across from them and remained there, looking at the Mullens as if waiting for them to speak, so Peg did.

"Where was your son in Vietnam?" Peg asked.

"I don't know," the woman said.

"You don't?" Peg asked, astonished.

The woman didn't answer.

Gene asked, "You mean, he never wrote to you from Vietnam?"

"He wrote me."

"But didn't you write him?" Peg said. "Didn't you ask where he was?"

"I wrote to his APO address in San Francisco," she said.

"Didn't he tell you anything in his letters?" Peg asked.

"Yes, but he never said where he was."

"And you don't know what unit he was with?" Gene asked.

"No, I don't."

"I can't understand this," Peg said. "You mean you never asked your son where he was or . . . or what unit he was with, or what he was doing?"

"Yes, I asked him."

"And he didn't tell you?"

"He told me," the woman said.

"But then you say you don't know," Gene said. "You said—"

"He told you where he was and what he was doing and you say you don't know where he was or what he was doing," Peg said. *What is the matter with you?*

The woman stiffened. "I can't talk."

"What do you mean?" Peg asked.

"I just can't," she said.

"But your son is missing in action," Peg insisted.

80

"He was in a tank that was burned and you say, you say you can't talk. What on earth is wrong with you?"

"Well, now I'll tell you," the woman said. "We've been informed by the Army that we can't discuss this with anyone because it might—it might 'aid and abet the enemy.' Until they confirm or deny that my son is dead or wounded, I'm simply not allowed to talk to anyone. And I won't."

"Well, if I were you," Peg said, "I'd get down on my knees and pray to God that they find your son, because I read in the newspapers—"

"Peg!" Gene warned.

"—about the battle he was in, and I don't think your son could have surv—"

"PEG!" Gene took his wife firmly by the hand and pulled her to her feet before she could finish. "We'd better be going, Mrs. F_____," Gene said. "If there's anything we can do for you, please let us know. We hope we haven't upset you. . . ." He got Peg out the door, then turned back. "It's so very sad, so hard. . . ." The woman closed the door on them and turned away.

"What was the matter with her?" Peg asked as she got into the car. "Her son is dead! He was burned to death in a tank! For God's sake, they're not going to find her son, there's nothing *left* of him. And she still does what they tell her!"

From Waverly, the Mullens drove due east on Route 3 through Fayette County, then south to Dundee, a tiny town on the banks of the Maquoketa River, the home of the mother of a boy who had been killed the same day as Michael. The Mullens stopped at the general store to ask directions, and a man there said, "It's so kind of you to come to see those people that I'll take you out to where they live myself."

"You don't have to do that," Gene said. "Just tell us the way."

"Nope, I'll take you," the man said. "You'd never find it otherwise."

The Mullens followed the man along the dirt section line roads, zigged and zagged until finally they reached a dilapidated and paint-peeled farmhouse and a broken-down barn. When Peg and Gene came up to the door, the woman invited them in right away. The Mullens explained why they had come, that Michael had died the same day as her son, and Peg noticed that here, too, no one had visited or brought any food. The mother thanked and thanked them for coming, explained that she was on welfare, that it had been very hard for them lately, but she hoped things would be better.

"You know, Mrs. Mullen"—the woman sighed —"this was the third of my sons to go to Vietnam."

"Your *third?*" Peg asked.

"I have seven sons," she explained, "and I prayed the first two out of the war, but when they drafted my third son, I was so discouraged. . . . He was my best son, mentally, physically, in every way, and when they drafted him, too, well I kind of lost faith in God. I guess I couldn't pray hard enough to pray him back home. But," she said, smiling bravely, "the draft board is so kind. When I went to visit with them, they told me they would only draft five of my sons for Vietnam."

Chapter Seven

It was now Friday morning, February 27, the seventh day since the Mullens had learned of their son's death and the third day since Captain Pringle had told Peg Mullen to call the Pentagon herself. The Mullens had not heard from the captain since. They knew neither who would be escorting Michael's body nor when it would arrive. The Mullen family, anxious, tired of waiting, was beginning to grow angry with Peg. In their impatience, they blamed Peg, she felt, because she had "defied the Pentagon and demanded our rights."

That morning Peg recalled that Senator Hughes' aide had told her to wait no longer than three days, that if no word had come from the Army concerning their request for the special escort by then, the Senator would have Michael's remains released and sent home. It was the third day, so Peg telephoned the Senator's office to find out what she should do. The aide told her to wait a little longer; he would contact the Pentagon himself to see what was going on. He called back almost immediately. One of the escorts had, in fact, been located and was in the air on his way to Oakland. The aide did not, however, know which one. Peg thanked him and told him not to worry, that Captain Pringle would be able to tell them when he got in touch.

By four o'clock that afternoon, when the captain had still not called, Peg decided to telephone his office herself. She was told that Captain Pringle was not in, was not expected back, and that she might try him later at his home.

Moments later one of the ladies of Father Shimon's Sacred Heart Catholic Church telephoned that they were making their preparations for the dinner to be served those attending the funeral on Saturday, the next day.

"You're getting the dinner ready?" Peg asked, surprised. "But there isn't going to be any funeral tomorrow!"

"What do you mean?" the lady asked. "We thought you told Father Shimon—"

"I told him—I told Father Shimon yesterday morning that if we heard anything, if Michael's body arrived yesterday, we would hold the funeral Saturday," Peg said. "But Michael's body isn't here yet, and . . . well, we just don't know when it will be."

"Then you won't be holding the funeral tomorrow?"

"I don't see how we can," Peg said tersely.

"Peg, I don't understand. What are you *doing* to Father Shimon?"

"What do you mean?"

"I mean he's so . . . so disturbed by all this."

"I don't know what I'm doing to him," Peg said, "but I do know what he's doing to me."

"I think it's terribly cruel," the lady said. "Father Shimon built the hall for this sort of thing, and now you don't even want to use it."

"Look," Peg said, "if we have the crowd we're expecting for the funeral, then we'll probably need the whole space, the dining room back of the church and all. If we have the Don Bosco Chorus and John's high school class, they'll simply overflow the church. We'll need all that extra room. That's why we sort of decided among ourselves today that we'd be better off if we go to dinner at the country club—that's where we went before the church was built anyway."

"What do you want me to tell Father Shimon?"

"I don't care what you say," Peg replied. "Tell him we can't make plans yet. We don't know when Michael's—when the funeral will be held. How many will attend. We just don't know."

"So you don't want to have dinner down here?"

"We don't really care whether we have the dinner or not. Do what you want," Peg said. "All we're sure of is that the funeral will not be tomorrow."

When Peg did try Captain Pringle's home, there was no answer, so she called his office again. The office phone was busy. For the next hour Peg tried both phones. The office continued busy, and there was no answer at the house. Peg began to worry.

Captain Pringle told Peg he would have to contact the four other families that week whose sons had been killed in Vietnam. She could tell how these deaths disturbed him, how much he hated his job. She believed him to be a compassionate man, and she began to worry that, like the Waterloo Marine survivors' assistance officer they'd heard about, Pringle might have suffered a nervous breakdown. Maybe even taken his own life. She discussed her concern with the telephone operator, who suggested Peg call a Mrs. Mason with the Red Cross. Mrs. Mason did everything in her power to locate the captain but was unable to find him. When Pringle's office phone remained busy for several hours that evening, Peg called a friend in the Waterloo telephone company to ask whether there might be something wrong with the captain's line. Peg continued trying to reach Captain Pringle before finally giving up that night at eleven o'clock.

Peg's friend with Northwestern Bell in Waterloo reported early Saturday morning that Captain Pringle's office phone had, in fact, been taken off its hook. The Mullens decided to help themselves. They first contacted Ozark Airlines, one of the airlines servicing their part of the Midwest, and explained that they were entering their second weekend since having received notification of their son's death. Might Ozark Airlines, they asked, have any record of an advance booking indicating when their son's body would return? Within minutes an Ozark employee was able to tell the Mullens that Michael's body was scheduled to arrive at the Waterloo Airport on their 7:45 P.M. Sunday evening flight.

At about ten o'clock that same morning, Sergeant Fitzgerald checked in. He told the Mullens that the captain should not have gone off without notifying Sergeant Fitzgerald that he was to act for him. Peg

85

said they had been able to learn when Michael was to reach Waterloo, but could the sergeant discover which of the two boys they had requested as the escort would be the one to accompany him? The sergeant explained there was no way for him to find out; he knew only that the body would be escorted.

Gene called Ozark Airlines again, and the same employee who had assisted them before was able again within minutes to check the passenger manifest and tell them that Tom Hurley, Michael's classmate at Rockhurst, would be coming. The Mullens telephoned Hurley's parents in Missouri and informed them that their son would be arriving in Waterloo the next night. His parents could barely conceal their delight and surprise, although, they were quick to add, they were terribly sorry for the circumstances which had permitted him to return. The Mullens understood.

At 7:45 P.M. on Sunday the Ozark Airlines flight carrying Michael's casket touched down at the far end of the Waterloo runway. The airplane braked, reversed its thrust, shuddered, slowed, braked some more and taxied in toward the terminal.

Peg was not there to see it. She simply could not make herself drive out to the airport where six months earlier Michael had kissed her good-bye and told her not to worry, saying, "Come on now, Mom, please? It'll all be over March first." It *was* March 1, and it *was* all over. Peg, therefore, remained behind, and her daughter Patricia stayed to keep her company.

Gene Mullen, his son John and daughter Mary went with the Hurleys and Sergeant Fitzgerald to meet the plane. The six of them stood by the picture window looking out at the nearly deserted airfield. As the airliner braked to a stop next to the terminal and shut down its engines, Gene Mullen asked Sergeant Fitzgerald what had impressed him most about Vietnam.

Without turning away from the window, Fitzgerald replied, "The corruption."

Tom Hurley was the last passenger to leave the plane. As his parents crowded forward to watch, Hurley walked down the boarding steps and stood next to the freight bay, watching while Michael's casket, cov-

86

ered by an American flag, was slid onto a baggage cart. The cart backed away from the plane, turned and gently lowered and guided Michael's casket into the hearse. Only when the hearse's back doors were closed did Hurley enter the terminal to embrace his family.

The Hurleys departed together, and the Mullens and Sergeant Fitzgerald followed the hearse to Waterloo. Michael's casket was taken inside the Loomis Funeral Home, and Tom Loomis, the director, asked Gene to wait in the vestibule while the casket was opened. Sergeant Fitzgerald followed Loomis, and Gene, Mary and John stayed behind. They sat silently, patiently in the vestibule wondering whether they could be certain it was Michael, worried that his body would have been so shattered by the artillery shell's explosion that they might never be able to know. After about twenty minutes Tom Loomis called down to Gene that he could now view the body. Gene rose and glanced, stricken, at his children.

"We'll be all right, Dad. You go ahead," John said.

Mary gave her father's hand a gentle squeeze. "We'll come up after a while."

Gene Mullen nodded and slowly turned away. He took a few steps and paused at the doorway of the funeral parlor's viewing room. The casket was in a far corner, and he forced himself to raise his eyes to look at it. The casket's lid was up, and Gene noticed Tom Loomis standing somberly to one side. Feeling apprehensive and ill, Gene walked forward until he could see a uniformed body inside. Despairingly, haltingly, he took another step. And another. Then Gene stopped, looked reluctantly at the face and quickly away.

It was Michael, his son. There was no question about it.

Gene Mullen steeled himself, made himself move right next to the coffin, close enough to touch the cold hands so carefully folded across his son's chest. Gene examined the military tunic, the strangeness of its brass buttons, the uniform jacket's lapels with the brass infantry and U.S. insignia, the black Army tie, the starched khaki collar's points, the throat, the lower jaw, the still blue lips, the mustache—the *mustache?*

Michael had a mustache! When had he grown a mustache? But it wasn't the mustache that bothered Gene. There was something else. Gene wasn't sure what; he just sensed there was something wrong. Suddenly Gene realized there wasn't a mark on his son.

Gene looked up at the funeral director in bewilderment, then back down. He noticed that Michael's face was a little puffy, his neck seemed swollen, but if it weren't for the uniform, there would be no sign that Michael had been in a war at all. In exasperation and puzzlement, Gene removed his glasses and wiped his hands across his eyes.

"Something wrong, Gene?" the funeral director asked.

"But, Tom, he was supposed to have been killed by *artil-tilery!*"

"When we lifted the body up out of the casket—we had to," Loomis explained; "because it had settled into it a little—I couldn't feel any broken bones or abrasions. . . ."

"Do you think he could have been killed by the concussion?"

"I couldn't say," Loomis said. "I just couldn't tell you that. I don't know." The funeral director leaned forward and traced his finger beneath Michael's khaki shirt collar. "There's some tape along here," he said, "but that's where they embalmed him."

Gene looked again at his son. For some reason Michael's coal black hair (which even when he had left was already thickly flecked with white) had now become a strange and alien brown. He noticed that his son's complexion, which had always been dark, almost mahogany-colored, seemed gray, chalky, a pallor foreign even to death. But Michael's hair and complexion were the only things that seemed wrong, and Gene kept asking himself how could Michael have been killed by an artillery burst, an explosion of burning jagged chunks of shrapnel, and still be perfectly whole? The more Gene tried to understand it, the more agitated and suspicious he became until finally, unable to tolerate it any longer, Gene asked the funeral director where Sergeant Fitzgerald had gone.

"I'm right here, Mr. Mullen," Fitzgerald said. The sergeant had been standing out of the way at the back of the room. He now came forward.

Gene scowled at the sergeant. "Now I want to know *how*-my-son-*died!* I want a death certificate. I want a death certificate stating how my son was killed!"

While Gene waited impatiently, Sergeant Fitzgerald opened an accordion-pleated manila file folder. He fiddled through the papers while Gene grew angrier and angrier, and when the sergeant pulled a sheet of paper from the folder, it was the same paper from which he had read the official casualty message to the Mullens. Fitzgerald simply began to cover it again: ". . . died while at a night defensive position when artillery fire from friendly forces—"

"That's not it! You know that isn't it!" Gene interrupted indignantly. "Look at him! Look at his body! There isn't a mark on him. Now let's get down to the bottom of that stack of papers and find out. I want to know—I want a death certificate. I want this confirmed before I bury that boy, or I'm going to have that body held."

The sergeant began leafing through the folder again. "I don't have a death certificate, Mr. Mullen. All I have is the original message I read to you . . . that and the notes I made when I received the information over the phone. That's this, here. . . ." Sergeant Fitzgerald resignedly handed Gene a piece of white typing paper upon which he'd handwritten the message: "Sgt. Michael E. Mullen, son of Oscar and Margaret Mullen, RFD #3, La Porte City, Iowa. Killed 18 Feb 70 near the village of Chu Lai. Nonbattle."

Gene studied the page for a long moment, and then, in a howl that compressed all the rage and confusion and pain he felt into one anguished question, he asked, "What does this mean: *'Nonbattle'?*"

"It means a casualty not the result of action by hostile forces," Sergeant Fitzgerald replied.

When Gene Mullen returned to the farm that night, Peg's first question was: "Is it Michael?"

"Yes," he said and dashed the one desperate remaining hope she had been nurturing all along.

Early Monday morning Gene drove back to the Loomis Funeral Home with Peg and Patricia. They had wanted to be alone with Michael's body and were surprised to find that a number of people were already there. Some were elderly friends of Michael's grandparents, some were Peg's friends—people she had met through her work on the County Democratic Committee—some were families who had sons currently serving in Vietnam, some were from John's high school class at Don Bosco, and others were families who too had lost sons in Vietnam. In all, about 145 persons signed the register. They had come because they had heard on the radio that Michael's body was to be brought back to the Mullen farm that afternoon, and not wanting to intrude on the family, they had nevertheless wanted to pay their respects. Peg particularly remembered the parents whose sons had died in the war. Their anguish was so real, they were so clearly reliving their own personal tragedies, that Peg felt they were the only people who really understood the despair that she and Gene felt.

When Gene and Peg Mullen and their daughter Patricia entered the funeral home, Captain Pringle met them at the vestibule. He reached inside his brief case and lifted out a small satin-covered box which he started to present to Gene. Thinking the box contained Michael's Army medals, Gene pushed the captain's hand away before Pringle could speak.

"We don't want them now," Gene said. "Maybe in time we'll change our opinion, but we don't want them now."

The box contained not medals but a small gold star symbolic of their son's death.

At first, more than anything else, Peg was upset by Michael's hair. She had heard that the malaria pills the boys took in Vietnam and the sun and water affected coloring; but now she saw that Michael had no white hair at all. She wondered whether the Army had

90

been embarrassed to show the Mullens that their son's hair had turned whiter, whether some well-meaning mortician hadn't dyed it. Peg couldn't stand its strange "taffy" color. But, other than that, as Gene had reported, Michael looked absolutely natural. There wasn't a mark on him.

Peg was suddenly overwhelmed by anger. The depth of her anger, of her outrage, its force and fury, stunned her. Gripping the velvet-draped platform upon which Michael's casket rested, Peg began to shiver. Her trembling transmitted itself down her shoulders, through her arms to the platform, so that it, too, vibrated slightly and the aluminum and brass-fitted handles on the casket began inexcusably to rattle—a thin, high, metallic pinging like a moored sailboat's rigging in a wind. Peg, unable at first to identify the source of the sound, glanced in amazement at the coffin and next at her hands, her arms until she realized that she herself was responsible for that outrageous noise. She jerked her hands off the platform as though burned.

"Mother?" Patricia put her arm around Peg. "You all right?"

Peg clamped her hands beneath her upper arms to still the trembling and bit her lip.

"Are you all right?" Patricia repeated, and Peg's look, when she turned to her daughter, was that of a frightened child.

"Daddy!" Patricia called. Gene hurried over and, sensing that Peg was for the first time about to break down, seized her other arm.

"Get me to the car, quick!" Peg said urgently. Her voice was a thin, compressed whisper. Gene and Patricia hurried Peg past the others in the funeral home, through the vestibule, where Captain Pringle called out, "Mr. Mullen, I need your—"

"Not now, wait. Be back," Gene answered over his shoulder.

Once outside Peg inhaled great gulps of air. She reached their car without stumbling, got in, and Patricia slid in next to her. Gene remained standing by the open door.

"Gene, you go ahead," Peg told him. "Go see what Pringle wants. I'll be all right now."

"You sure?" he asked.

"I'm all right," Peg repeated. "Patricia will stay with me. I just need to sit for a while."

Gene, leaning down so he could see Peg's face, nodded reluctantly and closed the car door. He walked back toward the funeral home entrance, paused at the stairs to look once more at the car. Peg gave him a little wave. Gene waved back and continued on in.

"You feel better now?" Patricia asked worriedly. "Is there anything I can get you? Some water?"

Peg shook her head no. She reached into her purse and pulled out a handkerchief.

"Are you sure?" Patricia said. "Isn't there anything you want?"

Peg continued to sit there in silence. After a moment, with obvious difficulty, she started to talk. She did not look up. Instead, she stared down at the plain white cotton handkerchief she had twisted into little knots in her hand.

"When . . . I . . . saw . . . Michael . . . whole. . . . When I saw Michael without a mark on him, I wanted —I don't know what I wanted, but I don't think . . . I don't think. . . ." Peg paused to clear her mind. "I don't think I wanted to see him . . . *whole,* you know? I got so angry . . . so furious because he . . . Mikey doesn't look as if he . . . as if he. . . ." Peg shook her head and took a deep breath. She faced Patricia, and for a moment, her voice became very matter-of-fact. "I don't think I wanted him whole, see? Because I've got to believe that he died in a war—and I can't. I can't believe it. And that's why I sort of went to pieces in there, do you understand?"

Patricia nodded. "I think so."

Peg studied her daughter, noted her worry, her concern, Patricia's strength. Peg's face softened, the whiteness around her lips started to fade, and she spoke quietly. "I do think I wanted him to have been blown to bits."

Because it was the first time she had let herself relax, become vulnerable, Peg suddenly began to cry.

Not since she had learned of Michael's death had she displayed any emotion but anger. "I do think I wanted him to have been blown to bits . . . I do! . . . I know I did," she said, and anguish flooded her face as she wept. "He was *all whole! All whole!* . . . Oh-h-h, why? . . . Why couldn't he have been blown to bits? So I could believe he . . . died . . . in . . . a . . . *war?*"

Inside the funeral home, Captain Pringle was signing the release papers that gave Gene Mullen and Tom Loomis final possession of Michael's body; in turn, Captain Pringle took Michael's Army dog tags.

Gene had wanted to keep the dog tags, but the captain explained that they were part of Michael's military equipment and, as such, were retained for record by the United States Army. Gene made up his mind that from that moment on he owed no more allegiance to the cause that had taken his son. He had had it with the Army, with the Vietnam War and with the U.S. government.

Peg never did understand why Michael's dog tags meant so much to Gene nor why he had saved his own dog tags from World War II. But Gene knew the expression, "If you can't make it in the Army, you won't make it on the outside," and dog tags represented not so much a souvenir of war with an enemy (the Army gives men medals for that), but war with oneself. To Gene Mullen, Michael's dog tags were a symbol that when called upon to accept and perform his responsibilities as a man among his fellowmen, his son had done his duty.

Tom Loomis was saying, "Gene, I understand you've decided not to have a military funeral."

"That's right," Gene answered, looking straight at Captain Pringle.

"When the coffin is brought to your home this afternoon, will you be wanting a flag draped across it?"

Gene thought for a moment. "Yes. . . . Yes, I want a flag."

"Flag to be on casket," Tom Loomis said. He made a little entry in his notebook. "And, let's see, we plan to have the coffin out to your house around noon. Will that be suitable?"

"Noon will be fine," Gene said.

"And the funeral mass is scheduled for ten o'clock at the Sacred Heart in La Porte City?"

Gene nodded. "Michael is to be buried in the family plot at Mount Carmel in Eagle Center."

"Mr. Mullen, pardon me?" Captain Pringle said. "I can come to the service—I *have* to be there," Pringle corrected himself, "but I mean, well, I can come to the service in civilian clothing, if you'd like. . . ."

"Certainly not, Captain," Gene said. "I want you there in the uniform you represent."

"Fine, sir," Pringle said. He paused for a moment, then he added, "I have one more question. . . ."

"Yes?"

"Where would you like me to sit?"

"*Sit?*" Gene asked.

"During the church service, sir," Pringle explained.

"Oh," Gene said. "I want you to sit right up in the front of the church where everybody can see you."

"All right, sir, fine," Pringle replied.

When Gene and Peg and Patricia returned to the farm, the mail awaiting them consisted of letters from friends and still more families who had lost husbands and sons. Eleven days had passed since Michael had been killed so far and the only expression of regret from the United States government had been the telegram from Major General Wickham which had arrived the week before and the 9-by-12-inch White House envelope containing President Nixon's speeches on how capably and efficiently the South Vietnamese were carrying out their share of the war. They still knew no more about how Michael had died than the information given in Wickham's telegram. If "artillery fire from friendly forces landed in the area," why, then, did Michael appear to be totally unmarked?

In Michael's next to last letter, dated February 11, he had written his parents, "We are still at bunker line—will be here a couple more days—will move out on a search mission for a week." The Mullens, therefore, knew their son was on a combat assignment, that he was in the field conducting a search mission February 18 when he died. Now the Army was telling them that although he was killed by artillery "while at a night defensive position," he was considered a non-battle casualty. The Mullens wanted to know why.

At noon on Monday, Michael Mullen's casket was brought to the farm and placed in front of the picture window in the Mullens' living room. The strained relationship between the family and their parish priest had not lessened. Father Shimon had neither offered them any assistance in planning their son's funeral nor made any effort to contact Father Hemesath, the priest whom the Mullens wished to have officiate at the mass. The only help the Mullens had received had been from the priests and sisters associated with the Don Bosco parochial school.

When Peg and Gene had asked that the music be sung by the Don Bosco Chorus, Father Shimon suggested they instead use the Sacred Heart Choir, whose experience singing together was evidently limited to Christmas, Easter and a few other occasions. When the Mullens persisted in their request for the Don Bosco Chorus, Father Shimon refused to permit the chorus to sing with the organ at the front of the church. He instead required that they stand at the back, where they would be "out of the way," and, he said, if the chorus wished to have music accompany them, they would have to provide their own.

Tom Loomis had never had a funeral at La Porte's Sacred Heart Church before, and after he delivered Michael's body to the farm, he continued into town to inspect the layout of the church. Sacred Heart is a modern brick building with pews divided into three sections, narrow at the front, then fanning wider toward the rear as in a movie theater. Loomis checked the interior and was preparing to leave when Father Shimon handed him a twenty-pound tub of soft butter which the women of the parish had dropped off in preparation for the lunch now scheduled to be served following Michael's burial the next day. When Loomis asked the priest what he was expected to do with the butter, Father Shimon said he didn't care so long as he got it out of the church. The priest suggested Loomis take it back to the Mullens' farm. That is why not more than an hour after Tom Loomis had brought the Mullens their son's body, he reappeared with a twenty-pound tub of soft butter.

That morning Michael's former girlfriend, Caroline Roby, was also at the farm. She had been driven to La Porte the afternoon before by John Stagg. Although the relationship between Michael and Caroline had evidently cooled prior to his being sent to Vietnam (one had the impression that it had cooled primarily on Caroline's part—at first Caroline wasn't going to attend the funeral. She later relented and called John Stagg, explaining, "I have to go. I couldn't live with myself if I didn't"), there was no strain between her and Michael's family. It was, in fact, Caroline who, along with the Mullens' daughter Mary and Mary's boyfriend, Rick DeJana, drove the tub of butter back to the Sacred Heart Church.

Mary carried the butter into the refectory kitchen and placed it in the refrigerator. Afterward she and Caroline and Rick DeJana began setting up the tables for the next day's lunch. A few minutes later Father Shimon entered and told Mary he didn't want the tables set up until after the service. Mary said there wouldn't be time; they all would have so much on their minds she didn't feel her family would want to worry about dinner preparations left until the last minute. Therefore, they had thought it best to get it done and out of the way.

Father Shimon told several women of the church who were present that if the Mullens wanted to do it, then they could do it on their own and instructed the ladies not to offer them any assistance.

Caroline turned to Mary Mullen in astonishment and asked, "Is he a *priest?*"

By the time the two girls and Rick DeJana returned to the farm the Mullens' house was filled with flowers and friends.

Peg's older brother, Bill Goodyear, was pacing in front of Michael's casket. Finally, he pulled his sister aside and agitatedly told her, "Peg, you've got to find out what happened to him. *Look* at Michael! Look at him. He could have had a stroke from the way he looks. . . ."

Gene overheard Peg's brother and asked, "What's this about a stroke?"

"Our mother's side of the family has a history of strokes in young people," Bill Goodyear explained.

"No-o-o," Gene said. "Tom Loomis told me when he brought Michael here, he took me into the bedroom and said that the shell had hit him back here." Gene pointed above his right kidney. "There was a hole no bigger than a pen top, 'bout as big as that," he said, holding up the tip of his thumb.

Peg shrugged. "Yeah, Gene, but he couldn't have looked because he—"

"Yes, he did!" Gene insisted quietly. "He wouldn't do it until I told Sergeant Fitzgerald, 'Now I want to know how my boy died.' He examined Michael up to the funeral home."

"Do you really think he looked, Gene?" Peg asked. "He couldn't have. How could—"

"HE DID NOT!" Peg answered angrily. "He couldn't have—"

"It was before Michael left the undertaker's parlor. Before they moved him out here."

"How could they? They only had twenty-four hours. We were—you were with Michael last night. You saw the crowd when we went back out there this morning. When did he have time?"

"Mother, he left—when he was up to the funeral home, he checked Michael," Gene said.

"When? When?"

"After everybody left last night," Gene said.

"Well, all I can say is look at him," Bill Goodyear insisted. "I say you ought to check Michael yourself."

97

Gene, stricken, gestured toward their house filled with friends, relatives, young people. *"How?"* he asked. "How can we check him now?"

For the rest of that afternoon and well into that evening a steady stream of friends and neighbors, townspeople, relatives, classmates arrived to attend Michael's wake. Some of Gene's coworkers stopped in, too, as did the general supervisor at John Deere. All the supervisors that Gene dealt with attended but one. The men and women and young people took turns that evening by Michael's casket, bowed their heads and said a rosary for Michael's soul.

Chapter Eight

Shortly before Michael's coffin was closed, his brother and sisters each placed a small envelope in Michael's crossed hands. None of the children ever revealed to their parents what they had written, nor did their parents ask. The coffin was sealed and taken to La Porte City.

Estep Motor Company, the local Ford dealer, provided three automobiles to transport the Mullen family to the Sacred Heart Church. Peg and Gene, their son John and his cousin Kathy Partridge rode in the first car. Mary and Patricia, Mary's boyfriend, Rick DeJana, and Patricia's fiancé, Alan Hulting, rode in the second. The third car carried Michael's uncles and aunts.

It was overcast, damp and chilly at ten o'clock when the Mullen family pulled up at the church and walked inside the vestibule. Tom Loomis had stationed three attendants from his funeral home on either side of the wheeled coffin truck upon which Michael's flag-covered casket rested. He then positioned the six honorary pallbearers chosen from among John's and Michael's friends behind the casket. Tom Hurley, in uniform with a black armband upon his sleeve, was one of them. As soon as the processional cross bearer saw the coffin brought into the church, he hastened up the aisle toward it.

The mass was concelebrated by Father Shimon, Father Ronald Friedell of the Don Bosco faculty, Father William Schwartz, a former Don Bosco teacher and a longtime friend of the Mullens, and Father Robert Hirsch, principal of the Don Bosco High School, who had been invited to deliver the homily. Father Hemesath was not present; Father Shimon had never been in touch with him. The Don Bosco Chorus, led by Sister

Richard, were standing around the portable organ she had brought from the school. Mr. Loomis nodded that he was ready, the young boy carrying the cross positioned himself at Michael's casket's head, facing down the aisle toward the altar, and the four priests, wearing the vestments indicative of a Black Funeral, entered from behind the sacristy and gathered in the sanctuary. With their entrance the congregation rose to their feet, the Don Bosco Chorus began "How Great Thou Art," a hymn chosen by Gene, and the cross bearer led the procession down the aisle toward the altar. Michael's family followed the six honorary pallbearers, and when the coffin reached the altar, Peg and Gene were guided into the frontrow center pew directly behind the casket. John, Mary and Patricia filed into the second row behind their parents, and the uncles and aunts were directed into the row behind that.

Father Shimon made the sign of the cross and said, "In the name of the Father, and of the Son, and of the Holy Spirit. . . ."

The congregation responded, *"Amen."*

Shimon extended his arms out from his sides. "The grace of our Lord Jesus Christ and the love of God and the fellowship of the Holy Spirit be with you all."

"And also with you."

"The grace and peace of God our Father and the Lord Jesus be with you all."

"And also with you."

Peg suddenly stiffened and poked Gene in the ribs.

"What's the matter?" Gene asked.

"The Lord be with you," Shimon was saying.

"And also with you," the congregation responded. Peg dipped her head toward Captain Ralph T. Pringle, who was standing in uniform all alone in the front-row right-hand pew.

"I told him to sit there," Gene told Peg.

"You did?" Peg said. "Oh, I was going to blame it on the undertaker."

"Peace be with you," Shimon was saying.

"And also with you."

"My brothers and sisters," Shimon said, "to pre-

100

pare ourselves to celebrate the sacred mysteries, let us call to mind our sins."

There was a moment of silence; then the congregation together prayed, *"I confess to almighty God, and to you, my brothers and sisters, that I have sinned through my own fault"*—they struck their chests—*"in my thoughts and in my words . . . in what I have done . . . and in what I failed to do; and I ask blessed Mary, ever virgin, all the angels and saints, and you, my brothers and sisters, to pray for me to the Lord our God."*

"May almighty God have mercy on us," Father Shimon prayed, "forgive us our sins, and bring us to everlasting life."

"Amen."

When it was time for Father Hirsch to deliver the homily, he smiled at the congregation, most of whom he knew, and as he spoke, he leaned forward comfortably to rest his elbows on the lectern. He talked about Michael's school record, the scholarships and fellowships he had received, his assistantship at the University of Missouri and the project he was working on there. Father Hirsch spoke of Michael's 4-H Club activities, the interest and enthusiasm evidenced in all his work. He tried to show how Michael's twenty-five years had been rich years, filled with joy and love for his fellowman. And then, to Peg's astonishment, Father Hirsch gave her a little wink, launched into a short speech in behalf of the need for continued support of parochial education, and the homily ended.

The congregation stood as the priests together spoke the general intercessions and the Don Bosco Chorus sang the offertory hymn, "Shalom."

When the last communicant had been served and while the chorus sang another of Gene's favorites, "The Impossible Dream" from *Man of La Mancha*, Father Shimon, assisted by the altar boy, cleaned the silver paten and chalice used in the celebration of the eucharist. Father Shimon then faced the congregation, saying, "Let us pray." He paused a moment and asked, "O almighty God, may this sacrifice purify the soul of your servant, Michael, which has departed from the world today. Grant that once delivered from his sins, he may receive forgiveness and eternal rest. . . . Through Christ our Lord. . . ."

"Amen," the congregation answered.

Father Shimon stepped down to Michael's casket, where he was joined by the other priests and the processional cross bearer. The Don Bosco Chorus began their final hymn, "America the Beautiful." It, too, had been specially requested by Gene Mullen, and Sister Richard's heavy stressing of the bass chords lent the hymn an almost martial air. The cross bearer moved to the head of the procession, and the funeral director with the help of the six Loomis Funeral Home attendants turned Michael's casket around so that it now faced up the aisle. The four priests arranged themselves behind the cross bearer. The Loomis attendants took up positions on either side of the casket, and the six honorary pallbearers lined up directly behind Michael's body. Next came Peg and Gene, followed by Patricia and Mary and John, and the uncles and aunts after that. As soon as everyone was ready, the cross bearer stepped off and the procession moved slowly up the aisle. As the chorus now sang the third verse, a young tenor's voice cracked, and Sister Richard saw the boy had begun to cry.

The small well-kept Catholic cemetery at Eagle Center is about ten miles from La Porte City. The cars slowed, then entered the drive and continued up the slight hill past the Mount Carmel Catholic Church,* past the Case backhoe machine used to dig Michael's grave, and then, at the crest of the hill, the hearse stopped. The Mullens' cars pulled in behind it. The other mourners parked their cars as best they could nearby.

During the journey from La Porte the sun broke through the overcast and now shone brightly down upon the cemetery. The sun remained out throughout the burial service.

---

*The first Catholic church, completed in 1868, was destroyed by a tornado the following year. The present building, constructed upon the foundations of the first, has stood since 1870.

Michael's grave was at the top of the slight hill within the Mullen family plot. Father Shimon waited while the family gathered around the open grave, then said, "Let us pray. . . ."

Peg slipped her arm through Gene's, and he gently rested his hand on hers. As the first prayers were spoken, Gene began to cry. Peg had wept only at the beginning of the church service. She had pulled herself together and remained dry-eyed through the rest. Now, as she stood at the graveside, the bright sunlight added to her strength, and when she felt Gene's hand tremble on top of her own, she squeezed his arm in sympathy.

"Give our brother peaceful rest in this grave," Father Shimon was praying, "until that day when you, the resurrection and the life, will raise him up in glory. Then may he see the light of your presence, Lord Jesus, in the kingdom where you live for ever . . . and ever. . . ."

"Amen," Peg said. Gene had to clear his throat, and his "Amen" followed a little after.

The honorary pallbearers held the American flag taut as Michael's casket was slowly lowered beneath it into the grave.

"Since almighty God has called our brother, Michael, from this life to Himself," Father Shimon continued, "we commit his body to the earth from which it was made. . . . Christ was the first to rise from the dead, and we know that He will raise up our mortal bodies to be like His in glory. . . . We commend our brother to the Lord; may the Lord receive him into his peace and raise up his body on the last day."

The flag was awkwardly folded by Michael's friends with Father Shimon's help while Captain Pringle stood by. The triangle was not crisp, bits of flag stuck out, the folds and the stars did not end up quite right, but it was presented to the Mullens anyway. There were no middle-aged men in VFW or American Legion uniforms with polished rifles to fire a salute over the grave. No bugler played "Taps."

Michael Eugene Mullen was buried in his Army uniform near the gravestones of John and Ellen Dobshire (1852–1886); Patrick J. and Mary Ann Dobshire Mullen (1886–1927); Oscar L. and Mary Ann Mullen

(1927–1951); Gene's sister, Lois Wenner; Daniel Mullen, Peg and Gene Mullen's second child; and the stone reserving the plot for Peg and Gene: Oscar E. and Margaret E. Mullen (1951–   ).

The dates on the stones are not those of the family's life spans, but of their title to their Iowa lands.

From Michael's grave only the Mount Carmel Church and a few parish buildings are visible nearby. Everything else is farmland, and when the sun sets, the shadows rush across the rolling hills like an incoming ocean tide.

After the burial the family returned to the Sacred Heart Church in La Porte for the lunch. There Captain Pringle neatly refolded the flag before saying good-bye. Tom Hurley, too, had to leave and drew Peg aside. All he said was: "Mrs. Mullen, whatever you do, don't stop fighting this war!" There was one other young man besides Hurley and Captain Pringle who attended the service in uniform. The Mullens never found out who he was, but they believe he was a soldier home on leave.

By late afternoon the uncles and aunts had departed, the friends had gone back to their own homes, and Peg and Gene and their three surviving children were finally alone on their farm. It was the first opportunity Peg had had to open the mail; a new letter had arrived that morning from Washington. The letter read as follows:

WASHINGTON

25 February 1970

Dear Mr. and Mrs. Mullen:

Please accept my deepest sympathy in the loss of your son, Sergeant Michael E. Mullen, on 18 February in Vietnam.

I know that the passing of a loved one is one of life's most tragic moments, but sincerely hope that you will find some measure of comfort in knowing that your son served his Nation with honor. His devoted service was in the finest traditions of American soldiers who on other battlefields and in other times of national peril have

104

given the priceless gift of life to safeguard the blessings of freedom for their loved ones and for future generations. In Vietnam today brave Americans are defending the rights of men to choose their own destiny and to live in dignity and freedom.

All members of the United States Army join in sharing your burden of grief.

Sincerely,

s/W. C. WESTMORELAND
General, United States Army
Chief of Staff

With a look of disgust, Peg skimmed the letter over to Gene.

Chapter Nine

The day after Michael's funeral Gene Mullen returned to work at John Deere. He was performing the final inspection on one of the big green and yellow tractors that had reached the end of the assembly line when he was approached by the supervisor who had failed to attend the wake or the funeral services. "Say, Oscar," the man said (at John Deere, Gene is addressed by his given name), "say, Oscar, I'm awfully sorry to hear about your tough luck...."

"Well, thank you, Arnold," Gene said over his shoulder.

The supervisor stood there while Gene made a note on his clipboard checklist; then he said, "I couldn't get out there to your farm, Oscar. I just couldn't. I was too busy."

"You were *'too busy'*?" Gene asked, turning now to face the man. "You sonuvabitch! My boy wasn't too busy to die for you, was he?"

The supervisor looked down at his feet.

"My boy died because you were too busy," Gene said. "How many others are you now going to let die for you?"

The supervisor blinked sadly at Gene. "All I meant was I'm awfully sorry...."

"So am I," Gene said, "so am I." He turned his back upon the supervisor and returned to work.

Back at their farm, Peg was reading the letter that had arrived that day from Vietnam:

DEPARTMENT OF THE ARMY
Headquarters, 1st Battalion, 6th Infantry
198th Infantry Brigade, Americal Division
APO San Francisco 96219

Mr. and Mrs. Oscar E. Mullen
Rural Route 3,
La Porte City, Iowa 50651

Dear Mr. and Mrs. Mullen:

It is with deepest sorrow that I extend to you the sympathy of the men of the 1st Battalion, 6th Infantry, for the loss of your son, Michael.

On the early morning of February 18, 1970, Michael's unit was located in their night defensive position near the village of Tu Chanh, approximately 13 miles south of Tam Ky City, in Quan Tin Province, Republic of Vietnam. At 2:50 AM, the unit was adjusting artillery to provide a predetermined range of fire in the event of enemy contact. During the testing, Michael received a fatal missile wound when an artillery round fell short of its intended target and detonated near his position. May you gain some consolation in knowing that Michael was not subjected to any prolonged suffering.

I sincerely hope that the knowledge that Michael was an exemplary soldier who gave his life assisting his fellowman and in the service of his country will comfort you in this hour of great sorrow.

A memorial service was conducted for your son. Michael's comrades joined me in rendering military honors and final tribute to him. You were in our thoughts and prayers at that time also.

The sincere sympathy of this unit is extended to you in your bereavement.

Sincerely yours,

s/H. NORMAN SCHWARZKOPF
LTC, Infantry
Commanding

The second paragraph was the only one that interested Peg. The others were mere formalities. She picked up a ball-point pen and carefully read that paragraph again, this time underlining key words: "Tu

Chanh . . . 13 . . . Tam Ky . . . Quan Tin . . ." and then, after a pause, she underlined "prolonged."

What did that mean? It could mean that Michael had suffered from anywhere from a few seconds to fifteen minutes or more. Peg abruptly pushed herself away from the kitchen table and walked to the bookcase in the living room. She searched until she found one of her children's paperback pocket dictionaries.

Prolong, vb 1. to lengthen in time: continue (a meeting)
2. to lengthen in extent or range (a line)
syn: protract, extend, elongate

She returned to the letter and tried the sentence again. Michael was not subjected to any *lengthened in time* suffering . . . subjected to any *continued* suffering . . . any *protracted* suffering . . . *extended* suffering, *elongated* suffering. . . . She covered her eyes with her hands. *But he had suffered nevertheless.*

"Near the village of Tu Chanh approximately 13 miles south of Tam Ky City in Quan Tin Province, Republic of Vietnam."

Peg's Hammond map of "VIETNAM and Neighboring Countries" showed Tam Ky about twenty miles north of Chu Lai.

Chu Lai was where Michael got his haircut; it was where he had been when he had telephoned his mother.

"Michael's unit was located in their night defensive position," the letter stated. ". . . At 2:50 AM, the unit was adjusting artillery to provide a predetermined range of fire in the event of enemy contact. . . ." Peg read those two lines again: "Michael's unit was located. . . . The unit was adjusting artillery. . . ." It could only mean that Michael's unit was adjusting the artillery. In other words, someone in Michael's own outfit had called in the artillery that had killed her son. Why? And why at two fifty—nearly three o'clock in the morning? It didn't make sense unless, *unless* they were under attack. And yet they said Michael was a nonbattle casualty. The letter clearly implied that the unit hadn't been under attack, that the artillery was called for "in

108

the event of enemy contact," *in case of* enemy contact. There was nothing in the letter about Vietcong infiltrating radio channels, no mention of the artillery having been from a South Vietnamese unit. In fact, as Peg studied that paragraph, she became more and more suspicious.

Why had Michael's unit, which was not under attack, asked for artillery to be fired over its position at three o'clock in the morning?

How could the one shell have "detonated near his position," have exploded next to Michael and have left him virtually unmarked except for a small hole in his back the size of a pen top or . . . or a bullet?

Why, if Michael's unit had called in the artillery, wasn't he in a foxhole? Why hadn't he been wearing his flak jacket?

Why had the shell fallen short?

Why had the only letter received by the Mullens from anyone even remotely connected with their son been from the battalion commander? Why had they not heard from his company commander? His platoon leader? Why had she not heard from anyone in Michael's unit? He had been dead more than two weeks. Hadn't Michael had any friends?

Was no one else hurt?

There had not been any newspaper accounts of an accidental shelling, nothing on the evening news. The casualty list released the week Michael died reported only eighty-eight deaths, and yet three planeloads, planes supposedly carrying seventy-five bodies each, had flown into California in just the first two days of that week.

Peg looked at the letter again. "Approximately 13 miles south of Tam Ky City. . . ." There was something familiar about "Tam Ky." Michael had mentioned it in a letter somewhere. Peg went to the box in which she kept all of Michael's correspondence. Perhaps, she felt, if she read all his letters again very carefully, she might discover some clue she had overlooked, some hint to what really might have happened to her son.

Chapter Ten

++++++++++

Michael Mullen regularly corresponded with his family from Vietnam. Sometimes he wrote letters, but for the most part, he simply jotted a few lines on a postcard. Michael had left for Vietnam on September 11, 1969, his twenty-fifth birthday, and after two weeks training at Cam Ranh Bay in the different weapons, the starlite scope and booby traps—the booby traps, Michael wrote, were "rather hairy"—he was assigned to the 1st Platoon of C ("Charlie") Company, 1st Battalion, 6th Infantry, 198th Infantry Brigade of the Americal Division headquartered at Chu Lai.

Because Michael's arrival coincided with the start of the monsoon season, his early correspondence dealt primarily with his efforts to stay warm and dry. The notes were bright, factual, uncomplaining and indicative of Michael's characteristic willingness to get unpleasant tasks done. October 5: "Today I got a rubber wet-suit —they keep you dry, but you sweat yourself wet." October 8: "Same old stuff—am drying socks over a peanut butter jar." October 16: "Only have a minute to say 'Hi.' Am going to mts for a spell and have to hump everything. Have a ROTC lieutenant giving orders by the book and the book doesn't mean a damn thing here."

Late in October, however, Michael's attitude perceptibly changed. His unit, he wrote, was burning out villages during search and destroy missions—operations which the Nixon administration claimed had been suspended. He began complaining about their maps which, because of inaccuracies, nearly caused his platoon on October 24 to be shelled by their supporting artillery. Even Michael's innate respect for authority began to deteriorate. October 27: "We are supposed to have the BN Co [battalion commander] out here sometime this week—kind of a laugh, for they live in a dream world! They have to have figures [body count] and nobody knows what is a VC or a plain ignorant villager, at least in this area." By November Michael was writing, "Nixon's Vietnamization will eventually fail. Our front-line troops here have little faith in the ARVN." And after his mother sent the newspaper accounts of 250,000 protesters arriving in Washington for the November 15 Moratorium Day, he responded, "Most of the grunts, E-6's and below, are pulling that things get wilder at home."

In mid-December Michael wrote: "Am tired right now—sitting next to my foxhole which is facing into a hedgerow. The stupidity of it all sort of makes me laugh at times." December 22: "Can't say much more other than Christmas is only a couple of days away—or another way of saying eight months left in this hole." On January 16 Michael wrote: "All is well, am in second day of stand down—all is bullshit. In fact, made up my mind to apply for an early out, wrote letter to Dr. O'Dell [Michael's faculty adviser] and admissions at Missouri. I hope to get out by May 25th. Am now a platoon sergeant."

That letter, more than any other, convinced Peg and Gene that their son had become disgusted with his participation in the war, an impression confirmed as much by his desire for an early release as having written "all is bullshit." They had never known Michael to swear. Peg wrote Michael an anxious letter about two young men who had reenlisted to get out of combat and, she asked, had he considered doing that himself? Michael's reply startled his family:

February 2:
   Let's get one thing straight, Mom. For God's sake, stop the worrying bit. Will you? If you worry, don't write me about it. As for those two chicken shits, it seems if they weren't happy in their jobs they can get out of them if they want to bad enough. I've seen too many too many of these soft, smart kids writing home exaggerated letters, crying and complaining, writing Congressmen and Senators and Mama, too. I have no

111

stomach for their type. The main problem in this mess is nobody wants to do his job and do it the best he can.

Now to try for an early out—should not be hard to do—one E-5 in our company had no trouble in getting one for night school. All it took was a letter of acceptance. Ran into a boy from Waterloo by name of Culpepper. . . .

What astonished the Mullens was the vehemence with which Michael reacted to the young men who had reenlisted out of combat; surprising, too, was his absolute unwillingness to hear any more on that subject. But most baffling of all was how in the next paragraph he had turned around and expressed the equivalent desire by applying for an early out.

On February 7 Michael wrote, "All is well! Got a letter from Dr. O'Dell. All is okay! Also got a letter from University of Missouri admissions office. Have sent in my enrollment card—should, in about three weeks, get an acceptance."

Michael wrote again on the eleventh and thirteenth of that month, but of course, by the time Peg and Gene received his last letter he was dead.

Rereading Michael's letters only exacerbated Peg's anguish. Not only had his correspondence failed to provide any clues whatsoever to how he might have died, but worse, each time she had come upon some thought, some word or phrase that was unmistakably his own, Michael would spring back to life for one joyous instant. Then the pain of her loss would rush back, and she would have to catch her breath to bear the ache. Nevertheless, even as she would be finishing one, her hand would be reaching for the next. And as the stack of un-reread letters diminished, Peg found herself reading more slowly, as if to retard the inevitable.

But the end came: "So 'til later, hang loose." Reading Michael's last line, Peg recalled Gene's bemused " 'Hang loose'?" and all the optimism of that moment, for Michael was clearly determined to get an early release. Almost immediately that bright image was replaced by Gene's raw, wounded face, his eyes gutted by the sergeant's awful message and Michael's distant electronic voice saying, "Good-bye, Mom, it's so sticky here. . . ."

"Sticky here? Peg thought to herself, *Was that really what he said? Or, was it, "Good-bye, Mom, it's so bad here . . ."?* It was suddenly terribly important to remember exactly what he had said, to get it right. She closed her eyes and concentrated. Only then did Peg realize she could no longer be positive she recalled even the sound of Michael's voice.

When Gene returned around midnight from John Deere, Peg was still answering letters of sympathy from complete strangers who had read of Michael's loss in the papers or heard it on the news and felt compelled to write that they shared her grief. Peg dreaded having to speak with Gene. He would want to talk about Michael's death, and each letter she had answered had forced her to try to articulate why her son had died. She didn't know why. She didn't even know *how.* General William C. Westmoreland, the Army Chief of Staff, had written Michael died, "defending the rights of men to choose their own destiny and to live in dignity and freedom." The only appropriate response to that, she felt, was Michael's comment: bullshit. Michael himself hadn't had the right to choose his own destiny; he had been drafted. Killed.

Gene paused at the bottom of the kitchen steps to scrape his muddy workshoes, then continued up. Waving wearily at Peg, he said, "Hello, Mother, what are you doing awake?"

"Couldn't sleep."

Gene put his lunch bucket by the side of the sink, and Peg asked if he would like a cup of coffee.

"No, I don't think so," Gene said. "Any mail today?"

"Letter from a Colonel Schwarzkopf. Michael's battalion commander."

"Oh-h?" Gene crossed to the kitchen table and sat down. "Did he say how Mikey died?"

"You read it. Tell me what you think." She pushed the letter toward him, then got up and washed his lunch bucket out at the sink. When she turned back around,

113

she saw Gene had put the letter down, removed his glasses and was rubbing his eyes.

"You look tired," Peg said.

"I am . . . I am. . . ." Gene told her about the supervisor who had said he couldn't come to Michael's funeral because he had been "too busy" and what he had told the supervisor in return.

"Oh, Gene"—Peg sighed—"you shouldn't have called him that."

"He made me mad."

"I know, but he really doesn't understand." Peg sat across the table from Gene and moved some papers about. "Did you finish Schwarzkopf's letter?"

Gene nodded. "It was very nice."

"*Nice?*" Peg asked impatiently. "What was '*nice*' about it?"

"That part about the memorial service with Mikey's friends," Gene said. "About our being in their thoughts."

"Oh, Gene that's . . . that's all just part of the form letter. You don't really think they held a memorial service, do you? What about how he died? Why was the artillery fired at three o'clock in the morning? Who called in that round? How come nothing was ever in the paper about this? Why wasn't there an investigation? Don't you understand?" She looked sharply at Gene. "Schwarzkopf's letter doesn't tell us anything! The Army doesn't believe people should really know how their sons died. That people don't really want to know."

"We'll find out," Gene said.

"But how?" Peg asked. "Who can we write? You know the Army won't tell us anything."

"The *official* Army won't," Gene said, "but we could write one of Mikey's friends."

"Who? We don't know any of his friends. The Army won't give us any names. Michael never told us any—no wait! Wait a minute!" Peg said. "There was somebody." She went to the box containing Michael's letters and began sifting through it. "He mentioned one boy. Someone from Waterloo. . . . In one of his last letters. . . . Here! Here it is: 'Ran into a boy from Waterloo by name of Culpepper.' C-U-L-P-E-P-P-E-R."

114

Gene walked over to the Waterloo-Cedar Falls telephone directory and riffled through the pages. "There are four Culpeppers in the book."

"Call them," Peg said. "See if one of them has a son in Vietnam."

Gene looked up at the kitchen clock over the oven. "Peg, it's after midnight."

The following morning Peg Mullen wrote Martin Culpepper, a young man she had never met, and asked him to help find out what had happened to her son in Vietnam. That same morning a letter arrived from Major General Kenneth G. Wickham, the Army Adjutant General:

DEPARTMENT OF THE ARMY
OFFICE OF THE ADJUTANT GENERAL
WASHINGTON, D.C. 20315

20 Apr 1970

I have the honor to inform you that your son has been awarded posthumously the Bronze Star Medal and the Good Conduct Medal.

Prior to death, Michael had been awarded the National Defense Service Medal, Vietnam Service Medal, Vietnam Campaign Medal, Combat Infantryman Badge, and the Marksman Badge with rifle, automatic rifle, and machine gun bars.

Arrangements are being made to have these awards presented to you in the near future by a representative of the Commanding General, Fifth United States Army.

The representative selected will communicate with you in the next few weeks to arrange for presentation. Any inquiry or correspondence concerning presentation should be addressed to the Commanding General, Fifth United States Army, Fort Sheridan, Illinois, 60037.

My continued sympathy is with you.

Sincerely,
S/Kenneth G. Wickham
Major General, USA
The Adjutant General

115

"What do you think of the Army suddenly offering us medals?" Peg asked Gene. "That Good Conduct Medal, I mean *really!*"

"It's only a piece of ribbon." Gene shrugged. "We used to laugh about getting them during the war."

"Posthumously? Why would they award Michael a Good Conduct Medal after he was dead? It's as though they were giving it to him for not—for not complaining about what they did to him!"

Gene reread the list of medals. "Well, these others, the National Defense Medal, the Vietnam medals, he got those for just being in the Army, for being in Vietnam. But the Bronze Star"—Gene brushed his hand through his silver hair—"that's supposed to be for bravery."

"That doesn't make sense either," Peg said. "Mikey said he'd only ever seen the enemy, what? Three times? I'll tell you why I think they gave him the Bronze Star. It's because he *died!* I'm sure of it."

The Mullens refused their son's medals.

That same morning friends who had attended the funeral telephoned to ask Peg if, by any chance, she had watched Chet Huntley and David Brinkley on last night's NBC-TV evening news. The caller said that he and his wife both thought a news clip had shown Michael.

"What do you mean?" Peg asked.

"The camera zeroed in on two boys in stretchers, and we were sure one of them was Michael," the man said. "I'm positive it was."

"But why would it have been shown last night?"

"I don't know. They explained that the film had been shot around the eighteenth of February, but they hadn't released it until it had been cleared or something. . . . Peg," he said. "I *know* it was Michael."

The caller was an engineer at John Deere, someone Gene described who would "not go off the deep end about anything."

"But, Gene," Peg protested, "the only time he ever saw Michael was here in the casket. How could he be so sure?"

"Well, I only know he's a very down-to-earth man," Gene said. "And if he thinks he saw Michael, then it probably was. We ought to at least try to get a look at the film ourselves."

KWWL-TV, the Black Hawk Broadcasting Company in Waterloo, was the nearest NBC affiliate. The person Peg spoke with explained that the evening news broadcast originated in New York City and the NBC studios there would be the only ones to have any information on the film. Gene was at John Deere by the time Peg got through to Chet Huntley's secretary in New York. "You're the fifth mother to call us on that film," the secretary said. "Are you *sure* you want to look at it?"

"Well, no, I don't think I want to see it," Peg said, "but my husband does. We want to know if it was our son. We don't know what happened to him, and maybe the film. . . ."

"Well, okay," the secretary said. "We'll do what we can. We'll have to send back to Vietnam to find out more about it."

"We'd appreciate it," Peg said. (About six weeks later NBC-TV contacted the Mullens to say that the newscast film had, in fact, been shot February 17, 18, or 19, but that the two killed and seven wounded had been from the 25th Infantry Division, not Michael's Americal. No enemy had been involved in that incident either.)

That afternoon at work a John Deere supervisor sat down next to Gene during a break and spoke to him about the funeral service and Vietnam, and then the supervisor said, "You know, Oscar, we've got to have this war. We've got to stop the Communists!"

"Joe, are you worried about the North Vietnamese? They're just seventeen million people! You say, 'Stop the Communists.' " Gene shook his head. "If we ever have any real conflict with the Communist nations it'll all be over in forty-eight hours. This won't be any hand-to-hand conflict!"

"What about Red China?"

"Red China? They couldn't come within a thou-

117

sand miles of our coast. They don't have the fleet to carry their men. If Red China was going to attack us, they'd use a nuclear bomb and you wouldn't be around to read it in the newspapers. . . . Why are you so worried about the North Vietnamese? Do you even know what they were called before World War Two?"

The supervisor shook his head, "No-o-o."

"Joe, what do you do? Why don't you read up on what's going on over there? Don't tell me my boy died for a 'just cause'—or that any of the forty thousand died for that either because," Gene said, "because, Joe, you know you're only saying that to protect yourself from feeling guilty about what you've let go on and on."

On Friday, March 6, Army Finance asked the Mullens to sign a blank pay voucher for Michael's final eighteen days of pay. Gene wrote back: "Never in my life have I signed a blank pay voucher and I am not going to at this sad point in my life. We have no real interest in any money due Michael today, so until you can give us a concrete figure that is due him, we shall not sign this Standard Form 1174." But no matter how angry Gene was at the Army for having killed his son, he was still too polite to forget it was staffed by ordinary men. Gene closed his letter, "We look forward to hearing from you again at your convenience," signed it, "Oscar E. Mullen, Father of Michael, Killed in Vietnam on February 18th," and added: "P.S., No need now for top priority in this matter."

The following week's mail brought letters of consolation from the commanding general of Michael's Americal Division, Lloyd B. Ramsey, and from Stanley R. Resor, the Secretary of the Army. The Mullens read them searching for a sign that their son's sacrifice had had some meaning. "We sincerely hope that your burden may be lightened by the knowledge that Michael was a model soldier," Major General Ramsey wrote, "whose actions and conduct brought credit to himself, the Division and the United States Army. . . . Michael was an exemplary soldier whose ability, spirit

118

and dedication to the service earned for him the respect of his associates and superiors alike. . . . We share your burden and we pray that you will find consolation in the sympathy of your friends, your family and your faith." Peg later sent Major General Ramsey copies of Michael's letters "so that you can see what one of your model, exemplary soldiers thought of you and your war."

Secretary of the Army Resor wrote, "We are proud of his military accomplishments and grateful to him for his contribution to our Nation's strength."

Peg tossed both letters onto the kitchen table pile she reserved for "official mail." The letters landed in such a way that Major General Ramsey's overlapped Lieutenant Colonel Schwarzkopf's just enough to display the date "2 Mar 1970" stamped on both. The rubber stamp infuriated her; it was, to Peg, as if some anonymous Army bureaucrat had simply decided, "Okay, on March 2, send all these letters out." Suddenly she noticed something even more disturbing: the "1970" on the two rubber stamps printed just a hair lower than the "2 Mar" and both "Mar's" seemed to tilt slightly to the left. Of course, Peg realized, the Army purchased rubber date stamps by the thousands, but was it mere coincidence that the battalion's rubber stamp and the division's contained identical flaws? The more likely explanation, she felt, was that the two letters had originated from the same office. The correspondence had been coordinated for but one reason: the Army had something to hide.

Peg had cause to be skeptical. During the week Michael was killed, seven other Iowans died in Vietnam. If Iowa's eight casualties were about average for the losses from the other forty-nine states, it would indicate that at least 400 Americans died that week in Vietnam. Peg already knew that one planeload of bodies had landed in Oakland on Monday and two more landed Tuesday the week Michael's body arrived. The planes carried 75 bodies each. And yet the official casualty figure released for that entire week listed only 88 Americans killed in Vietnam.

When Peg had contacted the parents of that

119

week's seven other Iowa casualties, she discovered the majority of them, too, had been told their sons were "nonbattle" casualties. But not until she learned that the weekly casualty figure reported on the evening television news was for those killed in action only did Peg begin to suspect why the nonbattle casualties were so high. Nonbattle casualties, such as Michael, weren't counted, and she wondered just how many other so-called nonbattle casualties there might have been. (Correspondents covering the Vietnam War in 1970 were already aware that the Army was classifying as nonbattle casualties any soldiers who died in the hospitals as a result of wounds.) Peg was convinced the Army was deliberately disguising the number of casualties suffered to prevent the American people from learning their true losses in the war.

That evening the Waterloo *Daily Courier* published a letter critical of the poor turnout given a Vietnam veteran who had come to Waterloo to give a booster talk on the war. The lady accused her fellow citizens of lacking patriotism. Peg's furious reply appeared on Sunday, March 15, under the heading "Parents of G.I. Killed in Viet—'Immoral War' ":

> Please get down and pray for the boys in Vietnam and for the boys and girls who are not waving the flag in defiance of this cruel and immoral war.
>
> Our boy was buried on March 3 in a beautiful, Christian, "non-military" funeral. We have been criticized because we did not have a military funeral and our decision was made on the fact that the Army took our boy (who was a chemist and not a soldier), trained him to kill, sent him to Vietnam and on February 21st, they told us, he was killed by friendly forces—accidentally, we will never believe.
>
> Do you realize how many thousands of American boys have been lost in this manner—denied the decency of being killed by the enemy? These boys' deaths are listed as "non-battle"—are they included in the casualty lists? Do we know how many bodies come back to Oakland each week—does the number of deaths tie in

120

with the casualty lists? Think about this. Please.
. . . "Think." . . . "Read." . . . "Study." . . .
Evaluate this war.

Mrs. and Mrs. Gene Mullen
Rt. 3

On Wednesday, March 18, three days after their letter appeared, Nick Lamberto, a feature writer for the Des Moines *Register,* telephoned wanting to know why Peg had questioned the casualty lists. She explained how Michael had been on a search and destroy mission, was at a night defensive position when the artillery shell had killed him and "wasn't considered a battle casualty, so he wasn't counted." Peg told Lamberto about the other area families who had been informed their sons were nonbattle casualties, too.

Because of Peg's letter, a *Register* researcher had gone through the newspaper files and compared the Pentagon's casualty count against the newspaper's own. As of March 1, Lamberto told Peg, the Pentagon listed 532 Iowans killed in Vietnam. According to the researcher, the *Register* files indicated the Pentagon figure was 129 casualties short.

121

Chapter Eleven

The morning after Nick Lamberto's telephone call, Peg Mullen returned from the mailbox with a letter from Martin Culpepper in Vietnam. Culpepper's letter was the first the Mullens had received from anyone who had served in Charlie Company with their son. Michael had been dead a month, and they still had not heard from any members of Michael's platoon or from the ROTC lieutenant he had mentioned in his letter or his company commander. Peg had written the Pentagon complaining, "It's just too damned bad that we can't find out who lived and died with our son. There's simply no communication and I firmly believe my son had at least *one* friend in Vietnam." The Pentagon never answered.

Through Culpepper Peg discovered for the first time that six or seven other soldiers had been wounded and one other young man had been killed:

> It was an air burst, it hit in between your son's bunker and another bunker. The round burst in the air when it hit a tree in between the fox holes. This was about 2:15 AM on Feb 18 before daylight. It was a short round that killed him. Meaning the round didn't travel the distance it was supposed to travel. He was not killed by enemy forces, but an accident.

Culpepper explained that DTs (defensive targets) were set up in advance in "an area or place where they call in artillery for support in case you are attack. From this area they can direct it to any place they want." One line of Culpepper's particularly intrigued Peg: "They normal shot about 200 to 300 meters away from you, they use to do this almost every night until that accident." They *used* to, but they stopped. Two killed, six or seven wounded, never anything in the newspaper about it, no investigation, no communication with anyone but Culpepper—whom Peg had discovered only by chance—and after that accident the Army didn't fire DTs again. Why not?

The obvious reason, Peg believed, was that what had happened was so wrong, so inexcusable the Army didn't want anybody to find out about it. That is why no one had been permitted to write, why the newspaper stories had been blacked out, and why the letters from the battalion and division commander had been coordinated. In a postscript to his three-page handwritten letter Culpepper added, "If the army's story is different please let me know." Clearly Culpepper would not be surprised to learn that the Army had lied. His letter closed:

> Even though the Lord has taken him away from you, we both will carry the memory of him in our hearts. The loss is great and nothing can replace him, but I hope the Lord will find peace in your heart. I would appreciate it if you would read in the New Testament, I Thessalonians, Chapter 4. The sixteenth through the eighteen verse and may it comfort your heart.
>
> Love,
> Martin L. Culpepper

Peg wondered whether Culpepper had found some passage in the Bible which would provide her with even more information, something which he dared not write openly but instead could only hint at.

Peg located the section in their family Bible:

> 16. For the Lord himself shall descend from heaven with a shout, with the voice of the archangel, and with the trump of God: and the dead in Christ shall rise first;
> 17. Then we which are alive and remain shall be caught up together with them in the clouds, to meet the Lord in the air; and so shall we ever be with the Lord.
> 18. Wherefore comfort one another with these words.

She studied the three verses for a few minutes, then gave up. Except for the "descend from heaven with a shout," which *might* have referred to the artillery shell, there didn't seem to be anything interpretable as a code.

On Tuesday, March 17, the death certificate demanded by the Mullens arrived. The document, a standard DA form 10–249, forwarded from the U.S. Army Mortuary at Danang, was dated 18 February 1970, and below the statement "I have viewed the remains of the deceased and death occurred at the time indicated and from the causes as stated above" was the signature of John S. Schechter, MD, Captain, Co D. 23D Medical Bn. The certificate listed Mr. and Mrs. Oscar *T*. Mullen as next of kin, the mode of death, "accident," the interval between onset and death, "unknown," and the cause of death ("enter only one cause per line"), "missile wound of chest." The space reserved for "circumstances surrounding death due to external causes" was blank, as was the space indicating whether or not an autopsy had been performed. Although the date and hour of death, *0250 hrs 18 Feb 70,* and the map coordinates for the place of death, *BT 366015* (the hillside overlooking the village of Tu Chanh), confirmed the information given them in Lieutenant Colonel Schwarzkopf's letter, the death certificate did nothing to allay the Mullens' suspicions.

Why was the space reserved for "circumstances surrounding death" blank? Michael, the Mullens had been told, was killed when an artillery round fell short. Why, if Michael had not been "subjected to any prolonged suffering" was the "interval between onset and death" unknown? Most disturbing of all, however, was the question why, if Michael's only wound according to Tom Loomis, the funeral director, had been that small hole in his back near his right kidney, did Captain Schechter list Michael's cause of death a "missile wound of *chest?*" The Mullens wrote back requesting a complete medical report on their son's death.

Two days later the Mullens received notification from First Lieutenant Arthur A. Belefonte of the U.S. Army Personal Property Depot in Saigon that Michael's possessions had been collected and sent and would reach them soon. Enclosed was a USARV form 438 inventory of Michael's belongings. Nowhere on the list was the $200 dollar camera sent Michael by his uncle Howard Goodyear. Although the inventory did list a "watch, Seiko without band," neither the wristwatch nor the camera was ever returned.

The simple cardboard carton reached Waterloo on Saturday morning, March 21. A friend who worked in the post office voluntarily drove the package to the farm himself. He refused Peg's offer of a cup of coffee, explaining that he had to return to work, but Gene and Peg knew he understood they would want to be alone.

The carton lay on the kitchen table between Michael's parents. Neither moved toward it until finally Peg pushed it over to Gene and said, "You do it. Go on."

Gene carefully untied the package's knotted strings, then slowly, almost reverently, removed the top. They began to sift through the empty, folded *clothing, 2 Shirts, khaki; 1 cap, Garrison; 1 Necktie; 1 Pair of gloves.* They found the fingernail file and clippers they had joked about (Michael had always kept himself so immaculate that his parents had speculated he would even clean his fingernails in the jungle); Michael's shaving kit with his worn, soft-bristled toothbrush inside; a pair of sunglasses; *1 belt, web with buckle; 1 Coin purse with 2 souvenir U.S. pennies: 1 Insignia, U.S. brass; 1 Nameplate, plastic;* a hairbrush which someone had cleaned; Michael's prayerbook, sweat-stained and bent to the contours of his hip. There were three rosaries; one was simply string tied in knots for each of the ten prayers. Gene decided he would give that one to Johnny; the other two to Patricia and Mary.

Peg was silently sorting through the papers, and the driver's licenses, addresses, receipts, the two photographs of Caroline Roby. She pulled out the *1 Pair of shoes, dress oxfords* and put them aside, and then she lifted up a small bronze-colored religious medallion hanging from a chain. "Oh-h, Gene. . . ."

It was the medal Gene had given Michael at the

125

airport. He took it from Peg and gently, tenderly, sadly lowered it around his neck again.

A letter from Creighton W. Abrams, the commanding general of the United States Military Assistance Command in Vietnam, arrived the following week. Peg sat holding it in both hands: "It is my hope that you will find a measure of solace in knowing your son gave his life for a noble cause, the defense of liberty in the free world. Rest assured that we who remain here in Vietnam will continue our efforts to bring peace to this troubled land so that your son's sacrifice will not have been in vain." Peg crumpled the paper in a rage; then, because she thought Gene might like to read it, she carefully smoothed out the page again.

Peg was still disturbed that with the exception of Culpepper none of Michael's friends had written. She was now certain that at least half the casualties in Vietnam were due to mysterious circumstances, "accidents," because maps were wrong, because someone high on drugs was shooting off his gun or because men were being killed by their own artillery. That was why no communication was permitted. What was it that Waverly mother said, the one whose son was missing in the burned-out tank? "We've been told by the Army that we can't discuss this with anyone because it might 'aid and abet' the enemy."

The enemy, it had begun to appear, was anyone who opposed the war. Almost a month had passed since Peg had written the Pentagon asking who had served with her son. She knew only from Culpepper's letter that at least one other young man had been killed. And then, suddenly, a woman in Kentucky wrote saying that the Pentagon had asked her to communicate with the Mullens since her son and Michael had died together and had been close friends.

The young Kentuckian was Leroy Hamilton. He had dropped out of school in the eighth grade after his father was badly injured in a lumber accident. The Hamiltons cultivated more than 100 acres and kept dairy cattle and Leroy, the oldest, was needed to work the farm. After Leroy was drafted, his mother, his six-

126

teen-year-old sister and fourteen-year-old brother were left to do all the haying and milking themselves. Peg was convinced that the Army had written Mrs. Hamilton confident she would be just a mountaineer mother of a high school dropout son and wouldn't know enough to write a letter to anyone.

What the Army failed to take into account was the estrangement people whose sons had died in Vietnam felt toward the government, the military and, in many cases, the neighbors in their own communities. Families of Vietnam casualties wanted to know each other, sought out each other because they had nothing in common anymore with the neighbor down the road whose son didn't have to go to war, who were never going to experience the anguish and bitterness such a loss brought.

A Gold Star family from north of La Porte celebrated their twenty-fifth wedding anniversary and, in addition to their friends, invited other families whose sons had died in Vietnam. They had asked them, the mother wrote Peg, because she and her husband needed to have others who appreciated how empty they felt celebrating their anniversary without the laughter of their firstborn son.

A few days after Peg wrote Leroy Hamilton's mother back, she and Gene went to dinner at a friend's house, and the husband, a veteran of World War II, after listening to Peg talk about the young people's opposition to the war, said, "Well, I don't know what's the matter with those kids. I went, why shouldn't they go?" Peg couldn't wait to leave. She decided from that moment on she would seek out only people who shared her views. She no longer understood anyone who felt there should be a war on; to be pro-war was, to Peg, synonymous with being pro-Michael's death. As she later explained to Gene, "There's only one side when you lose your son."

Peg had mailed Michael's letters to the Des Moines *Register*, and the editors decided to run them in their Easter Sunday edition. On March 27, Good Friday, a *Register* editorial headed "Why? And for What?" devoted to Michael's letters concluded:

127

He was in a night defensive position when artillery fire from friendly forces landed in the area and killed him.

Why? and For what? his parents still ask.

So far some 41,000 Americans and 102,000 "friendlies" have been killed in this futile war. These are not statistics, they are individual human beings—sons and husbands and brothers.

Nick Lamberto, the *Register* reporter who had earlier interviewed Peg about her Waterloo *Courier* letter questioning the casualty figures, telephoned Peg again. He called at a bad time.

Earlier that day Peg had argued with a representative of the United States Army over Michael's headstone. The Army insisted that if the Mullens were to accept the free government-provided headstone, the words "U.S. Army," "Sergeant" and "Vietnam" would have to be on it. Peg was so disgusted she made up her mind to buy her own. She went to a La Porte memorial carver and related her quarrel with the military; the near-sixty-year-old stone carver replied, "Goddamn the Army! Good for you, Peg, I'll give it to you at cost."

Peg had the stone engraved:

Michael E. Mullen
Born Sept. 11, 1944
Killed Feb. 18, 1970
Son of Gene & Peg
"He dared to ripple my pond"

The quote was lifted from a letter written by Caroline Roby. Although Peg worried the phrase might appear mawkish, she considered it the most appropriate sentiment they had received. It described Michael. He never left anything undone. "If someone needed their pond rippled," Peg said, "Michael did it." Far more indicative of Peg's mood at this time was the word "Killed." Michael had not died in the war; he had been *killed*.

Lamberto telephoned shortly after Peg returned from the stone carver, and she was still furious. Peg complained that only "the cream of the crop" were sent to Vietnam, that "if you got a girl in trouble, or were too fat, or too thin, you didn't have to go." She spoke to Lamberto for about fifteen minutes, and it wasn't until she had hung up the telephone and cooled off that she began to worry about what she had said. By the time Gene returned from John Deere she had telephoned her sister Louise, who lived next door to Lamberto in Des Moines, to find out more about him.

"Lamberto's going to kill me, Gene," Peg said that night. "He really is. I didn't find out until this afternoon that he was a hawk on the war."

"What can he do to you?" Gene asked.

"I just think he's going to print things that will cause me trouble." Peg thought for a moment, "Maybe I'll drive to Des Moines tomorrow and see if I can talk to him in person."

Peg did meet with Lamberto and asked if he would delete a couple of statements.

"Lamberto just laughed at me," she reported back to Gene. "And when I left, he said, 'Well, have faith, hope and charity, Peg Mullen.' "

Michael's letters and Lamberto's interview appeared in the *Register* on Easter Sunday. Lamberto's piece began: "A distraught mother, bitter over the death of her son in South Vietnam, has vowed to use his insurance money 'to save the boys still over there.' "

By this time the Mullens had received the bulk of Michael's insurance policies. The $10,000 U.S. Army policy had been split four ways: $2,500 each to Gene, Peg, Caroline Roby and the Don Bosco High School. In addition, Michael carried a $10,000 policy with the Knights of Columbus (Gene Mullen later tried to invoke the double indemnity clause since the Army had ruled Michael's death "accidental." He did not collect) and $980 from a $1,000 policy with the Federal Life Insurance Company.

The Mullens had also received the money Michael had withdrawn and converted to traveler's checks five days before he was killed and a U.S. Army check for $2,014.20, a gratuity payment representing six months' projected salary to defray the cost of his funeral. It was this gratuity pay and not, as Lamberto reported, the insurance money which the Mullens had decided to utilize in their fight against the war. Lamberto wrote that Peg had vowed to use $5,000 "to ferret out the truth about the war. I have no organzied plan," he quoted her as saying, "but I'm writing letters and making phone calls, telling our story." Lamberto then reprinted the majority of Peg's letter to the Waterloo paper but added two sections based on his telephone interview of one of which Peg denies ever having said: "They accuse us of a massacre at My Lai. That's a farce. Our boys had a right to kill those people. How many Americans have been killed by 'local' citizens over there?"

The other passage was the one Peg had tried to have him delete, the part where she had spoken of the boys who had gotten girls into trouble or were too fat to be sent to Vietnam.

Monday, March 30, the day after Michael's letter and Lamberto's article appeared, two local television stations, KCRG-TV of Cedar Rapids and KWWL-TV of Waterloo, arrived at the Mullens' farm to interview them. Gene and Peg were good material: angry, articulate, emotional and defiantly opposed to the war. At a time when the American Midwest was the bastion of the Silent Majority and the only real opposition to the war existed among the draft-age young and their college professors, the Mullens represented a newsworthy exception. Still, if the media capitalized on the Mullens, the Mullens were quick to recognize they could take advantage of the media, too.

The television reporters had come only because of the interviews and letters which had already appeared in print. Peg and Gene realized that the newspapers therefore provided the cheapest and most effective platform from which other, broader outlets such as radio and television coverage became accessible. Gene now began to consider the possibility of purchasing newspaper space through an advertisement.

That afternoon a second *Register* reporter, Gordon

Gammack, suggested the Mullens take it easy on their activities. He advised Peg that the Army was "doing an excellent job in a very bad situation" and was "doing it as well as they could.

"If you really want to know the truth about the war, about Vietnam," Gammack told Peg, "the war correspondents will tell you. Don't spend your money trying to find out things that will only hurt you." He then added, "You can't believe a GI coming back from Vietnam. You just can't believe what they say."

With the exception of Culpepper, Peg hadn't heard from any GIs! She would soon, though. It had not occurred to her that hundreds of copies of the Des Moines *Register* interview and Michael's letters were already on their way to Vietnam. She had been too busy to think of that.

She was now spending several hours every day at her typewriter. Letters had become her major link to Michael, the only means she had of keeping him "alive," of making his death mean something. The frenzy with which she corresponded reflected an energy which she had to direct away from her anger and grief. She was so convinced the military was behind a deliberate conspiracy to prevent the American people and their representatives in Congress from learning the truth about the war she immediately copied any information she gained about Michael or any letter from any person containing any knowledge whatsoever about the war and forwarded those duplicates to Senators Fulbright and Hughes in Washington.

The Xerox machines in the library and bank cost a quarter for each copy, so Peg tried whenever possible to have her correspondence duplicated for free on the Xerox machine at the Don Bosco High School. But one afternoon she was in La Porte with six letters and called attorney William Wagner to ask if she might use one of his office machines.

Bill Wagner shared law offices with his brother, Roy, whose own son was serving with the Americal Division in Vietnam at this time. Bill Wagner is a square-jawed, iron-gray-haired, crew-cut ex-Marine in his mid-fifties who took part in the assaults on Guam,

Bougainville and Iwo Jima. Wagner had become active in patriotic organizations after the war and was now vice-commander of the La Porte City American Legion Post to which Gene had previously belonged. Wagner would later say, "There isn't anyone in this town who has more sympathy over the loss of their son than I have. I've been there. I've seen the smell and taste and sound of battle, and after thirty-eight months in combat you kind of learn a few things. You learn that this country is worth all it takes to keep it going. I believe in *this* country *first*. I'm not a 'superpatriot,' but if my country calls and has a use for me, by God I'll be the first guy out there with a bayonet to stab somebody!" He genuinely liked Peg and Gene, and they liked him, too. He did not, however, approve of their approach. He could not condone Peg's wearing a Moratorium armband, writing letters to Senators, Congressmen, newspapers protesting the war, saying the sort of things reported in that *Register* interview. It puzzled him. It was the sort of behavior which Wagner expected from some *damned radical,* not Peg and Gene. Still, he appreciated Peg's feelings. He knew that if he had lost a son, he couldn't be sure how he would have reacted.

The bookshelves of Wagner's office are lined with more than 200 Jim Beam commemorative whiskey bottles he has amassed as a hobby. His collection increased to such an extent over the years that his wife wouldn't let him keep them in their house. Wagner laughingly tells about his Iowa state trooper friend "who saves beer cans and thinks I'm crazy!"

Wagner rose from behind his massive desk as Peg entered and expressed again how sorry he was over Michael's loss. "He was a very nice boy, Peg, an exemplary boy, a credit to the community." Peg thanked him and said that both she and Gene appreciated his having called off old Peter Dobkin.

"So you'd like some letters copied?" Wagner asked as Peg sat down.

"I have six. You'd find them interesting, I think." She slid the letters across his desk. "It's the real story about Vietnam. . . ."

Wagner glanced quickly at the top letters, saw

132

they were to Senators Fulbright and Hughes and buzzed for his secretary. "She'll have these copied and back to you in a few minutes."

"Don't you want to read them?" Peg asked.

Wagner refused to be baited. He believed he knew as well as anyone what was going on in Vietnam. His old outfit was there, and he would receive a communication from the Marine Corps every two weeks. Although he was disturbed about the American involvement because Congress had never officially declared war, he disapproved most of all the limitations on the men doing the fighting. "You know," he would muse, "I've always wondered how my old comrades could sit back and get shot at and not fire back. Hell, we had guys who'd make Patton look like a Sunday school teacher!" Wagner simply didn't want to get involved in a discussion with Peg about the merits or lack of merits of the war. He admired the Mullens' concern, their courage and dedication. He believed in "standing up and being counted" and questioning one's Congressman "at the proper time and place as to why we are in Vietnam. Nobody's answered that one for me yet," he said, "but I wouldn't tear the flag down to find out. I still think our Congressmen, our leaders have a lot more information than I have." The only time Wagner did write his Senator was when Iwo Jima was given back to the Japanese. "We had four thousand kids who never walked off that place," he protested.

Wagner should have known it was impossible to talk with Peg without the Vietnam War entering in. Peg's opening came when Wagner asked whether Gene might not want to join the American Legion again.

"I know he doesn't, Bill," Peg said, "and he isn't going to."

"He's not?"

"Of course he isn't!" Peg said. "How can he join when the American Legion is upholding the war? Until you men wake up, I suppose we'll be there forever since you seem to have more influence on President Nixon than someone like myself."

"Well, that's your opinion," Wagner said. "I don't agree with you, of course."

The secretary returned with the copies, and Peg asked what she could pay for them.

"Happy to do it," Wagner said, holding up his hand. "You don't owe me a thing."

"Let me give you something," Peg insisted.

"You could give me all the money in the world," Wagner replied, "and I wouldn't take it. I'm glad to do it for you."

On April 1 Peg joined a group of Iowa antiwar activists on a plane trip around Iowa to publicize and campaign for the passage of the 609 amendment cosponsored by Iowa's Senator Harold Hughes, California's Senator Alan Cranston, New York's interim Senator Charles Goodell, Oregon's Senator Mark Hatfield and South Dakota's Senator George McGovern in an attempt to set a definite time limit on American presence in Vietnam. That same day, in Vietnam, the Communists launched their spring offensive. By the end of that week American forces had suffered their heaviest losses in seven months.

On Monday, April 3, Peg mimeographed the following letter to the many who had written who had expressed support or lost sons or husbands in Vietnam:

Dear Friends:

We wish it were possible to answer each letter personally, but it can't be done at this time. We'll try later. We have too much work to do in carrying on our protest—each hour that is lost haunts us.

Michael's story has also appeared in the Kansas City *Times* and the Columbia *Missourian*. We have someone taking it to the St. Louis *Globe-Democrat* and the Milwaukee *Sentinel*. If any of you have contacts with large newspapers such as Omaha, Minneapolis, etc., please let us know.

We feel that letter writing to Washington is a waste of time. I have done it for years and all of you seem to have been pouring out your anguish to Congress and to the President and it is like knocking your head against a stone wall. The only response I get is from Senator Hughes and he is certainly behind all of us.

We apologize to those parents who feel we played up the plight of the college graduates. . . . We felt we could not tell your story, only the one we know best, ours! Please tell YOUR story of the fine 19 or 20 year old boy you lost—only you can tell it. It costs no money . . . the news media seem to want to donate their facilities.

We need your ideas—not your money—and thanks so much.

s/Mr. and Mrs. Gene Mullen

Now when the Mullens drove into La Porte, they noticed people avoided them, ducked into stores when they saw Peg or Gene on the street. The townspeople knew the Mullens would want to talk only about the war. Gene would return to the farm fuming with rage. "It's time for us to speak out!" he would tell Peg. "I want people to know what it's like to walk down the streets of your own hometown and have your friends cast one look at you and turn their heads away. Why do *I* have to be the one to say hello first?"

"Oh, Gene," Peg said quietly, "you can't blame them. You know it's hard to be with us. This is something we've done to ourselves."

"What do you mean, 'done to ourselves'?"

"We have, Gene. You know we have."

"We have not!" Gene said angrily. "All we've done is what is right!"

"No, Gene, no. . . ." Peg shook her head sadly. "You know when you see them that you're terribly jealous that their kids didn't go, that they—"

"That's not so!" Gene interrupted. "I was, but I'm not anymore. I'm not, Peg. I'm just angry that they avoid me. *Why do they avoid me?*"

Not all of the Mullens' friends avoided them. Peg's card club tried over and over again to get her to come. She knew they wanted to help. She knew, also, that

135

there was nothing they could do. One afternoon, however, one of Peg's closest friends did stop by. She listened quietly as Peg went on and on about the inequities of the draft and then asked if Peg would have wanted Michael to have avoided his military obligations entirely.

Peg looked stung. "Oh, God," she said, biting her lower lip, "I think this is probably our real anguish." She looked through the kitchen window to the dirt road and the open fields beyond. "It's not that we didn't want Mikey to go, it's that we—we *let* him go!" Peg turned back to her friend, tears gathering in the corners of her eyes. "We raised Mikey in the belief that an individual, a man, *obeyed*. That you didn't question and, and"—Peg's tears were flowing freely now—"this was so wrong! So wrong. Mikey never went against an order. And this, this is our anguish! That we ever did such a thing to our child." Peg wiped her eyes with the back of her hand. "Oh-h-h, God!" She wept. "He was the best little guy that ever lived!"

For close to a week now the $2,014.20 gratuity paycheck had been lying on the kitchen table. Gene and Peg were determined to use the Army money to purchase space in the Des Moines *Register,* and although they had not yet decided what to say, they knew it was essential to make themselves heard. The response to their letter to the editor in the Waterloo paper three weeks earlier, the publication of Michael's letter and Lamberto's interview in the Des Moines *Register* a week before, had convinced the Mullens they were not alone, that all over Iowa there were families like themselves "just crying out." The Silent Majority's unwillingness to speak out was, the Mullens believed, more than anything else why the war had been allowed to drag on and on. And each night Gene and Peg would stay up late trying to figure out how to get their neighbors involved enough to care. The war obsessed the Mullens; they were unable to think or talk about anything else.

Gene had started looking into the Black Hawk County draft calls. Out of the county's population of

125,000, 25,000 young men were registered for the draft. Of that 25,000 only 2,000 were considered eligible to go. All the rest had managed deferments. As Gene began learning who had received deferments and how, he also discovered that the Iowa casualties were coming from the small farm communities where the boys had no access to the men on their draft boards. Peg was unable to forget Michael's phone call from the Des Moines draft headquarters "I simply didn't need to be drafted!" and his accusation that the whole draft setup was corrupt. And so each night, far into the night, Peg and Gene would sit at the kitchen table talking about the draft and the war. If anyone came to the house, the conversation would turn to the war. Every morning Gene would tune his transoceanic radio to a Sydney, Australia, station which carried the Vietnam news. At night the first thing he did when he returned from John Deere was listen to the local news. He would read the *Register* and *Courier* daily and attempt to piece together all the information he had received. Peg, during her day, would have culled what she could from the mail, telephone contacts and the television news. John, their only child who still lived at home, was finding it increasingly difficult to be around his parents. No longer able to bear hearing them go on and on about the war, he began giving one excuse after another to get out of the house.

One night in the middle of the first week of April Gene was sitting at the kitchen table making little marks on a yellow pad. He and Peg had been discussing their advertisement again. "How many Iowa deaths have there been now?" he asked.

"Altogether? Since the beginning of the war?" Peg thought for a moment. "I suppose somewhere around seven hundred by now. At least that many, don't you think?"

Gene did not answer. He continued to doodle on the pad. Suddenly he said, *"Crosses!"*

"What?"

"A page full of crosses!" Gene said excitedly.

137

"Think of it! Just crosses, a cross for every boy who died in Vietnam. A page full, a half page, whatever we can afford."

"Of just crosses?"

"Well, we'd need to explain what they mean. Something like 'Each cross represents an Iowa boy who has died—' no, who 'gave his life in Vietnam.' I don't know," Gene said. "You know what to say, Peg, you always put things better than I do."

Peg thought for a while. "Just a page full of crosses. . . ." She reached over and patted Gene's hand. "You know? I think that's a real good idea."

"Why, thank you, Mother," Gene said and smiled.

Chapter Twelve

The Mullens' half-page Des Moines *Register* advertisement appeared on April 12, 1970, on page five of the first news section, and exploded habitually taciturn Sunday breakfast table conversations throughout the state. There was a half-inch-high banner black headline:

A SILENT message to fathers and mothers of Iowa:

And below, in slightly smaller but still boldface type:

We have been dying for nine, long, miserable years in Vietnam in an undeclared war . . . how many more lives do you wish to sacrifice because of your SILENCE?

Two inches to the right of the "SILENCE?" was a small black cross and beneath it, the epitaph "Sgt. Michael E. Mullen—killed by friendly fire."

Then came the crosses. Rows upon rows of crosses. Fourteen rows containing forty-nine crosses each, a fifteenth row with twenty-seven and space left open for more. Their ranks, so starkly aligned and black against the bleak white page, suggested a photographic negative of some well-kept battlefield cemetery viewed from afar. The crosses blurred, vibrated, played optical tricks. There were too many for the eye to contain. One could only grasp blocks with white space in between. But as the eye moved across the page, ranks appeared to open up, re-form themselves into ghostly platoons, companies, battalions on parade.

"These 714 crosses," a legend explained, "represent the 714 Iowans who have died in Vietnam."

Near the bottom-left-hand corner of the page was

139

printed: *"In memory of Vietnam War Dead whom our son joined on February 17, 1970 . . . and to those awaiting the acceptable sacrifice in 1970. . . ."* On the opposite side appeared the credit: "Sponsored by Mr. and Mrs. Gene Mullen, La Porte City, Iowa."*

That Sunday morning Peg had attended the five o'clock mass at Father Shimon's Sacred Heart Church. Gene Mullen awoke at seven, carried the newspaper into the house and left it opened to the advertisement for Peg to see upon her return. She took a quick, satisfied look, asked Gene to wake her if there was any response and went back to bed. Peg got less than an hour's sleep.

Iowans were already busy telephoning neighbors, friends, relatives. College students were calling their parents; fathers were arguing with sons. The Mullens' telephone began ringing at eight o'clock and never let up. In La Porte, William Wagner caught sight of the advertisement, put down his breakfast cup of coffee, grimaced in shock and said, "Good God!" United Press International interviewed the Mullens at nine. At ten a Des Moines television station newscaster complained he had been trying to reach Peg all morning but had had so many incoming calls himself about their advertisement he hadn't been able to get an outside line. "Everybody wants to know what you meant by your ad."

Peg explained how the Army had drafted their son, a biochemistry student in graduate school, and made him a soldier, that Michael was on a combat mission when he was killed by his own artillery in Vietnam but was considered a "nonbattle casualty" and, therefore, "wasn't counted." She told him she was now convinced the casualties in Vietnam were much greater than the American people were being told, that the public didn't realize "how many thousands of American boys have been lost in this manner." Peg pointed out the discrepancy between the actual number of Iowa deaths and the Pentagon's "official casualty lists" and said that although she and her husband had once been members

---

*The Mullens thought the eighteenth in Vietnam was the seventeenth in the United States.

of the Silent Majority, the death of their son convinced them that "the time had come for us to speak out."

"Our advertisement," Peg explained, "was our way of telling the world what we feel about the draft, the war and the loss of life in Vietnam."

One by one broadcasting stations throughout Iowa telephoned, but the majority of the callers were people who simply wished to express their sympathy and agreement with the Mullens' views. They were of all age groups, from Iowa and neighboring states, and over and over again would say they were sure the Mullens would be receiving a lot of "crank calls" (or "outraged calls," or "negative calls"), that the Mullens would be accused of being "un-American" (or "Communists," or "deranged"), but that they had telephoned because "we just wanted to say, 'Good for you!' "

Peg would reply that they *hadn't received* any calls from people who didn't agree, that *all* the people had said that they were sick of the war, too. The person on the other end of the phone would pause, surprised, then say something like: "Well, I'll be darned!"

It would be a mistake to suggest that there weren't people who disagreed. Many persons in La Porte objected strongly to the Mullens' advertisement. They thought the protest brought discredit not only to the Mullens but, by association, to the town. However, they didn't call; they simply assumed, like Lamberto, that Peg was "distraught," that Michael's death prevented the Mullens from making sense. They were "crazed with grief." As one of the waitresses in La Porte's Mom's Cafe explained, "Other people have lost their sons, and they don't protest!"

The only objection the Mullens did receive was from a "Mr. and Mrs. P. J. Schultz" of 2113 Clinton Street, Iowa City, who tore the Mullens' protest out of the newspaper and mailed it back with the message, printed in red ink across the bottom:

MY SON BELIEVED IN WHAT HE WAS FIGHTING FOR IN VIETNAM, FREEDOM FROM THE COMMUNISTS; He believed that they are taking over country after country like

Lenin and Krushev said they would, and he believed it best to stop them in VIETNAM, rather than in the streets of U.S. If your son did not believe this, he was a fool to go, but *don't* drag the rest of our sons down to your son's level.

The "Schultzes" also printed "JU" in the lower left-hand corner.

Peg wrote the family, but her letter was returned. No one by that name lived at that address. And there was no "P. J. Schultz" in the Iowa City telephone directory.

The Mullens were overwhelmed by the response to their advertisement. Virtually every Iowa radio and television station featured it on their evening news. The UPI interview was carried by wire service newspapers throughout the country. Local television stations again sent reporters to the Mullens' farm. Television network commentator Paul Harvey, using the *Register* page as a backdrop, told how the Army's gratuity check had paid for the Mullens' antiwar protest and how the Iowa farm family's anger expressed his own growing dissatisfaction with the war.

Peg Mullen, with mixed feelings, discovered she had become a celebrity. Although she realized people now sought her views, that it was now easier for her to express her opposition to the war, she was deeply troubled that her new status as an "antiwar spokesman" would not have occurred had not Michael died. She knew that people in La Porte felt she was "cashing in" on Michael's death, that she was, in a sense, "displaying his bones for a profit." And it distressed her that their protest had had precisely the effect they had hoped for everywhere except their own hometown. La Porte resented the publicity she received. The estrangement the Mullens had begun to feel within their own community was growing worse. They saw fewer and fewer people, withdrew more and more into the isolation of their farm.

Peg continued to correspond with parents whose sons had been killed in the war. If a new casualty's family didn't live too far away, she would visit them and offer her help. But Peg's outspoken opposition alienated, in several instances, the very people she had most hoped to comfort. Many families were unprepared and unwilling to agree with Peg that their sons had sacrificed their lives for an unjust cause. They would not believe that their sons' lives had been "wasted." Peg was forced to accept exceptions to her conviction: "There's only one side when you lose your son."

Peg learned from Culpepper that publication of Michael's letters and the Lamberto interview in the *Register* had reached Vietnam. "I've just come from Bayonet to the field," Culpepper wrote Peg. "In the rear they told me about your articles. I'm glad to see that your son told how it was and you had it published so the public can see what goes on over here. I'm glad that you stand up for us boys in Vietnam." Culpepper also told Peg that if anyone asked where she was getting her information from, she should "tell them about me. They can't do anything. It might get me out of the field."

Peg was enormously gratified by Culpepper's letter. He had provided vindication for the antagonisms her outspokenness had generated. She was "stand[ing] up for us boys in Vietnam." She was even more encouraged when she subsequently learned that soldiers who had seen their advertisement were writing back for fifty more copies at a time. The Mullens' antiwar protest was being tacked up on orderly room walls all over South Vietnam.

Six weeks had passed since the Mullens received the Army Finance Center's request that they sign a blank pay voucher for Michael's final eighteen days of pay. They had not heard from Army Finance again. On April 21 Peg wrote Lieutenant Colonel William J. Cochran, chief of the Army Finance Center claims division: "It seems that we did not make ourselves clear to you in our letter to you of March 6, i.e., we want a detailed statement of monies due Michael for the 18 days of February, 1970. We want to know what deductions from pay were made, and what additional pay is due because of unused furlough, and allotment of $60 that did not arrive at destination on or about August 5.

"We are merely asking you for a statement of account," Peg's letter continued, "something I had to do April 15 as far as our government was concerned."

Peg explained that they had not worried about the money before but needed it now because "our 'Peace' campaign which has gone nationwide is beginning to become costly, and we have just begun."

Peg sent duplicates of this letter to Secretary of the Army Stanley Resor and Secretary of Defense Melvin Laird.

Peg had long felt frustrated by the total lack of response with which her correspondence to the White House, the Army and Congress had been met. Other sympathetic families had complained, too, over and over again that nobody seemed to read the letters they had sent and that writing Washington accomplished nothing. Peg cut a stencil explaining her new plan and mailed it to her friends and contacts. Everyone who wrote protesting the war was to send her a carbon of the letter. She hoped thereby to accumulate as many as 500,000 copies, which she could then present in bulk to one person at the Capitol in graphic demonstration that such letters did, in fact, exist. Carbon copies slowly began to trickle in, but the flood which Peg had anticipated never materialized.

Instead of being discouraged, Peg merely channeled her energy toward an already proved idea, a second advertisement, one which would reinforce the premise that the war and the deaths of young Iowans would continue until the citizens of the state had the courage to speak out. Because the crosses had been so effective, Peg and Gene decided to repeat the theme. A huge cross was formed by the intersection of the words "SILENT" and "SILENCE":

```
        S
        I
    SILENT
        E
        N
        C
        E
```

The accompanying text bludgeoned their message home: "Was there silence when you looked at your son and said, 'He is too young, it will soon be over.'" "Was there silence because you were afraid to speak out?" ". . . .you were afraid to be labeled un-American?" ". . . .you accepted the status quo?"

"Was there silence when you thought of your boy in Vietnam and said, 'It couldn't happen to him.'?

"Are you silent because 'You did your duty' in another conflict?" "Are you silent because you think the war doesn't involve you?" ". . . because you have a financial interest to protect?" ". . . because of political expediency?" "Are you silent because you have no CONSCIENCE?"

The Mullens had "THE FIGURE IS NOW 719 IOWANS DEAD IN VIETNAM" printed in large boldface letters across the bottom of the cross.

The advertisement then asked, "Vietnam deaths recorded in Defense Dept., Washington, D.C., only—not at State level—WHY?" Below that appeared five small black crosses with the legend: "number of crosses added to 714 since April 6, 1970."

The advertisement ended:

> To the hundreds who have written . . . or called in person, we agree—YOUR DECISION IS NOW. This nation under God shall have a new birth of freedom and that government of the people, by the people, for the people shall not perish from the earth.

The Mullens could afford to purchase only a quarter page this time. Their advertisement appeared on Sunday, April 26, 1970, again on page five of the first news section of the Des Moines *Register,* next to a Singer sewing machine advertisement. Its appearance met with practically no response. The Mullens don't know why that happened, whether it was the advertisement's location in the newspaper or its layout, but they were terribly disappointed.

The next day Secretary of State William Rogers, faced with almost unanimous bipartisan opposition within the Senate Foreign Relations Committee against giving military aid to the new Cambodian leaders, informed the committee members that the Nixon administration had not reached any decision on Cambodia's request for extensive military aid. He did suggest, however, that the President had authority to send at least limited amounts of military assistance with or without Congressional approval.

Two days later, only a few hours after thousands of South Vietnamese troops supported by American warplanes and heavy artillery crossed into Cambodia, the Defense Department announced United States advisers were being provided the ARVN forces fighting in Cambodia, but that "only a few hundred Americans" were involved. Peg felt sure the Defense Department was lying.

Mothers for the past several weeks had been worriedly writing and telephoning Peg. About a month previously, these mothers said, their sons had written that their units were heading for the Cambodian border. The young men were with the 198th Infantry Brigade of the Americal Division, the 25th Infantry Division, the 1st Air Cavalry Division and the 11th Armored. The mothers had heard nothing from their sons since. Peg, certain that those units had been sent into Cambodia, decided to forward the women's letters and comments to Senator Fulbright's Senate Foreign Relations Committee right away. She had intended to have them duplicated on the Don Bosco High School machine, but while in La Porte on an errand she noticed Bill Wagner and his brother, Roy, on the sidewalk in front of their law offices. She had the letters with her, Wagner had been nice enough to have had her letters copied three weeks before, so she parked her car, walked over to him and asked if she might rent his machine for about an hour. "I'll pay the girl whatever you pay her, or more than that," Peg told him, "if you'll let her run me off some work."

"I can't, Peg," Wagner said. "Today's the last day for filing state returns. You're aware how we work, that we get all the farmers out in the mail on March first. So we still have all the people who have

146

been gracious enough to wait until the farmers' papers are done."

"It'd only take an hour," Peg said.

"I can't." Wagner shook his head. "I just can't spare the hour you want—or the girls. A lot of these people are due refunds and they're anxious to get them back. These are people whose federal returns are due, not just the state returns. We've got to get them in the mail. We've got two girls tied up running these machines now all day long."

"That isn't the reason, and you know it!" Peg said bitterly. "You just don't want—"

"That's not so!" Wagner interrupted. "If you'd asked me any other day, you could've—"

"You don't want to let me use the machine because you know why I need it."

"It has absolutely no connection whatsoever with why you want to use it," Wagner said impatiently. "I wouldn't rent the machine to, to *the President of the United States* today if he asked me. I've got to use the machine today. It's packed with my business, and *that's it!*"

"That *isn't* it! You American Legion types—"

"That's ENOUGH!" Wagner shouted. "I don't want ANY PART of you or WHAT YOU'RE DOING! It's trash! JUST TRASH!" He whirled away from Peg and into his office.

"Roy?" Peg said, turning to Wagner's brother. "Can't you please—"

"I'm sorry, Peg," Roy Wagner said. He left her standing alone on the sidewalk.

She turned and saw that townspeople had stopped to watch the exchange, but they refused to meet Peg's look and moved away. She walked slowly back up the street, climbed inside her car and wept. Back at the farm later that afternoon Peg wrote Wagner she was sorry to have lost her temper. "I have cried very little since Michael died, but you can bet I cried today." She enclosed a dollar and a half for the six letters he had coped for her three weeks ago and mailed the letter.

When the canceled check was returned in their monthly bank statement, Peg saw that Wagner had endorsed it over to the American Legion as a donation from the Mullen family.

The next day, April 30, President Nixon announced that he had ordered American combat forces into action against Communist sanctuaries twenty miles within Cambodia. On nationwide television the President said, "Tonight American and South Vietnamese units will attack the headquarters for the entire Communist military operation in South Vietnam." Even as he spoke, more than 50,000 troops, half of them American, were pouring into Cambodia in eight separate thrusts from the highlands opposite Pleiku to the jungles west of Saigon. The President stressed that it was "not an invasion," he was taking this action "not for the purpose of expanding the war into Cambodia but for the purpose of ending the war in Vietnam and winning the just peace we all desire."

The President's speech provoked new antiwar protests, campus violence and moves in Congress to curb his powers. The President, the newspapers reported, referred to those on campuses who opposed his policies as "bums," compared with the American soldiers in Vietnam whom he called "the greatest."

It was apparent within only forty-eight hours of his speech that although the American and South Vietnamese troops were able to locate substantial rice stores and some abandoned medium-sized enemy bases, the Communists had evacuated the Cambodian Fishhook section being searched, and no indications whatsoever were found of any elaborate underground "headquarters for the entire Communist military operation in South Vietnam." The Defense Department announced that more than 100 U.S. fighter-bombers had attacked Hanoi's antiaircraft guns in "protective reaction" against the firing upon of unarmed U.S. reconnaissance planes. The raids were the biggest since the November, 1969, bombing halt.

College campuses throughout the nation were racked with antiwar protests. At Kent State in Ohio, after two nights of violent disruptions during which the ROTC building was burned to the ground, a 600-man contingent of the Ohio National Guard was sent to the campus to bring the university students back under control.

By this time Peg Mullen was dizzy with rage. The Cambodian invasion prompted a fusillade of letters—to and from Senator Fulbright, to and from Martin Culpepper, to and from the Army. Peg had earlier asked Fulbright to "inquire how nonbattle deaths are listed by the Department of Defense" and whether those deaths were released to the press. The Senator responded that he would let her know the results of his inquiry and added, "I certainly agree with you that it is important that the most accurate information be made available to the public." A few days later Peg wrote Fulbright again:

> Thank you for your letter of April 29 concerning the history of nonbattle deaths in Vietnam. Having checked into this from many angles I have learned that the names are released to the press listing them as hostile and non-hostile; however, on Thursday, when the total kill is given only those dying in hostile actions are included. . . . We believe the nonbattle count could run as high as one-third, not one-fifth as given out by the Pentagon.

Peg requested his office's assistance in obtaining the casualty list and next of kin of those who had died in Vietnam the week Michael was killed so that she could pursue her search for what had happened to her son. And because additional mothers with sons in Cambodia had since written, she included an updated list of their units.

On May 4, the afternoon Peg mailed her letter to Senator Fulbright, the Ohio National Guard tear-gassed a noon rally of Kent State students who had gathered in protest of the widening Southeast Asian war. When the students refused to disperse, when instead they turned angrily on the guardsmen, shouting obscenities and throwing rocks and the tear gas canisters back at them, the inexperienced and frightened young soldiers inexplicably and indiscriminately fired into the crowd. Four students were killed, and eight were

149

wounded. The dead students were Allison Krause, nineteen, of Pittsburgh, Pennsylvania; Sandra Lee Scheuer, twenty, of Youngstown, Ohio; Jeffrey Glenn Miller, twenty, of Plainview, New York; and William K. Schroeder, nineteen, of Lorain, Ohio. Their deaths appalled Peg Mullen; she saw them as four more non-battle casualties of the Vietnam War. Children were not safe from the U.S. Army even on their college campuses.

Near the end of that week, on the day the U.S. casualty figures were released indicating 168 Americans had been killed and 1,001 wounded (the highest figure in eight months), Peg Mullen heard from Martin Culpepper again. She had to read his letter twice to make sure she had understood it properly: anyone from Michael's old unit could be court-martialed for writing the Mullens. Any correspondence with the Mullens had to be copied and a duplicate retained by the Army. "Anything sent to you," Culpepper wrote, "can be censored as we are in a war zone." Culpepper had misspelled "censored" and someone, with a handwriting quite different, had crossed out Culpepper's misspelling and corrected it. Peg felt the entire tone of Culpepper's letter was so different from his previous ones she was sure it had been dictated—and dictated by whoever had corrected the spelling, presumably the censor. No one had ever opened or censored letters to the Mullens before; it was, to Peg, an indication of a new policy—a policy in response to the Des Moines *Register* interview, letters and advertisements confirming that the Army's attitude was that the Mullens, too, were the enemy.

Obsessed by her conviction that she and her family were the targets of a conspiracy on the part of the United States Army to prevent them from learning the details of their son's death, Peg fought back harder. She sought more proof that the military and the Nixon administration were deliberately preventing the American public from knowing the truth about the war. She had been able to locate Fred Wilson, Michael's friend from NCO school, who was now with an infantry company in Vietnam. Wilson wrote Peg

150

about Ed Gardiner, a young man who had gone through NCO school with Michael: "He is with a reconnaissance unit in the 3/22 working around Tay Ninh. He has been crossing the border into Cambodia since early April, when the 'Administration' was saying no U.S. troops were in Cambodia." Wilson also noted that lately the list of casualties "Killed as a Result of Hostile Action" and "Died not as a Result of Hostile Action" carried by the *Army Times* were of about equal length and that in the 4th Infantry Division "more people are being killed in accidents than by the enemy."

Peg had Culpepper's and Wilson's letters copied and forwarded to Senators Fulbright and Hughes.

Peg was now so upset with the Army that her fury spilled over into her renewed correspondence with the Army Finance Center. Her letter was filled with outrage and sarcasm and, atypical of Peg but clear evidence of the state of mind she was now in, error after error in simple arithmetic:

W. J. Cochran, LTC, FC
Chief, Claims Division
U.S. Army Finance Center
Indianapolis, Ind. 46249

Dear Sir:

It has been fourteen days since I last wrote you and asked that you send me [a] complete statement of account concerning Michael's last pay in Vietnam.

To help you along on this great task, I have worked out in minute detail what you owe him:

His pay was $335.70 per month—and using 30 days per month as [a] schedule, I have come up with the figure of $11.19 per day.

$11.19 per day x 18 days = $201.42
    Less $50.00 allotment
    Less $20.00 allotment
    Less $ 6.25 bond
    Less $12.50 bond
    Total deductions = $98.75
                    $102.37

Plus $60.00 allotment for
July never received: = $60.00
Plus seven days furlough
never used   = $78.33
Pay Due: = $230.70 [sic]

Is it going to take an act of Congress to get
this poor dead soldier's pay? I shudder how the
bereaved have been taken over the past nine
years on this one phase of military operation.

s/Mrs. Gene Mullen

Peg Mullen heard from the Army Finance Center on May 14 (the same day Mississippi state police
fired shotguns, rifles, machine guns and armor-piercing
shells into student groups and a women's dormitory at
Jackson State College, a black college, killing Philip
L. Gibbs, twenty-one, and James Earl Green, eighteen,
a high school student visiting the campus). The letter
from the Army Finance Center contained a recompu-
tation of Michael's basic pay rate and a recapitulation
of their efforts to track down Michael's $60 July
allotment, which had gone astray. A paragraph, near
the end however, read as follows:

Your son accumulated 44 days leave from 4
September 1968 through 18 February 1970. A
review of his military pay record shows he used
53 days leave, or an excess of 9 days leave. Members on excess leave are not entitled to pay and
allowances; therefore, pay and allowances were
collected for the period of 23–31 August 1969,
the period of excess leave.

As was entirely normal and legitimate, Michael
Mullen had taken twenty-one days' advance leave prior
to his departure for Vietnam, which, when added to
his previous Christmas and other leaves, came to a
total of fifty-three days. At the time of his death Michael had served only long enough to have earned
forty-four days' leave; *the Army, therefore, billed him
for the nine days he had taken but had not lived long
enough to earn back.*

Peg was so outraged she telephoned the Army

Finance Center and asked to speak with Lieutenant Colonel Cochran himself. She was shifted to an aide whom she told: "You can goddamn well keep that final paycheck as payment for embalming Michael's body—evidently you *forgot* to bill us for that!" She informed the aide that they would never accept Michael's final paycheck until the Army returned to him "the nine days' pay, nine days' clothing allowance and nine days' food ration you withheld from him!"

Peg realized that the deduction from Michael's final paycheck reflected only a certain terrible bureaucratic logic. The point was not that Michael did not live long enough to earn back his advance leave but that he simply did not earn back his leave. It did not matter that the organization which was deducting his pay was the same organization which had killed him, thereby making it impossible for him to earn it back. The Mullens were faced with the implacable logic of computers, of standard operating procedures. This demonstration that her son's death meant no more to the Army which killed him than it did to the actual artillery shell, the flyswat which did it, was, as Peg so aptly explained to Gene that night, "the last obscenity, really!"

Would that it had been.

Two weeks earlier Peg had castigated Iowa Senator Jack Miller for letting ten weeks pass since Michael's death without any expression of sympathy. "You always find time to vote in the Senate in favor of those issues which condemned our sons to death in Vietnam," Peg wrote, "how is it you are unable to find time to write these dead soldiers' grieving parents?"

The Senator's reply arrived one week after the Army Finance Center's letter deducting nine days from Michael's final pay:

May 18, 1970

Mrs. Gene Mullen
La Porte City, Iowa

Dear Mrs. Mullen:

Replying to your letter of May 5th, I naturally extend my deepest sympathy to you over the loss of your son. I have written a good many letters of sympathy—not only to people like you, but to parents and wives of our prisoners of war. Also, you should know that many Members of Congress have shared some tragedies and concerns of people like you. Our son-in-law flew over 120 combat missions in Vietnam, and fortunately returned.

It has been my observation that, with few exceptions, the persons bearing the real burden of this war—the men who have been doing the fighting, the wounded, their wives and parents—have been the least complaining of anyone over this tragic war.

I regret that you are one of the exceptions.

Very truly yours,
s/Jack Miller

Chapter Thirteen

Senator Jack Miller's letter reached Peg the day 150,000 blue-collar workers and hard hats carrying thousands of American flags marched in New York City in support of President Nixon. That morning's mail also contained Senator Fulbright's reply to Peg's request for the casualty list of the week Michael had died. The Senator had not yet been able to acquire that information, but he did enclose the Defense Department's response to his inquiry as to how "nonbattle" casualties as a result of artillery fire were arrived at. The communication read, in part:

> One cannot assume that all such [U.S.] casualties to [friendly artillery fire] are included in the category of "U.S. Casualties Not the Result of Action by Hostile Forces." If it is determined that such casualties occurred during an action with enemy forces, the casualty is placed in the category of "U.S. Casualties Killed as a Result of Action by Hostile Forces."

This meant if, for example, American troops were surrounded and in danger of being overrun, and they called in artillery over their own position, those Americans killed by their defensive artillery barrage would be considered killed as a "result of Action by Hostile Forces," or battle casualties. The same would hold true if American troops were advancing behind their own artillery screen and a round fell short, killing a few. Both these actions are more common than one would wish to believe; such casualties are, however, taken for granted as an ugly facet of war. At any rate, the major point was that just because a man was killed by his own artillery, he need not necessarily be considered a nonbattle casualty.

The letter from the office of the Department of Defense continued:

> All Vietnam deaths, hostile and non-hostile, are reported on the daily casualty lists which are available to the press. Only when the next of kin specifically object to the publication of the name of the deceased is that name withheld. The casualty is also included in the weekly statistical summary of casualties.

Local newspapers would report only local casualties and would not generally distinguish between battle and nonbattle deaths. Major metropolitan newspapers might include the total casualty count and might list battle and nonbattle deaths as such. But the bulk of the nation did not read those casualty lists. They would instead depend on the evening television news to provide them with the information about the war. The television networks did not include the nonbattle casualty count during this period. There was no deliberate network policy of omission as such; it reflected simply the national attitude that the number of nonbattle deaths was no real indication of the progress or lack of progress achieved in the war. Since the only means of "scoring" the war lay in the accumulation and comparison of body counts (if the evening news reported 750 Vietcong killed and 75 Americans, America was "winning" 10 to 1), it was to the military's advantage to keep the reported casualty figures as low as possible. North Vietnamese and Vietcong losses were inflated, American casualties disguised. Men who died in the hospitals as a result of wounds were likely to be listed as having died from postoperative complications; they were nonbattle casualties and not counted.

I am informed that each instance where Americans have been killed by friendly artillery fire is investigated. These are included in a category designated by the Military Assistance Command Vietnam (MACV) as "Misadventure," and are not tabulated separately.

The Mullens were so outraged to discover that the Army, with cosmic inappropriateness and unseeming levity, referred to the manner in which their son had been killed as a "Misadventure" that they almost missed the information that an investigation had been performed. If they were able to read the results of that investigation, then they would know exactly how their son had died. The Defense Department neglected to point out, however, that such investigations are classified "For Official Use Only" and not available for public scrutiny. The Mullens now knew that their son had been killed, in military terminology, by "friendly fire" and was, therefore, a "nonbattle" casualty as a result of an artillery incident officially referred to as a "misadventure" in a war which was never declared.

The casualties for the two weeks ending May 23 in South Vietnam and Cambodia were 359 U.S. dead and 2,084 wounded.

A couple of days later Peg was telephoned by a woman from Mason City, Iowa, a town about sixty miles to La Porte's northwest. The woman's son had been only eleven days with Delta Company, one of the five rifle companies in Lieutenant Colonel Schwarz-kopf's infantry battalion, when his patrol was caught by a booby trap. Thirteen members, himself included, had been wounded severely enough to require evacuation. The Mason City mother told Peg that her son, while at the hospital, had met Abe Aikins, a young black medic who had been with Charlie Company the night Michael was killed. Aikins had asked her son if he had known Michael. The Mason City boy hadn't. "Well, I've read some of Mrs. Mullen's letters," Aikins said, "and Michael's old lady is telling it like it is."

The mother admitted her family had spent several nights discussing whether or not they should call Peg. "We know how much you want to find out how your son died," she said, "so we decided to go ahead. Maybe this Abe Aikins will be able to help." Peg was

157

very grateful the woman had called. She wrote Abe Aikins that night.

A week later, on May 23, another Iowa family whose son was in Vietnam telephoned Peg. Gene had met them at the Loomis Funeral Home prior to Michael's service. The father had introduced himself, saying that their son had just been assigned as a medic to Michael's old unit. The mother had occasionally called Peg since to read parts of her son's letters home. Peg was convinced that the losses Charlie Company now seemed to be suffering were so terrible that had Michael not been killed that February night, he would not and could not have survived the next three months.

"Peg, what am I going to do?" the mother asked. "I'm so frightened for him. In his letter today, he said, 'Mother, I cannot pick up another body sack. Here I am tonight sitting by two of my friends in sacks from booby traps. And there was another one with both his legs gone. I don't think he'll live,' he says. 'They took him out in a helicopter and I don't know whether he will live or die. . . .' "

Peg spoke of the sort of operations Michael's unit had carried out. "They never saw any enemy, but," Peg said angrily, "these crazy Americal officers have this obsession with body counts. This Schwarzkopf, the battalion commander, is one. All any of them want is body counts so they can get their promotions!"

"Peg, what am I going to do?"

Peg explained how her son could enlist out of combat or try for a conscientious objector status. The mother said she didn't think her son would do that, that he would rather remain with his friends even if staying meant he might die.

"Well, just pray for him then."

" 'Pray for him'?" the mother said. "Oh, God, don't you think I am?"

Peg was convinced that the high casualties Charlie Company was suffering were entirely Lieutenant Colonel Schwarzkopf's fault. She recalled Michael's letter written late that previous October: "We are supposed

158

to have the BN Co. out here sometime this week—kind of a laugh, for they live in a dream world! They have to have figures and nobody knows what is a VC or a plain ignorant villager, at least in this area." And Culpepper in one of his earlier letters mentioned that Charlie Company had been "harassed a little bit and it wasn't much fun" during Michael's last stand-down. Peg wrote Schwarzkopf an angry condemnation of the Army in Vietnam, his harassment of Michael during the stand-down and swore her determination to avenge her son's death. She explained how she had taken Michael's gratuity pay and spent it on antiwar advertisements (which she enclosed along with excerpts from Michael's letters). She wrote that neither she nor Gene would rest until they learned who was responsible for Michael's loss. Although Peg did not accuse Schwarzkopf specifically, she left no doubt that she felt he was at least partially to blame not only for Michael's death but also for the high rate of casualties incurred by his battalion since.

What Peg did not realize was that Schwarzkopf had not taken command of the battalion until December. The battalion shortly, thereafter, received a new brigade commander as well: Colonel Joseph Clemons, whose unhappy assignment in a previous conflict, that of a young infantry lieutenant during the waning interminable peace negotiations of the Korean War, had been portrayed by Gregory Peck in the movie made from Brigadier General S. L. A. Marshall's book *Pork Chop Hill*. Shortly after Michael was killed, Colonel Clemons shifted Schwarzkopf's battalion out of the "Rocket Pocket" and sent them south to relieve the 5th Battalion of the 46th Infantry in the Batangan Peninsula. The new area of operations (AO) was a fifteen-by-twenty-five-square-kilometer section of the peninsula which included My Lai. The Batangan Peninsula had been notorious since the French Indochina colonial wars for its booby traps and overlapping minefields. Colonel Clemons had decided to rotate Schwartzkopf's 1st Battalion of the 6th Infantry with the 5th of the 46th because that battalion's men had become so leery, their morale so shattered by the minefields and

159

booby traps, the brigade commander no longer felt the 5/46th was effective.

Lieutenant Colonel Schwarzkopf requested and received from the 5/46th an overlay depicting the minefields in his new Batangan Peninsula AO. When the overlay was unrolled and positioned on his map, Schwarzkopf saw that the entire AO, from one end to the other, was filled with either suspected or confirmed minefields. Schwarzkopf, whose previous tour with the Vietnamese Airborne had taken him all across South Vietnam in 1965, would later remark that the Batangan Peninsula was the worst experience he had ever been through in his life. It was an entirely different sort of AO from the one in which Michael had been killed. The battalion's whole *modus operandi* changed. The primary enemy was no longer ambushes; it was minefields and booby traps. "It was terrifying to me," Schwarzkopf said about the Batangan Peninsula, "and I know, I know it was terrifying to the men."

On May 28 Bravo Company of Schwarzkopf's battalion became trapped in a minefield, and Schwarzkopf himself was wounded.

A portion of Bravo Company had been patrolling and suddenly one man and then another detonated mines. The company commander, a young captain, and the platoon leader, a young lieutenant, were both badly wounded. A medical evacuation helicopter was called for, and Lieutenant Colonel Schwarzkopf and his artillery liaison officer, Captain Bob Trabbert, immediately flew in their command helicopter to Bravo Company's area and landed. In order to save time, Schwarzkopf turned his helicopter over to be used for med-evac. After he helped load the wounded on board, he and Trabbert stayed behind as the helicopter flew out.

The remainder of the patrol was frozen in the middle of the minefield. The young soldiers were on the edge of panic. Their commanding officers had been evacuated; they felt leaderless, abandoned. Colonel Schwarzkopf began talking to them as calmly as possible. He told them that they were going to be all right, to walk back out the same way they had walked in. "Watch where you put your feet, keep to your old tracks, stay calm, keep your distance," he told them. They had just begun again to move when a young private off to Schwarzkopf's right stepped on another mine.

The same explosion that punched the kid up into the air slightly wounded both Captain Trabbert and Lieutenant Colonel Schwarzkopf. They felt the impact, the pain before the young soldier even hit the ground. The boy's right leg was flapping out to one side. "My leg! MY LEG!" he screamed, and Schwarzkopf saw the men around him begin to panic again.

"Keep STILL!" Schwarzkopf ordered. *"Stay where you are!"* Schwarzkopf called for the radio operator; someone else was yelling for a medic. The first sergeant, too, had been seriously injured by the blast and lay unconscious, the dust settling back over him. "Trabbert!" Schwarzkopf turned to the artillery liaison officer behind him. "Get that dust-off here in a hurry. We need that med-evac *now!*"

"My leg! Somebody help me!" the kid was screaming. "Oh, God, it hurts so much!" He was thrashing about on the ground, and the men all around him stood rigid with horror, terrified that the wounded private would trigger another mine. Schwarzkopf began inching across the minefield to reach him.

"Somebody help me, HELP ME!" The private was still flailing about.

"Don't move!" Schwarzkopf yelled at him. He was less worried that the young soldier would set off another mine than he was concerned that the boy would cause himself further injury and lose his leg. "You're going to be all right, just hang on," Schwarzkopf was maybe thirty feet from the wounded private. He carefully, slowly, slid one foot forward, testing the ground beneath his boot before placing his weight on that foot. There was absolute silence now except for Trabbert talking on the radio to the med-evac helicopter, telling them where Bravo Company was and what they would need. Schwarzkopf still had twenty feet of minefield to cross when the wounded private started panicking again: "I'm going to die! We're all going to die!"

Schwarzkopf's legs suddenly began to shake uncontrollably; his knees were so watery he had to reach down and grip them until they stilled. The perspiration was stinging his eyes. He straightened up and saw the men were watching him, waiting for him to move forward again. Schwarzkopf, to his astonishment, suddenly thought of the sign on Harry Truman's White House desk: "The buck stops here."

"I don't want to die," the kid was whimpering. "You've got to get me out of here."

"I'll get you out," Schwarzkopf said gently. "Just keep still. You're all right."

"I'm not! Goddamn you, can't you see my leg?"

"Take it easy son." Ten feet to go. "It's only broken; I can tell that from here." The colonel could see the boy had suffered an ugly compound fracture, pieces of bone were sticking out, but if the boy remained calm, he wouldn't lose the leg. "We'll come out just the way I'm walking in."

"Colonel," Trabbert called, "dust-off's in sight!"

"Hear that, son?" Schwarzkopf asked the private. "You'll be in the hospital before you know it."

"Hurry!" the boy said, and he began to writhe again.

Five feet . . . three feet. . . . Schwarzkopf gently lowered himself across the wounded boy's body to keep him still. "I don't want you to move around," Schwarzkopf told him. "We're going to have to set that leg."

"Am I going to lose it?"

"What's your name, son?"

"Miller, sir. Private Miller."

"You've got a broken leg, Miller, that's all."

"God, it hurts, sir!"

Schwarzkopf looked about for something he could use as a splint. There was a small waist-high tree back where he had left Trabbert and where three other men were standing still. Its branches would be perfect. All they'd need to do would be to snap the twigs off. "I'm going to need to splint Miller's leg," Schwarzkopf called back to them. "One of you cut me some splints off that tree there."

Trabbert pulled out his sheath knife and passed it to one of the men. The man took one step toward the tree and triggered another mine.

"Oh, my GOD!" Schwarzkopf cried, horrified. Trabbert had taken the full force of the exposion. One of his legs was blown off, an arm broken backward so that the white bone of the elbow socket showed, and a great hole was gouged in his head. He would survive, but the other three men were killed instantly. They lay where they had been flung. No one moved. Only the young private, pinned beneath Schwarzkopf, was twisting about to get a better look. "Are they all dead, sir?"

The following afternoon, in La Porte City, the American Legionnaires and Veterans of Foreign Wars visited the little cemeteries in the neighboring communities and placed American flags on each of the veterans' graves. Early the next morning Gene Mullen drove to the Eagle Center cemetery and removed the Legion's flag from Michael's headstone. He did not want to permit them to glorify the manner in which Michael had died. It was Memorial Day.

Toward ten o'clock the Boy Scouts and Girl Scouts, delegates from the local 4-H Clubs and Women's Relief Corps, the Saddle Clubs and Navy Auxiliary began assembling outside the American Legion Hall in La Porte, where the honor guards from the Legion and VFW had already formed. As they marched down Main Street toward the old steel-girdered bridge which crossed Big Creek, a high school band struck up "Anchors Aweigh." Ladies of the Navy Auxiliary moved closer to the bridge railing and waited until the band stopped before dropping bouquets of flowers into the rain-swollen waters. There was a moment of silence while the white blossoms, like tiny sailors' caps, bobbed and tumbled in the rushing current and were swept under and out of sight. Afterward the drum major hoisted his baton, blew his whistle, the strong-thighed majorettes marked time to the drumbeat, the Boy Scouts punched each other back into line, the baton dropped and the Legionnaires, the Veterans of Foreign Wars, the Saddle and 4-H Clubs and all the rest stepped briskly off, "Semper Fidelis" ringing in their ears, toward the first of the cemeteries. A brief service was held for the veterans buried there—veterans of Vicksburg, Chickamauga, of Sherman's March to the Sea, of Verdun, Okinawa, the Bastogne, Inchon.

Not all of La Porte, of course, attended the Memorial Day ceremonies; many of the citizens did not wish to remember any wars. And the farmers, who had had to wait for the late spring rains to absorb, were busy in their fields. They liked to have their corn planted by the second week of May, their soybeans in by the twentieth, but this Memorial Day farmers were still out planting the lower fields which only now had begun to dry. So the snare drummers' rim shot marching rhythms would be tempered by the deeper insistent thrumming of tractor motors beyond the gentle hills.

By midday the air rose thick and wet from the blacktop road, shimmered like gauze over the marchers' heads. The Boy Scouts teasing of the Girl Scouts grew more ill-tempered, severe. Black Angus, grazing like Japanese "Go" pebbles on lime-green pastureland gaming boards, would drift down to the fence lines and gaze curiously at the passersby. "Stars and Stripes forever!" the drum major ordered. "Pass it back!" The first blast of his silver whistle landed like lightning in the cattle's midst, and the steers had stampeded in panic beyond the next hillside before the drummers had even agreed on the beat.

If anyone at the Eagle Center cemetery noticed the little American flag had been removed from Michael Mullen's grave, no one mentioned it to his parents. Neither Peg nor Gene was present to hear "Taps" bugled. Gene was in his cornfields; Peg was typing a fresh stencil. Her letter, this time, was to be sent registered mail, return receipt requested, to each of the 100 United States Senators:

To:
Senator ——
From:
Mr. and Mrs. Gene Mullen, La Porte City, Ia., parents of Sgt. Michael E. Mullen, killed in Vietnam Feb. 18, 1970.
Subject:
Conduct of military concerning disposition of one soldier's death, burial and personal property.

Purpose: If 10% of you read this, we feel that we have not failed our son.

Feb. 21, 1970. Received message of son's death. Asked military to hold news from public until we had time to notify our family. Service officer said he was unable to do so. We pleaded with him, but he said he could not tell the army what to do.

Service officer told us we could request escort for our son. We did this and learned 24 hours later that Pentagon had chosen to ignore our request, making their own choice of escort. We demanded they honor our request, and through services of Senator Hughes' office the Pentagon was persuaded to grant our request.

Family asked for complete medical report on son's death. To date this has not been received.

Army Finance Dept. asked that family sign blank pay voucher for son's final 18 days of pay. Family refused and asked for audit.

Box of personal property returned from Vietnam, minus anything of value. Service office thinks family is the "exception" because they expected to have watches and $200.00 camera returned.

NOW WILL YOU PLEASE READ THE FOLLOWING . . . IT MIGHT HELP YOU TO UNDERSTAND WHY THE BITTERNESS GROWS AND GROWS IN THE HEARTS OF BEREAVED FATHERS AND MOTHERS.

"Your son accumulated 44 days leave from 4 Sept. 1969 through 18 Feb. 1970. A review of his military pay record shows he used 53 days leave or an excess of 9 days leave. Members on excess leave are not entitled to pay and allowances;

165

therefore, pay and allowances were collected for the period 23–31 August, 1969, the period of excess leave."

Michael was given a 21-day overseas furlough in August 1969. He only lived 5½ months in Vietnam, thus consuming 12 days leave. The computer indicates he should not have died before July, 1970.

Our son had two school loans which were cancelled because he died in the service of his country . . . but the organization that forced him into an immoral war . . . punched his card to Vietnam and his death, demands that he repay NINE OF his last 21 days of FREEDOM on earth. They are withholding the following: Base pay, $67.92; food rations, $11.18; clothing allow., $1.28; FICA adj. $12.19. We are wondering if there is some way Michael in his death could bill the AMERICAL DIVISION for the days in the jungle when they failed to resupply him with clothes, food, water and medication.

THROUGH YOUR OFFICE YOU HAVE BEEN ALLOWING THE MILITARY TO SPEND 36 MILLION DOLLARS A DAY. NOW WE LEARN THEY HAVE ANOTHER SLUSH FUND . . . REFUNDS FROM THE DEAD.

By four that afternoon Peg had had the stencil run off, the envelopes stuffed and addressed, and needed only to pack her suitcase for Washington.

Early in May the same week American troops were ordered into Cambodia, the Des Moines *Register* reported a group of Iowa clergy and laymen planned to travel to the Capitol to lobby in support of the Hatfield-McGovern amendment (609) which called for setting a definite time limit on American aid to the war. The group called themselves CALCAV, an acronym for Clergy and Laymen Concerned About Vietnam. A couple of days after the *Register* article, a man telephoned Peg that if she were willing to join the CALCAV group, he would pay her expenses to Washington. Peg did not know the man and declined, saying she did not think she was "the type clergymen would want along."

The man persisted, mentioning her involvement with the 609 group which had traveled by lightplane all over Iowa only six weeks before. Peg was just the sort of person the CALCAV group *would* want, he told her, since she had already demonstrated her effectiveness in protesting the war.

"Why don't you yourself go?" Peg asked.

"I can't. I'd *like* to," the man said. "But I can't stay away from my office that long. I wanted to do something, though. And I thought of you. I know you don't have a whole lot of money, Mrs. Mullen, and well, I thought I'd gladly pay your airfare from Waterloo to Washington and back if you'll say you'll go."

"No," Peg said. "I really appreciate your offer, but I can't go. I hate to fly."

The man urged Peg to reconsider, but when she seemed adamant, he told her, "If you should change your mind, my offer still stands."

During the next weeks, nothing whatsoever occurred to diminish Peg's suspicion that the military was deliberately falsifying the casualty counts. And when letters from soldiers spoke of deceptions and censorship and urged her to continue to "stand up for us boys in Vietnam," Peg knew she had to go to Washington, that she could not avoid going. It was her responsibility to go. She telephoned the CALCAV group's organizers in Iowa City and asked if she might join them. The group eagerly begged Peg to come. They had been worried that there would be too many college-age participants and that the seriousness of their purpose would be diminished if their image was that of just another college protest group. "To tell you the truth, Mrs. Mullen," the spokesman told her, "we want all the middle-aged people we can get."

Peg laughed. "Well, thanks. I guess."

She telephoned the man who had volunteered to pay her fare and said she would accept his offer, but she wouldn't fly. She would travel to Washington by bus. "God bless you, Peg," the man said. He sent her $50.

Peg was still packing when Gene returned from feeding the hogs. He stood watching her until Peg looked up from her suitcase and asked, "You don't mind my going, do you?"

"Peg, you have to go."

"Johnny's all packed, and we'll meet Patricia in Iowa City. You'll be all right, won't you?"

"Of course I will," Gene said. "What time do you have to leave?"

"Midnight. From Iowa City." Peg was folding some handkerchiefs. "You'll mail those letters for me?"

"You know I will."

Even in the midst of her preparations Peg could not forget her correspondence. Repeatedly she would interrupt her packing, her discussion of the trip to remind Gene that the letters were to be sent registered mail and not to forget to request a receipt. Almost as often as she mentioned the letters she expressed concern that Gene should take care of himself. "I've put some meat loaf in the freezer for you. Take it out before you leave for Deere's."

And Gene, proud of Peg as well as anxious about her, urged her to take care of herself.

"Oh, I will." She smiled. "Patricia and John will see to that."

Finally, as Peg was about to leave, Gene hugged her and told her, "Give 'em hell."

Chapter Fourteen

✚✚✚✚✚✚✚✚✚✚✚✚✚✚

Peg Mullen, her children John and Patricia, and Alan Hulting, Patricia's fiancé, boarded the first of the two buses chartered by the Iowa CALCAV group. Their bus left Iowa City a little past midnight, swung onto Interstate 80 and headed east toward the Mississippi River crossing at Davenport. Peg could not sleep. She stared out her window at the scattered farm lights until the broad, empty, darkened Illinois plains gave way to the glow of distant cities. Beyond Joliet, the swirl of Chicago's tollways, skyways, expressway interchanges appeared.

Peg's bus skirted Chicago, Hammond, the beaded lights of railway marshaling yards, Gary, East Bend, the fires of far-off steel mills lighting the sky. The high-tension lines swooped overhead to towers girdered like giant headless Amazons guarding the boundaries between factory towns. East of South Bend the sun rose and steamed the mist from Indiana. Peg watched the shadows shorten, saw the interstate begin to fill with campers as she passed through the Central Time Zone and into Monday's morning. Little children waved, flashed shy peace signs from the backs of station wagons.

And then her bus entered Ohio, flat, endless Ohio. Peg's restless mind broke loose, spun free, gave way to rages, daydreams. Unable to sleep, she sat staring out at silent, unprotesting, National Guard-drunk Ohio. By noon her bus reached western Pennsylvania. Peg did not sleep all the way through the Alleghanies, down to Maryland, east along the Potomac to Hagerstown and south again until the bus' headlights reflected against approaches marked "Washington." At Silver Spring the bus entered Alaska Avenue, and Peg

169

reached across to tap her son. "Wake up, John. We're almost there."

At 11 P.M. her bus stopped outside the Episcopal Church of St. Stephen and the Incarnation, where Peg and the CALCAV group were to spend the night. Peg had sat up for twenty-two hours. She felt chalky, irritable, dirty. All she wanted now was sleep.

Early in the antiwar movement St. Stephen's began providing "sanctuary" for protesters by permitting them to set up sleeping bags within the church and gymnasium. Its priest had concelebrated a mass in front of the Pentagon the fall before, and his senior warden had been among those arrested.

Peg and John unrolled their sleeping bags near the altar. Peg had never used a sleeping bag before. She slid herself inside it, tried to get comfortable, peeked out and saw John with his long hair settling down next to her. She worried whether that disreputable-looking crowd would be permitted inside the Senate to lobby. Patricia knelt over her mother to ask if she was all right. Peg told Patricia it was "the worst-looking bunch" she had ever seen. Her daughter laughed. "Mother, they're worried about *you!* About how you're going to get yourself in shape to go."

Just before Peg fell asleep, she wondered what all her conservative friends might say if they could see her now. As she drifted off, she smiled.

The next morning, Tuesday, June 2, Peg was the last to wake up. When she did, she couldn't believe what she saw. All the young men were wearing suits, white shirts, ties. Even their shoes were shined.

They met first that morning with the Moratorium Committee at the Mayflower Hotel, and Peg writhed while the Moratorium spokesman instructed the CALCAV group on how to lobby. Peg did not like anyone to tell her how to do anything. She was impatient to get inside those Senators' offices so she could tell them what she thought. After the meeting she hurried to the Senate Office Building ahead of the others. Their meeting with Senator Hughes was scheduled for one o'clock. Peg simply roamed the halls, killing time. She passed one open door and peered inside. The office was filled with Rath Ham advertisements and canned hams. Rath Hams was in Waterloo. Peg walked in and asked, "Whose office is this?"

A secretary looked up, "It's Senator Miller's of Iowa."

"Well," Peg said, "I should have known I guess."

"Are you with the CALCAV group?" the secretary asked.

"I sure am."

"May I ask who you are?"

"I'm Peg Mullen."

There was an audible groan among the office staff which the secretary ignored. "Your organization asked for a meeting with the Senator, but at the time we were unable to make any definite plans. However, you can tell them now that we will be able to see you all at three."

"That's fine," Peg said. "We've a meeting a few minutes from now with Senator Hughes."

"Oh, well, then, we'll arrange for the meeting to take place in the same hearing room."

"That would be very nice of you," Peg said, and she started to leave the office.

"Oh, Mrs. Mullen?" the secretary said.

Peg paused and turned back, "Yes?"

The secretary smiled. "Welcome to Washington."

The CALCAV's meeting with Senator Hughes lasted an hour and a half. Since the group knew that Hughes, as one of the sponsors, obviously favored what had come to be known as the Hatfield-McGovern (609) amendment, the discussion moved to other topics before the Senator excused himself saying he had to return to his work. Peg and the others had a few minutes to wait until Senator Miller was to join them. Before he arrived, his secretary entered and, walking directly to Peg, asked whether she would like to meet the Senator.

Peg, embarrassed to have been singled out, explained that she had met the Senator the year before. "If the Senator wants to meet anybody," Peg said, "I think he should be introduced to the young man who arranged the trip. He's sitting right up over there."

As the secretary went forward to meet the CAL-CAV organizer, an attractive middle-aged woman drifted into the hearing room and sat down beside Peg. They struck up a conversation, and the woman explained she was originally from Iowa but lived now in Virginia. They were still talking when Miller's secretary suddenly returned, took Peg by the arm and pulled her up to the front of the hearing room.

"Senator Miller?" the secretary said. "I want you to meet Peg Mullen."

Both Peg and the Senator were embarrassed. His face turned red and Peg's even redder. When she shook his hand, he gave her a limp, dead-fish handshake before turning away.

Unlike the meeting with Senator Hughes, the meeting with Senator Miller was filled with challenges and accusations. An indication of Miller's and Hughes' political differences is provided by ratings given them by certain political interest groups. The Americans for Democratic Action (ADA), for example, awarded Hughes a rating of 97 (out of a possible 100 percent total support of the ADA's position) while giving Miller a 13. The ADA, synonymous with the liberalism of a Galbraith-Schlesinger-New Deal-Great Society sort of legislation, represented staunch opposition to defense spending and any encroachments upon civil liberties. The National Security Index (NSI), on the other hand, which typified the belief that America's best interests are served by increasing the amount spent on the support and maintenance of large weapons systems and the defense of anti-Communist nations throughout the world, rated Senator Miller 100 and Hughes 0. Several times Miller became so furious he threatened to order the group to leave. "I know all about Vietnam!" Miller protested. "You can't tell me a thing about Vietnam! I've been there."

"Of course you were, *General* . . ." one young man said.

"Don't call me general!" the Senator replied.

"But you are a general, aren't you?" the boy quietly asked. He was referring to the Senator's commission as a brigadier general in the Air Force Reserve.

Peg told Miller she thought Congress should simply end the war immediately. "We should bring all the troops home bang! Right now! There's no need to stay another hour, another day or lose another life."

Senator Miller glared at Peg. "You're a dreamer, Mrs. Mullen!" he said, pointing a finger at her. "You live in a dreamworld with your theory on ending this war!"

"So do you, Senator," Peg replied.

"Well, Mrs. Mullen, your theory is an obsession with you," Senator Miller said angrily. "It would never work; it can't work. It won't work."

Peg shrugged and tuned the Senator out.

The meeting with Senator Miller ended just after five o'clock, and the woman from Virginia asked Peg if she might take her to dinner. "I miss Iowa so much," she said, "and it's so good to talk to someone from my home state. Can't I do something for you?"

"But I look like the devil!" Peg protested, patting her hair.

"You look fine," the woman insisted. "Please? Can't I take you to some place nice to eat?"

"Well. . . ." Peg thought for a moment, then smiled. "Oh, why, sure you could."

They ate at a seafood restaurant overlooking the Potomac River. During cocktails and red snapper the woman spoke of growing up in Iowa and Peg told her what had happened to Michael. Suddenly Peg put her fork down and laughed. "This just kills me!"

"Why?" the woman asked.

Peg gestured in dismay toward the elaborate dinner she had been served. "It's all so delicious and pleasant I feel guilty enjoying it."

"*Guilty?* Why? About what? Don't you think you deserve a decent meal?"

"Oh, sure"—Peg smiled—"but I couldn't help thinking about all those hungry kids." Peg explained how she had traveled from Iowa with two busloads of penniless students and how the money the man had given her for her bus fare was almost all gone.

"If that's all you're worried about," the woman

said, rummaging into her purse, "here." She gave Peg $30. "I'd gladly give you more, but that's all I have with me."

"I couldn't accept that!" Peg said.

"You sure can!" the woman said and pressed the money into Peg's hands. "Consider it my donation to your antiwar activities. Frankly, this is one donation I know will be doing someone some good. Besides, I'm not asking you to take it for yourself. It's for the students."

Peg gave the $30 to the CALCAV group. Several of the girls brought groceries with the money and that evening cooked dinner in the church kitchen for about sixty members of the group. Afterward Peg telephoned Gene to tell him what had happened since she had left the farm.

"I got the casualty list from Senator Fulbright's office," Gene told her, "the one for the week Michael died."

"Yes?"

"Michael's name wasn't on it."

"*Wasn't* on it? Are you sure?" Peg asked.

"Of course I'm sure—and I'll tell you who else wasn't on it," Gene said. "That Hamilton boy, Leroy Hamilton from Kentucky. He wasn't listed, nor was that boy from Illinois whose father called us and said his son had died the eighteenth."

They spoke for a while about others missing from that list as well. The day after they had been informed of Michael's death, Peg and Gene had started investigating other casualties which might have resulted from South Vietnamese artillery firing upon American forces. While they were getting in touch with other families whose sons had died on February 18, they learned four helicopters had been shot down with at least thirty men on board that same day and that there were at least five sites where mysterious shellings had occurred. But when it was confirmed that Michael had been killed by American, not ARVN, artillery, they had quit their search. Peg told Gene she would try to see Senator Fulbright the following morning and assured him she and the children were fine, just tired. Gene told her to go to bed.

The next morning, Wednesday, June 3, the Iowans visited more Senators and Congressmen. Peg was initially impressed by Senator Charles Percy of Illinois, whom she thought very handsome. Percy took time to shake hands with everyone in their group; he was the only Senator to do that.

"Of course I'm for the 609 amendment," Percy told the CALCAV listeners. "I thought you all knew that. But when the war ends, I'd like it to be my bill that ends the war."

Peg thought the Senator's comment so shallow she couldn't stand it.

Hugh Scott of Pennsylvania, the Senate minority leader, was too busy to meet with the group, but sent one of his aides. Peg and Patricia knew the Senator opposed the 609 amendment. Patricia, who spoke very emotionally about the morality of the war, received a standing ovation from the CALCAV group.

Peg went from Senator Scott's office to Senator Fulbright's. She spoke there with James Lowenstein, Fulbright's military liaison aide, and told him the casualty list sent her had been incomplete.

"What do you mean 'incomplete'?" Lowenstein asked.

"I mean," Peg said, pausing deliberately, "our . . . son's . . . name . . . isn't . . . on . . . it! I know something fishy's going on. Isn't there some way I could speak directly to whoever makes up these casualty lists?"

Lowenstein shrugged. "You could always try. . . ."

"I can't believe my son's death wouldn't be recorded somewhere," Peg said. "And if it isn't, then how many others have there been like him? How many boys have never been counted?"

Lowenstein seemed hesitant to contact the Pentagon any further about the casualty lists, so Peg suggested she would call them herself. A young man with the CALCAV group telephoned the Pentagon instead and was able to arrange a briefing for the following

175

afternoon. Peg left Lowenstein's office for the Senate gallery so she might sit in on the Cooper-Church amendment debate.*

The only time the CALCAV group were asked to leave their purses and briefcases behind was on entering the Capitol. Peg checked hers and moved up to the gallery. She listened to the debate for an hour; then she and Patricia went back down to the rotunda. Peg handed a guard the claim check for her briefcase, and he grunted lifting it over the counter.

"Your briefcase is certainly *full!*" he told Peg.

"It's interesting, too," Peg replied.

"What do you mean, 'interesting'?" the guard asked.

"It's full of antiwar literature."

"Oh? Can I have some?"

"Sure," Peg said, snapping her briefcase open, "that's what it's here for."

As the guard sifted through the papers, a second guard came over to look. Peg explained to him what was inside and the guard said, "Look, lady, I was there. I know what Vietnam's all about."

"Then you know how immoral the war is," Peg said.

"I don't know any such thing!"

Peg's briefcase was returned to her, and as she and Patricia were walking together out the Capitol, they fell in step with some men in hard hats who wore name tags identifying them with some Pittsburgh labor union group. Peg turned to the nearest one. "I suppose you're here lobbying against the war?"

"Mother!" Patricia said, taking her mother firmly by the arm. "You'd better start behaving yourself."

---

*The Cooper-Church amendment, co-sponsored by Senator John Sherman Cooper (R. Ky.) and Senator Frank Church (D. Ida.) would have barred the President from spending money to "retain" American forces in Cambodia, from sending advisers there, from providing combat air support for Cambodian forces and from paying any foreign troops who were assisting the Cambodians—this latter clause sprang from the disclosure in Senate testimony that a secret agreement had existed since 1967 between the governments of Thailand and the United States providing Bangkok with $50,000,000 a year in return for their sending one combat division to Vietnam.

The following afternoon, Peg's last day in Washington, she visited the Pentagon. Although the young CALCAV member had arranged the briefing for twenty members of the CALCAV group, twice that number showed up. To Peg's outrage, just within the front entrance a display booth had been set up to "sell" the Cambodian war. The rear projection screen showed American GIs chopping through the jungle and breaking open crates of captured supplies while a brisk and hearty narrator described how successful the operation was. Patricia, standing next to her mother, said, "They're neglecting to show one thing: the American boys dying there. There aren't any pictures of dead bodies."

Roger Simpson, one of the organizers of the CALCAV group and a chaplain at the University of Iowa, walked up behind Peg and Patricia and was so visibly shaken by the display booth's merchandising of the war that he was not sure he wanted to go further. Peg told him he must. Simpson later described Peg as "the spiritual focus of the whole effort."

"Those of us with the university were up on the intellectual issues, question-oriented, prepared to discuss things objectively," he explained "We needed the emotional balance Peg provided. She was such a good communicator, so open and friendly. She accepted sort of a mother-sister role to us all and was largely responsible for creating among us a family spirit in the best sense."

"Peg," Simpson asked, turning his back on the Cambodian display, "is it all going to be like this?"

A Pentagon public relations officer in civilian clothes approached before Peg could answer. "Will you come with me, please?" he said. He led the group down one corridor after another, deeper and deeper into the Pentagon where their briefing was to be held. Peg, oppressed and alienated by the vastness of the building, lagged behind and finally slumped onto a bench along the wall. She did not want to follow the group anymore. All during the march down the corridor she had felt the animosity of the Defense Department guards and the military personnel. She had not missed the anger in their eyes when their glances flashed upon the peace buttons the Iowans wore. The antagonism depressed Peg even more. She did not want to be there. She did not want to have to listen to the Pentagon spokesmen's words. She knew how futile the briefing would be. They would not be told anything because addressing them would be considered "aiding and abetting the enemy." Peg, seeing that she had fallen far behind, forced herself to her feet. She reminded herself that she had come to Washington after all to find out about the casualty lists, and as she trudged along after the group, she was determined not to relax until after she had done that.

As she rounded a corner, she saw that a young curly-headed boy she had nicknamed Harpo was waiting for her to catch up. Peg hurried toward the boy, and while they walked on together, she had the eerie sensation that she was being "shadowed." A tall man in black trousers and a white shirt was walking behind her. Whenever Peg and Harpo walked a little faster, the man would speed up. When Peg dropped back, the man dropped back. An Army major came out of an office, grimaced at Peg's peace button, and hurried past. "Harpo," Peg said, "I'm getting ill."

"What's the matter?" the boy asked warily.

"Well, if I had thought that just the sight of an American military uniform would make me sick, I wouldn't have come here."

The man in the black trousers suddenly came abreast of Peg and cut her off, preventing her from continuing up the corridor toward the CALCAV group. "Did you say something back there?" he asked.

"What?" Peg tried to step around him.

"I repeat," the man said, "did you say something back there?"

Peg attempted to push past him. "Will you get out of my way?" she asked impatiently. "I've got nothing to say to you."

The man refused to let her by. "Did you say that the sight of an American uniform makes you ill?"

Peg glared at the man. "I'm afraid it does. Now will you—"

"Oh, it does, does it?" he asked. "Well, just what is your bitch?"

"Mister," Peg said coldly, "some man in one of those American uniforms killed my son! I'm afraid the sight of an Army uniform is going to make me sick forever."

"Come off it, my son was all shot up in Vietnam, and you don't see me acting the way you do."

"Your son was all shot up?" Peg asked. "Then what are you doing here? You sound almost glad of it, as though you were bragging! What kind of man are you to brag about your son's wounds?" Harpo began nervously tugging Peg's sleeve, but Peg was furious. She told the man exactly what she thought of him, the Pentagon and the war.

Finally the guard said, "All right, lady, that's enough! I'm afraid I'm going to have to ask you to leave."

"You can ask all you want," Peg told him. "I don't even know or care who you are—"

"I'm a guard," the man said. "Now will you leave the Pentagon right now? Or am I going to have to escort you out?" He reached for Peg's arm, and she slapped his hand away.

"Mister, I'll leave the Pentagon when I'm goddamn good and ready, escorted or not. Now get the hell out of my way because I'm with a group." She simply bullied past the guard, dragging Harpo with her, and hurried down the corridor. At the briefing room door she looked back, but the guard was nowhere in sight.

The briefing room appeared familiar. It was the same one, she thought, they used for their briefings on TV. Since the seats were nearly filled, Peg perched on an oak table near the back. A man asked Peg if she wouldn't like them to bring her a chair, but she declined. Then she leaned toward a colonel standing next to her and asked whether the three men on the podium would be delivering the briefing. The colonel said they would and identified them as Daniel Z. Henkin, an Assistant Secretary of Defense for Public Affairs; Jerry W. Friedheim, Henkin's deputy assistant; and then

Brigadier General Daniel "Chappie" James, Jr., USAF, the senior military officer in Henkin's office and chief of information at the Pentagon.

"And what is your name, sir?" Peg asked.

"I'm Lieutenant Colonel Giorgi, Air Force."

" 'Georgey?' " Peg asked.

"G-I-O-R-G-I," the colonel spelled out.

Assistant Secretary Henkin commenced with a discussion of the Cambodian operation. Peg had the feeling she had heard it all before, that it was, in effect, the same justification delivered by the President on TV. Henkin showed the same maps, the same photographs, the same rationale. Peg listened wearily to the same promises of success. Throughout Henkin's talk Peg had the sensation that the CALCAV group was being photographed, that the briefing was being taped. Although no evidence was in sight, she learned that others in her group had had the same reaction. At Henkin's conclusion he asked if there were any questions. Peg's hand shot into the air. "Why didn't you tell us we've been in Cambodia for weeks, for months before Nixon went on television and said we were?"

"How do you know we were?" Henkin asked.

"Because every mother who had a son there was written by her boy that he was in Cambodia. I found out because when something like this happens, these people will write or call me. It seems to be a way of life now. I heard from mothers whose sons"—Peg shuffled through some papers in her lap—"whose sons were with the 198th Brigade of the Americal, the 25th Infantry, the Marines—"

"Ma'am?" Henkin interrupted.

"The 5th Infantry, the 47th, the 1st Air Cav, the 11th Armored—"

"Yes, ma'am," Henkin said, "and what is your question?"

"My question, Mr. Henkin, is do you *deny* that American boys were in Cambodia for weeks or months before the President said they were?"

"No, you're right," Henkin said. "American troops were there."

"I don't know why we're even talking about Cam-

180

bodia at all," Peg continued. "My son lived and died in 'Eye' Corps, First Corps. You people have been fighting a war there for almost ten years now and you haven't accomplished a thing! You still can't go a mile from the beach without getting your head blown off! So what are you worrying about Cambodia for? Why don't you clean up 'Eye' Corps first?"

"You seem to be quite well informed about the war," Henkin said. "Next question, please."

The CALCAV group began asking about secret operations in neighboring countries. All secret operations were categorically denied. Persistent questioning led to the questioner being cut off. One young man had photographs of unmarked American aircraft bombing Laos during 1969 and asked General James about it.

"Never happened," James said. "I was there, and it never happened."

"Of course it didn't happen to you, General," the young man said. "You're a general. You wouldn't have gone."

"Well, I can tell you this," James said angrily, "any reports of our bombing Laos are a lie!"

American bombing of the Laotian countryside had, in fact, begun in 1964. This bombing was confined at first to that part of Laos sharing a border with North Vietnam and later expanded so that by 1969, the time the young man's photographs were taken, Laos had become the most heavily bombed country in the world— ever.

For about two hours the Iowans questioned the Pentagon briefers. Each member of the group had some special area of interest, some aspect of the Southeast Asian war which he had studied. Peg leaned over to the Air Force lieutenant colonel by her side and asked him to supply her with that week's casualty list in Vietnam. "I haven't had a chance to read this morning's paper," Peg said, "but I know the figures are released today."

Lieutenant Colonel Giorgi leaned back and asked a man in civilian clothes sitting behind Peg if releasing that information would be all right. Peg was already suspicious of the civilian's function. Throughout the briefing he had been taking notes, and several times Peg had caught him pointing to one member of the CALCAV group or another so that Henkin would know who to let talk. When one of the Iowans would get out of hand, it had been the civilian who would signal Henkin to cut the questioner off. Peg turned to look at the man and their eyes met. He appraised Peg coolly, then nodded. Lieutenant Colonel Giorgi excused himself and left the room.

Several minutes later Giorgi returned and told Peg that the number of men killed that week in Vietnam was 125.

"Is that *all* who died, Colonel?" Peg asked.

"What do you mean?"

"I want the *total* casualty list of those who died this past week."

"I still don't understand," Giorgi said.

"All right," Peg said impatiently, "this is what I mean: I want the total number of people who died there, *not* just the number that you publish."

Lieutenant Colonel Giorgi again leaned back to the man in civilian clothes and a moment later left the room a second time. When he returned, he whispered to Peg that the figure would be twenty-five more. Peg's hand shot back up. "I have a question," she said.

Henkin recognized her, saying, "May I ask *you* something first?"

"Sure," Peg said. "What?"

"Are you a newspaperwoman?"

"A what?" Peg asked, surprised.

"Are you a newspaperwoman?"

"No, sir." Peg laughed. "I'm only a simple farmer's wife. As a matter of fact, we finished planting the corn just before I came down here."

Henkin looked embarrassed and asked what her question had been.

"There's something I want to know about these casualty lists," Peg said. "Who isn't telling us the truth? Is it your office? Or is it the press who isn't telling us each week how many died in Vietnam?"

"I'm not sure I understand what you mean," Henkin said.

"Here's what I mean," Peg said coldly, "I just asked this gentleman sitting next to me, Colonel Giorgi, how many died this week and he gave me two different figures. First he said one hundred and twenty-five died. A few minutes later he came back and added twenty-five more. This is what I mean. As far as the public is concerned, one hundred twenty-five died, but," Peg said, "one hundred and fifty mothers and fathers know their sons died! This is what I just . . . can't . . . stand! I happen to be the mother of one of those boys you didn't count!"

"I still don't think I understand," Henkin said, but Lieutenant Colonel Giorgi did. He suggested Peg accompany him to his office and he would try to straighten her out.

"No," Peg said. "I don't want to go to anybody's office. I want to know who's telling us these lies?"

"Won't you please come, Mrs. Mullen?" Giorgi asked. He was joined by another younger man in civilian clothes. "We can take you directly to the office where these casualty lists are compiled. Any question you might have, all the information will be right there on hand."

Peg relented and was led down more Pentagon corridors until she was halted before a door which opened into a huge tan room, a room so large Peg believed her entire La Porte City farmhouse might have fitted inside.

Five silent secretaries worked at desks set against the windowed far side of the room, the steady *plick-plick-plick* of their electric typewriters interrupted only by the faint wind-chime *ting!* of their typewriter carriage return bells. The only other noise was the droning buzz of the fluorescent ceiling lights. Packed against each other along the other walls and pressed into any available space between the secretaries' desks were the filing cabinets—row upon row of identical slate-gray government-issue four-drawer filing cabinets. The open space in the middle of the room was filled by long oak tables, plain, sturdy office tables lined up end to end like flatcars spanning the entire length of the room. On the tops of these tables papers had been stacked so tightly that practically no wood showed. When Peg stepped closer to see what these papers might be, she suddenly realized to her horror that each paper was a casualty list, and she sagged back against the door-frame for support. She could not even count how many tables there were. She saw only that the room was filled with tables, the tables filled with casualty lists, the single-spaced casualty lists filled with dead boys' names. And still, on the far side of the room, the secretaries' typewriters were clacking away, each delicate *ting!* sounding the death knell, a new line, another dead boy's name.

Peg wished to God she had never let them bring her to this room. It was more terrible than she had believed it could be, more inhumane than anything her imagination thought existed. She turned in agony to Lieutenant Colonel Giorgi and cried, "What kind of man are you that this is your life? How can you work on these lists day after day after day?"

"Mrs. Mullen, I——"

"And you?" Peg said, turning to the secretaries, who, sensing a scene, had stopped their work to look. "What kind of women are you? Don't any of you have sons of your own?"

"Mrs. Mullen," Lieutenant Colonel Giorgi said, "you can't believe we enjoy——"

"Colonel, please," Peg said, holding up her hand to stop him. "Please, I don't want to hear or see any more." She hurried past him out the door.

"Mrs. Mullen," he called after her, and caught up with Peg in the corridor, "Mrs. Mullen? What did you really want to know?"

Peg leaned back against the corridor wall. She could hear the secretaries typing again. "I wanted to know. . . ." She paused, dreading that she would hear a faint *ting!* "I wanted to know why you lied to Senator Fulbright. Why you sent him half a list instead of a whole one?"

"Mrs. Mullen," Giorgi said unhappily, "I still don't understand. I don't know what you want. What you mean."

"All right, Colonel," Peg said wearily, "I want you
184

to send me the names of all the boys who died the week of February 15, 1970, in Vietnam. I want the names of both the battle and nonbattle casualties. I want all the names and that's all I want—except to get out of here."

Later that night Peg Mullen, her children and Patricia's fiancé boarded their bus outside the Church of St. Stephen and the Incarnation for the twenty-two-hour drive to Iowa. She arrived back at her farm late Friday night.

Waiting for her on the kitchen table was the mail in response to the 100 registered letters she had sent each United States Senator. Two Senators, Birch Bayh of Indiana and Ralph T. Smith of Illnois, had telephoned. Sixteen others had written. They were:

Senator Thomas J. Dodd of Connecticut
Senator Edward J. Gurney of Florida
Senator Frank Church of Idaho
Senator Vance Hartke of Indiana
Senator Harold E. Hughes of Iowa
Senator Charles McC. Mathias, Jr., of Maryland
Senator Edward M. Kennedy of Massachusetts
Senator Walter F. Mondale of Minnesota
Senator Thomas F. Eagleton of Missouri
Senator Carl T. Curtis of Nebraska
Senator Stephen M. Young of Ohio
Senator Fred R. Harris of Oklahoma
Senator Mark O. Hatfield of Oregon
Senators George McGovern and Karl E. Mundt of South
    Dakota
Senator William B. Spong, Jr., of Virginia

Each Senator agreed that the deduction of unearned leave from a dead soldier's pay was a grievous wrong; not one of them, however, proposed legislation to change it.

Senator Hughes later told Peg his office telephone had rung continually with calls from other Senators who pointed out Peg was his constituent and they expected him to handle it.

When Gene returned that night from John Deere, Peg told him about her trip to Washington and Gene told her that Larry Phelps, his cousin's son-in-law, was home on leave. Gene had watched Larry's wife, Kathy, grow up with a mixture of sorrow and pride—sorrow because Kathy, at two, was severely crippled by polio and had had to suffer through countless agonizing and immobilizing operations, pride because of Kathy's determination to lead a normal life. Kathy and Larry Phelps now had an infant son, and Larry had just received his orders for Vietnam.

"If he goes, Peg," Gene was saying, "you know he'll meet with Michael's end."

"Then we'll simply have to prevent them from making Larry go," she said.

"How? What can we do?"

"I don't know yet," Peg said. "Kathy shouldn't have to live alone and take care of that baby all by herself. . . . Maybe he could qualify as a hardship case."

There was a racket outside, and Gene sprang out of his chair. "Goddamn it!"

The hogs had broken through the wire-fence pigpen by the barn and were rooting about the lawn.

"John?" Gene called. "You awake?"

"Yeah, Dad," John answered. "I'm getting up now."

John and his father spent forty-five minutes rounding up the hogs and repairing the fence. John went back to bed, and Gene rejoined Peg at the kitchen table. She was still too tense from the bus trip to sleep. She was telling Gene about the casualty room in the Pentagon when Gene sprang to his feet again and began massaging his calf muscle.

"What's the matter?" Peg asked. "What've you got? A cramp?"

"Oh, yeah!" Gene winced. "Oh, Mary!"

"What can you do about it?"

"Nothing," Gene said, shaking his head. He continued to massage his calf. "Just live with it, I guess."

Peg smiled. "That's what you get for chasing after those hogs. You're just getting old."

For the next week Peg worried over how she might best help Larry Phelps. Although she would never forgive herself for letting Michael go, Peg hoped she might alleviate, at least to some degree, the guilt she felt by preventing the loss of another young man's life in Vietnam. By helping Phelps, Peg was helping herself. Finally, on June 11, she wrote Assistant Secretary of Defense for Public Affairs Daniel Z. Henkin himself. Before leaving Washington, Peg had looked up Henkin's home address in a telephone directory. Peg mailed her letter to his house, not the Pentagon.

She wrote she had come home "weary and very much concerned with the futility of mothers, like myself, thinking they can say or do anything to change the militaristic attitude of the administrative branch of the government today." Peg explained that both she and Patricia had come away from the briefing "with the thought that we both liked you. We have been asking ourselves why you are in that position, and why did you stay on in the change of administration. You can't believe what you say." She speculated that perhaps Henkin believed he might have "a leveling influence on the military monster which threatens to destroy this country" but added she had "no faith in Mr. Nixon at all. . . . It is his lack of intellect that really scares me.

"Because you were the only bright spot in the Pentagon," Peg's letter continued, "I am going to ask you to do something." She related Kathy's battle with polio, the birth six months ago of their "beautiful baby" and Larry's orders for Vietnam. "I'm sure he will walk the same path my son did, and you know the kill ratio among these young men. . . . How can a government close its eyes to a handicap such as this and send a young husband to Vietnam and possible death? Isn't there someone who can save this family from such a fate? You know the fighting is going to worsen there, and he'll have little chance of coming home."

Peg explained she had not mentioned to either Larry or Kathy that she was writing Henkin in an effort to help, "but I couldn't live with myself if I didn't." Phelps, she added, was due to leave for Vietnam in eighteen days.

187

"Today I sorted out two footlockers of my son's books," Peg's letter concluded. "Among them was his thesis to be finished this summer, the first leg of his doctorate in bio-chemistry. His plan was to save the world in his research for agriculture nutrition not to destroy it. I am sure there are very few minds in that edifice called the Pentagon that would be equal to his. . . ."

The letter was typical of Peg Mullen: touching, infuriating, melodramatic, but honest above all.

John Mullen's draft classification had arrived in that morning's mail. Peg knew his 1-A category, "Available for Military Service," was wrong, that he should have been given a 4-A classification: "Sole Surviving Son."

John argued with his mother. He did not want her to change the classification. He preferred the drama of confronting the draft board with their error when they attempted to induct him—although there were moments, too, when the idea of escaping to Canada appealed to him. "Mother," he said, "leave the draft board alone!"

Also in that morning's mail was a letter from Abe Aikins, the young black medic who had been with Michael on the hilltop that night in Vietnam:

Dear Mrs. Mullen:

   I guess you can say that it is ironic that I received your letter today, Memorial Day. Memories are difficult when one thinks of loved ones who have died in wars. It is even more difficult when one feels that a life was lost in vain. This is an unjust and inhuman war, for men to give their lives for a cause that is dubious, for ideals that are talked of but never sought, those lives were given in vain. . . .

Aikins explained that although he and Michael had not been very close, he had known Michael as well as anyone in the company and had had several discussions about the war. He then added a few details

188

about Michael's death. Aikins did not really tell the Mullens anything they did not already know. He did mention that "Mike never knew what hit him. The explosion was directly over his head. He died in his sleep." Peg was relieved to know that; she had continued to worry over how much Michael might have suffered. There was nothing very heartening, however, in Aikins' confirmation that Michael's "life was lost in vain." Aikins repeated that it had been a short round fired by U.S. forces. When Peg and Gene discussed Aikins' letter that night, they recalled that Schwarzkopf and Culpepper had each written that it was a "short round," too. So far, however, no one had explained why the round had fallen short.

Two days later, Saturday, June 13, Peg heard from the Air Force lieutenant colonel who had taken her to the Pentagon casualty room.

"I am sorry to say that nowhere is there a list of U.S. casualties which is kept by the date," Giorgi wrote. "Your request is the only one to develop such a listing for the week [your son died]."

Lieutenant Colonel Giorgi did, however, enclose a "List of Casualties Incurred by U.S. Military Personnel in connection with the Conflict in Vietnam by Home State of Record." The document listed those Iowans who had died in Vietnam between January 1 and April 30, 1970. Twenty-seven Army men, four Marines, and one sailor had been killed in action. Six soldiers and one sailor were nonbattle casualties. They were from Mississippi River cities like Davenport, Keokuk and Dubuque, from small farm towns like Victor, Letts, Dunlap and Coin. They came from Rockwell city, Newton, Knoxville, Clarion, Algona—Iowa county seats. They had grown up in Bonaparte, Eldorado and DeSoto in big cities like Des Moines and Sioux City and crossroad towns like Portsmouth and Dumont. The boys had come from towns all over central Iowa and Missouri River communities like Thurman and Mondamin. These young men had names of simple grace: Atkinson, Carson, Davis, Earlywine, Johnson . . . Marlin, Porter, Reilly, Rogers . . . Carter, Gardner, Wilson, Roth. They were boys with country names: Dean and Earl and Gary and LaRoy. And they were all dead. Gerald, Jeffrey, Jesse, Jimmy, John E., John M., John W. . . . There, too, was "Mullen, Michael Eugene . . . Sgt . . . 480628411 . . . Date of Birth: 11 Sep 44 . . . Date of Casualty: 18 Feb 70 . . . Home of Record: La Porte City." Not far from Michael's name was that of the Waverly mother's boy who had died in the burned-out tank.

The following week a letter arrived from Lieutenant Colonel H. Norman Schwarzkopf in Vietnam. The letter, written in response to Peg's angry blast of three weeks before, told the Mullens nothing at all. Its whole tone was strange, guarded, impersonal: "I sincerely hope that I can be of some assistance in answering your questions. . . ." That was the sort of line one expected from a salesclerk in response to some shopper's query. "Michael's platoon leader was in a defensive position approximately eight to ten feet away from him. . . . The Company Commander, the Company First Sergeant, and the Battalion Chaplain were also located within thirty feet of Michael's position. . . ." No names. Just their titles. Why weren't the Mullens told who those people were? To Peg the answer was obvious: if she knew their names, she could write them. "Unfortunately, United States Army, Vietnam policy," Schwarzkopf's letter continued, "does not allow me to release the names of its servicemen," a convenient policy, Peg felt, should the Army have something to hide. "I have learned that Michael's closest friend was killed in the same tragic accident. . . ." That, too, struck the Mullens as a bit too convenient. If Michael's closest friend—an obvious reference to Leroy Hamilton—was dead, the one young man most likely to tell the Mullens the truth was lost. And according to Culpepper's letter, those who had survived were threatened with punitive action should they attempt to write.

Schwarzkopf's response to Peg's outrage at Michael's harassment during his final stand-down read as if it had been copied from some training circular: "It is the policy of this command to utilize stand-downs for training and relaxation," to "maintain the health and welfare of our men," to "maintain the proficiency and skill of each soldier. . . ." What sort of man would write such an insensitive, detached letter to grieving parents? What sort of man would write a letter such as this at all unless he had something to hide? The Mullens were now convinced more than ever that Schwarzkopf had been instrumental in both the death of their son and the subsequent cover-up.

Imagine what the Mullens would have felt had they known that the two letters they had thus far received signed by H. Norman Schwarzkopf had not, in fact, been written by him at all.

Chapter Fifteen

On Wednesday, June 24, 1970, the United States Senate by a vote of 81 to 10 repealed the Gulf of Tonkin Resolution. The Senate's August 7, 1964, passage of the resolution—in clear defiance of the 1964 electoral mandate to seek no wider war—provided the sole legal basis for the Vietnam War's escalation and the inevitable acceptance by American forces of the major burden of the ground, sea and air war in Southeast Asia, which resulted in the deaths of Michael Mullen and Leroy Hamilton and, by the end of June, 1970, more than 50,000 other Americans as well. The repeal of the resolution was backed by the Nixon administration, which stated it did not need the Gulf of Tonkin Resolution to justify current U.S. involvement in Vietnam.

Earlier that same day Daniel Z. Henkin, the Assistant Secretary of Defense for Public Affairs, telephoned Peg. After graciously complimenting her letter (and expressing surprise she had sent it to his home), he reported having spoken to an Army general in personnel who agreed Larry Phelps should be send not to Vietnam but to some post in the United States. Henkin asked Peg to find out Phelps' service number, prior assignments, current orders and to forward as much information as she could to Henkin's Pentagon office as soon as possible.

Peg was ecstatic. She left for Kathy Phelps' home right away.

Larry had been spending his advance leave with his wife's family, the Rosauers. Kathy Phelps' mother, Nona Mullen Rosauer, was Skinny Mullen's sister and Gene's first cousin. And, like Gene and Skinny, had grown up visiting their grandfather, Patrick J. Mullen's house. Nona Mullen married Alfred Rosauer, who, like his father before him, worked the blacksmith shop at Eagle Center a mile west of the cemetery in which Michael Mullen now lay. Peg and Gene had always been friendly with the Rosauers, but lately, because of Michael's death, a strain existed. When Peg arrived at the Rosauers' she found Nona very upset and Kathy in tears. They explained they had just returned from Waterloo, where Larry had boarded an airplane for the first leg of his trip to Vietnam.

"Then we haven't got a moment to lose!" Peg said. "I need all the information on Larry I can get. I can keep him from being sent to Vietnam."

"Oh-h, Peg." Nona sighed. "Please don't start all that. Not now."

"What do you mean?" Peg asked. "I'm trying to tell you I've got the most wonderful news. I just finished speaking with a Mr. Daniel Henkin, an Assistant Secretary of Defense at the Pentagon—I met him in Washington, see?—and he called me this morning to say Larry wouldn't have to go."

Kathy looked at Peg apprehensively.

"What's the matter with you two?" Peg asked. "Don't you believe me?"

"Oh, sure, Peg," Nona said, unconvinced. "It's just that we're all pretty upset right now, and, well, we know how upset you've been and. . . ." Her voice trailed off.

"But I tell you I can help!" Peg insisted. "I can keep Larry out of Vietnam!"

"You can?" Kathy asked. "How?"

"What do you think *you* can do?" Nona asked.

"As soon as I heard Larry had been ordered to Vietnam, I wrote Henkin a letter and—"

"You wrote this man at the Pentagon about Larry?" Kathy interrupted.

"And he telephoned me not more than a half hour ago," Peg continued. "He told me he'd talked to some general in personnel who said Larry would not have to go to Vietnam, that he should be reassigned to

193

some place here in the United States. But they need more information so they can give him new orders. That's why—"

"Peg, please," Nona begged gently. "Larry's already gone. You can see how heartbroken Kathy is, how worried we all are. You're only making it worse."

"This man you wrote about Larry, he called you back?" Kathy asked. She looked over at her mother, not sure whether to believe Peg or not.

"I don't understand why he called you, Peg," Nona said. "Why didn't he call—"

"He telephoned me," Peg said a little impatiently, "because I was the one who wrote him about keeping Larry out of Vietnam. Look, I have a copy of the letter I sent him back at the farm."

"Why didn't you say anything to us about this before?" Nona asked. "Why did you wait until we'd put him on the plane?"

"I didn't know you were putting him on the plane!" Peg said. "I didn't want to say anything before because I didn't want to get your hopes up. I wasn't sure I could do anything to help. Besides, it doesn't matter that you put him on the plane. He still has to process through Oakland. That takes a couple of days. The only thing is that you've got to give me the information so I can call Henkin back at the Pentagon. I need Larry's rank, his serial number, orders, things like that."

Kathy leaned forward hopefully. "Do you really think you can keep them from sending Larry to Vietnam?"

"Of course I do," Peg said. "I wouldn't have come here if I didn't think so. Don't you believe me?"

"I want to," Kathy said. "It's just that, how can you be so sure?"

"I simply believe Michael will help."

"Michael who?" Nona asked uneasily.

"My Michael in heaven."

Nona Rosauer looked dismayed, but Kathy asked Peg again to tell her again what information was needed. Afterward Peg suggested Kathy come back to the farm so she could be there when Peg telephoned Henkin's office.

"Oh, yes, Mrs. Mullen," Henkin's secretary said, "we were expecting your call. Mr. Henkin asked me to take down the information, so go ahead."

Peg gave her what details she knew, and the secretary told Peg if Larry telephoned that evening, she was to ask if he had ever filed for compassionate reassignment, and, if so, how many times and where. Peg was also to tell Larry he would be met by a personnel officer at Oakland that the personnel officer would know Phelps had had a "hold" put on him by the Pentagon, and all Larry would need to do would be to file the necessary reassignment forms there. The papers would then be forwarded to the Pentagon for approval, and in about ten days his reassignment would come through.

"See?" Peg asked triumphantly.

Kathy smiled uncertainly. "I still don't know whether to believe it or not."

Peg returned that evening to the Rosauers and waited with them for Larry's call. Peg brought Nona the letter she had written Henkin, and Kathy confirmed that she herself had heard Henkin's secretary on the phone. When Larry finally did telephone, Kathy answered it saying, "Honey, I've got the most wonderful news!"

Larry had not known that Peg was trying to help either, so initially he, too, found the story difficult to believe. But when he spoke with Peg, he agreed to do whatever she said, adding he would try anything to keep out of Vietnam. Phelps said he had applied three times for compassionate reassignment, once each at Fort Polk, Fort Benning and Fort Ord. His requests, however, had never been forwarded beyond the desks of the lieutenants who had handled the forms. Peg told him not to worry; a personnel officer would meet him when he went through processing the next morning and that the Pentagon had put a hold on his orders for Vietnam.

"Well, I can't believe it, Mrs. Mullen," Larry said. "I don't know how to thank you."

"Call me collect if you run into any snags," she said and handed the phone back to Kathy, quietly gathered up her papers and left. She was asleep when Gene came home.

The next morning Peg received letters from Martin Culpepper and Abe Aikins in Vietnam. Peg had written them both after her trip to Washington. She opened Culpepper's first:

> It was very interesting to read about your trip to D.C. with some ralliers who think the same about the war here. The army couldn't answer your questions or all of them anyhow. For them to do so is to quote "break your back." The truth is they can only beat around the so long but I pray it's not too long or late for our sake.

Peg read the last sentence again: "The army couldn't answer your questions . . . for to do so is to 'break your back.' The truth is they can only beat around the so long," the *what* so long? Culpepper had omitted a word. "Beat around the *bush?*" "Around the *truth?*" Was he saying that if the Army told Peg the truth, it would break her back? Her spirit? Was Culpepper not telling Peg what had really happened? She wondered whether she was being overly suspicious, or had Culpepper been trying to hint at something? She recalled having told him some of the questions her CALCAV group had asked about the secret treaties, the border crossings, the secret operations and bombings. That line about the Army's being unable to answer her questions, was he referring to her questions about Michael or those asked at the Pentagon? It was infuriating not knowing what Culpepper really meant and frustrating, too, getting just one little nugget of information at a time. Culpepper's letter continued:

> I knew Doc Aikins personally, he was and still is a good friend of mine. It's true what he said about Michael. If he said it, you can believe it!

Peg had written Culpepper that according to Aikins, Michael had died in his sleep and had never
known what hit him. She had never ceased worrying
over whether or not Michael had suffered and Culpepper's confirmation gave her some relief.

Aikins' letter simply thanked Peg for her offer to
help by sending him the procedure for enlisting out of
combat, and he wrote her of his plans for going to
school. He was just twenty-one credits short of his BA
degree. "I will complete my education after I leave the
Army," Aikins said. His letter reminded Peg that Michael, too, had planned to return to school, that Michael had anticipated being home in June and, if
everything had gone the way they had all expected, he
would have been sitting across from her at the kitchen
table right now. Peg got up and walked outside.

The lawn still showed the ravages of the hogs'
escape nearly three weeks before. Great chunks of
turf had been rooted up, rolled back like sod strips. In
other places the lawn had been humped as if moles had
broken through to the surface, then kept on going. Peg
could not prevent herself from thinking how Michael
would have been upset had he seen the lawn. She
heard the well pump start. Gene was awake and running water. She took one last look around the lawn and
barn. The farm was beginning to show Michael's absence. She went back inside the house.

"Hello, Mother," Gene said cheerfully. "Been taking a morning constitutional?"

"What are you so happy about?"

"Why, it's a beautiful day!"

"You wouldn't think so if you saw the lawn,"
Peg said sourly.

"Now, Mother," Gene chided her, "let me have
my coffee first."

That evening when Larry Phelps telephoned from
Oakland, he told Peg *no* personnel officer had met him,
no hold had been put on him, and he had been processed for Vietnam. "It was a nice try, Mrs. Mullen,"
he said. "You've opened my eyes to what goes on."

"Don't give up, Larry. There are still things we
can do."

Peg immediately called Daniel Henkin at his home. It was about ten o'clock Washington time. Henkin assured Peg that everything would work out, that no one could ship Phelps to Vietnam without first contacting the Pentagon. A "hold" had been put on him. But Henkins then said, "Still, Mrs. Mullen, you must remember it is in the hands of the military."

Peg's heart sank. She hung up convinced she'd been duped, that Henkin had no actual authority at all. She pictured that general from personnel blithely nodding up and down, agreeing with everything Henkin said without the slightest intention of helping Phelps at all. She was so discouraged she called one of Senator Hughes' aides. The aide explained there was nothing he or the Senator could do for Phelps unless Phelps himself asked for assistance.

"How can he do that?" Peg asked impatiently. "He's in the Army! He's all the way across the country in California. They're getting ready to ship him to Vietnam! You know he's going to get killed!"

"Peg, I'm sorry. Unless Phelps gets in touch with the Senator personally, there's nothing we can do."

"You're no different from the goddamn Army!" Peg swore. "None of you care one bit what happens to your people. The only thing you care about are yourselves!" She hung up on him.

The following morning, Friday, June 26, Phelps called with good news. A hold had been put on him, and he had been assigned a job. Best of all, he had an appointment Monday morning with the personnel officer to file his reassignment papers. "A Lieutenant Steven Davies interviewed me," Phelps told Peg, "and he said my chances for a reassignment were about ninety-nine percent!"

"Is he the officer who was supposed to meet you yesterday?"

"He was supposed to, but yesterday was his day off."

"So in the meantime you were processed for Vietnam?"

"Yeah," Phelps said, "but he had about three pages of papers from the Pentagon on me stuck away in his desk."

"A lot of good they would have done you there," Peg said bitterly.

"Well, they're doing me good now." Phelps paused for a moment, and then he added, "You know? I'm beginning to think for the first time you may really be able to keep me from going to Vietnam."

Monday morning, when Larry Phelps was interviewed by the personnel officer, he filed his compassionate reassignment papers and was turned down cold. He telephoned Peg. "They said it's not an emergency case. I'm scheduled to leave for Vietnam either tomorrow or the day after."

"We'll see about that," Peg replied.

She immediately placed a person-to-person telephone call to Lieutenant Steven G. Davies, the personnel officer Phelps had dealt with at the Oakland Army Terminal. She asked him what he had done with the orders from Daniel Henkin's office and those from the Pentagon general with whom Henkin had spoken. Lieutenant Davies very courteously explained that their orders did not mean a thing to him; he had his own orders to follow. If the general wanted to rewrite them, he could. Until then, however, he had to follow "the book." And Larry Phelps' problem, as defined by "the book," was "not of an emergency nature" since it had existed for a long time in advance. Nor did Phelps' problem "meet the minimum criteria established by the Department of the Army for a compassionate reassignment." Larry Phelps was therefore processed for Vietnam.

Peg then contacted Daniel Henkin's office at the Pentagon, and a Lieutenant Colonel William Taylor there insisted Phelps could not leave Oakland until his papers had reached Washington. Not satisfied, Peg alerted Senator Hughes' aide about what was going on. He again told Peg there was nothing the Senator could do unless Phelps contacted Hughes himself.

199

Later that afternoon in Oakland, Lieutenant Davies sent for Phelps. Davies, visibly disturbed, told Phelps that he had spoken with both 6th Army Headquarters and Peg, but nothing could be changed. Phelps felt Davies simply wanted to talk, to try to defend his position. When Phelps reported this conversation to Peg, she was so convinced she had lost her battle to save Phelps that she drove into Waterloo to see a lawyer there. She hoped he might know of an attorney in Oakland who could help. Peg's friend mentioned an attorney in San Francisco who, he had heard, for $1,000 might be able to get Phelps out of Oakland. She decided to borrow $1,000 and worry about paying it back later.

When by two o'clock that morning she had still been unable to reach the San Francisco attorney, Peg gave up and drove back to the farm. Her final act was to send a night letter to President Nixon, pleading with him to save Larry Phelps' life.

Tuesday morning Larry Phelps telephoned Peg to say good-bye. He said that he had been able to get through to Senator Hughes' office and that the Senator had promised to help. He also told Peg that Lieutenant Davies had given him a typed statement confirming that his request for compassionate reassignment did not qualify as an emergency situation since it was not, in fact, of an emergency nature. The statement, typed up in triplicate, was signed by Davies and Phelps.

"All right, Larry," Peg said, "send me a copy, and make sure you guard your own copies carefully."

"I will. And Mrs. Mullen? . . . Peg? Thanks for your help."

"I wasn't much help, I'm afraid."

"You did more than anyone else ever could."

"When do you leave?"

"This afternoon."

Peg closed her eyes. "I'll pray for you, Larry. Take care of yourself."

"You, too, Peg. And I mean it, thanks again for everything. Keep an eye on Kathy for me, will you? I worry about her at times."

"Don't, Larry. She'll be fine. The baby, too."

"I sure hope so. . . . Well, I guess this is good-bye."

"We'll get you home before long," Peg said firmly.

Peg was in such despair that she didn't even bother to listen to the evening news on television. She didn't find out until the next day that the Cooper-Church amendment had passed the Senate after thirty-four days of debate. Nor did she listen to President Nixon's speech on how the Cambodian operation had been a success. She simply drove into Waterloo to "get lost." Peg did not return to the farm until after 10 P.M. On the kitchen table was a note left by Gene saying there had been "an urgent call from the Pentagon," which she was to return "no later than nine." She was too late.

Peg did not sleep that night. Instead, she waited up until the Pentagon was open. At 7 A.M. Iowa time, she placed a call to the Pentagon number given her and discovered it belonged to Lieutenant Colonel William Taylor of Henkin's office. Taylor said the reason he had called was to explain why the Pentagon had been unable to help Larry Phelps.

"It's very simple," he told Peg. "Phelps neither requested nor applied for reassignment."

She rested her brow against a kitchen cabinet and squeezed the telephone receiver to her ear. "Would you say that again?" She could not believe what the Pentagon colonel had told her.

Taylor again said that Phelps had not requested or applied for reassignment, and Peg said, "I don't believe you."

"Mrs. Mullen, I contacted Sixth Army Headquarters myself. They are forwarding me a statement signed by Larry Phelps indicating he did not want a reassignment."

"You're now telling me Phelps did not want a reassignment?" Peg asked incredulously.

"That is correct."

"Well, Colonel, I simply do not believe such a statement exists. I think this whole business I've had with you people in the Pentagon is a farce. You never did intend to reassign that boy! And I'll tell you something else: Larry Phelps is sending me a statement typed up and signed by Lieutenant Steven Davies, the Personnel Officer at Oakland, which will prove that Phelps did apply for compassionate reassignment and that Davies turned him down because his circumstances were 'not of an emergency nature.' "

Lieutenant Colonel Taylor hesitated for a moment, then said, "Well, Mrs. Mullen, I'd be very interested in seeing a copy of that statement if, in fact, such a statement does exist."

"Oh, it exists all right!"

"Then will you send me a copy?"

"I sure will!"

The statement signed by Lieutenant Davies and Larry Phelps arrived two days later, on July 3, 1970:

AMPCO-ORP   Compassionate
              Reassignment

Larry G. Phelps   Personnel Officer   29 Jun 70
470–60–0059   ORS, USAPERSCEN

1. AR 612–2, Para 4–8a, states that action will be taken to resolve emergency personnel problems of overseas replacements at the overseas replacement station.

2. After a thorough review of your case and a personal interview with Lt. Davies this station, it was found that your problem is not of an emergency nature, and has existed well over five months.

3. Should the situation become aggravated or should you accumulate any additional information you may submit your request for compassionate reassignment to your personnel officer at your permanent unit of assignment.

                    s/STEVEN G. DAVIES
                    1/Lt, AGC
                    Personnel Officer

I have read and I acknowledge receipt of a copy of this DF

                    s/Larry G. Phelps

The first thing Peg did was call Lieutenant Colonel Taylor at the Pentagon to tell him that the statement was in her hands. She then told him that in her opinion Lieutenant Davies "had simply cut off the top half of the sheet of paper and typed in a new statement from the Pentagon above Phelps' signature." Her reaction is difficult to understand. Davies' statement clearly indicated the young lieutenant was covering himself because, according to "the book," Phelps did not have grounds for a compassionate reassignment *at this time*. It is not clear what sort of "new" statement Peg believed the lieutenant might have typed over Phelps' signature, especially since it was Phelps himself and not Lieutenant Davies who forwarded her the statement.

Perhaps Peg's confusion might be partially explained by the communication she had received from Lieutenant Colonel Dominic Giorgi in that same day's mail. His letter, in response to Peg's request for more information on how the casualty reporting system functioned, reads like a celebration of Pentagonese:

> As I have mentioned to you in my previous letter to you the casualty lists are available in alphabetical order and alphabetically by state. We do not maintain lists by those who were casualties on a specific date. To get such a list would require an extraordinary amount of time and personnel resources which are not available.
>
> However, I am sending you the official casualty releases of February 25, 26, and 27, as you requested. As I discussed with you these lists do not necessarily indicate that those are names of U.S. servicemen who died the previous week or on a specific date. Quite possibly some died the previous week but you cannot determine if this is the case by reading the release. The attached explanation will clarify this point.

There followed a typed single-spaced "Procedure for Reporting U.S. Casualties in Southeast Asia," which filled one-half of a sheet of regular office typewriter paper:

> The number of casualties as they are reported, is expressed as a cumulative number beginning in

January, 1961. At the end of each week the previous cumulative number is subtracted from the new cumulative number and the difference is referred to as the number reported for the week. This statistical process permits us to make necessary changes; such as, from non-hostile to hostile, missing to died-while-missing, etc., and still preserve the accuracy of the published totals. Everyone of the dead, missing, and captured are on our lists, with date of casualty. Note that the weekly number represents the number reported during that week and will almost always contain reports of a few whose date of casualty was earlier.

There are two principal reasons for this: One, some men are initially reported as missing and as evidence is later received are changed to dead although the date of death is established as the date they were reported as missing. Secondly, in some instances the circumstances are such that a determination as to cause of casualty cannot immediately be made and the report would then usually be classified as non-hostile and later changed, if necessary, according to information in the final report. Some of these cases take quite a while.

The foregoing is to explain why we would find in the list of names of those reported as having died during any week some who would have an official date of death which was earlier. Conversely, some who actually died during the week in question could not be reported until later.

Over and over again, while reading the procedure, Peg had had to remind herself that the "casualties" and "cumulative numbers" and "statistical processes" referred to dealt with human beings, young men once as alive and as vital as her son. The vocabularly, with its businesslike detachment, offended her as much as the message itself.

Several points should be made about Giorgi's letter and the enclosed casualty reporting procedure. His assertion that "to get such a list [of casualties on a specific date] would require an extraordinary amount of time and personnel resources" was probably correct. Since, however, lists were available by alphabetical order and alphabetically by state, and since "every one of the dead, missing, and captured are on our lists, with date of casualty," there is a means by which a computer search by date could have been made—were the military to have wanted such a thing done. The computer might not have been programmed to provide such information, and the creation of a new program is what might have taken the time and personnel resources.

Secondly, the procedures Giorgi outlined permit considerable flexibility in reporting the actual number of casualties. Heavy losses on any given week could be delayed in filing and thereby spread out over a series of weeks, hidden away, or at least dispersed so that no one state adjutant need become overly alarmed by having to report a large number of area casualties at one time.

Thirdly, as the procedure document points out, in those instances where "the cause of casualty cannot immediately be made," that casualty would "usually be classified as non-hostile." Why? Nonbattle casualties were not included in the casualty count given on the evening news. This policy, therefore, facilitated keeping the "reported" casualties as low as possible. By the end of June, 1970, the actual casualty figure for the Vietnam War was 42,754 deaths as a result of hostile action, 8,122 deaths from "non-hostile" causes.

On July 7 Lieutenant Colonel Taylor acknowledged having received Lieutenant Davies' and Larry Phelps' signed application for compassionate reassignment papers and wrote Peg, "We hope that the case will be resolved favorably and without delay."

On July 10 Major General F. W. Boye, responding to Peg's night letter to President Nixon pleading for Phelps' life, explained that Phelps' request could not be honored because the problem was long-term and could not be resolved in the one-year period authorized. "Physical conditions which are of a long term duration," the general explained, "do not satisfy the criteria for compassionate reassignment." In other words, if young Kathy Phelps had been stricken with polio recently rather than when she was two years old, her husband could have been reassigned.

On July 17, six weeks after Peg had mailed her angry registered letter to each United States Senator denouncing the deductions taken from her son's final paycheck, Senator Jack Miller introduced the following bill, S.4099, before Congress:

A BILL

To amend section 2771 of title 10, United States Code, relating to final settlement of accounts of deceased members of the armed forces.
1. *Be it enacted by the Senate and House*
2. *of Representatives of the United States of*
3. *America in Congress assembled.*
4. That section 2771 of title 10, United
5. States Code, is amended by adding the
6. following new subsection:
7. "(e) A setoff may not be made
8. against an amount otherwise due under
9. this section to recover pay and allowances
10. for any period the deceased was on excess
11. leave if the member was killed by hostile
12. fire, explosion of a hostile mine, or any
13. other hostile action."
14. Sec. 2. This act is effective as of January 1,
15. 1964. A

(page 2)

1. person who is entitled to payment of an
2. amount by virtue of the enactment of this
3. act based upon a final settlement made under
4. section 2771 of title 10, United States Code,
5. before the date of enactment of this Act
6. shall be paid that amount if application is
7. made therefore to the Secretary concerned
8. before the first anniversary of that date.

Jack Miller's bill was read twice to the Senate and referred to the Armed Services Committee. From the Armed Services Committee the bill was forwarded to

206

the Pentagon for further study. The bill never re-emerged, nor has it been passed.

Even if it had passed, Michael Mullen would not have been covered, nor would any other "nonbattle" casualty.

Chapter Sixteen

++++++++++++++++++

Five months had now gone by since Michael's death. A Midwestern father whose son had been killed in Vietnam the same day as Michael wrote Peg:

> I know how you feel and especially the sense of total frustration in dealing with the Pentagon. We have a huge military-industrial complex now who couldn't care less.
>
> You are familiar with the form letter sent out: "The President deeply regrets—" blah, blah. The President couldn't care less; nor the Pentagon. Your son and my son are just ciphers, just a number who unfortunately stopped an enemy bullet and now are gone forever out of our lives.
>
> Harry went into combat two days after arriving in Vietnam. He was on combat duty six months when wounded by shrapnel—some of it so deep they were unable to dig it out. However the medics sewed him up, and away he went right back into combat, shrapnel and all. I wrote to Nixon and received a reply from some general who said that the Army medics are the people who make these decisions, and like all doctors in America, *never* make a mistake. That letter, of course, was tantamount to a death sentence.
>
> Harry was riding in a helicopter on a reinforcement mission around the Song Bhe area. They were shot down and all were killed immediately. After Harry was killed we received long distance calls from different parts of the country inquiring about Harry. All were from people who had sons who were killed on that day. All had phoned the Pentagon and, for some reason, all had been given our phone number. Anyway, if the Pentagon had been correct, Harry

would have been killed in three different helicopter crashes on that day.

Pardon this scrawl, but I have been under medication four years after two major operations. So we still have five in our family with two boys coming up—one almost sixteen. Another couple of years it will be time to flee the country. I am sure my wife and I would never survive another military funeral in the family.

We can only say God helps us all in our sorrow and anguish. We must accept the cross. God bless you and comfort you.

For more than nine years the war in Vietnam had been on the front pages of every metropolitan newspaper, inside every newsmagazine, brought nightly into American living rooms on the television news. By now the casualty figures slipped through the nation's consciousness with no more significance than those windstrewn calendar pages used by early cinematic directors as a device to indicate the passage of time. The casualties weren't human beings; they weren't even *grunts* or *dinks* or *slopes* or *gooks*. They were, as the Midwestern father had written Peg, "just ciphers, just a number." And America had reached a surfeit of numbers.

Even though concerned citizens continued to read their newspapers and tried to keep informed, it became increasingly apparent that their government did not want them to know the truth and that the executive branch in particular was willing to go to extraordinary lengths to prevent the American people from learning the full extent of United States involvement in the Southeast Asian war. Instead of honesty, Americans were given numbers: body counts, tonnage counts, mission counts, truck counts, troop counts, weapons counts . . . counts? *Kownts?* The word had become alien and meaningless in its repetitions. It was as if the government believed numbers, through their inviolability, could sanctify and shore up a policy which large numbers of Americans had already come to question and protest.

In mid-July, 1970, in response to the growing an-

209

tiwar movement President Nixon approved the Huston Plan for expanded domestic intelligence operations, even after being warned that parts of the plan were "clearly illegal" and involved "serious risks" to his administration. The plan, developed by a thin, balding twenty-nine-year-old aide to the President, Tom Charles Huston, called for the stepped-up spying upon of private American citizens by electronic means, the opening and resealing of citizens' mail, surreptitious entry into and burglary of citizens' homes and offices and the continued and increased surveillance of American student groups at home and abroad. Authorization for the Huston Plan was rescinded five days after Nixon initated it only because of objections raised by the director of the Federal Bureau of Investigation, J. Edgar Hoover, whose opposition seemed based less on the infringement on citizens' constitutional rights than on the threat such an expanded domestic intelligence operations might have had upon the autonomy of the FBI and his role as chief. Nixon's approval of the plan came just two weeks after disclosures that the names of thousands of law-abiding American citizens—termed "persons of interest"—were being fed into large government computers for use by law enforcement agencies. These "persons of interest" were Americans who had made their anguish over government policy known. They were Americans who despaired of not only why we were in Vietnam, but how we were there as well. They were sickened by what the American government was doing to the Vietnamese and ourselves. They were not pro-North Vietnamese, pro-Communist, pro-anything except putting an end to the horrible slaughter of human beings of both sides in the Vietnam War.

The Vietnam War was not only making people like the Mullens believe that their sons had died in vain, but also making them ask if they themselves had lived in vain. What was the point of five generations of a family working the same land if they had become as enemies to that nation upon which their land rested? The Mullens did not believe that they were unpatriotic. The government was unpatriotic. And the only means

210

by which the Mullens could demonstrate their love for this country was by continuing to protest those policies which, they felt, were inhumane and un-American and by proceeding with their efforts to help those still in Vietnam. The more they protested, the lonelier they became. Few people visited the farm. If anyone did stop by, the conversation would always turn to the war. John stayed out in the fields for as long as he could, and when he came home, it would be to change.

"Are you going out tonight too, John?" his mother would ask.

And John would say, "Mom, I got to. You can get turned off by shouting too much. I got to get away."

Iowa was hot now, muggy. The cornstalks had burned a dark shade of green; lawns were browning out. Larry Phelps had been assigned to "C" Company, 2nd Battalion of the 7th Infantry, 1st Cavalry Division and had gone directly into combat with them. A month had passed, and still no action had been taken to get Phelps out. Peg asked Henkin if "the saga of Larry Phelps is now a closed book."

Brigadier General Bertram K. Corwitz responded that an investigation indicated "Sgt. Larry Phelps had not applied in writing for a compassionate discharge" and that when the Army had learned Phelps might have had "justification for such a discharge," he was interviewed at Oakland "and rejected." Corwitz's letter infuriated Peg. At no time had Phelps applied for a *discharge;* he had requested only a *reassignment*. She immediately telephoned General Corwitz at the Pentagon. The general was busy, and she was transferred to Colonel Alan Thompson, his aide.

Peg became progressively more angry as she related Phelps' story. She said she was "weary of lies" being told her by the Pentagon "every which way [she] turned." There was no pacifying her. The more furious she became, the more she cursed the Pentagon and the men who worked there until she finally called Colonel Thompson "a goddamn liar" himself.

211

"I've never told a lie in my life!" Colonel Thompson protested angrily.

"Well," Peg said, "then you're certainly in the wrong building and job if that's the case! You mean to tell me your office has been telling us the truth all this time about the war? Are you now saying that no American troops were in Cambodia before the President said they were? That we never sent a bomber over Laos? Colonel, we can read. We're not just stupid farmers out here!"

"Mrs. Mullen, I—"

"I have letters from boys in Vietnam," Peg continued, ignoring the colonel. "I know about Cambodia. I know, too, about the American and Laotian bombing missions being coordinated out of a joint center in Vietnam—"

"Vientiane," the colonel corrected gently.

"*Vientiane,* then," Peg said. "The point, Colonel, is that I know what's going on, and I know, too, enough not to believe all the stuff coming out of your office."

"All right, Mrs. Mullen," Colonel Thompson said patiently, "I don't think either of us will get anywhere if we argue the merits of the war. I agree with you that there are elements which are worse than the American people are being told about. But I do not feel that it is a question of the people in the Pentagon deliberately lying. There are elements of security involved. I know you understand that. . . ."

"I suppose so, yes," Peg said, unconvinced.

"But this is not why you called me, right?"

"Right," Peg said. "I called to find out what needs to be done to get Sergeant Larry Phelps home from Vietnam."

"Fine. This is an area in which we can work together. In the first place, I am very concerned that from what you've told me Phelps has not tried to file any reassignment papers since his arrival in Vietnam. Before we can do anyth—"

"Colonel," Peg interrupted, "two days after Larry arrived in Vietnam he was sent into combat. He was assigned to Charlie Company in the 1st Cav, the one

212

CBS-TV did the documentary on, the infantry company which refused to go out on patrol. I don't think you fully appreciate the position of a draftee in an outfit like that. You tell me how he's going to file any papers from there?"

Thompson explained there was no legal basis to deny Phelps the request and "if the boy does get an opportunity to file those papers," the colonel said, "I, personally, will expedite their progress through the Pentagon."

Peg was so disarmed by Colonel Thompson's willingness to cooperate that she apologized for having called him a liar.

"These are difficult times, Mrs. Mullen," Thompson said. "We are all under a strain."

"Well, I want to thank you," Peg said. "I appreciate your kindness, and I'll be back in touch with you again."

Peg composed a long letter to Larry Phelps. "No one cares whether you live or die except your family," she wrote. "If you lose your life you'll just be another statistic, so don't think you'll be giving your life for any great cause." She begged him to file his reassignment papers and promised to help all she could at her end.

Three months passed before Peg heard from or about Larry Phelps again. During that period Father Daniel Berrigan, the Jesuit priest, was captured by the FBI on Block Island. A violent explosion destroyed most of the U.S. Army Mathematics Research Center on the University of Wisconsin campus. The Hatfield-McGovern (609) "Amendment to end the war" was defeated in the Senate 55 to 39. Vice President Spiro Agnew described liberal Congressional Democrats as "Troglodytic leftists," coined "Radiclibs" for Radical Liberals, accused them of "whimpering isolationism" in foreign policy and "mulish obstructionism" in domestic policy, and "pusillanimous pussy-footing" on law and order. The Soviet Union, the United States and Communist China all exploded nuclear devices on the same day (October 14). The Atomic Energy Commission called it "pure coincidence." The Portage

County (Ohio) Grand Jury indicted twenty-five persons in connection with the Kent State disturbances, and not one of them was a member of the Ohio National Guard. Highly placed sources in Saigon reported that American Special Forces units had been leading secret operations inside Laos, and their casualties had not been made public.

By the time, in early November, Peg Mullen read in the local newspaper that Larry Phelps had received a routine decoration in Vietnam, the 43,962nd U.S. soldier had been killed in combat and the 291,118th had been wounded. When Peg brought the clipping to Kathy Phelps, Kathy said she didn't need to worry about Larry for a while. He was in the hospital with malaria.

The Iowa summer was over. Black funnel clouds had been sighted twice over Black Hawk County, but no tornado touched down. Gene Mullen received 20 cents more per 100 pounds for his hogs than he had the year before; the increase, however, did not cover his rising cost of feed, and he lost $1,000 on his hogs in all. The price for corn and soybeans had risen, too, however, and the yield had been good. His profits from his fields offset his losses with his hogs. But the Mullen farm was beginning to show further effects of Michael's absence.

There is an Iowa saying: "You can tell a farmer by his fences." Gene's fences were sagging, and those around the hogpen were patched with baling wire. Another Iowa saying is: "If you take care of the land, the land takes care of the barn. Take care of the barn, and the barn takes care of the house." Gene's barn and outbuildings lacked paint, although they were sound otherwise. He and John had plowed down the fields to aerate the soil. Some of the machinery was in need of repair. The lawn still showed scars from the hogs' rampage. The farm's slow deterioration reflected not only a lack of interest but a failure of the spirit. When Michael died, Gene's devotion to the land died with his son. He still went through the motions: he ordered seed, tended the chickens, patched up what needed work most, but Gene's heart wasn't in it. Michael was

214

to have inherited the farm; John didn't want it. Whom was Gene supposed to be preserving the farm for? Not Mary. She was off in Kansas City. And certainly not Patricia. Patricia, unwilling to wait any longer, had married Alan Hulting that summer.

Patricia and Alan had wanted to marry that previous spring before the school year was out. She was finishing her senior year at the University of Iowa, and Alan, who had dropped out for one semester, had found a temporary job as a guard at the Iowa Medical Security Facility, the maximum-security prison hospital for the violent, the hopelessly retarded and the criminally insane.

Patricia had written Michael in Vietnam over Christmas about her wedding plans and asked if he could serve as best man. With characteristic common sense, he had urged her to get her degree first without the disruptions and responsibilities of marriage. Besides, Michael had added, if she would wait until June, he would surely be home to attend. And so that winter Patricia and Alan agreed to delay their wedding until June. But as the June date approached, the Mullen family's emotions were still in such turmoil that the wedding was put off again.

Normally that summer, Patricia would have left Iowa City to spend weekends at her family's farm, but like John, she had come to dread being home. It wasn't that she didn't want to have to think about the war and Michael's death—besides her marriage, she had thought of little else. What hurt and confused her so deeply was the anguish her proposed marriage caused her father. Gene would simply refuse to discuss her wedding plans with Patricia.

Gene Mullen loved his daughter very much; Patricia had always been a unique child to him, in a sense his favorite of them all. A special bond existed between them, and now it was threatened. Gene felt betrayed by Patricia's marriage, perhaps even jealous of Alan Hulting. He utterly rejected any well-meaning suggestion that he wouldn't be "losing a daughter, but gaining a son." He had convinced himself that once

215

Patricia married, he would never see her again. His daughter's wedding promised only the same aching loss he had suffered with Michael's death. That is why up to the very day of their marriage Gene would call her fiancé Alan Hu*t*ling, as if to deny the seriousness of Patricia's intentions by deliberately mispronouncing Alan Hulting's name.

Alan appreciated the agony Gene Mullen was going through and was careful not to impose himself in any way upon his future father-in-law. But when, near the end of July, it became clear that Gene's attitude was not going to change and that Peg showed no signs whatsoever of moderating her battle against the war, Alan and Patricia decided to get married as quietly and quickly as possible just to get it over with. They also decided it would be easier if they were married in Iowa City instead of at Father Shimon's Sacred Heart Church in La Porte. Patricia shared her family's estrangement from their local priest. She was aware, too, of the feelings in their community of La Porte. Remarks passed by local people had worked their way back to the family, comments like: "Why does Peg Mullen think she's so different? Michael's not the only boy who died." And, "If Michael Mullen was so damned smart, what was he doing in the Army?" Patricia knew, also, that La Porte considered Peg's anti-war activities attempts for special recognition and treatment and her protests nothing more than "whining about the war." By holding the ceremony in Iowa City, Patricia and her mother would have a convenient excuse for limiting the guest list. The young couple chose August 28 as the date to be married. When Patricia attempted to telephone her mother of their decision, the line, of course, was busy. Peg was on the telephone with the local draft board director's secretary.

Peg had abided by John's request that she not interfere with his draft board for as long as she could. But she worried that John might be inducted before his 1-A draft classification could be proved an error. Peg's experiences with the Pentagon had convinced her that nothing could prevent the military from sending a young man to Vietnam if that was the Army's wish. And so when Patricia called, the draft board secretary was telling Peg, "Mullen, John, Rural Route Number Three, La Porte City, yes, we have your son registered. His classification is One-A. Now, what is your question?"

"My question," Peg said coldly, "is what does the Four-A draft category include?"

"Four-A? . . . That would be anybody who has had some service."

"Is that *all* it is? I'm certain it has more meaning than that."

"Oh, sure. It's also the category for sole surviving son, but," she quickly added, "we never have any of those in Black Hawk County."

"You happen to be talking to the mother of one," Peg said angrily. "My oldest son, Michael, was killed in Vietnam on February eighteenth of this year, and that same week, madam, you registered his younger brother, my son, John. If I had worked for the twenty years I understand you have in your position, and a young boy came in to register the same week his older brother died, I think I would have tied those two names together. But you later sent John a classification of One-A."

"Well," the secretary said crisply, "we're entitled to make one mistake in twenty-five thousand!"

"Lady, a draft board isn't entitled to make any mistakes!"

The secretary paused for a moment and then, in prissy, clerical tones, said, "If you want to certify that your son is a sole surviving son, we will have him listed in that category."

"I don't have to certify any such thing! All the 'certification' you need is lying right now in the Eagle Center cemetery," Peg said and hung up.

Moments later Patricia telephoned and had to hear all about the draft board, of course, but when her mother started in about the war, Patricia interrupted. "Mother! Alan and I have decided to get married August twenty-eighth in Iowa City."

"This August twenty-eighth?" Peg asked, startled. "That's not quite a month from now."

Patricia explained why they wanted to hold the wedding in Iowa City rather than La Porte, and to Patricia's relief, her mother was in complete agreement that it would be "easier all around." They talked about the wedding dress and bridesmaids' dresses, which Peg volunteered to help make. During their conversation Patricia suddenly realized that it was the first time in a long while she and her mother had laughed together. The only thing she was worried about, Patricia told her mother, was her father, and Peg said, "Don't worry. I'll talk to your father and everything will be all right." Afterward, when Patricia repeated the conversation to Alan, she was smiling.

For the next month, Peg lost herself in preparations for Patricia's wedding. She spent hours over her sewing machine making her daughter's wedding dress, three bridesmaids' dresses, new curtains for the living room. In addition, Peg wallpapered the kitchen, cleaned the house from top to bottom and, the night before the wedding, prepared a buffet supper for the anticipated 100 guests.

Patricia Mullen and Alan Hulting were married at the St. Thomas More Church in Iowa City on August 28, 1970, a hot, breezeless, humid Friday afternoon. Patricia wore the heavy white silk wedding dress her mother had helped her make. Alan Hulting was in a black double-breasted Edwardian jacket and tuxedo pants. Dr. Jon Hulting had driven from Davenport to serve as his brother's best man, and Mary Mullen was the maid of honor.

At the opening chords of the Wedding March Patricia rested her hand on her father's extended forearm and squeezed it gently. Gene Mullen turned to her, attempting to smile, but the expression on his face— half pride, half agony—was the same as when he and Michael had stood together at the Waterloo Airport just before Michael left for Vietnam. Patricia had to nudge her father to start him on the slow march down the aisle to where Alan Hulting waited. The closer they came to the altar, the lighter Patricia's hand seemed to rest on Gene's arm, and when it was time to surrender her, Gene pressed her fingers against his chest. Their eyes met, a smile flickered at the corners of Patricia's lips, and then her glance slid from her father to the dark-haired young man waiting at her other side.

The service was a simple wedding mass with prayers chosen by Patricia and Alan from the Song of Solomon: "Behold, thou art fair, my love; Behold, thou art fair; thou hast doves' eyes. . . ." When the organist played the first full, rich notes of the hymn "How Great Thou Art," Patricia heard her father suddenly gasp behind her.

Patricia had chosen the hymn simply because it was her father's favorite and she had wanted to please him. She had forgotten, however, that it had been played last at Michael's funeral. When Gene recognized the hymn, he broke down and wept throughout the rest of the service for the son he had lost and the daughter he expected never to see again.

Patricia, too, began to cry. She couldn't help it. She cried out of frustration that her marriage was something her father could find no pleasure in, that it was something which her family seemed only able to endure. She wept because Michael was not there, and she missed him. And, too, she cried for Alan Hulting, who stood so worriedly at her side. She loved him so and wanted for his sake as much as her own for their wedding to be nice. But instead there was now this layer of gloom, the constant awareness of Michael's death, the sense that her parents' thoughts kept straying elsewhere on what was to have been this, her most important day.

When, as Mr. and Mrs. Alan Hulting, the young couple turned back up the aisle, Peg looked up at her tearstained daughter and scolded, "For God's sake, Patricia, stop crying!"

A small coffee and cake reception was held following the ceremony at the University of Iowa's Student Union cafeteria where Patricia had worked, and afterward about seventy-five persons drove back to the Mullens' farm for a buffet dinner. Alan Hulting, sweltering in his tuxedo, found himself at one point trapped by an intoxicated friend of the Mullens' in their base-

219

ment recreation room. When the man finally turned to Alan and asked, "By the way, who are you?" Alan replied, "I'm the groom," and went back upstairs to find his bride. Patricia was in the living room worriedly watching her father corner one guest after another to talk about the war.

When it was time for Alan and Patricia to leave, Gene and Peg followed the young couple out to their car. Gene held the door for his daughter and kissed her lightly on the cheek. Patricia got in, and Gene and Peg walked beside the automobile as Alan slowly maneuvered out of the Mullens' driveway and turned onto John Dobshire's dirt road. When Patricia twisted in the front seat to wave out the back window at her parents, she saw they had continued across the dirt road to the mailbox. Patricia sadly realized that whatever little reprieve her wedding might have provided her parents, it was now over. The "cease-fire" had ended, and her parents' private, lonely war with the United States government had resumed.

Chapter Seventeen

The Mullens' obsessive correspondence, their bitterness, their inability to talk or think about anything but the war, their utter impatience with any divergent points of view were symptoms of their continuing belief that a conspiracy existed to prevent them from discovering the details of their son's death. The letter they brought back from the mailbox as Patricia and Alan drove away had been forwarded them by Senator Jacob K. Javits of New York.

Javits had redirected his copy of Peg's registered special delivery letter to each Senator to the Pentagon, where Major Thomas F. McMorrow, a General Staff officer in the Chief of Legislative Liaison Office, was assigned the task of providing answers. McMorrow's point-by-point response was mailed to Javits on August 20 and reached him, after the weekend, on the twenty-fourth.

McMorrow confirmed that Michael's "death was caused by a missile wound to the chest which was the result of an artillery round which exploded when it hit a tree in his company area." But because McMorrow then added, "He died before he could be removed to a medical facility," the Mullens now wondered if Michael had *not* been killed instantly as they had been told and instead had lingered, suffering for an unspecified amount of time. McMorrow's letter continued: "Accordingly, the only medical record available is the Certificate of Death which was completed at the mortuary, signed by a medical officer and a mortician. A copy of this document, which confirms the cause of death, is enclosed."

The enclosure was the same DA form 10-249 the Mullens had received that previous March 17 listing the mode of death as "accident," the interval between onset and death as "unknown" and the cause of death "missile wound of chest." The Mullens still questioned how it was possible for their son to have been killed by artillery and be perfectly whole. If the only wound Tom Loomis at the funeral home had found was a small puncture above his right kidney, why did the Army insist the wound was in Michael's chest? Michael, they believed, had been asleep when the shell hit. They knew their son usually slept on his left side. Loomis' placement of the wound made the most sense. Because of this confusion, the Mullens had requested a complete medical report. It was never sent because no such report ever existed.

"On 22 February the Chief of Support Services, Department of the Army, sent a message to Private Mullen's father. . . ." McMorrow's listing of their son as a "Private," not "Sergeant," was the sort of needless error which so infuriated the Mullens. The telegram containing information on the return of Michael's body also mistakenly listed his rank as "private." The indifference to the details of their son's life suggested to the Mullens an equal indifference to the details of Michael's death.

The remainder of McMorrow's letter dealt with specifics: the problem the Army had had in securing the special escort requested by the Mullens, the Army's attempts to locate Michael's missing camera, the procedures the Mullens should follow to file their claim. Then a brief section was devoted to the itemization of Michael's final paycheck including the deduction for unearned leave.

> Payment of the sum of $97.46, reflecting net unpaid pay and allowances, has been held in abeyance by the Finance Center pending receipt of the claim form signed by Mr. Mullen. That sum reflects a careful determination of remaining monies due him as beneficiary.
> Your interest in this matter is appreciated.
> Sincerely,
>
> s/THOMAS F. McMORROW
> Major, GS
> Office, Chief of Legislative Liaison

Gene and Peg never did sign the claim form; to have signed it would have meant they accepted the Army's right to deduct nine days' leave from Michael's final pay.

Iowa's summer had given way to fall by the time the Mullens heard from Major McMorrow again. The first Arctic winds had come down to cool the gentle hills, the cottonwoods had begun to drop their leaves, and the pheasant hunters were back out in the fields yelling at their dogs to hunt close. McMorrow's second letter, written to Senator Harold Hughes in response to the Senator's request for information, was, like Javits' letter, forwarded to the Mullens in La Porte.

McMorrow repeated the previous details of Michael's death, then continued:.

> Added information from the oversea command revealed that the artillery fire had been requested by the forward observer assigned to that company from the supporting artillery unit. It should be noted that an assigned forward observer for a company habitually lives and works with the supported unit at all times.
> At the time of Sergeant Mullen's death, the forward observer was within the overall defensive area and was preparing to adjust fire on four specific locations. This is a standard precautionary measure, even though there was no contact with the enemy at the time. The preparatory action assures the rapid and accurate delivery of artillery fire at predetermined locations in the event of an enemy attack without requirement for the adjustment of fire during the attack itself. It is confirmed that the unit firing was a platoon of a U.S. Army artillery battery.

The Army, for the first time, had admitted an American forward observer had called in the artillery which had killed Michael Mullen. Peg realized that the one young man who could answer all their questions would be that forward observer—but, of course, the Mullens did not know his name. Remembering Lieutenant Colonel H. Norman Schwarzkopf's second letter

223

—"Unfortunately, United States Army, Vietnam policy does not allow me to release the names of its servicemen"—Peg knew she'd never learn the name through the Army. McMorrow's letter continued: "Michael was not the acting platoon sergeant at the time of the incident, but he had previously performed in that capacity since he was a ranking enlisted man."

McMorrow's allegation was in direct refutation of Culpepper's letter of March 16: "Your son was acting platoon sergeant at that time. He was a soldier like us all, but he was fair to everyone because he believed in right." The Mullens thought if Michael had been the acting platoon sergeant, he would have been due more pay, but more than the denial of extra pay the Mullens resented the Army's repudiation of the accolade, the honor of the higher rank.

> At the time of the accident, his platoon leader was in a defensive position approximately eight to ten feet from him. Other members of the unit within the immediate area included the company Commander, the Company First Sergeant, and the battalion chaplain, who were located within 30 feet of Sergeant Mullen's position.

Peg read that paragraph twice. At first she wasn't even sure what bothered her about it. It wasn't simply the lack of names; she was accustomed to that. It was something more. Then she recalled the description of the incident in Lieutenant Colonel Schwarzkopf's second letter and searched through her papers until she found it:

> When the tragic incident occurred [Schwarzkopf had written] Michael's platoon leader was in a defensive position approximately eight to ten feet away from him. Other members of the unit were within the immediate area. The Company Commander, the Company First Sergeant, and the Battalion Chaplain were also located within thirty feet of Michael's position.

The almost exact duplication of the wording was more than coincidence, Peg felt; certainly the descriptions had been coordinated, but whether or not the similarities provided concrete evidence of a cover-up conspiracy, Peg couldn't be sure.

> Every incident in which our personnel are fired upon by friendly forces is thoroughly investigated so that any warranted corrective action may be taken to preclude any recurrence. The loss of life of an Army member under such circumstances is a matter of deep concern to all commanders and is a source of untold grief to all those immediately involved.

Peg seized upon that first sentence. In May Senator Fulbright had forwarded to Peg Daniel Henkin's letter on how nonbattle casualties are listed. In that letter the Mullens had learned the accident was termed a "misadventure." Henkin had also written, "I am informed that each instance where Americans have been killed by friendly artillery fire is investigated." McMorrow's letter confirmed this fact. Somewhere, therefore, a report of such an investigation must exist. If Peg could read it, she would know exactly what had happened to her son.

McMorrow's next paragraph was in response to the Mullens' demand to know why no one was permitted to write them and why they had not heard from any of the other officers in Michael's unit:

> Under established procedures the commander of a deceased or missing member's unit of assignment, the chaplain servicing that unit, or the installation commander will write a letter of sympathy to the next of kin and to his parents if they are not the designated next of kin. In accordance with the policy of the 1st Battalion, 6th Infantry, the battalion commander sent letters of sympathy in behalf of the battalion. In addition to the letter of sympathy, the battalion commander forwarded a letter dated 10 June 1970 to Mrs. Mullen in response to an inquiry he had received.

> There is no censorship of mail from Vietnam. A serviceman who wants to communicate with the next of kin of a deceased comrade is not

225

prevented from doing so; he is often encouraged. However, the member is under no obligation to correspond, and the extent of his communication is a matter of personal choice.

The Mullens did not believe this. They had Culpepper's letter of May 9: "Today we were informed of rights in the army. If any people have written to you in mail, the future is in jeparody. . . . For they can be courtmarshalled for mutiny and undermining the army. Don't publish any article of such writing for it would bring harm to people and their future. Anything sent to you can be censored as we are in a war zone." Lieutenant Colonel Schwarzkopf, himself, later confirmed that Division had written the letters sent out under his signatures and that he had not been permitted to answer the Mullens' letters, although he had wished to.

McMorrow then defended the Army's classification of Michael as a nonbattle casualty: "It has been definitely established that Sergeant Mullen's death was not directly related to hostile action, nor was the presence of the enemy a contributing factor. Therefore, his death was correctly classified as non-hostile."

The Mullens still smarted over that judgment. Michael, they knew, had been going out on a combat mission. With increasing bitterness and irritation, Peg Mullen read on:

> At all levels the Army is keenly aware of the human feelings that are involved. Individuals designated to act as official representatives of the Army are carefully selected for their ability to perform this difficult task with tact and understanding. In view of the seriousness of allegations that Master Sergeant Waldo T. Fitzgerald made certain comments, a full report was requested from the Commanding General Fifth U.S. Army.
>
> Information received indicates that when the parents saw the notifier in uniform accompanied by a Catholic priest, they immediately sensed the purpose of the visit and became very emotional. Approximately one-half hour later, when they were sufficiently composed, Sergeant

226

Fitzgerald read the official casualty message he had received by telephone. It stated only that Sergeant Mullen died at a night defensive position when artillery fire from friendly forces landed in the area.

During the conversation that followed, Mrs. Mullen recalled a radio broadcast reporting the shelling of friendly patrols by personnel of the Army of the Republic of Vietnam (ARVN), and it was noted by the family that Michael's unit may have been one of those allegedly so shelled. Reverend Otto B. Shimon, the priest who was present, says Sergeant Fitzgerald mentioned that the enemy may have gotten into friendly communication channels and caused the friendly unit to fire on the patrol, but he gave this only as a possibility.

Sergeant Fitzgerald states that he did not at any time say, suggest, or imply that Sergeant Mullen or any base camp mentioned on the radio had been deliberately shelled by ARVN forces. This statement is confirmed by Father Shimon. In his opinion Sergeant Fitzgerald was in control of his feelings and performed a difficult task as well as could be expected under trying conditions.

I realize how deeply Mr. and Mrs. Mullen have been hurt and how lasting will be their sorrow. It is most unfortunate that misunderstandings added to their distress. Michael was a brave and dedicated soldier, and my deepest sympathy is with all the members of the Mullen family in their great loss.

Sincerely,

s/THOMAS F. McMORROW
Major, GS
Office, Chief of
Legislative Liaison

"Of course," Peg told Gene that night after he had read the letter, too, "it's just between whether I'm crazy or Sergeant Fitzgerald is. I know I didn't make it up! I can see him standing there with his back to me and he was ready to go, remember? And I said, 'Sit down!' I said, 'We're going to talk about this wire. What do you mean by "friendly"? How is it the word

227

"American" isn't there?' And he said, 'Because it wasn't American fire.' I know I didn't make that up!"

Gene nodded. "And when you asked the sergeant why the word 'accident' wasn't in there, he said, 'Because it was no accident.' "

"And that's what Father Shimon denies! I couldn't have made all that up because I went downstairs and typed it up so I'd have it. I typed it that day, remember?"

"Shimon was so shook he wouldn't have known what anybody said," Gene flatly stated.

"Another thing," Peg said, "I'm sure they'd been talking about the Bien Hoa shelling at Fifth Army when this message about Michael came through. Someone probably said, 'What's this deal about "friendly fire"?' And another person said, "Well, that's probably another deal like Bien Hoa.' That's the way I think it all came about—and the whole Bien Hoa story, the whole thing about Michael being killed by ARVN artillery was printed in the Des Moines paper. Why didn't Sergeant Fitzgerald deny it then? He was here several times, and I told that same Bien Hoa story over and over again in those next few days to anybody who would listen, and he never once made any effort to correct me. I was so damned mad I told everybody who came the same story, and Fitzgerald or that captain—"

"Captain Pringle."

"That's right, Pringle. They were here. They never made any effort to correct me." Peg returned from the sink with a damp sponge and began wiping the top of the kitchen table.

Gene lifted the letter out of the way. "What are you gonna do about that investigation report?" Gene asked. "Do you think they'll ever let us see it?"

Peg shrugged. "I'm going to write General Ramsay and tell him to send it to us. I don't know what else we can do."

Several weeks passed, and then, to the Mullens' astonishment, a telegram from General Ramsay's adjutant was forwarded by the Veterans Hospital in Iowa

City saying that the artillery investigation report was on file at Long Binh and a copy would be sent them. The Mullens waited.

The report was never sent.

In mid-September the Mullens left La Porte to drive east to Pittsburgh for Peg's annual visit with her brother Howard Goodyear. They stopped on the way at Champaign, Illinois, to talk with Fred Wilson, the young man who had gone through the Fort Benning Noncommissioned Officers School with their son Michael.

Wilson, who was now released from the Army and attending the University of Illinois, had been the first soldier to write Peg of his unit's operations in Cambodia a month before President Nixon admitted troops were there. The Mullens visited Wilson at his rooming house near the university campus. They sat on his front porch talking together for about three hours. Peg was alarmed at how difficult it was for him to speak. She would ask a question, and Wilson would pause, struggle to answer and often in the middle of a sentence simply stop and stare off into space. She couldn't help wondering whether Michael would have been like that, too, had he come home.

"How many enemy did you see during your year in Vietnam?" Gene asked.

"I saw one," Wilson said. "One Vietcong. And he was dead. . . . I didn't kill him. I don't know who did."

"Fred," Peg asked, "what was it like over there?"

Wilson shrugged. "What can I tell you? We were mortared every night by local villagers. . . ."

"*Local* villagers?" Gene asked. "What did you do?"

Wilson turned slowly and looked at Gene. "One night we went out and did our own My Lai. We killed maybe—we." Wilson stopped and lit a cigarette. His hand was shaking so badly the top of his Zippo lighter rattled. He sat with his cigarette in one hand, the lighter in the other, not saying anything; then he took a deep breath and exhaled slowly. "After that we lived

229

three, maybe four months before we were mortared again." He looked uneasily at Peg and Gene. "We had to, see? Because night after night we kept losing. . . ." His voice trailed off.

Peg knew Wilson didn't want to talk about the war, that it was torturing him to bring it all up again, and she hated putting him through it. But she had to know. Wilson had been there. Peg needed to understand what it had been like for Michael.

"What are you going to do now?" Peg asked him.

"About what?"

"The war."

"Nothing," Wilson said. "Nothing for now." He shut his eyes. "I'm going to close it completely out of my mind. But when I've got myself under control again, when I've got my head straight, then God help them. God help them!"

The Mullens reached Pittsburgh late Sunday night, September 20. They stayed four days. Peg straightened up her brother's apartment, dusted, vacuumed under couches and chairs, defrosted his refrigerator, did those tasks which she knew her bachelor brother had neglected. And while she cleaned, Gene and Howard Goodyear talked about the war. Howard loved his sister and honestly admired and respected Gene. Because he grieved, too, over Michael's loss, he listened patiently, sympathetically and, for the most part, agreed.

"The people in La Porte," Gene was saying, "they see me coming and look at me like 'You sonuvabitchin' Communist, you traitor!' and turn away, head in some other direction. And you know, Howard, you know they don't even try to think about what's going on."

"Don't want to!" Peg corrected.

"See, Iowa's a very patriotic state. We have all these people who were brought up pledging allegiance to the flag, and they don't believe it's possible that the government could be telling lies."

"Oh, our government's always told lies, don't you think?" Peg asked.

230

"Never so many so deliberately since Johnson and Nixon. Just tell me one thing," Gene said. "What are they trying to hide? What are they so scared of? Why are they so afraid to tell the truth?"

"They can't admit they've made a mistake," Peg said. "We should never have become involved in Southeast Asia. Never sent American boys to Vietnam. It should never have been our war."

"That's right," Gene said. "We can't be policemen for the whole world. You know all these people who accuse—who think Peg and me are Communists, well maybe being a Communist in Vietnam isn't such a bad thing. I'm not *pro*-Communist. I'm not pro-anything except putting a stop to this war. I talk to the fellows at the plant, and I try to explain to them that what's going on now in Vietnam is the same thing that's been going on for a thousand years. It isn't a Communist revolution; it's a nationalist revolution. The leaders on the other side just happen to be Communists, and all they want is to unite their country and kick us out the same way they did the French. And they say, 'But, Oscar, what about the Chinese?' I tell them, 'Read Vietnam's history. The Vietnamese have been resisting the Chinese for a thousand years!' "

"Nixon doesn't understand what's going on," Peg said. "He thinks all we need to do is drop more bombs. Did you know more bombs have been dropped on Vietnam and Laos and Cambodia than were dropped throughout Europe and Japan the entire Second World War?"

"Now, I'll tell you this, Howard," Gene said, "the thing that really gets me, that really burns me up is these people whose sons never had to go to Vietnam, these American Legion types who never saw any combat themselves, these so-called Good Americans who think Peg and me are unpatriotic!"

Howard smiled sadly. "My country right or wrong?"

"When your country's wrong," Gene said, "the real patriot damn well tries to do something about it!"

On Thursday, September 24, the Mullens left Pittsburgh and drove south following Interstate 79 to

231

Charleston, West Virginia, then west on Interstate 64 paralleling the Ohio River north of Huntington and across the Big Sandy River into Kentucky. They soon left the interstate and followed county roads until they came to the small oilfield town on the ridge above which Leroy Hamilton's family lived. When Peg had first heard from Mrs. Hamilton that her son had died with Michael, Peg had written back spilling out her frustration and rage. Mrs. Hamilton initially asked that neither she, her husband nor Leroy's memory be involved in Peg's protests against the war. Later, as a sense of confidence and trust developed between them, Mrs. Hamilton in subsequent letters came more and more to agree with Peg's opposition to the war. Peg was the first person Leroy's mother had ever carried on an extended correspondence with, and eventually, when Peg wrote that she and Gene were driving east and would like to meet her, Mrs. Hamilton unhesitatingly invited them to come.

Peg and Gene followed the black macadam road which snaked back and forth up the hillside to the ridge top. The macadam gave way to dirt at the Hamiltons' property line; the dirt became a worn track. The Mullens' old car bounced and bumped across the stones and potholes, continued the last few yards around the corner of the barn and stopped. It was almost six o'clock, milking time; the Hamiltons were at work inside the barn.

Peg and Gene waited inside their car for the Hamiltons to come out; but no one moved. The Hamiltons were expecting them and must have heard their car drive up. Peg suspected that the Hamiltons simply did not know what to say to an Iowa family who might have nothing more in common with them than grief and horror at the deaths of their sons.

"Come on, Gene," Peg said and led her husband into the barn.

Mrs. Hamilton rose from beside a cow, wiped her hands and looked hesitatingly at Peg.

"Hello," Peg said, stepping forward. "I'm Michael's mother."

"I'm Leroy's mother," Mrs. Hamilton said.

The two women did not touch each other, did not embrace until Mrs. Hamilton suddenly started to cry. Peg quickly hugged her, comforted her, patted her gently on the back. A cow's hoof scraped across the cement floor; there was the slight ping of a metal pail; then Leroy's father emerged from the back of the barn and held out his hand to Gene. "We thank you for coming," Mr. Hamilton said.

Inside the Hamiltons' simple house, an added-onto mountain shack without indoor plumbing of any kind, the family's youngest daughter, Elsie, rushed up, smiling. "Hello, you must be Peg," she said. "I knew you'd come sometime, I knew it!"

They ate dinner right away. Gene and Mr. Hamilton talked farming, how hard the Kentucky land was compared to Iowa, the yields one might expect, the advantages and disadvantages of raising dairy cattle compared with hogs. Mr. Hamilton told how the tree had fallen on him and hurt his back.

"I suppose you miss your son very much," Gene said to him.

Mr. Hamilton looked away and talked instead about his hunting dogs, the four or five hounds Gene had noticed earlier roaming about the yard. Each time Gene attempted to talk to Leroy's father about the war, the man would become guarded, suspicious and change the subject back to farming or his hunting dogs again.

"Tomorrow I'll show you my garden," Mrs. Hamilton was telling Peg. "And I'll take you down to our root cellar. It's just jammed with canned vegetables and fruit."

"Let's set outside on the porch," Mr. Hamilton said.

The autumnal Kentucky evening was dank, humid, oily. Crickets and frogs filled the air with challenges and song. A small flock of doves raced in from the trees, circled briefly above the barn, then settled in to roost. A cow mooed complacently. One by one the dogs approached Mr. Hamilton's chair to have themselves scratched behind their ears. Mrs. Hamilton sat down next to Peg with a photograph album, and as they looked at the pictures of Leroy, she spoke of the past.

"We used to hunt deer," Mrs. Hamilton said. "Climbing these hills together was one of our greatest joys. He loved these hills, especially this time of year, the fall. The leaves would turn, and we'd go out together to hunt some venison for the table. He was a good shot. . . . And then when he was killed, I just went out to the hills alone." She began to cry telling Peg how day after day that winter she would take her rifle and climb the same hills she had climbed with her son, tramp the same trails to keep her sanity, to cry in privacy, to let the deep snow muffle her wounds. "I cried all that winter, Peg," she said. "I'm crying still," she added, smiling slightly. She held a photograph of Leroy in her hands, and as she spoke, her fingers would move along its borders in the sort of gentle, absentminded caress a mother makes when soothing a fevered child. "You know he stayed beyond his time during his final leave? He already had his orders for Vietnam, and he didn't want to go. He reported back to the Army after Christmas. He was killed less than two months after his arrival in Vietnam." She looked down at the photograph of her tall, handsome young son. "Leroy's buried up there," she said, gesturing toward the top of the ridge. "There's a little cemetery up above. It's real pretty."

Mrs. Hamilton told how hard she had had to work this past summer, how, because of her husband's injuries, she had had to bring in the hay. She had done most of the gardening and milking herself.

"You know," Gene said to Mr. Hamilton, "the one thing you keep thinking when you have a son in combat is that it can't happen to him. But it did. It did. When I think of the reason, the causes that took our sons. . . ." He saw that Mr. Hamilton's face had tightened again.

"Leroy was a wonderful boy," he replied. And that was all he would say.

When it was time to go back inside, Mrs. Hamilton showed Peg the pieced quilts she made during the winters, two or three each year. She opened a trunk and lifted out and unfolded the one she had made especially for Leroy. When she spread it out for Peg to look at, she began to cry again.

The Mullens left early the next morning for their Iowa farm.

Six days after their return, Peg and Gene were listening to the morning news about the Vietnam War when there was a knock at their kitchen door.

"I'll get it, Mother," Gene said. He walked down the back steps and peered through the storm door. A young black man looked at him from the other side. Gene opened the door a crack and said, "Yes? Can I help you?"

"Mr. Mullen? Mr. Gene Mullen?" the young man said.

"Yes, that's right."

"I'm Martin Culpepper."

Gene took Martin's hand in both of his and squeezed it in joy. He whirled around and shouted up the stairway, "Mother? Mother? It's Martin! Martin Culpepper. He's back from Vietnam!"

"For heaven's sakes, Gene," Peg called back, "don't just stand there, let Martin come on in!"

Martin Luther Culpepper was then twenty-one years old. He had been born in Mississippi, but three months later his family had moved to Waterloo, Iowa, where his father, the Reverend G. L. Culpepper, took a job with the Rath Packing Company and became the pastor of the New Zion Baptist Church. Martin attended local schools, and upon receiving his high school diploma, too, went to work for Rath. At night Martin attended the Hawkeye Institute of Technology, where he was learning welding with the hope that this skill would keep him out of the Army. It didn't. He was drafted six months later.

"It's the only way they would have gotten me,"

235

he told the Mullens. Culpepper was nineteen when he was inducted. Like Michael, Martin was sent to Fort Polk, Louisiana, for basic and advanced infantry training. He arrived in Vietnam a week after Michael Mullen.

Culpepper was pleased to be assigned to Charlie Company. He had been told that more Iowans were there and that "if things got hot, Charlie Company had the most dependable people. They didn't get rattled." That is how, he told the Mullens, he came to be with their son on that steep, wooded hilltop on that terrible night five months later when Michael Mullen died.

"All right now, Martin," Gene said, hitching his chair up to the kitchen table so that he and Culpepper could sit close. "We want to know what happened. Who was responsible that night? Who called in the shot? *Who-killed-our-boy?*"

Peg had a pad of paper and pencil and was prepared to take notes. "We want you to tell it like it really is, Martin. Give us their names," Peg said. "What were you doing that night? There was no enemy around. Why were you in the mountains? Why did they call in artillery? Start at the beginning, and tell us everything."

"Well, we heard it might have been any one of three things," Culpepper said. "We were told that the gun was the same gun that had killed some guys in Bravo Company a couple of months before—"

"The same gun!" Peg interrupted. "There was something wrong with it?"

"We heard something about a gun that always fired low," Culpepper said. "We also heard that the officer in charge of the guns was drunk, or that the guys firing were drunk and—"

BLAM! Gene's fist slammed the table in rage. He pointed his finger in Martin's face. "Now, I want you to tell me this, Martin: Who was drunk? WHO WAS DRUNK and killed my boy?"

"I don't know who it was, Mr. Mullen. Nobody ever told us any names."

"You heard the officer was drunk, am I right?" Gene asked.

"Well, we heard that, yes. But we also heard there was something wrong with the gun."

"Martin, you said it could have been any one of three reasons," Peg said. "What was the third?"

"There was a rumor that someone back on the hill they were firing from had failed to correct for the height of our hill," Culpepper said. "When the lifers came out the next day, they tried to get us to say it had been Vietcong."

"That's typical," Peg said disgustedly. "They wouldn't want to accept the blame. Because somebody was drunk or high on drugs or something."

"Was there a lot of drugs around?" Gene asked.

Culpepper looked uncomfortable. "While I was there, they called us in the Third Platoon a bunch of dope addicts, pot heads, acid freaks—you name it. But we weren't really. We smoked, sure. At one time everybody in the platoon had smoked pot except the lieutenant."

"Did Michael?" Peg asked.

"Smoke? No, no. Mike never smoked," Culpepper said. "I didn't know Mike all that well—I knew him, you understand, but we were in different platoons. I liked him. He was just a regular guy, calm and quiet. He didn't do too many things to excess. He didn't gamble or anything like the normal guys did. Everybody on payday—well, somebody would get out the dice, they'd scrape some place out on the ground, get out the money and the dice. Mike would come around and watch once in a while, but he didn't gamble. There was one kid nicknamed Perfect—everybody had nicknames." Culpepper smiled. "There was Perfect and Razzle-Dazzle and the Prince. . . . Nobody ever calls you by your full or last name. You get a nickname, and everybody sort of adopts it. Everybody called me Pep, for instance, or Pepper. . . ."

"Did Mike have a nickname?" Gene asked.

Culpepper thought for a moment. "No, I don't think so. Everybody just called him Mike. This one
237

guy, though, Perfect, he could gamble damned good. He'd sometimes send home as much as a thousand dollars a month. Bought himself a brand-new Dodge Charger with it. It was waiting for him when he came home—only he got killed." Culpepper began to fiddle with a pencil. "He got hit sixteen or seventeen times—not the same night as Michael. It was later on." He looked up at the Mullens. "People don't realize the feelings of people who have been to Vietnam and what happens afterward. The average GI when he comes back, he don't say nothing about the war. The first thing everybody asked me when I got back was, 'Hey, man, did you kill somebody, man?' That's the first thing my old buddies asked me last night. They always want to know if you killed somebody. 'No, you didn't,' they'd say. 'You didn't kill nobody. I don't believe you.' . . . They want to know, 'Did you see any action?'

"I said, 'Yeah, we got shot at.'

" 'Really?' they'd want to know.

" 'Yeah,' I'd say, 'I saw some action,' but you don't want to talk about it," Culpepper told the Mullens. "It brings up bad memories. Like the night Perfect got killed. And Cocoanut. They were two of my best buddies." Culpepper was rolling the pencil between his palms, looking down at the table. "I just got through talking to them," he said. "They'd walked out to set up some Claymores, and I'd said, 'Okay, I'll pass the word around that you're out there.' It had just gotten dark." Culpepper pushed away from the table and stood up. He went over to the sink and looked out the kitchen window.

"What happened to them, Martin?" Gene asked quietly.

Culpepper turned back. "We didn't even see the dinks, Mr. Mullen. They'd crawled almost up to us and I was just sitting there, and suddenly all hell breaks loose!" He cradled an imaginary machine gun in his hands. *"Buh-buh-buh-Bam! Buh-buh-buh-Bam!* Probably three, four machine guns. We didn't—my gun was back at the foxhole, I didn't even, hell, I didn't

238

have a chance to do anything. I ran for my foxhole, and the others thought I'd been killed because I disappeared in a bunch of dust. Perfect and Cocoanut were out front. Just as I got into my hole, I heard Cocoanut say, 'Hey, man, I'm hit! *I'm hit!*' I went to get up, and that's when they started firing RPG rounds—"

"What's that?" Peg asked.

"Those armor-piercing grenades they got," Culpepper said. "One hit in front of my position, one hit to the left. Cocoanut said, *'I'm hit!'* and oh, God, I heard Perfect groan from real low in his throat, 'I'm h-h-hit *unh-h-h-h*,' like that, and I knew he was hit bad. Then another RPG hit right beside Cocoanut, BOOM! He never knew what hit him . . . and Perfect, he's out there, and guys run out through all this damn fire and stuff and grab him, start dragging him back, but they couldn't get back to the bunkers." Culpepper remained standing, looking down at Peg and Gene seated at their kitchen table. "We couldn't even shoot back. They caught us lax, the way they wanted. Everybody goofing off, nobody paying attention, people just sitting around. . . ." He slid back into his chair and turned to the Mullens in agony. "We'd been searching for them all day long! And we couldn't find them. We were all relaxed; nobody was watching, no more than just watching out front. It wasn't quite dark. You could sort of see. I guess they'd been crawling along the ground. We figured some of them must have been as close as fifteen, twenty feet before everything broke loose." Culpepper wrung his hands together. "Perfect lay out there moaning. He kept moaning and *moaning* and MOANING! Things like that, you know, guys who . . . people. . . ." He pulled his hands apart and wiped them on his trouser legs. "You don't want to tell people about it because it brings all these bad memories back. . . ."

"You don't have to tell us, Martin," Peg said. "Not if you don't want to."

But Culpepper did want to tell the Mullens. He wanted them to know what it had been like in Vietnam.

With tears in his eyes he described Perfect's wounds, how Perfect had lain in the open for ten minutes, been hit over and over again until he had no back left and the medics couldn't understand how he hadn't been killed right away.

Cocoanut, too, had been hit several times in one leg, had three holes in his arm when the RPG round exploded beside him, tore off his unwounded leg and killed him. Both Perfect and Cocoanut had been in Vietnam for a long time. One had spent ten months there; the other had less than thirty days left in his tour. Martin tried to explain the anguish their deaths had caused him, how he had felt the pain one experienced losing a close member of the family. "It hurts so much," he told Peg, "but you know the kind of hurt I mean."

"I know," she said. "So does Gene."

Culpepper glanced at Gene. "I wanted to kill people after that."

"Did you?" Gene asked.

"Yes." Culpepper nodded.

He told them about the time his machine-gun squad had been sent out with a different infantry company and set up along a hedgerow. Culpepper's assistant machine gunner had spotted a North Vietnamese Army (NVA) regular crawling toward a young unsuspecting American soldier who had been sitting helmetless, his M-79 grenade launcher open on his lap. Culpepper could tell that the NVA soldier would emerge from the hedgerow between the unwary American soldier and his own position. Two other GIs were at the other end of the hedgerow. The NVA soldier would be trapped between them. Culpepper and the others could walk up behind him and capture him alive. "The kid with the M-79 was just sitting there playing," Culpepper said. "The gook got right up to the corner and saw him. He didn't run. He just stopped and froze. I was standing in a crouch. All I could see was the top part of him; then he saw me and made a quick move toward his shoulder, whirled around toward me, and I stitched him, *buh-buh-buh-*

bup! I felt so damned *good!* I'd killed me one of them sonuvabitchin' gooks!" Martin paused, half embarrassed by his language. Gene indicated with a little wave of his hand that it was all right, that Martin should go on.

Culpepper told how he had fired fourteen times, knew he'd hit the North Vietnamese soldier in the chest. "I saw him dead and I realized I'd killed another human being, you know? It made me want to cry. I can't explain the feeling. . . . I haven't gotten over it yet." He looked up at Gene. "He had had two grenades. I thought he'd had a pistol. That he was reaching for a pistol, see? There was no way to tell. I felt *so bad* about killing him. Here I was sinking down lower and lower, feeling worse and worse about it all the time because I'd killed a human being and everybody was pounding me on the back, saying, 'Man, you got that sonuvabitch! You killed one!' After that I started getting scared."

Culpepper explained how they then started seeing the enemy all over the place. Three here, four there. The men began shooting. They could hear semiautomatic fire coming from the village, more shots from the company perimeter behind them to their right. Culpepper and his machine-gun squad picked up and moved back to the safety of the company line. He didn't sleep that night. "I thought every little noise was an elephant coming through the bushes. Your nerves can only take so much. They say people turn into animals in a war," he told Peg, "but not really. You get so your body changes. Your senses change so that the least little noise wakes you up automatically. When I got out of the field and back to the rear, I'd sit down to eat and my nerves were so bad my hands would start shaking, and I'd have to stop in the middle of the meal. Put my hands under the table because I was embarrassed, you know? I didn't want people to see. . . . My hands still shake. My nerves are still bad. I guess I'm going to be that way for a long time."

"Martin?" Peg said quietly.

"People don't realize the feelings of people who

241

have been there. What happened to them afterward," Culpepper was saying. "They don't understand. They can't."

"Martin?" Peg repeated. "What was it like the night Michael was killed?"

Chapter Eighteen

For the rest of the day the Mullens' kitchen became that jungle hilltop in Vietnam. The more Martin Culpepper spoke, the less he seemed aware of his surroundings. Culpepper wasn't just talking about what had happened that terrible night; he was *there*. As Peg and Gene watched uneasily, Culpepper stormed about the table, hacking and chopping at the imagined dense jungle growth. The Mullens could only try to visualize what the young man still so clearly saw: helicopter swooping down for a combat assault, shark-faced Cobra gunships circling beyond their kitchen window, a white phosphorus artillery marking round exploding with a soft, plushy *foop!* above their stove. Flares popped high in the night sky illuminating the horribly wounded, who lay groaning and bleeding about the Mullens' yard. Vietnam's tight coil within Culpepper had not yet unwound.

The Mullens would, for the most part, wait patiently when Martin Culpepper's narrative would begin to ramble. At other times when he wandered off on some unrelated tangent, they would interrupt, ask a specific question and gently nudge him back on course. Throughout it all Peg was taking notes.

"Did you know about the boy who went berserk?" Culpepper asked.

Gene looked at Peg, who shook her head.

"His name was Polk," Culpepper said. "He was a black private in the First Platoon. He was asleep between Mike and Leroy Hamilton when they died. Polk wasn't even touched. He went crazy that night."

"What happened to him?" Peg asked.

"He's in jail at Leavenworth," Culpepper said. "He was court-martialed."

"Polk, black private, went berserk," Peg wrote in her notebook. *"Court-martialed. Leavenworth."*

"Mike was always looking out for Polk," Culpepper was saying. "Whenever Polk got in an argument, Mike would try to calm him down, say something like, 'Man, you're here. We're all here. We can't do anything about it.' Mike and Sergeant Gregory would try to talk to him sensible. But the other guys in the First Platoon wouldn't have much to do with Polk. They said he was a troublemaker."

"Friend of Mike's," Peg added to her notes. And on the line below she wrote, "Sgt. Gregory, 1st Platoon."

"We need names, Martin," Gene said. "We want to know who was with our son."

Peg's list began to grow:

General Lloyd Ramsey, Commanding General. Americal Division
Colonel Joseph Clemons, 198th Infantry Brigade Commander
Lieutenant Colonel H. Norman Schwarzkopf, 1/6th Battalion Commander Captain
(—) Cameron, Company Commander, Charlie Company
Lieutenant (—) Rocamora (sp?), Forward Observer w/Charlie Co.
Lieutenant (—) Joslin, Platoon Leader, 1st Plt. Mike's.
Sgt. Webb, 3rd Platoon, now in Des Moines.
Russell Schumacher, 3rd Plt. Still in Vietnam. Iowa boy.
Albert Gaynor, 3rd Plt. Back in States. Still in Army.
Abe Aikins, Black medic. Probably back in States.
Prince (nickname?), 1st Platoon. Wounded. Lost leg, maybe two.
Polk, Black Private, went berserk. Court-martialed. Leavenworth.
      Friend of Mike's
Sgt. Gregory, 1st Platoon

"Did you know that our platoon and Mike's platoon traded positions that night?" Culpepper asked.

"We were originally supposed to set up on their side of the hill."

"Whose decision was that?" Gene asked. "Schwarzkopf's?"

"No, it was the lieutenant's," Culpepper said. He told them how the 3rd Platoon had already dropped their equipment off and begun digging in when the order came to switch positions. The 1st Platoon was emplaced on the south side of the hilltop, and the 3rd Platoon to the north where there was a cliff. "I was set up right on the edge of it," Culpepper said. "It was about eighty feet straight down."

"Martin, what was Schwarzkopf really like?" Peg asked.

"He was a real gung-ho sort of man. He just wanted to get promoted."

"How old a man is he?" Peg asked.

"Thirty-two, thirty-three? He was a young man for a lieutenant colonel," Culpepper said. "The kind who want to make brigadier general by the time he was thirty-five."

"No matter how many boys he lost?" Peg said.

"We hardly lost none until the night Mike and Leroy died," Culpepper said. "After that we started losing a lot."

"We heard Charlie Company had about one hundred twenty casualties in the next three months," Gene said. "Could that be so?"

"Could be," Culpepper said. "I don't really know. It was a lot, though."

"Another thing, Martin," Gene said. "Why did they fire the artillery so late?"

"They told everybody as soon as we were dug in to put on their steel pots because they were going to fire the DTs. That's when everybody started making smart cracks about the helmets: 'They aren't any good nohow.' 'What good do they do? Don't stop nothing.' Things like that. That would have been about five thirty-six o'clock, somewhere in there. It wasn't dark yet, I remember.

"They said Rocamora was going to call them in," Culpepper continued. "And everybody was to get into their foxholes in case the arty wasn't right. But they didn't fire them. They called the DTs off. We all know the DTs were for our protection. As Schwarzkopf told us, 'If they want to get to you, let them come through a ring of steel.' . . . *Ring of steel!*" Culpepper laughed, shaking his head. "All this gung-ho stuff they used to feed us!"

"But, Martin," Gene asked again, "why did they fire the DTs so late?"

"I don't know," Culpepper admitted. He explained how the artillery investigators had arrived on the hill the following morning. They had looked at where the shell had hit and asked if the men were sure it hadn't been a Vietcong mortar round. "Everybody just started cussin' at them," Culpepper told the Mullens. "Someone said, 'It wasn't no mortar round,' real quietlike. 'You know what it was! You know who fired it!' finally they ordered us to be quiet, to return to our side of the perimeter. But even as we were walking back, we heard the artillery experts saying things like, 'Well, it could have been an ARVN round. . . .'"

"*An ARVN round?*" Peg asked, glancing at Gene. Could the original message, the Bien Hoa story, have been true after all?

"We know it wasn't the South Vietnamese," Culpepper was saying. "Those lifers were going around. 'Well, we have to examine all the possibilities,' they said. 'It may not have been an error. It could have been the enemy.' We know it wasn't."

The moment Culpepper left that evening, Peg threw a quick dinner together for Gene, swept the kitchen table top clean, and sat down to write Russell Schumacher, an Iowa boy, who was still with Charlie Company in Vietnam. He would tell her the truth. Hank Webb, according to Culpepper, was back in Des Moines—Webb had formed a sniper unit along with two other men so that he could move separately from the company. He carried an accurized M-14 with a telescopic sight and, Culpepper told the Mullens, was wounded a third time before being rotated out—Webb would, however, probably know Albert Gaynor's address. So Peg now had the names of three other young men who had been on that hill the night Michael was killed. She had specific questions to ask them and, for the first time, could expect to receive specific answers. Peg heard first from Russell Schumacher:

Yes I remember the night of February 18th when your son was killed. I was on guard talking with Albert Gaynor at his foxhole. I think Al & I were talking about how close they were firing defensive targets, "DTs." I was telling Al how funny it was to fire them at all much less at around 2:30. Then the 5th artillery round came in & hit in the trees near your sons hole. We knew it was in the perimeter and seconds later we heard guys in pain. . . . Your son died in a few minutes after he was hit. He probably never woke up to feel any pain. Leroy Hamilton died very shortly after being hit, too. It was a bad night that sure none of the guys that were there will ever forget.

The next morning the lifers came out to investigate. I think they said that morning that the officer in charge of the artillary mite have been drunk. Then later a roomer was it was the same gun that killed a guy—maybe two—in another company earlier this year. . . . Then later we were told that someone mite not have figured out the elevations of the hill the artillary gun was on and the hill we were on right. How ever it happened there was no reason at all to be firing artillery at that time in the morning. There was no fresh signs of enemy around.

When death comes its allmost to much for ones heart. I think your very brave in checking into your sons death. I truly hope you can help GIs out by learning the truth.

Maybe when the army & leaders find out that people care about the soldiers safety they will care. Many of the guys who knew Mike and know what you're trying to do believe you're right. Do what you can and may God give you a hand.

Truly,
s/Russell

During the first week in November the Mullens visited Hank Webb in Des Moines. Webb repeated the rumors Culpepper and Schumacher had mentioned: a faulty gun, the men were drunk, or the elevation had been incorrectly figured. But, he added, he didn't think the forward observer, Lieutenant Rocamora, had called in the shots. Webb explained to the Mullens while his parents sat listening that Rocamora wasn't a lifer and had no great loyalty to the Regular Army. Rocamora always alerted the men when the DTs were to be fired. If Rocamora had called in the artillery and not alerted the men, the men would have blamed him. "They would have made it so uncomfortable for Rocamora," Webb said, "he wouldn't have wanted to remain with the company."

"Did he stay?" Gene asked.

"Oh, sure," Webb said. "Everyone liked him. When the shell hit, there wasn't any warning. I thought it was an attack. I can remember sweeping, just throwing the men into their foxholes!"

Like Michael, Webb had been an acting platoon sergeant. He had been in the 3rd Platoon along with Culpepper, Gaynor and Schumacher. Polk, however, had been in Michael's 1st Platoon.

Schumacher wrote that he remembered Polk: "He had been afraid and quite a troublesome guy before. I think he had bad nerves for one thing. On the night your son died, Polk was sleeping right next to him. That really got to his mind. I could see how he cracked up. He was almost in shock that night."

Webb, that afternoon in Des Moines, told the Mullens Polk had "gone crazy." Some of the men from Webb's platoon had had to knock Polk out, restrain him, before he could be loaded onto a helicopter and flown out of there.

Gaynor, however, wrote:

As to your question about Pvt. Polk, it seems there's some sort of mix up. As far as I know nothing happened that night with Polk. I'm not sure, but I heard nothing of it. To my knowledge he was sentenced because of incidents a few days following the night of the 18th. Possibly the

20th or 21st. There were charges brought against him for a number of things. Hitting an officer and a non-commissioned officer, firing his weapon at civilians, and some other things which I do not know. Anything related to the night in question, I'm not aware of.

Gaynor had rotated out of Vietnam and was stationed at Fort Hood, Texas, when he wrote. His letter was the most explicit the Mullens received:

As I remember that night we were set up in a night defensive perimeter, which was located on a ridge line quite a few miles from Chu Lai. We dug foxholes as usual and set up for the night. Each platoon having its own sector of the perimeter. At about 8:30 PM we were informed over the radio that D.T.'s were going to be shot out in the next five minutes. . . . Most of the men in the company usually felt quite uneasy about the firing of these because they thought it was possible something could go wrong, and possibly somebody could get hurt. This is one of the reasons we were usually informed shortly before they were fired. So if some of the men wanted to get into their foxholes, they could do so. Some of the men did, but no artillery came. Finally it seemed that they were going to cancel the D.T.'s that night. Then about 3:00 AM, or some time around there, they started firing them. I know, because I was on guard that night. They fired some on our left and right which were a safe distance away. A safe distance is usually about 600 meters away.

They fire two rounds for each D.T. One round is a white phosphorus which explodes in the air and gives off white smoke. This is to make sure of the exact location where the round is to hit because the next round is H.E. (High Explosive) which is an extremely destructive round. The third set of D.T.'s was the one that hit inside the perimeter. A white phosphorus was fired first. It went directly over the middle of the perimeter. I heard it explode and saw the white smoke. It looked to me like it was in the right spot. A bit close possibly. Then the next round came in, this is the H.E. It sounded so close I hit the ground.

249

I heard the explosion and I remember thinking to myself it sounded awfully close. That round hit 50 yards inside our perimeter. You already know the rest. Mike and another man were killed, 6 others were wounded.

In your letter you said you were told Lt. Rocamora called in the artillery at 2:50 AM. Personally, I can't believe that. Of course I never asked him. But looking at it from my point of view it would seem foolish of him to do such a thing. Especially since most of the men like to be warned before it came and at 3:00 AM in the morning everybody would be asleep except for the guards. I was on guard, as I said before, and no for-warning was given.

We were told that it was the artillery people's fault. They told us that some officer and some sargent were being held responsible. There were rumors going round about the people firing the artillery being drunk and some sort of neglect was evident. Neglect isn't uncommon in Vietnam. This wasn't the last instance of it. There was much, much more to come in the following months.

I don't know if Hank Webb told you, but at one time we wrote a letter to you about the February 18 incident and some of the conditions afterward. It was signed by about 60 men in the company. That letter was never mailed because the Company Commander got word of it. We were threatened with reprisals and also he said that our mail could be censored. The letter was destroyed. When your in the army you don't have quite the freedom civilians have.

Mrs. Mullen, I think you are doing the right thing. If more people in the United States were as concerned as you are about the war, possibly something could be done.

s/Albert Gaynor

Gaynor's corroboration that censorship had been imposed on the men of Charlie Company infuriated the Mullens. Peg had now spoken or corresponded directly with four men present the night Michael had died; each of them had verified that American artillery had killed their son. They possessed, in addition, Lieu-

250

tenant Colonel H. Norman Schwarzkopf's letter written March 2 stating that "during the testing Michael received a fatal missile wound when an artillery round fell short of its intended target and detonated near his position."

Over and over again the Mullens had been told that Michael was killed because an artillery round had fallen short. Both Peg and Gene would have understood and might even have been able to accept that this was what had happened to their son were it not for the Army's unwillingness to provide them with the details as to why it had happened. It was obvious to the Mullens that it wasn't *what* had happened, but how it happened that the Army was so determined to hide.

The Mullens were now certain an American artillery unit had, for no apparent reason, suddenly and without warning, commenced firing over Charlie Company's night defensive perimeter at approximately three o'clock in the morning, taking Charlie Company by surprise. None of the men Peg had communicated with believed that the artillery had been requested by Rocamora, the company's forward observer. There was no reason for the artillery to have been fired at that hour; there were no signs of enemy activity around. One of the artillery shells fell short, detonated when it hit a tree above the company perimeter and killed Leroy Hamilton and Michael Mullen and wounded six others.

The Mullens were also now certain they knew why: the men back at the guns were drunk.

Peg was invited to be a guest speaker at the November 15 Black Hawk County Moratorium. She accepted and had her first brush with the FBI.

From the moment she stepped out of her car until she returned home Peg Mullen was photographed. No matter whom she stood next to or spoke with her picture was taken. At least eight men with cameras were among the protesters, and the thought of FBI agents photographing a peaceful gathering of American citizens was so repugnant, so absolutely *foreign* to Peg that when it was time for her to speak she was shaking with rage. She was outraged that she, Peg Mullen,

251

whose own son had given his life in support of his government's war, should be considered a potential subversive by the very government which had killed him.

Peg rose before the protesters and related step by step what had happened to her son in Vietnam, how he had been "killed by some drunken officer shooting off an artillery gun." She told how the Army's first reports had placed their son 400 miles from where he had actually died, how they had lied, led them to believe that Michael had been killed by South Vietnamese, not American, artillery. She explained how Michael was a "nonbattle casualty and, therefore, not counted," how the young men he had served with had been threatened with court-martial and reprisals if they attempted to write. She described how callously and insensitively the Army and Congress had treated her family from the moment they were notified of their son's death and her outrage at the deduction of nine days' leave from his final pay. She expressed her utter contempt with the White House for having included the President's Vietnamization speeches at a time when the family still believed their son had been killed by the South Vietnamese. She told of the letters she had received from young men who admitted to being in Cambodia a month before the President announced they were, and looking directly into the closest upturned camera lens, she said, "We are tired of President Nixon's lies! We were good members of the Silent Majority, but we cannot remain silent any longer. We are determined to speak out, to expose the government's lies. And we are not alone. All across America there are mothers and fathers, young men and women, *good Americans,* who feel the same way we do about this immoral war! We have come here today, all of us, to make our opposition known. We are not afraid." The photographer turned away and joined the others drifting through the crowd. Peg defied the government to draft her one remaining son, her son-in-law and any future son-in-law she might have. She vowed to continue her battle in behalf of the 44,000 killed in combat and the 9,000 nonbattle deaths like her son, so

252

that "those dead shall not have died in vain," she said, quoting, as she had in their second *Register* advertisement, the passage from Lincoln's Second Inaugural Address, "that this nation under God shall have a new birth of freedom, and that government *of* the people, *by* the people, *for* the people, shall not perish from the earth!"

About one week after Peg addressed the Moratorium, John Mullen received his corrected 4-A draft classification in the mail.

Early in December Peg, returning from marketing in La Porte, crept slowly along the ice-glazed dirt road and paused at the mailbox in front of their farm. She found a letter from Larry Phelps that had been dropped off by his mother while Peg had been in town. Larry again wanted help in getting out of Vietnam. He asked Peg to contact the Red Cross to find out the procedure. He was certain that his request this time would be forwarded through the proper channels because he now had a sympathetic first sergeant who believed Larry could be sent home. It took two days for Kathy and her mother to assemble the necessary documents and affidavits. On December 29, Kathy Phelps called Peg to say that Larry had received all the papers and had had them properly processed in Vietnam. He was waiting only to hear from the Pentagon. Peg immediately telephoned Colonel Alan Thompson and reintroduced herself. Thompson said, "Yes, Mrs. Mullen, I remember you very well." He promised to look into Larry Phelps' case right away and to let Peg know as soon as he had any news.

As 1970 ended, it was estimated that 4,727 American GIs had died in battle, 1,818 had died of "nonbattle" causes, and 34,774 had required hospitalization as a result of wounds suffered that year in Vietnam.

On January 4, 1971, Colonel Alan Thompson telephoned to say, "I have the best news in the world for
253

you! Your young friend should be getting on a plane today in Vietnam and will be home tomorrow."

Peg did not speak for a moment. Then she said, "Colonel, I find it very hard to believe. I don't think I'll tell Larry's family yet. I don't want to subject them to the same heartache I put them through seven months ago."

"Do call them, Mrs. Mullen," Colonel Thompson said. "Don't worry. Nothing this time can go wrong."

Black Hawk County was wrapped in a heavy blizzard, and ice accumulation between the Mullens' farm and Eagle Center, where Kathy's family lived, had pulled the telephone wires down. Peg looked out of her kitchen window. The wind-driven snow had pushed deep drifts against the fences, barns and silo and had so glazed the road she was hesitant to drive. Peg decided to telephone Larry's mother, whom she'd never met, and perhaps Mrs. Phelps could relay the news.

"I have just spoken with Colonel Alan Thompson in the Pentagon," Peg told her, "and he said that Larry's orders for reassignment reached Vietnam last week. Larry is supposed to leave Vietnam today and will be home tomorrow night. . . ." Peg paused, but when Mrs. Phelps did not say anything, Peg added, "So you can expect a phone call from Oakland some time tomorrow night." Peg waited again, and when there was still no response, she asked, "Mrs. Phelps? Are you there? Are you all right?"

Larry's mother was crying. Peg realized that Mrs. Phelps was trying to speak, to thank her, but no words would come out. "Don't try to say anything, don't worry about it," Peg told her. "Just try to call Kathy for me, would you?" And she hung up.

About thirty minutes later Larry's mother had regained her composure and called Peg back. She reported that she had been able to reach Kathy, that they all were very excited and grateful and couldn't wait for the following evening when Larry was to call.

Larry Phelps did not call the following evening, or the next, or the day after that. Four days after Peg had spoken with Mrs. Phelps Larry finally did call.

And at ten thirty that night, Kathy telephoned Peg to say that Larry had arrived in Oakland and had booked himself out on the first flight east that night.

"Thank God," Peg said. "I was so worried. I was sure some other second lieutenant had put the screws to him."

Two days later, on Sunday, January 10, Larry Phelps drove over to the Mullens' farm. Peg was there to meet him. Some young Lieutenant, Phelps told her, had indeed sat upon his orders. The day his orders had arrived Phelps had been sent on a ten-day search and destroy mission. He had not even known about his orders until the seventh, three days after Colonel Thompson had telephoned Peg. A helicopter had picked him out of the field, and he was immediately placed on a plane for the United States.

"Peg," Larry said, "I don't know how to thank you."

She hugged the young man and said, "I'm just glad you could come home."

The following spring Peg found herself with two flat tires on the road to Waterloo and limped into a gas station on the edge of town. The service attendant there, she discovered, was Larry Phelps' older brother. Peg introduced herself and explained how she had helped Larry out of Vietnam. "Isn't it great," she asked, "that he could come home?"

"So what?" Phelps' brother said. "I was there for two years, and it didn't hurt me any."

Chapter Nineteen

As the Mullens approached the first anniversary of their son's death, still disillusioned, angry, suspicious, wounded and confused by all they had suffered and learned, they did not believe the government had singled them out *specifically* for mistreatment. They accepted, instead, that the government was willing to treat any of its citizens in the same manner if given the chance. That is why the Mullens felt it their duty to alert their fellow Americans to what might befall them by holding themselves up as examples. Gene wanted to focus attention on what had happened not merely on that jungle hilltop in Vietnam and rolling farmland in Iowa but, by association, all over Southeast Asia and the United States as well. The Mullens were horrified that never before in the history of this nation they so loved had its government so rigorously dedicated itself to the accumulation of power at the expense of its citizenry. And what dismayed the Mullens so much was the ease with which Americans acquiesced and refused to speak out.

On February 20, at a press conference preceding a $50-a-plate Lincoln Day Dinner in Des Moines, Senator Robert Dole, of Kansas, chairman of the Republican National Committee, asserted that by May 80 percent of the U.S. ground troops would be out of Vietnam. Peg Mullen, watching him make that statement on the evening's television news, saw that not one of the reporters present had questioned Dole's remark. She couldn't stand it.

At a press conference in Sacramento several days before, Dole had said, "The issue with Muskie, McGovern and Bayh is deciding which was against the war first, and by then the war will be over." Peg had written him then:

> You are following the impression given by our President that the war can be over whenever the Republicans desire. It is this pattern of thinking that simply tears at the hearts of fathers and mothers whose sons have died since Mr. Nixon campaigned to end the war, whose sons today are going endlessly to Vietnam and into combat, whose sons will die there this week, next week, next month, next year.

"It is difficult for me to understand your reasoning on this issue," Dole replied. "I am a veteran of World War II and am well acquainted with what involvement in war means to an individual. I strongly support President Nixon's program to bring the war in Southeast Asia to a successful conclusion with our national honor and integrity intact."

What national honor? What national integrity was left? Peg discovered which Des Moines hotel Dole was staying at following his Lincoln Day Dinner and telephoned his room. It was eleven o'clock at night, and the Senator either wasn't in or wouldn't answer. At seven thirty the following morning Peg placed the call again. Dole answered the telephone, and Peg explained who she was. Dole said, "I don't have time to talk to you. I have to catch a plane."

"They'll hold the plane for the Republican National Chairman," Peg said. "You can wait. You can talk to me."

"Only for a moment. What is it you wanted to say?"

"Last night you said eighty percent of the ground troops would be out of Vietnam by May," Peg said. "That's a lie."

"Don't call me a liar!"

"That's a lie, Senator," Peg repeated.

"It isn't. I received that figure from the White House this week."

"Well, I don't believe it," Peg said. "How many ground troops are there now?"

"About two hundred and eighty thousand."

"I don't believe that either. I think there are more troops there than that."

"That's the figure," Dole said.

"Okay then, eighty percent of that is two hundred thousand. Do you honestly believe you can get two hundred thousand troops out of there in two months?"

"I do."

"Senator Dole, Nixon doesn't have the one hundred fifty thousand he promised out of there last April, yet," Peg said. "He isn't even much over one hundred thousand."

"I can't help that. That's what the President is going to do."

"Well, your saying it doesn't make me nearly as ill as the fact that everybody simply sat there and listened to you. Nobody challenged you or said a word. I mean it burns me up that people sit and swallow that stuff and never ask a question. They don't know anyth—"

"Mrs. Mullen, I—"

"—ing, or maybe they don't care. But I've even got nuns over at the local parochial school reading antiwar books. Some of th—"

"Mrs. Mullen, I've got to go."

"—old ones who didn't even know there was a war on, Senator. But the people of this nation will soon find out. . . ." Peg's voice trailed off. The Senator had hung up on her.

About this time the Mullens became convinced their telephone line was tapped. They had been suspicious ever since that summer when a lady had called Peg and asked, "What goes on at your house? I called you direct and got the third degree. Someone broke in on the line and wanted to know who I was, where I was calling from and so on. I've never had that happen before."

The Mullens share a party line, and one of their neighbors, too, thought the line was tapped. Peg had laughed off the suggestion because she suspected the neighbor was just paranoid. On the last day of February, however, the Mullens received what they considered proof.

All that week Peg had been making tapes for radio stations to play in advance of President Nixon's March 1 visit to Des Moines. On these tapes Peg asked mothers and other concened citizens to join her in peaceful protest of the continuing Vietnam War and the recent Dewey Canyon II incursion into Laos.* Although American ground forces were forbidden by congressional ban to cross the border into Laos—a legislative action which had grown out of congressional and public outrage at the President's invasion of Cambodia ten months before—more than 20,000 South Vietnamese troops supported by U.S. Air Force B-52 bombers, Navy and Marine fighter-bombers, 2,600 U.S. helicopters and American artillery had launched an invasion into Laos to cut the Ho Chi Minh supply routes and Communist supply lines. On that last Sunday before the President's arrival, the Mullens received a great many telephone calls from other organizers, including several from the Another Mother for Peace group confirming their plans to visit the Mullen farm to make a short film. That evening Mary Mullen called her mother from Kansas City and suddenly asked, "Mother, what's the matter with your phone?"

Immediately they heard a man say, "Shut that thing off!"

"Mother, what is it?"

"Oh, it's just more of the same that goes on here all the time," Peg said.

Later that same evening the Moratorium Committee telephoned from Des Moines. They told Peg that a young Iowa state representative planned to present a peace petition containing 15,000 signatures to President Nixon when he addressed the state legislature in Des Moines. The next day that young state representative was approached by the Secret Service and told if he even tried to move in his seat while the President spoke, he would be escorted out of the Capitol. The

*Dewey Canyon I was the code name for the 3rd Marine Division's invasion of Laos during January and February, 1969.

Moratorium Committee could not understand how advance word of the young man's plans had reached the Secret Service.

"I can tell you how," Peg informed them later. "You mentioned over my telephone what you were going to do."

The conversation with Peg Mullen was the only leak the Moratorium Committee could discover.

That Sunday night, moreover, during her phone call with her daughter Mary, there was a continuous click-click-click on Peg's telephone and Mary's voice would fade in and out. Peg wasn't surprised that her telephone might be tapped; Peg's experience with the government made such a violation of her civil rights seem absolutely natural and inevitable.* She simply

---

*During the spring of 1973 the Mullens, still convinced their telephone was tapped, discussed reporting their suspicions to the proper authorities. Patricia Mullen Hulting, then attending the University of Iowa College of Law, was advised by a criminal law professor that Federal Judge William C. Hanson in Fort Dodge would have had to sign the court order approving the tap. Peg put off writing Hanson until June, when, because of Gene's insistence (and that of a neighbor, tired of the constant interruptions, fading signal and clicking sounds, who shared their party line), Peg telephoned the judge directly.

Hanson was irritated that Peg had asked his assistance and suggested she not discuss her suspicions over the telephone. "If you want to talk to me come to my office," he told her. "But I must inform you that if we do talk about possible taps on your telephone, our conversation will be taped. I don't want you to be offended, but I will not have you saying things, then distorting what I've said when you repeat our conversation in return." Later that summer while visiting her sister Isabel Strathman in Fort Dodge, Peg stopped in at the Federal District Courthouse. Hanson was not in, but Peg was able to speak to his clerk, who chided her for having waited so long before speaking to them. The proper man to contact, the clerk told Peg, would be the U.S. Attorney, for the Northern District of Iowa; Evan L. "Curly" Hultman.

When Peg called Hultman from La Porte, she was told he would be away for two weeks. Several weeks passed when Hultman returned Peg's call and, according to Peg, was "quite incensed at even the thought of my phone being tapped." Hultman, too, added that Peg should have contacted him several years before. He promised he would get in touch with the Federal Bureau of Investigation and would have them send an agent out to see her.

Late that August Peg returned from Davenport and found FBI Agent Jim Gibson waiting at her farm. Gibson denied the FBI had instigated the taps. "If your phone had been tapped by the FBI," he told Peg, "you never would have known about it. Besides, there

shrugged it off and returned to painting the protest sign she would carry with her the next day during the President's visit: 55,000 DEAD, 300,000 WOUNDED. MY SON, JUST ONE.

At eight o'clock, Monday morning, March 1, 1971, Peg Mullen left to rendezvous with the President of the United States in Des Moines. During the hour and a half drive to the state capital Peg could not shake the memory of that March 1 one year before. No crowds greeted Michael. No Secret Service guarded his body. No one cheered or waved a flag. No newspapers or posters marked the sacrifice he had made in the war.

Peg was anxious and depressed about participating in any public gathering protesting the United States. In spite of her abhorrence of Richard M. Nixon, she continued to hold his office in high esteem. Like her fellow Iowans, she had been brought up to believe in the inherent goodness of the United States. Respect for the presidency dies hard . . . but it dies.

Peg, too, felt a fierce elation that she was directly to confront the one man who, to her, epitomized the dark forces which had taken her son. She wanted to stand before Nixon face-to-face, wanted him to see her sign, feel her rage. She dared even hope she might speak to him, tell the President exactly what she thought.

When Peg, carrying her sign, reached the snow-covered lawn in front of the Statehouse, where the President was scheduled to speak, she was relieved to see not only young people there. There were farmers from Iowa, South Dakota, Missouri, Nebraska, their wives and children and even some elderly grandmothers. Although Peg realized many of them had come not to protest the war but simply to see the President or to

---

was no need to tap your telephone. Anything you had to say you always spilled right out in the open."

Peg believed him. She had always been convinced that their phone tap had been initiated by the military.

Gibson and Peg spoke for several hours that afternoon. At one point Gibson smiled and told Peg, "As a matter of fact, when the U.S. Attorney called me about you, I told him, 'Oh, sure, I know who she is. I've had her under surveillance for three years.' "

261

protest some farm or labor legislation which they felt should or should not have been passed, she was comforted by their presence. The President, his advisers and the press would find it hard to ignore so large a turnout of middle-aged Americans.

Protest signs were everywhere. The labor groups' signs reflected their resentment at administration efforts to keep their wages low. The farmers were bitter about the years of hardship they had put into their farms without profits of any kind. But the majority of placards were peace signs, protest banners, Another Mother for Peace posters reading WAR IS UNHEALTHY FOR CHILDREN AND OTHER LIVING THINGS.

Peg positioned herself on the steps leading to the west entrance to the Statehouse and looked down Walnut Avenue, the street selected as the President's route. It was practically deserted. Where were the flag wavers, the greeters who might normally have been expected to provide a huge turnout for whatever visit an American President might make to a Midwestern state? Did the poor attendance reflect the cold or the President's lack of support? President Nixon, Peg felt, had demonstrated how little he cared for what the people thought; perhaps the people were showing how little they thought of him. The President would certainly know what *she* felt. There would be no way for him to climb those steps without passing directly by Peg Mullen and her sign.

Peg heard, before she could see, the President's motorcade. The motorcycle outriders were the first to come into view, followed by a Secret Service automobile, the huge black bulletproof presidential limousine and another Secret Service automobile. Suddenly it became clear that the President would not be arriving at the west entrance as announced, and the crowds, angry and frustrated, surged around the Capitol to reach the other side. By the time the protesters reassembled the President had already disappeared within.

During the next thirty minutes, while the President addressed the assembled Iowa legislators and the young state representative with the peace petition remained motionless in his seat, the protesters outside

262

stamped their feet and blew into their hands to keep warm. Union representatives, farmers, clergymen, anti-war spokesmen took turns addressing the crowd, but the speakers were soon drowned out by the young gathered along the police barricades, who had pushed as close as possible to the President's parked car. They were chanting, *"One-Two-Three-Four, We don't want your FUCKING WAR!"* Peg winced at the obscenity, not only for herself but for the older people there.

The east doors opened, and Secret Service men emerged. The President was preparing to leave. Peg dreaded what might happen. If Nixon went into one of his typical arm-waving V signs, there was no predicting what this cold and angry crowd might do. Peg had abandoned any hope of actually confronting the President; when he had been driven to the east entrance instead of the west, she had lost her vantage point of being near where he would pass.

As Nixon started to raise his arms in salute, a roar of outrage climbed the steps toward him. The President jerked his arms down as if stung and was swiftly hustled by the Secret Service into the presidential car. Peg was surprised to find herself shocked that the President had been booed. She herself, stilled by some apparent, hidden reserve, had not uttered a word. Half amused, half angry, she watched the President's automobile depart while the younger protesters flung snowballs after it.

Peg walked slowly away from the Statehouse. She decided to follow the crowds to the President's next stop, the Hotel Fort Des Moines. Upon her arrival she discovered the entire north wall of the hotel was lined with more protesters. Again, they were of all ages, and many carried private messages on hand-painted signs. Peg was distracted by the presence of an ambulance parked at the hotel's front entrance. A chief of state's appearance now generated an all too familiar dread. One could not witness a presidential motorcade without remembering what had occurred in Dallas eight years before. American tragedy had written itself a new score with music provided by electric generator trucks, winding down jet engines, reporters' motor-driven reflex cameras, hot arc lights hissing in gentle, misty rains. Peg forced herself to look away.

More and more people were arriving. The crowds spilled over onto adjoining blocks. The young began chanting again, *"One-Two-Three-Four, We don't want your FUCKING WAR!"* Some of the older people joined in. The chanting had grown so loud Peg was certain it could penetrate the thick walls of whichever conference room contained the President. All about Peg stood the farmers with stern, worn, weather-etched faces, and their middle-aged women, some wearing veils of mourning.

Suddenly, out of the corner of her eye, Peg saw something white arc out of the crowd toward the hotel entrance. At first she thought it was another snowball or a wad of paper. But Peg saw the next egg clearly. The photographers quickly moved to get their shots. Peg wondered how many of them might be from the FBI. She twisted about to see if she recognized any of the cameramen from her Moratorium Day speech in Waterloo. When she turned back toward the hotel, the police had started moving into the crowd.

A line of policemen carrying a length of 1-by-14-inch lumber as a wedge was heading toward where Peg stood. "Move back! Move back!" the police were shouting. "Clear the street!" Peg was pushed backward against a street barricade and pinned. As much out of defense as defiance she held her sign out toward the advancing police. She wondered if this was how it had started at Kent State. A plainclothesman grabbed her sign, and Peg, feeling the rush of adrenalin, held on. They began to wrestle. In Peg's mind the confrontation choreographed itself into a symbolic ballet. The sign, held high, became her own son, her vision of America; the plainclothesman became the government's imperturbable façade. At last Peg was fighting an enemy she could see and touch. She made up her mind that no power on earth could make her release her poster. The plainclothesman unexpectedly lifted his right arm and smashed Peg across the face with his elbow. Peg's vision blurred, her knees buckled, but she

264

didn't fall, couldn't fall because she was still trapped against the street barricade. Two young student marshalls rushed forward to assist her. They took Peg's arms and begged her to move back for her own sake, but she shook them off. Still furious, shivering with tension and rage, she defied the plainclothesman to strike her again. "Next time there will be a thousand mothers like me," she shouted at him. "A thousand! Not just one!"

"Lady," the man said wearily, "would you please just move back?"

Peg, still panting from fright and exertion, knew from the man's tone that his hitting her hadn't been anything personal, that he had a job to do. He was there to protect the President insulated deep within the hotel. The plainclothesman's attitude was all too understandable. It was the same dispassionate sentiment with which the government had reacted to the death of her son. The plainclothesman was typical; that was what so frustrated Peg. What did it take to make Michael's death, his family's grief and bitterness, meaningful to people like him?

Peg saw that there was something symbolic, too, about this President's visit to the heartland. In a speech delivered at Kansas State not long before, President Nixon had told his audience, "The heart of America is sound. . . . The heart of America is good. . . ." How could he know? He remained hidden behind barricades, behind sturdy hotel walls, behind barriers of bumper-to-bumper buses, armored steel and bulletproof cars. Did he not look outside because he didn't want to see? Was he unaware that everywhere he went Americans were being roped off, pushed back, struck, driven away? On this visit to the heartland, had he looked, the President would have seen Peg Mullen punched, seen the middle-aged woman standing next to Peg dragged backward by her hair. He would have seen some other American rush to the woman's aid, knock the plainclothesman away and carry the woman to safety inside the Firestone Building. The President would have seen the weeping, near-hysterical older woman shouting that she'd seen it all in Germany forty

265

years before. Peg, safely out of the path of the police, glared up at the hotel's brick facade.

"Won't you take one of these?" an old woman asked her.

Peg looked down at the piece of literature the woman had thrust into her hand. "What is it?"

"Everyone should return to God," the old woman said, smiling. "Only He can right such wrongs. Communism is the true enemy of free nations and free people. Their atheistic dogma is anti-Christ."

"I agree, madam," Peg said, "but we should devote our energies to fighting our enemies here at home—not in Indochina. The best place to fight the anti-Christ would be the Pentagon."

"What's the Pentagon?" the woman asked.

The President of the United States, shielded from view by the wall of buses, had already climbed into his limousine and was gone.

Later that night Peg Mullen, home again, looked at the Des Moines *Register* newspaper photographs of American helicopter crewmen kicking and punching the wounded and panic-stricken South Vietnamese Dewey Canyon II soldiers away from the landing skids so that their helicopters could take off. During the Laotian operation the ARVN troops suffered close to 45 percent casualties. More than 3,800 South Vietnamese soldiers were killed, 5,200 wounded, and eight battalions were put out of action. Ninety-four American helicopters and five aircraft were destroyed. Sixty-six American crewmen were killed; seventy-nine were wounded. Peg pushed the newspaper aside and got out her box of stationery.

Dear President Nixon:

It is now just over a year since our son died a needless death in Vietnam, died while he was continually questioning what the administration was doing and going to do about the insane war in Vietnam.

As I listen to the news this week, I can only thank God that we have no more to give, *ie:* We

266

will give no more young men to war. I personally feel that only the mothers of the world can
stop this conflict. When I am asked to speak before groups this is my theme: "Mothers, please
don't let your sons go—don't live with the guilt
for a lifetime that you stood back and let your
innocent son die in Vietnam."

Michael's father and I find it very difficult
to live these days, but because we do have faith
in God, we feel that there will be a special hell
for the men and governments that have allowed
the war to continue . . . there will be a judgment
to be faced and it will be as swift as was the
death of our son.

Mr. President, your plan [to end the war] is
now going into the third year. Did you ever really
have one?

In the name of God, stop the insane killing
—haven't there been enough heads served on
platters?

Sincerely
s/Mrs. Gene Mullen

Peg received the following reply:

DEPARTMENT Of STATE
Washington, D.C. 20520

Mrs. Peggy Mullen
La Porte City, Iowa

Dear Mrs. Mullen

President Nixon has asked me to reply to your
comments on Viet-Nam, where your son gave his
life in our country's service.

President Nixon and all of us are deeply con-
scious of your sorrow and that of other parents
who have lost a son in Viet-Nam. We share in
your loss. The young men chosen to fight our
battles are the pick of our youth; America has
always relied on the citizen soldier. The question
of why young Americans must fight, suffer and
sometimes die in a distant country is not an easy
one. But two World Wars and the conflict in
Korea have taught us that retreat before ag-

gression does not assure our security or that of the free world.

When a just and honorable peace is achieved in Viet-Nam, free men everywhere will owe an immeasurable debt to America's sons who gave their lives in defense of freedom. We pray that God will grant this nation the wisdom and strength to redeem their sacrifice by making the kind of peace that the next generation will be able to keep.

> Sincerely yours,
>
> s/Michael Collins
> Assistant Secretary
> for Public Affairs

Collins, of course, was the command module pilot who had orbited the moon while Neil A. Armstrong and Colonel Edwin E. Aldrin made man's first lunar landing on July 16, 1968. Peg was thrilled to have received a letter from the astronaut, but unimpressed by its contents. Peg's next plea to the President for an end to the war was also answered by Collins:

> I can understand your desire for peace but the question of a withdrawal must be considered in the light of our purpose in Viet-Nam. We are fighting to assist the people and the Government of the Republic of Viet-Nam to defend themselves against aggression by North Viet-Nam. We are there, at their request, to help them maintain their right to direct their own affairs free from external interference. This is what we are trying to achieve at the peace talks in Paris and on the battlefield in Viet-Nam.

Collins described how the troop level had dropped from 549,000 in the beginning of 1969 to 434,000 fifteen months later. He added that the President planned to lower the troop level by a further 150,000 before the summer of 1971. Collins mentioned the various peace proposals offered, and Peg knew it was the same old line. She assumed Collins wrote what he was told to write and had no intention of any further contact. But a few days later Peg had reason to address Collins directly:

Dear Mr. Collins:

There are very few stories in the newspapers these days to bring a smile to my face . . . but the announcement that you were resigning from the State Department actually made me chuckle.

Having been the recipient of letters from Washington following the Cambodian invasion, I found it very difficult to associate your signature with the propaganda that went out from Mr. Nixon's office.

Good luck in your new assignment. You are a credit to your ancestry.

Sincerely,
s/Mrs. Gene Mullen

Collins was quick to reply:

Dear Mrs. Mullen:

Thank you for your note concerning my change of jobs.

However, I very much resent any letter I sent you concerning Cambodia being called "propaganda that went out from Mr. Nixon's office." Our publications are in fact true; and I think events since Cambodia, such as American casualty rates, prove that what we said at the time was absolutely correct.

Sincerely,
s/Michael Collins

There has been no correspondence between them since.

Peg spent the remainder of March attending meetings of her local Another Mother for Peace group. She asked that she be appointed chairman of the Committee on Abolishing the Draft. In a letter to Senator Hughes she explained, "I intend to work hard and endlessly in this endeavor." Although the inequities Peg saw in the draft had largely been eliminated on

269

May 13, 1969, when President Nixon by executive order signed the random selection lottery system coupled with the one-year vulnerability clause into law, one of Peg's charges bears mentioning: "Only 3.2% of Congressmen's sons and grandsons," she wrote Senator Hughes, "have been drafted to serve in the Vietnam War."

Of the 234 draft-eligible sons (grandsons not included) of Members of Congress during the Vietnam period, 118—or just over 50 percent—received deferments. Forty-eight congressional sons served in the military during this period, but not in Vietnam. Twenty-six—or just over 11 percent—did serve in Vietnam. Peg's 3.2 percent figure was the correct amount for those who saw combat. None was killed or missing, and only Captain Clarence D. Long III, son of Representative Clarence D. Long, (D. Md.), was wounded.

Snow still covered the Mullens' fields in the middle of that month when a film crew from Another Mother for Peace came to La Porte City to interview and photograph the Mullens. The filmmakers had already completed their work on four other families who they felt best represented the personal anguish caused by the war. The first family's son was killed on Mother's Day. The second family's son had surrendered to federal marshals rather than serve in the Army. The third family's son was a Navy pilot spending his third year as a prisoner of war. The fourth was from a ranching family from Texas; the young father returned from Vietnam without his leg. The film released under the title *Another Family for Peace* was photographed by Joan Churchill and directed by Donald MacDonald. It was edited down to thirty minutes, the final ten minutes of which was the Mullens. To get those ten minutes, the film crew stayed four days at the Mullens' farm.

The film, photographed in black and white, opened with a long shot of the Mullens' farm taken from the field next to the stand of timber which had once held "The Old Eagle Tree." The camera held that

270

shot until the vastness and isolation of that bleak, wintry Iowa landscape seeped in. The only sound was the barking of a neighbor's dog seemingly far, far away. Perhaps the most extraordinary facet of the film was how unself-conscious the Mullens were. Peg had insisted on being permitted to fix up her hair, but other than that, there was no indication that the Mullens were "acting." There was a great deal of voice-over dubbing, exterior action shots with an imposed sound track: "My reaction to the death of my son was twenty-five years of my life torn out of me," one hears Gene saying as he carries a huge bucket of feed on his shoulder to his hogs. He is calling, "Pig! Pig! Pig!" and is bundled up against the cold. "I was stunned. I couldn't see it because I had great hopes for him. He had a great future. I couldn't see why it had to happen. I felt this very strong bitterness. I couldn't accept it. My boy—it was only when they brought the body back and I was asked to view it, that I could accept it. That it was Mike. . . ." Gene has put the bucket down and is now walking over to the old plum red Farmall Michael had driven his last night. "When I went to the airport," Gene is saying as he climbs into the seat, "and I escorted my boy's body back to the funeral parlor"—he presses the ignition and holds it—"I asked to have his dog tags and the military said, 'They still belong to the United States Army.'" The tractor starts, and Gene advances the spark. "I said, 'That's enough! From now on the boy is gone! And I'll bury him as my son and not as a military soldier anymore," Gene puts the tractor into gear and drives off. The camera shifts to the Mullens' downstairs recreation room where Peg has set up a table and is writing a letter to Senator Edward M. Kennedy. Throughout her typing one hears her voice dubbed over saying, "I have to live with this thing. . . . I have to make Michael's death a cause in my household. This is what I'm doing now. Michael has to have died for something! I think it's my duty to see that he *did* die for something."

The camera pans across the recreation room wall containing photographs of Patrick and Mary Ann Mullen, a photo duplicate of John Dobshire's original land grant, yearbook photographs of the Mullen daughters; then the camera closes in and holds a tight shot of Michael's photograph as Peg's voice-over continues: "If my protesting of the war is that 'something,' then that's what I'll continue to do. My feeling now is a feeling of guilt. I feel I didn't do enough to enlighten my son. A mother who loses a son simply feels she didn't protect him, I suppose. . . . Even though he's a man, he's twenty-five years old, you feel you still should have been in there fighting for him. A mother can't let her son go there. It isn't the 'patriotism' thing anymore. This son is yours! He's part of you! . . . They'd have to drag him over my dead body to get him to go now. . . ."

The final sequence was filmed at the Mount Carmel Catholic Cemetery at Eagle Center. The Mullens drive into the cemetery, stop their car and get out. It is a long shot. Gene reaches into the backseat for a snow shovel, and then, with Peg wrapped up in a fur coat following slightly behind him, Gene walks up the slight hill to the grave. The wind-drifted snow has blown across Michael's flat headstone and Gene chips away at the ice with the edge of the shovel blade. There is no sound except the harsh grating of the steel shovel across the ice. Peg crosses herself, then kneels in the ice beside Michael's grave to pray. It is an awkward shot, too set-up, and Peg, shivering with cold and discomfort, stands without ever actually having looked at her son's grave. Gene is still chipping away at the ice. He kneels and wipes at the snow with his gloved hand, but a crust diagonally crossing the headstone will not come free. Gene straightens, picks up his shovel again, but before he can use it, he doubles over with grief. His shoulders shake, he buries his face in the back of his gloved hand, and Peg, seeing him weeping, lays a hand across his arm. She touches him for only a moment. Gene pulls himself together and begins shoveling again. The ice will not budge, and Gene crosses himself and prepares to leave. Peg, too, turns away from the grave but pauses and turns back. For the first time she looks at Michael's headstone. The camera is not in tight on her face, and she looks at his stone for only a second, but if one stops the projector entirely so that that one instant is frozen in a single frame one cannot help recognizing her expression. It is not anguish or sorrow; it is a terrible rage.

The camera follows the Mullens as they cautiously make their way down the glazed hill to their car; then it pans slowly back across the desolate Iowa landscape, back up the hill to the gravesite, and dips down for one last tight focus on the ice-locked stone:

-ael E. Mullen
-n Sept 11, 1944
-illed Feb 18, 1970
Son of Gene & Peg
-ared to ripple my pond"

(In June that year the Another Mother for Peace Committee arranged a showing of the film in an auditorium at the United States Capitol. All the Senators and Congressmen were invited to attend. The only Senators present were Senators Harold Hughes and Jack Miller of Iowa and former Senator Ernest Gruening of Alaska. Miller left before the Mullens' portion of the film was shown.)

Chapter Twenty

+++++++++++++++++++++

On April 12, 1971, a Monday about three weeks after the Another Mother for Peace film crew had departed, I drove up John Dobshire's dirt road to meet Peg and Gene Mullen for the first time.

For two and a half years, from the fall of 1967 through the spring of 1969, my wife and I had lived surrounded by cornfields in a small white frame two-story tenant farmhouse a few miles east of Iowa City. We rented the house from the Reverend and Mrs. Louis Penningroth, whose much grander house and barns stood at the top of the rolling hill about three-quarters of a mile to our southwest. The house and barns of Mr. and Mrs. Flowery Smith, our only other visible neighbors, lay in the opposite direction, across Rural Route 5, our dirt section line road, beyond the little stand of dead timber, atop the rolling hill to our northeast. In the late summer before the corn was cut, our tenant farmhouse seemed to ride like a chip of flotsam between two deep-green giant ocean swells. In the fall, however, when the corn was down, we could climb the pony pasture behind our house to the hilltop from which we flew our kites and, holding our arms straight out from our bodies, be pointing at nothing but sky. With the exception of our two neighbors' barns, there simply wasn't anything in the way. We could see for miles down the dirt road that passed our house, follow it with our eyes over the crest of the first hill, see it reappear as a thinner stripe crossing the hill after that, still thinner crossing the hill after that, and the one after that, like the road in a children's book. A children's book, exactly. We were very happy in Iowa. Life on that farm seemed pastoral, edenic, almost too good to be true.

In April, 1969, the month before we left Iowa to return East, President Nixon visiting Vietnam told some American ground troops about to go out on patrol, "I think history will record that this may have been one of America's finest hours because we took a difficult job and we succeeded." How was one to respond to that? Write another angry letter? March in another antiwar parade? To be honest, I didn't do a thing.

Iowa was a respite from that sort of activity; the crises in the rest of the world didn't seem so urgent there. Iowa was a return to the quiet tree-lined small-town streets of old *Saturday Evening Post* covers, rolled-up newspapers cast upon one's lawn, state fairs and soda pops, of being neighborly. The rest of America has always had a bemused, somewhat patronizing attitude toward Iowa. Perhaps this is because the state's ambience suggests the nineteenth century more than the twentieth. The majority of Iowa's 95.5 percent white population still lives in small towns or on farms. There are no large military installations in Iowa; Collins Radio in Cedar Rapids is practically the state's only industry linked with defense. Agriculture continues to be its primary business. Most Iowans depend directly or indirectly on farming for their livelihood, just as their ancestors did at the turn of the century. The eleven o'clock news is broadcast at ten o'clock Central Time so early-rising farmers can get their sleep.

While I was living there, I believed Iowa to be at least ten years behind the tensions, the conflicts, the polarizations of a California or a New York. I was wrong, of course. The 1968 Chicago Democratic Convention with its riots, tear gas, police clubs and sell-outs changed all that—changed it for many of the younger generation at any rate.

I was teaching at the University of Iowa's Writers Workshop, and a coed in one of my classes went to the Chicago convention to assist in Senator Eugene McCarthy's presidential campaign. She was the daughter of a central Iowa farmer and not an especially promising student; she would write extremely tense and anxious papers filled with "hences" and "thuses," but she was an exceptionally hard worker and terribly nice. Whenever we would throw a Sunday kite-flying party, she would show up with more food than she could possibly afford. And she would arrive later than the others because she would have attended church services and have had to return to her dormitory to change. After our first class following the Chicago convention she said she wanted to talk to me about what had taken place. We walked down to my office, and she took a seat opposite my desk. "Well," she said, taking a deep breath, "we arrived there in the afternoon. . . ." and that's all she said. She burst into tears, and each time she would try to speak, her words would emerge as cries instead. She would take another deep breath, swallow hard, shake her head and try again. For at least five minutes she sat across from me gasping for breath, her great shoulders heaving, tears coursing down her cheeks, fingers shredding the Kleenex tissues I had passed. Finally she pulled herself together and in a low, wounded voice said, "Oh, those sons of bitches! Those dirty sons of bitches!" and got up and left. What more could she say? What could any of us say?

During my three years in Iowa, 33,384 Americans had died in Vietnam; another 112,110 had been wounded. What could any of us do?

I didn't know of the Mullens when we lived in Iowa: La Porte City was about seventy-five miles to our north, and we had no reason to travel there. The Mullens' half-page advertisement appeared in the Des Moines *Register* almost a year after we had left. It wasn't until November, 1970, when I stopped off in Iowa for a few days to visit friends, that I heard about the Mullens at all.

Vance Bourjaily, the writer, and his wife, Tina, and I were sitting by the fireplace of their Iowa farmhouse having a drink and watching the late-afternoon

276

sky make up its mind whether to snow or not. We had been talking, naturally, about other writers and their books, but inevitably our conversation drifted to the Vietnam War. Tina asked me if I had heard of Peg Mullen. Vance had met her when they had flown about Iowa in behalf of the 609 amendment. Tina told me how Mrs. Mullen's son had been killed in Vietnam and instead of shutting up about it like a good patriotic Gold Star mother, she had angrily published an anti-war ad. Both Vance and Tina thought Mrs. Mullen might be worth looking into, that it sounded like a good story. "Mom's Apple Pie Gone Sour," I remember, was Tina's phrase. Still, I couldn't help asking myself who was left in America who would be willing to read a story which in any way touched the Vietnam War. I certainly didn't want to write one. Like everybody else, I was sick to death of hearing about Vietnam.

It took me six months to change my mind, six more months of watching the casualty figures on the evening television news before I realized that I was losing my capacity for outrage and shock, that I was simply acquiescing in what this nation's leaders were permitting our country to become. The police and volunteer firemen in the old New England town to which we had moved had suddenly taken to wearing American flags on their uniforms. Why? The wife of a local psychiatrist wanted to pull her son out of the Memorial Day parade because, like the others in his Boy Scout troop, he would have had to carry an American flag. Why? Bumper stickers read AMERICA! LOVE IT OR LEAVE IT! or depicted the flag with the legend THESE COLORS DO NOT RUN!

The turning point came for me when the President went out to Kansas State and told his audience, "The heart of America is sound. . . . The heart of America is good!" This simply wasn't true.

The heart of America was broken over the deaths of its young in Vietnamese jungles, in bunkers along the Cambodian border, in helicopters over Laos, on campus hilltops in Ohio and in dormitories at Jackson State. If the President thought otherwise, then, it seemed to me, it was a clear case of "The Emperor's Clothes." Could he be so out of touch that he was unaware of the growing hostility and frustration throughout the country? Wherever he went, he was met by protesters and picket signs. It further seemed to me that Mr. Nixon should have come away from his Kansas State experience impressed not, as he had bragged, that it was still possible for him to receive a resounding ovation from college students, but that he should have had to go to a Kansas State to receive one.

I felt there had to be some way to articulate the people's discontent, their estrangement from their government, their increasing paranoia and distrust. And what better way was there than to return to Iowa? Iowans are among the most open, honest, friendly, trusting people in the country. If they seemed unsophisticated, then they were unsophisticated in the best possible sense: they believed in personal honor, that a man's word had meaning and that he was responsible for his acts. If the government of the United States had lost the loyalty and support of an Iowa farm family, then it indicated, to me at least, that the government was in very grave trouble indeed.

The editor of the magazine with which I first discussed the possibility of doing an article on the Mullens asked if I thought Peg Mullen might be "deranged." He did not ask this because he felt Peg's protesting of her son's death was a symptom of any derangement, but rather out of concern for her health. If she were deranged, then any exploitation of her grief could only contribute to whatever imbalance she might have. And it was precisely the exploitation of her grief upon which any article would have to depend.

And yet when I first telephoned Peg Mullen, introduced myself and explained what it was I wanted to do, she was willing to have me come. In fact, I was a little startled and dismayed by how eagerly she had invited me. I left for Iowa two days later.

While driving out, I saw, opposite an Indiana Turnpike service station, a German shepherd just after it had been struck by a car. The impact must have broken the dog's hip because I watched it half drag,

278

half claw itself to the side of the road. And as I passed, I saw it twisting back to bite its hip where it had been struck.

I did not stop. I told myself I couldn't have even had I wanted to. A tractor trailer was highballing right behind me. Besides, what could I have done to help? The dog would probably have bitten me had I approached. There were people in the service area. Someone must have let him escape from a car. I drove on without slowing, ashamed that I hadn't stopped, incapable of shaking the image which to this day is so clearly imprinted on my mind: the grimace on that German shepherd's lips as it arced back to attack the terrible hurt.

There is a line in Nathanael West's *Miss Lonelyhearts* describing the advice-to-the-lovelorn columnist forcing himself to read the anguished letter from a woman who signed herself "Broadshoulders." "He read it," West explained, "for the same reason that an animal tears at a wounded foot: to hurt the pain."

I found myself wondering if something like that did not also partially explain the eagerness with which Peg Mullen invited me to come. In a strange way I still think it did. Peg Mullen, of course, disagrees. She invited me, she said, because the war was still raging, young men were still dying, and I was supposedly just writing a magazine piece which would have appeared a few months later when it might have been able to do someone, somewhere some good.

I turned into the Mullens' farm a little after twelve noon. I parked my car by the shed in which rested the old Farmall H-series tractor Michael had used to pull out the tree stumps his last night of leave. Peg Mullen, wearing slacks and a yellow short-sleeved sweat shirt with a SLIPPERY WHEN WET traffic sign printed in black on its front, met me at the farmhouse door. We had barely introduced ourselves when she said, "Michael would have just died if he had seen this lawn!" We both winced slightly. The hogs had broken through the fence again the night before and rooted up the spring rain-softened yard. The late March snows had melted away from the fields, but there was still snow in the ditches on either side of the section line roads. Since Gene was out in the lower field with his son John, Peg brought me into the kitchen and offered me lunch and coffee, apologizing for the papers covering the kitchen table.

There were dozens of sheets of stationery with letterheads from the Department of the Army, the Department of State, the United States Senate, Another Mother for Peace, various universities and business groups. There were newspaper clippings, stacks of typing paper, blue second sheets and carbons, a roll of stamps, several laboriously printed letters on ruled tablet paper. Peg cleared a space for me. I began pulling out my own papers and pens as Peg asked me how my trip had been, what I felt might happen to Captain Ernest Medina now that he had been formally accused of responsibility for the "alleged" murders committed by his infantry company at My Lai, and what the people "back East" thought of Richard Nixon and his "latest invasion of Laos."

I was trying to answer Peg's questions as best I could when Gene Mullen came up the back stairs followed by John. Gene agitatedly paced from the window by the sink to the side window facing the barns. His hands were constantly working, tapping the windowsill, tugging at his belt, adjusting his half-frame glasses, brushing back his silver hair. He patted the shoulder of his son John, who had seated himself quietly in a corner. Then, impatient to get on with it, Gene sat at the kitchen table, swept some papers aside with his arm, gestured for me to pull my chair closer, took one of my yellow pads and a pen and started right in.

"One boy was on guard here," he said. He drew an oval on the legal pad and placed a small circle near one edge. "Each platoon had their own guard. Schumacher, he was Third Platoon." He circled Schumacher's position again. "Culpepper was in the Third Platoon. Platoon Sergeant Webb was Third Platoon. . . ." Gene drew two more circles.

"Gaynor was Third Platoon," Peg said. "We've heard only from Third Platoon boys."

"And Abe Aikins, the medic, was stationed here." He drew another circle. "We have letters from all these boys. We can tie it all in. Wherever you set up a defensive perimeter, your forward observer radios back to your artillery unit to get your coordinates in case of an enemy attack. The boys tell us they fired a little around eight o'clock."

"There's a conflict in their stories there," Peg said. "One boy says they never fired at all. That they called off the artillery and didn't test it that night. Two of the boys said they did fire artillery around eight o'clock and finished. But the shot that killed them came in at two thirty, and nobody believes it was called in."

"It wasn't called in," Gene stated flatly.

"We're searching for this Lieutenant Rocamora because he was the forward observer who would have requested the artillery."

"Now whenever you have artillery," Gene said, "you can fire from this point here. . . ." He made an X on the yellow pad below and to one side of the oval "hill." "Or from this point here," Gene continued, marking another X above and to the other side of the "hill."

"It's against the Army Code to fire over a group," Peg explained. "But this is what they did. They were firing right over the boys' heads evidently."

"The shell came in, and it killed Michael, here." Gene drew an X within the oval. "Leroy Hamilton, here." He marked an X near Michael's. "And a colored boy name of Polk, Private Polk from Detroit, was right between them and wasn't even scarred. There were seven boys wounded in the First Platoon. We know of a boy name of Prince who lost his leg—"

"—We're trying to locate him, too."

"—and this boy Polk went berserk. He tried to kill the artillery forward observer for calling in the shot. They handcuffed him. And that morning when the choppers came in to pick up the dead and wounded—"

"Gene," Peg interrupted, "that was over a period of about three days."

"Just be quiet, please. After the helicopters came in, Charlie Company was moved over to another ridge

281

for the boys to cool off. Sergeant Webb, who lives down to Des Moines, was guarding this boy Polk, but Polk got loose and took a machine gun and started spraying some Vietnamese working in a rice paddy. He also evidently struck a couple officers. So a helicopter came in and picked Polk up. They gave him a shot of sedatives that almost killed him—"

"The medic saved Polk's life!" Peg said. "He went into shock from the sedatives."

"The medic had to revive him. When they got back to Chu Lai, they had twenty-seven charges against Polk. Now here's his letter." Gene pushed a letter across the table to me. The rush of voices ceased.

Polk's letter, dated four days earlier, had a "Drawer 'A,' Fort Leavenworth, Kansas" return address.

Dear Mrs. Gene:

I received your letter today. I must say that your letter brought back some sad memory. Yes I was in Michael platoon, He was my platoon sergeant at the time of his Death.

You might have been told this, but I'll like to tell you again. I was with your son at the time of his Death. Michael Died in his sleep, he never woke up. Before his Death him and I became very close friend. I was the only Black in our Squad, and I can honestly say I had heard the word Nigger enough to last me a life time. You see I could talk with Michael, he didn't care if you was Black or White. He was a good guy and we both had a Great Deal of Respect for each other.

You know I almost went to jail the night of the Accident. I was trying to get to our Fire Detection Officer. Today I still believe he call the rounds in short. Anyway the guys in the Company keep me away from him.

You might like to know, if you don't already know, the reason why I'm in jail. Well it started right after Michael Died. I was out in the field when this E-5 call me a Nigger, I came close to shooting him. But I was talk out of it buy the Officer in our Company. I was treated unfair because of my color. People dislike me in the Company with out full knowledge of the type of person I was. I was Prejudg the day I got into Co. C., 1/6, 198th. Your son Michael, and Prince, and a few other Blacks who names I can no longer remember, were the only People in the Company I could communicate with. Well, on the 26th of Feb 1971 I woke up in the hospital with a concussion and a contusion on the side of my face. They said I shot at some Friendly Vietnamese and hit a Lt. (Officer) and a E-6. All the while I was in the field and saw the Death of your son I was Depress. I often have Dream about that night, and sometimes I can't sleep for thinking about them guys and how young they were. Please excuse me, but you are the first person I have talk with fully about that night and it Feel Good To Do So.

I have been lock up for 14 months and I'm tired of this. All I want is to get out of jail and see my Family. I haven't seen them in 16 month. I'll be so glad to see them (smile). I guess I'll have to wait until June 1, 1972. I wish you could Be of some help to me, Mrs. Gene, but you see I don't know what to ask you. If you could stop by and visited me I would like that Very Much. Oh yes! I try to get your address in March 1970 to write you to tell you how Sorry I was. But they wouldn't give me your address.

Well, until I hear from you may God blessing be with you and your family.

Sincerely yours,
s/Willard

P.S.: Happy Easter.

"The clue to everything is Private Polk at Leavenworth," Peg said when she saw I'd finished the letter. "We asked him to send us the name of Prince, the white boy who Culpepper told us had lost a leg that night—they didn't think he would live, but he did. We want to meet Prince because he was in the First Platoon. . . . The thing is, I don't know whether we are just suspicious characters or whatever, but right away we didn't believe what we were told. And this

283

whole story we were first told by the service officer about the ARVN artillery, we repeated it, of course. So when the boys in Vietnam read about us in the newspaper, how I'd said Michael had been killed by South Vietnamese artillery, that's when we found out the truth. They wrote back that Michael had been killed by *our* artillery. That there had been investigations made."

Speaking very slowly, Gene said, "We have asked for the artillery log. You see a record of every shot fired has to be kept for one year. We wrote Senator Fulbright—"

"He and Senator Hughes are trying to get it for us."

"We want to know if that shot was scheduled, see? Who called it in? That information has to be in the artillery log. It has to be in there!" Gene sorted through some papers and pushed one to me. "Read this. It's the death certificate for my son."

Before I had a chance to finish it, Gene said, "Michael did *not* have a missile wound in the chest. He was lying on his left side. He used to sleep on his left side." Gene pushed himself back from the table and stood up. "The wound was right through here," he said, pointing at his right kidney. "The undertaker told us that."

"This is something we'll never, never be sure of. We don't know why we. . . ." Peg paused and rubbed the corners of her eyes wearily. "About a month ago we met a couple, and this is what the father did. After everybody left the funeral home, he undressed his boy from head to foot to see if it was his boy. They couldn't tell because their son had been hurt in the face. The father undressed him because he knew his boy had a birthmark on his shoulder. He didn't know where he got the strength to do that. He said it took superhuman power, and he couldn't do it again, but he said, 'I did it that night. I had to know.' And, see, my older brother when we brought Michael back here said, 'Peg, you've got to find out what happened to him. Look at him!' he said. 'He could have had a stroke the way he looks!' "

284

"The shock I got when we opened the casket and there wasn't a mark on him!" Gene said. "I'll never forget it. Never!"

I spent five days with the Mullens that April out on their farm for the most part listening to them talk about their son, Michael, what a fine, hardworking young man he had been, how he had been active in 4-H projects, had worked his way through college and into graduate school, how he would have been the fifth generation of his family to work the same land homesteaded by his great-great-grandfather John Dobshire, 120 years before. What impressed me most was how positive and unshakable they were in their opinions, as though they were responding to issues the morality of which could be clearly and unmistakenly determined—issues which were, therefore, capable of being judged against existing standards of right and wrong.

The intensity of their indignation wasn't all that overwhelmed me. I was astonished, too, by the seemingly inexhaustible volume of sources their outrage fed upon. Local school board elections, telephone company stock manipulations, draft inequities, Nixon's Vietnamization policies, farm subsidy programs, the voting records of incumbent Congressmen and Senators, the machinations of the military-industrial complex, each seemed to contribute to some consummate proof of a conspiracy on the part of the United States government deliberately to deceive and defraud Mr. and Mrs. Oscar Eugene Mullen of La Porte City, Iowa. It became clear, however, that the Mullens' indignation, their sense of betrayal, stemmed from a vision of an America better fitted, perhaps, to an innocent history primer, one capable of expressing a faith in a simpler America—an America which probably never even used to be. One other thing became clear, too, those first five days: the Mullens' surviving son and daughters would never possess so naïve a confidence in this nation's purpose or its leaders. This, in a very real sense, is as great a tragedy as the loss of a son.

The Mullens rarely needed to be prompted or

285

asked; too much time had passed since anyone had encouraged them to talk. Sometimes their voices were soft, gentle; at other times, they spoke so angrily their words seemed to darken the air about us. Equally expressive would be those sounds which were not spoken at all: the slam of a hand hitting the table in rage, the breath caught because an onrushing memory was causing too much pain, the sigh. Mixed in with their charges and complaints would be numbers: the numbers of dead, of wounded, of nonbattle casualties, unit designations, congressional amendments, the numbers of bills pending, votes needed, letters received or sent, postage paid out, friends who had defected, friends made anew, the number of documents received, copies run off, dollars spent, days used up, weeks waiting, months passed, years wasted. Papers were always rustling in the background, letters, documents, telegrams, carbons, Xeroxes, corroborating evidence shifting about. And, too, there was that full panoply of emotions exposed: Gene belligerent, furious, impatient, confused, exhausted, tender and, in the next instant, anguished, unsure of himself, inchoate, in tears. And Peg: abrasive, demanding, cocky, maternal, protective and then so suddenly lonely and gutted, defensive and vulnerable, so tired and exiled by anger and grief.

During those five days on their farm they would over and over again describe themselves as "typical." Their detachment about themselves was what had, at first, seemed so puzzling about their unself-consciousness in that Another Family for Peace film. It was as though they viewed themselves as representative rather than actual and, by so doing, eliminated any presumable inhibitions. They abdicated privacy in favor of exposure, and yet they seemed not to have any sense of exposing themselves because "they" did not exist as individuals. "They" were indistinguishable from people like them.

"We want people to know," Gene said that first afternoon, "what it's like to walk down the streets of your own town and have your friends cast one look at you, then turn their heads away because they have a

286

guilt complex that your son died in this war. We want to know why we have to say hello *first!*"

"Well"—Peg sighed—"as I said to Gene before, this is something we've done to ourselves. . . . You don't realize the depth to which in Iowa, a farm state, a conservative state, one is taught to respect the flag, the government. It involves our whole school syst—" Peg paused. She saw me turn off the small tape recorder I had brought to put in a fresh cassette.

It was not the first time that day the Mullens halted in midsentence when I had had to change tapes. It bothered me initially that they could seemingly "turn on and off" at will, but I simply did not recognize the obvious: the Mullens stopped because the tape stopped. There was nothing studied or playacting about it. They stopped because the recorder, like the pens and yellow legal pads with which I wrote, were instruments of record, a means of capturing, preserving and disseminating everything that had happened to them. With the exception of the Another Mother for Peace film crew, no one had shown any interest in them for a long, long time. Therefore, each hour spent, each page covered, each cassette filled encouraged them, comforted them in their need to believe that the anguish they had been through might somehow prove to have been worthwhile.

"It involves our whole school system from the kindergarten on up," Peg continued when the tape resumed. "Iowa is a very patriotic state. People here took great pride in being a member of the Silent Majority. That is why we decided to run that first advertisement. We were driven by the fact that we had to speak out in some way. We had to rouse the people, waken them, warn them that since it happened to us, it could happen to them."

"There've been a hunnert and twelve killed since we ran—no, wait," Gene said.

"Hundred and eighteen," Peg corrected him. "Eighteen since the first of this year and a hundred during the year before."

"It's so hard to talk to people," Gene said, shaking his head.

287

"They don't want to talk to us. They don't. They know the war is wrong, and now a hunnert and eighteen more are dead. Well, what do you do! . . . All these parents. . . . What do you say when a man tells you your boy is *dead?*"

Peg had been invited to address an Another Mother for Peace meeting my last evening with the Mullens. We arrived at the basement of the Catholic Student Center near the campus of the University of Northern Iowa in Cedar Falls just after eight o'clock. Card tables had been set up against one orange-brown cinder-block wall to display Another Mother for Peace literature, posters, sample cards and letters to be sent Congress in support of holding public hearings into the granting of offshore oil leases throughout Indochina and those proposed specifically off the coast of Vietnam.

Approximately fifty persons were present; although a few men and children stood about, the vast majority were women in slacks and pantsuits. The younger women wore their hair long, natural, the middle-aged women had spray-set bouffants, and the older women simple, almost boyish haircuts. Many of them greeted Peg by name and spoke with her briefly before drifting away.

The chairwoman called the meeting to order, and everyone moved to the folding chairs set up for the showing of Bess Myerson's *You Don't Have to Buy War, Mrs. Smith,* an Another Mother for Peace film.

The film urged women to boycott those companies which also manufactured war goods: Alcoa, for example, built rocket tubes; General Electric made the multiple individually targetable reentry vehicle (MIRV); Bulova, metal parts for high explosive shell fuses; Honeywell, antipersonnel mines; and so forth. The film proposed that Dow, for example, should cease manufacturing napalm and create, instead, a nonpolluting detergent. Over and over again the point emphasized was: "Whirlpool, get out of the beehive projectile business and build us a washing machine that doesn't self-destruct and we'll buy it. General Motors, instead of building electronic assemblies for torpedoes, build us an automobile that doesn't pollute and we'll buy it."

Following the film there were announcements on the need to send those postcards off to Congress, and then a young man in a black and yellow striped T-shirt and blue jeans, stepped barefoot up to the center of the room and discussed the upcoming April 24 anti-war march in Washington. "What we need from you," he explained, "is food, moral support and forty dollars for bus fare."

I leaned over and asked Peg if she planned to attend. She shook her head no.

Next an earnest young mother proposed planting a tree for peace on Memorial Day. "Some living symbol," she said, "which we can dedicate to ourselves, our children and peace. . . ."

She was succeeded by the chairwoman, who introduced Peg: "If you don't know her personally, I'm sure you've heard of her." The chairwoman mentioned the Another Mother for Peace film crew's visit to the Mullen farm and then, turning to Peg, said, "Peg's lost her voice, but can you muster enough to tell us about the film being made?"

Peg was suffering from a mild case of laryngitis caused as much by five days of constant conversation as the onset of a cold.

Peg walked up to the podium. "Nothing has ever stopped me from talking yet," she said hoarsely. She spoke briefly about the film, how the film crew had stayed four days at the farm and seemed pleased with the footage they had shot. "I'm not going to look much like Bess Myerson." She laughed. "In fact, I had to fight with them to let me comb my hair." She then told of the mother and father she had recently heard about whose son was in Vietnam. After learning that the mother had voted for Nixon in the 1968 presidential election, the father had said, "I hope I won't ever have to say, 'I told you so.'" At that exact moment their doorbell rang. It was the survivors' assistance officer, come to tell them that their son was dead.

Peg reported having been invited by the Vietnam

289

Veterans Against the War to march with them in Washington and that "the Boston people have something called S.O.S., meaning Save Our Sons. The plan," Peg explained, "is for everyone to send Nixon a photograph of your son whether he's eighteen months or eighteen years with the message that you're not going to let him go to war." She spoke about that plan for a while and of her own letter-writing campaign shortly after Michael had died, how they had hoped to accumulate 100,000 carbons of letters protesting the war. She told how she had been able to get Larry Phelps out of Vietnam. The audience was beginning to stir. One could hear pocketbooks opening and snapping shut, papers rustling.

". . . and from September on, Phelps neither gave nor obeyed an order," Peg was saying. "He had been sent to the First Cav Division, and there were then only sixty men left who would even shoulder or fire a gun. Those sixty, he told me, were just mercenaries. They'd kill anybody. But Senator Goodell* when he spoke here last Sunday, he said, 'If you save one life, you've accomplished something.' And I thought to myself, 'Well, gee, I have!' All that I've done, all the enemies, friends I have made were worth getting that one boy, Larry Phelps, out of Vietnam."

Peg's voice became stronger. "We've searched since last summer for a boy named Polk who was with our son," she said. "He was asleep next to Michael when Michael and the boy on the other side were killed. Polk woke up and went berserk. . . ." Peg talked on and on about Polk, and the woman to my right took a long and sour look at her wristwatch. It was after ten o'clock; Peg had been speaking for half an hour.

Peg turned her attention to the percentage of Congressmen's sons drafted. When Peg started on Senator Hughes' position on the draft, a man stood up and walked to the back of the room for his coat. By the time she covered Senator Goodell's comments about all the young men in prison because of court-martials

---

*Senator Charles E. Goodell (R. N.Y.), defeated in 1970 by Republican Conservative Party candidate James L. Buckley.

and how all aid was cut off to their families, there was a low hum of voices in the room.

"Oh, and another thing," Peg said, "This could go on. This is somewhat of an obsession with me." Peg began talking about the deduction from Michael's final paycheck, and the woman on my right groaned and stood up. She reached behind her folding chair for her purse and coat and walked out. "I threatened them with a congressional investigation," Peg was saying. "They deducted nine days' pay, nine days' rations, nine days' leave. . . ."

More people were standing. A man began winding up the motion-picture projector cord.

"We had requested an audit, see," Peg continued, "and when they sent it to us, well, it was the first time in my whole life I lost control."

A man in front of me stood and tapped the woman next to him. She rose also.

"Well, I never have a good ending," Peg said ruefully. "I never know when to stop. . . ." She stepped away from the podium to a smattering of polite applause. The people with their coats on in the back of the room clapped without interrupting their conversations. The chairwoman stepped forward and thanked Peg. Suddenly there was a stir in the back by the door, and a group swirled into the room talking excitedly. Someone hurried up to the podium and whispered to the chairwoman who then rapped for attention.

"Ladies and gentlemen, please," she said, "we have some very thrilling news. Eqbal Ahmad, who was addressing the college tonight and who is one of the Harrisburg Six on trial with the Berrigan brothers,* is

---

The Reverend Philip F. Berrigan, forty-seven, already serving a six-year term in the Federal Prison at Danbury, Connecticut, on charges of destroying draft records (Catonsville 9 trial), was then, along with five others, indicted by a Harrisburg, Pennsylvania, grand jury on charges of conspiring to kidnap then-Presidential Adviser Henry A. Kissinger and of plotting to blow up the heating tunnels of federal buildings in Washington, D.C. Among those indicted with Philip Berrigan were his brother, the Reverend Daniel Berrigan, the Reverend Joseph R. Wenderoth, the Reverend Neil R. McLaughlin, former priest Anthony Scoblick, Sister Elizabeth McAlister of Marymount College and Eqbal Ahmad, a fellow of the Adlai Stevenson Institute of Public Affairs.

291

coming here in a few moments and has consented to say a few words to us!"

Peg watched the people in the back of the room removing their overcoats and moved back against a wall, utterly alone.

Moments later Eqbal Ahmad bounced in like a puppy full of enthusiasm and joy. He declined to use the podium and spoke instead from the center of the room where the motion-picture projector had been set up. In a soft, melodic voice he laughingly told of his mother's concern that her forty-year old Hindu son had been placed on trial with "two ungodlies."

" 'Mama,' I said, 'you know that in every human being there is something good and something evil,' " Ahmad was saying. " 'It is the difference between the saints and the devils. But this fellow, Nixon, Mama,' I said, 'he is trying to bring out the worst in the country.' " Ahmad remarked upon the paranoia of contemporary American politics and how no conspiracy could be complete without "foreign agitators."

"But our writings and our actions speak for themselves," Ahmad said. "We have denied the substance of the charges against us. In principle and in fact we abhor violence and the kind of acts of which we are accused. We are challenging the government outside the court and inside the court to prove one instance where we have lied to the American people. None of us has ever told a lie or betrayed the government. And we are challenging the United States government to prove one instance in which the Presidents of the United States between 1965 and now have told a single instance of truth to the American people about our involvement in Vietnam. We have challenged the government. And in return, these criminals of war have challenged we men of peace."

Someone asked what could be done to aid the Berrigans.

"The best way to help them," Ahmad replied, "is to work more to get this war to stop. If only fifty thousand show up in Washington next week, Nixon will see it as a victory. Go to Washington," Ahmad urged. "Go to Washington and work very hard for the people's peace treaty."

As the crowd shifted around Eqbal Ahmad, I caught sight of Peg Mullen again. She was still alone, seated on an aisle folding chair and looked tired, sad.

Ahmad was urging public hearings into the FBI and compared the imprisonment of Angela Davis to that of Lieutenant Calley.* Calley was free in his quarters at Fort Benning. "There is an imbalance here," Ahmad was saying. "The crimes Calley committed were crimes against humanity, crimes committed in pursuit of obeying orders given him by his President, the Cabinet and presidential advisers. And yet," Ahmad said quietly, "it was Calley who was made the scapegoat. . . . Aren't you shocked the American people are now trying to make a hero out of him? Why do you suppose they are doing this? Why are these Americans protesting Calley's sentence?" Ahmad cocked his head to one side and smiled. "Because they sense that Calley's trial is their trial as well. They are crying to the President, 'Get us off the hook, too!' "

Ahmad mentioned where he would be speaking

---

*On March 29, 1971, a court-martial jury of six officers convicted First Lieutenant William L. Calley, Jr., of premeditated murder of 22 South Vietnamese men, women and children at the hamlet of My Lai on March 16, 1968. The jury, following thirteen days of deliberation, convicted Calley of 22 deaths rather than the 102 deaths he had been charged with, because witnesses disputed the number during the trial. On March 31, the same jury sentenced Calley to life imprisonment, along with dismissal from the service and forfeiture of pay and allowances.

The guilty verdict brought on enormous public reaction. The Calley case became a rallying symbol for debates over the morality of the Indochina War. The verdict was denounced in Congress, state legislatures, at public meetings, and resolutions demanding Calley's release were passed. Vietnam veterans attempted to turn themselves in claiming they were just as guilty as Calley. Draft boards resigned. In Indiana the state flag was flown at half-mast.

Many saw Calley as a "scapegoat" for others higher in the chain of command. As the public outcry continued, President Nixon ordered Calley on April 1 to be moved from the stockade to his quarters at Fort Benning until his case could be reviewed. Nixon added he would personally review Calley's case "before any final sentence is carried out." The President was accused of "unprecedented intervention." Others defended Nixon's action as his legal right as Commander in Chief of the armed forces.

next, thanked everyone for listening and was immediately surrounded by a crowd of well-wishers. Peg stood up, took one step toward Ahmad, hesitated, then remained forlorn and forgotten by her chair.

I walked over, and immediately she asked if I was ready to return to La Porte.

"Whenever you are," I said.

She looked over at Eqbal Ahmad, the center of attention. "Why don't we leave now?"

A few of Peg's friends stopped by as she put on her coat. The woman thanked Peg for her talk, and Peg replied she felt she had spoken too long. The chairwoman smiled, patted Peg's arm and told her to go home and rest her voice.

We spoke little during the drive back to the farm. Peg was obviously tired. I was thinking over what she had said. Throughout her telling of how Michael had died, what had happened to her family, her role in getting Larry Phelps out of Vietnam, the court-martial of Private Willard Polk, I had recognized instances in which her version of the events had differed from what she had initially told me, instances that night at Cedar Falls where the truth had been slightly embroidered. I wondered why she had felt this necessary. The truth was offensive enough. I came to understand that the truth was no longer adequately outrageous to Peg.

She had lived with the truth for more than a year. Now a darker conspiracy had to be hinted at; the Army's behavior had to seem more callous; the government's indifference more deliberate, the survivors' assistance officers more inept. By so doing, Peg could refuel her anger, sustain that high level of outrage necessary to battle those forces responsible for taking away from her forever her firstborn child. It was the only way she could cope with the awful grief she felt. The one time during those five days I spent with the Mullens that Peg ever cried was when she spoke of having reared Michael to accept unquestioningly the authority of the United States government. By magnifying the military's guilt, she could minimize this, the source of her own. She and Gene had let their son be

294

drafted. As a result, Peg's was the sort of grief which transcends tears; it was an arid, furied Medean grief, one in which anguish is indistinguishable from rage. And, to a lesser extent, I believe it was clear by this time even to Peg that the longer she could remain angry and actively fight the war, the longer she could prolong the illusion that she was helping Michael, she might postpone that crushing moment when she would be forced to admit that there was nothing, nothing whatsoever, she could do for Michael Mullen anymore. Michael was dead.

We turned off Route 218 and onto John Dobshire's dirt road. Our headlights swept too high to illuminate the drainage ditches on either side. The road, silvered by the frost, lay isolated by the darkness and seemingly floated above the land. As Peg pulled into the farm and parked, she asked, "Do you really have to go back tomorrow?"

"I think I'd better," I said.

"You'll come by in the morning, won't you? Have breakfast with us at least?"

"I'd like to very much."

We got out of the car, and I caught up with Peg, who was standing by the path leading to the kitchen door. She brushed a hand across the top of one of the little evergreens Michael had planted his last day on the farm. "Was I awful?" she asked. "Did I talk too much? Go on too long?" She did not wait for me to answer. "I always do," she said. "I never seem to know when to stop."

"Peg, you were fine."

"Do you think they listened?"

"Of course they listened."

"But do you think they cared?"

Friday morning, April 16, Gene and I were sitting at the kitchen table drinking coffee, and he said, "People ask us have we done anything? What have we accomplished? . . . Well, I think we've helped break through to the Silent Majority on Vietnam." He leaned back in his chair so that its front legs were off the ground. "When I went to work after Michael's funeral up to Deere's, the men would look at me and it was still, 'We've got to have this war, Oscar. We've got to do it!' But in the last four, five months the attitude has changed. Now they come up to me and tell me, 'Oscar, we're *wrong!*' They say, 'We've got to get out of there. How can we get out?'

"I tell them, 'Write a letter,' " Gene continued. "They say, 'They won't listen to my letter.'

"I tell them, 'Write a thousand of them! Two, three, *four* thousand letters,' " Gene said. "But the attitude is changing here in Iowa. I had one hard-core Republican, one of those loyal to the party, tell me just two weeks ago, the day after the President's decision to release Calley from the stockade, he said, 'Oscar, I'm ashamed of my country. I'm ashamed that I voted for that man in the White House. What's wrong with my country?' "

Gene smiled. "I said, 'Warren, what's wrong with my country and your country is you allowed it to happen.' "

"It's what's wrong with us all," Peg added.

"I told Warren, 'You allowed it to happen so long as it didn't affect your boy. You were hoping and praying this war would get over with, but,' I said, 'it isn't going to be over with. This Nixon was a bug about Communism. He figures himself a second General Patton. A hero. But,' I said, 'you look at his past record. Even in 1954 he wanted to send U.S. troops to fight in Vietnam.* Eisenhower had to shut him up.' "

"It's the same all over the country," Peg said. "If you don't have a son in Vietnam—well, you've seen for yourself how they react around here."

"People keep telling us, 'You're going to destroy yourselves,' " Gene said. "They say—"

---

*In April, 1954, during the desperate battle for Dienbienphu, then-Vice President Richard M. Nixon stated that if the French were unable to hold, Indochina "would become Communist dominated within a month. The United States . . cannot afford further retreat in Asia. It is hoped the United States will not have to send troops there, but if this government cannot avoid it, the Administration must face up to the situation and dispatch forces."—*New York Times*, April 17, 1954.

"I don't care," Peg said.

"They say over and over again, 'You must stop. You're going to destroy yourselves!' But we don't think so."

"I don't care!" Peg repeated.

"Do you think the past year has changed you?" I asked.

Gene shrugged and looked over at Peg.

"Yes," Peg replied, "Yes, Gene, you've changed. I haven't. I don't think I've changed."

Gene pushed himself away from the table and walked into the living room. He returned with a framed photograph of Michael. Wedged in the bottom, between the wooden frame and the glass, was a poem from one of the consolation cards sent them after Michael's death. "When I think of my boy," Gene said, "I say that poem about him being happy in heaven fifteen, twenty times a day."

Peg sighed. "Gene gets consolation from the fact that he thinks Michael is in heaven. I don't. . . ." Peg paused for a moment. "See, Gene has accepted Michael's death. I haven't." She began pushing some of the letters back and forth across the kitchen table. "I don't know if I ever will."

No one spoke. Peg remained with her head lowered. Gene was rubbing his chin, looking down at the photograph of Michael, which lay flat on the table before him. He took a deep breath, let it out slowly and turned to me. "I know you have to be leaving us soon," he said, "but I'd like to ask one favor of you before you go. I'd like you to drive over to the cemetery again to see Mikey with me. Will you do that?"

"Of course," I said. I looked over at Peg.

She shook her head. "I've got some letters to write."

Gene and I left the house together, and he paused by his car. "See that tractor in the shed there, the old red Farmall?" he asked me. "Mike was so small when he was six years old that when he used to go down after the cattle, down that eighty acres back there that my great-grandfather acquired from those two German

297

Walker boys, I'd put Mikey on the tractor, start him out on the road, put the tractor in low gear. He used to have to stand up. He could not sit in the seat and steer. So he'd stand up, and I'd say, 'Now, Mikey, if anything happens, take your knee and push in that button there and that'll stop the tractor immediately.' See, it'd stall out in low gear. Well, at six years of age," Gene continued, "he used to go down to the pasture and bring the cattle back up here for milking time and —oh! I had some shorthorns. Great, big cows. Well, they'd be up here in the cattle yard all winter, and they'd know that day in the spring of the year when they were supposed to go down to the blue grass pasture. I had an old, big white cow who was the lead cow. . . . We used to take them down the road there, and the cattle had to make a right turn to get to the pasture. Well, Mikey would have to run ahead to get them to turn, and the cows would always run faster than him and scatter all over. So we bought him an English racing bike for Christmas, and all winter he was planning. 'Boy, I'm going to beat those cows down to the corner! Well"—Gene smiled—"the day we put the cattle down to the pasture, we got them out onto the road, and Mike gets on his bicycle and tries to beat that old lead cow—he tried, but the cow was still faster than he was on that English racing bike!" Gene lifted his cap and ran his fingers through his hair. "I'll never forget it." He laughed, replacing his cap. "Never forget it!"

He was looking down the road at where the cows would have to be turned to reach the pasture, but he was seeing a small dark-haired six-year-old boy, hunched over a racing bike, elbows akimbo, knees pumping crazily, trying to beat an old white lead cow to the corner.

Walking up the slight hill to Michael's grave, Gene said, "I've been thinking about what you asked, had we changed? And Peg said I had. Well, she's right. I'm a very changed man. I'm not afraid to die. I go on and don't worry about the crops getting in. It seems like someone is watching over us all the time. . . ." He glanced at me quickly. "Maybe I sound foolish to think that?"

Gene prayed silently, then crossed himself at the foot of Michael's grave. "He was so loved by his brother and sisters, so *loved!*" Gene stooped over and picked up a piece of scrap paper that had blown onto Michael's grave. "I'll never forget that forlorn look on his face at the airport when he told us not to stick around." He crumpled the paper and shoved it into his pocket. "Peg used to put him out in the sandbox behind the house where he played for hours and hours. 'Hoggy house,' he used to say. 'Maduder.' He couldn't say 'manure.' Because I was working, I watched him grow up as if from far away, but I was so proud of him!" Gene paused, determined not to cry. "I just opened the fields to him, you know? I was so very proud of my son. . . ."

He looked up from the grave to the rolling hills that stretched to the distant horizon. "I could justify Mike's death if he had died of an illness. I could justify it if he had died in an accident. I can't justify the way he was killed—I didn't say 'died,' I said *'killed.'* You can see what it says on the headstone. . . . That's what we put there because we can't justify the death of any boy in Vietnam."

We stood by Michael's grave in silence; then Gene placed his hand upon my shoulder. "I thank you for coming." His hand fell away, and we both turned toward the car.

On the drive back to the farm Gene said, "You've spent some time with us now. You've gotten to know Peg. She's a very forceful, righteous person. She's critical not because she sees evil, but because she wants to see goodness. . . . She has so much compassion for people. Everybody calls her Peg. Everybody. Little kids. Older people. She got mail delivered simply addressed 'Peg. La Porte City.' Even some came 'Concerned Parent, La Porte City.' You've seen what she does all day long," he continued. "Answering those letters. You saw how many phone calls we get a day and the sort of people they come from. Good, decent people. Peg has to do this. *She has to fight this war!* Oh! Over there," Gene said, pointing through the windshield at the field to our right, "that's where my grandfather, Patrick J. Mullen, had his barn with all the horses. Each boy had eight working horses and his own driving team. Can you imagine the names they gave them?" He smiled. "It's all gone now." We drove on in silence for a few minutes, then turned onto the dirt road past Hubbard Frost's old place with the huge boulder in the field, turned again onto John Dobshire's dirt road and into the Mullens' farm.

"The only time Peg has trouble with her grief is when she sees things that Mike did, like that basketball backstop behind the house." Gene switched off the engine and sat gripping the steering wheel, looking through the windshield at the backstop. "He was about fourteen when he put it up," Gene told me. "I said, 'Mikey, the wind'll blow it down. It'll never stand.' I wasn't trying to ridicule him. I was only trying to save him from failure. But he wasn't going to fail. He was going to put it up there. He was *determined*. And look at it. It's staying up there still. . . ." He turned to me. "You know, people think we're crazy. That we couldn't have had a boy like Michael, like we say he was. But we did. God gave me a boy like that and . . . and. . . ." His grip tightened on the wheel, and he looked away from me. "I don't know why! That's what hurts. . . . It hurts so much!"

Gene's hands dropped from the steering wheel. He removed the key from the ignition and opened his door. "I wish you'd known him," he said.

The instant we entered the house Peg handed me a letter. "Here, read this," she said. "I just finished it."

The letter was addressed to the Director of the Internal Revenue Service, Des Moines, Iowa, and contained a check for the balance due on the Mullens' 1970 federal income tax:

I pay this tax under protest, and with a sickened heart. I do not like the heavy hand of the law forcing me to buy materials to rain more death and destruction on friend and foe alike. I

300

find it almost impossible to live with the thought that my money paid the tax that bought the artillery shell that killed our son in Vietnam.

If it were my choice alone, whether or not to pay this tax, I would not pay it, and gladly go to jail to dramatize my point. . . . But I have a family . . . a husband who would in all probability lose his job . . . and children who would be forced to leave college.

I am sure that the "computer" who handles income tax monies is very grateful that it cannot think.

Sincerely,
s/Mrs. O. E. Mullen

"I'm sending a carbon to Nixon and Senator Hughes," Peg said. "But you don't think anybody'll read it, do you?"

"Senator Hughes will," Gene said.

"Peg, once you get in touch with Private Polk at Leavenworth and the others," I said, "what do you plan to do with the information they give you? What's next?"

"We're waiting for one letter, to find one man," Gene answered. "Lieutenant Rocamora."

"We don't believe Rocamora called in the round that killed Michael," Peg said. "We want Rocamora to tell us he didn't call it in. Mike's death was investigated the following day, as we've said. But we've never been sent the results of that investigation, even though they promised us they would. Several of the boys we've been in touch with indicated that either the officer and the men on the gun were drunk—"

"Or they think it was an old gun," Gene said. "Or that someone else called in the target coordinates wrong."

"Those three things," Peg said. "That's right. But, see, there's nothing we can prove. . . ." Her voice trailed off.

"But assuming you found out the worst," I said, "that the artillery forward observer was drunk or that the battery commander and his men back at the guns

301

were drunk and had been firing off shells as a lark and one of them exploded and killed Michael. What are you going to do then?"

Without a moment's hesitation Peg replied, "We're going to demand about five hundred thousand dollars."

"Michael was in the citizens' army," Gene said.

"His potential, even with just the degree he had at the time he went to Vietnam, was from thirty to forty thousand dollars a year in his field. We don't want the money for ourselves," Peg said. "But we think they destroyed somebody with a terrific future for no reason."

"We know *something* happened there that night," Gene said, "and we know they're trying to cover it up."

"The fact that it was never a news item," Peg said. "We feel that with the one platoon being practically wiped out, the two men killed and seven wounded, that alone would have been a news release."

"If Mike had died on the streets of La Porte City," Gene said, "if some drunk had run over him, that would have been manslaughter, and there would have been a trial. Well, we're just tired of the military excusing themselves. That's what they've done in thousands of deaths in Vietnam."

"Like the mother whose son was in Special Services," Peg said. "He was murdered in his bunk, and the Army told her he'd been killed in battle!"

I began gathering up my notebooks, pads, pens, the tape casettes. Gene said, "I guess you've got to be going?"

"You won't forget about us, will you?" Peg asked.

"No." I smiled. "I certainly won't do that."

Peg handed me a pen I'd overlooked and followed Gene and me to my car. Gene held the door as I got in. "What are you going to do now?" he asked.

"I guess, the same as the two of you," I said. "I'm going to try to find out what happened to your son."

On my way out of La Porte City on Route 218 I heard on the radio that the 45,000th United States

302

soldier had been killed in Vietnam. I happened to glance into my rearview mirror and caught sight of the town's paint-chipped and faded sign. It took me a moment to decipher La Porte's motto, its print backward in my rearview mirror. It was PROGRESSING WITH AMERICA.

Chapter Twenty-One

On Monday, April 19, one week after I first met the Mullens, Operation Dewey Canyon III commenced in Washington, D.C. This "limited incursion into the country of Congress" was staged by a little more than 1,000 Vietnam Veterans Against the War (VVAW). Although their number was small—out of the perhaps 3,000,000 American men who served in Vietnam, only 12,000 joined the VVAW and fewer than 1,200 took part in the protest—the veterans made a dramatic impression. It was the first time American men who had fought in one of this nation's wars had come to Washington to demand its end while that war was still going on.

The veterans remained in Washington for five days. They laid wreaths at Arlington National Cemetery, conducted mock search and destroy missions and took "prisoners" on the Capitol steps; some demanded a Supreme Court ruling on the constitutionality of the war; others attempted to turn themselves in as war criminals at the Pentagon. (They were met there by Brigadier General Daniel "Chappie" James, USAF, the Pentagon briefing officer who had denied in front of Peg's CALCAV peace group that American planes were bombing Laos. James told the young veterans, "We don't take American prisoners of war here. Why don't you try the Justice Department?") The most formidable impact, however, was achieved through former Navy Lieutenant John Kerry's speech before Congress on Thursday, April 22. Kerry, in his fatigue uniform, wearing the Silver Star and other decorations he had received for his bravery in Vietnam, sat in a leather chair studded with brass nails facing the assembled members of the Senate Foreign Relations Committee and the television cameras.

"Each day to facilitate the process by which the United States washes its hands of Vietnam," Kerry said, "someone has to give up his life so that the United States doesn't have to admit something the entire world already knows, so that we can't say we have made a mistake. Someone has to die so that President Nixon won't be—and these are his words—'the first American President to lose a war.'

"We are asking Americans to think about that because," Kerry said, leaning forward in his chair, "how do you ask a man to be the last to die in Vietnam? *How do you ask a man to be the last man to die for a mistake?* But we are trying to do that, and we are doing it with thousands of rationalizations. And if you read the President's last speech to the people of this country, you can see that he says, and says clearly, 'but the issue is communism, and the question is whether or not we will leave that country to the communists, or whether or not we will try to give it the hope to be a free people.' But the point is that they are not a free people now, and we cannot fight communism all over the world. I think we should have learned that lesson by now."

Two days earlier, the Nixon administration had anonymously suggested that fewer than 30 percent of the veterans present in Washington had actually ever seen any service in Vietnam. Kerry, like the others, was furious. "This administration has done us the ultimate dishonor," he told the Senators. "They have attempted to disown us and the sacrifices we made for this country. In their blindness and fear they have tried to deny that we are veterans or that we served in 'Nam. We do not need their testimony. Our own scars and stumps of limbs are witness enough for others and for ourselves.

"We wish that a merciful God could wipe away our own memories of that service as easily as this administration has wiped away their memories of us. But all that they have done and all that they can do

305

by this denial is to make more clear than ever our own determination to undertake one last mission—to search out and destroy the last vestige of this barbaric war, to pacify our own hearts, to conquer the hate and the fear that have driven this country these last ten years and more, so when thirty years from now our brothers go down the street without a leg, without an arm, or a face, and small boys ask why, we will be able to say 'Vietnam' and not mean a desert, not a filthy, obscene memory, but mean instead the place where America finally turned and where soldiers like us helped it in the turning."

Kerry gathered up his papers and leaned back in the leather chair. He looked up at the Senators, and they back down at him. Then the television lights were extinguished.

That night Peg Mullen telephoned me from a restaurant on the Indiana Turnpike. She was part of an Iowa group heading by bus for Washington to take part in Saturday's march.

On Friday, April 23, while Peg's bus was speeding east, the Vietnam Veterans Against the War were once more marching to the steps of the Capitol. Accompanying them were Anne Pine, Evelyn Carrasquillo and Neil Olsen, Gold Star parents whose sons had died in Vietnam. Both Mrs. Pine and Mrs. Carrasquillo had brought with them the flags which had covered their sons' coffins. Mr. Olsen wore his dead son's field jacket and carried a trumpet. The veterans, as a final gesture of contempt, had decided to throw their medals earned in Vietnam over the wire fence so hastily erected on the Capitol steps to thwart them.

Neil Olsen stopped before the fence, lifted the trumpet to his lips and, with terrible, trembling determination, blew "Taps." He had a kind face, the sort of gentle small-town American face one saw on druggists, grocers. He held the last note for as long as he could while the newspaper and television cameramen jockeyed about for a better angle from the far side of the fence.

"Hold the horn up! Hold it higher!" a photog-

306

rapher was shouting. Olsen ignored him and brought the trumpet smartly and with as much dignity as he could down to his side.

The fence was a simple wire grille nailed to 2-by-4 boards. Microphones had been arranged in front of it, and one by one the veterans came forward. "I'd like to say one thing for the people of Vietnam," one said. "I'm sorry. I hope someday I can return to Vietnam and help rebuild that country we tore apart." He threw his medals over the fence.

The next veteran curled his fingers tightly around his Bronze Star. "I wish I could make them eat it!" he said. He flung his across the fence.

An ex-sergeant from New York City discarded all but two of his medals. He held aloft two Purple Hearts. "I'm keeping these in memory of friends," he explained.

The next veteran flung away his cane; another bitterly threw his medals, saying, "Here's my merit badges for murder." The next, a veteran with a surprisingly young face, paused before the microphones and softly said, "I just want to ask for the war to end, please?" And on the far side of the wire the discarded medals pinged against the Capitol's marble steps like small pieces of shrapnel.

Rusty Sachs, a former helicopter pilot with the 1st Marine Division, stood tense with emotion in his leather flight jacket with the Marine Medium Helicopter Squadron 362 patch sewn above his right breast pocket and captain's bars pinned to his shirt collar. He cocked his arm, pegged his Bronze Star over the fence and moved away. Suddenly he saw a newsman pick up one of the medals. Sachs whirled back to the microphones. "Listen, you newsmen," he warned. "We're not giving *you* the medals! We're turning them back to the country. *Don't touch them!*" Even as he spoke, he saw another newsman lean down, pick up someone's Purple Heart and slip it inside his pocket. Sachs rushed up to the fence, reached through the wire and jerked the closest newsman up against the grille. "Listen," Sachs threatened, "you tell every motherfucker back

307

there that if somebody touches another medal, I'm going to be over there breaking the fingers off his fucking hand!"

"Hey, hey, calm down a little, brother," said another vet, taking Sachs by the shoulder, "it's okay."

Sachs moved back, but not far.

Ron Ferrizzi was wearing khaki pants, an Army fatigue jacket, a black Stetson hat looped behind his shoulder blades. "My parents," he said, looking at the veterans gathered around him and then up at the Capitol dome, "my parents told me that if I really did come down here and turn in my medals that they . . . well, they never wanted anything more to do with me. That's not an easy thing to take," he said, looking down at the microphones. "I still love my parents."

Rusty Sachs was watching Ferrizzi closely.

"My wife doesn't understand what happened to me when I came home from 'Nam," Ferrizzi continued. "She said she would divorce me if I came down here because she wanted my medals for our son to see when he grew up." He glanced at the medals he held and shook his head sadly. "I'm not proud of these medals . . . of what I did to receive them. . . ."

He was speaking so softly now it was difficult to hear what he said. He was explaining how three men had died so that he might receive these decorations, and all around him the veterans strained to hear, their faces stiff and tight with memories. Rusty Sachs suddenly began to cry, and when Ferrizzi stepped back from the microphones and flung his medals as far and as hard as he could, the former Marine helicopter pilot grabbed him and hugged him. The two men stood weeping, clinging to each other while the news photographers shouted at the other veterans to get out of the way, they were blocking the shots.

I met Peg Mullen at about two o'clock Saturday afternoon in Washington in the American Friends Office on Second Street, four blocks from the Capitol. I was shocked by how drained and exhausted she looked. I asked her if she felt all right. Peg replied all she wanted was to sit down. We walked to a nearby hotel and took a table in its restaurant-bar. Peg's bus had arrived in Washington at three that morning. "The bus driver was so worried about us," Peg explained, "that he raced to Washington and arrived here five hours early. We were supposed to have been able to sleep on the bus, but he was so frightened by what he had driven into that he made us get out."

Peg and the other passengers had been discharged at the Washington Monument and had to walk more than two miles to an Episcopal church in which arrangements had been made for the group to spend the night. Peg, wrapped in a blanket she had brought with her from Iowa, stretched out on the floor and slept poorly. When, this morning, she had walked the two-plus miles back to the Washington Monument, where the march route was scheduled to begin, the crowds were already so heavy she became separated from her Iowa friends. "I just walked with whatever group happened by," Peg said. "I think it was a teachers' group. Something like Teachers for Peace."

The march contained many different groups—Clergy for Peace, Doctors for Peace, Lawyers for Peace—and for the first time, organized labor joined the protest, too. Although Peg saw several young men wearing the Vietnam Veterans Against the War Button, she never met up with any of the leaders who had invited her to join them. "I did see some American Legion types, though," she told me. "One of the men I marched with said he was a dentist and started singing that song, 'One-Two-Three-Four, we don't want your,' you know. I was so shocked I turned to him and said, 'How can you sing a song like that?' He was such a handsome man, too!" Peg laughed. " 'It's not so hard,' he said. 'Try it.' But I didn't. I couldn't. I just—oh! And there was another. . . ." Peg paused and tried to suppress a yawn. "There was another old man in an American Legion cap. He and his wife. They must have been around seventy-five. And about every block or so they'd sit down on the curb and rest. He looked exactly like Pat O'Brien, really. I was dying to ask him if he was. Anyway, they'd sit on the curb and rest, but the next thing you'd know they'd be right back up there marching with you."

Many more older people attended this peace march than I'd seen at any other. Of course, the majority of the demonstrators were young. They were, after all, the ones being asked to sacrifice their lives. At least 30 percent of the crowd and perhaps more, however, were in their mid-thirties and older. But that vast sea of blue denim was so deceptive (a hundred different shades of blue in a score of different styles: bib overalls, blue jean shirts, boot-top Levi's, cut-off shorts, skirts) from a distance everyone looked alike. Only when one was within that Levi sea could one discern sport-shirted businessmen, young mothers in cotton dresses with infants strapped to their backs, fathers in turtlenecks and tweeds. And, too, among the ministers and priests one might see an elegant elderly woman in a flowered garden party hat.

"I couldn't even get close to the Capitol," Peg said, watching the color television set nestled in a corner above the bar. The TV was tuned to the demonstration taking place not more than three blocks away. "Did you hear John Denver?" she asked me. "The wind was blowing just right, and I could hear him sing that song about dreaming there would be no more war. It was so pretty. . . ." Peg yawned again and apologized.

I asked Peg when she had eaten last.

"I ate a piece of chicken this morning," she said. "I dropped out of the march at one point and was sitting on the curb when two ladies sat down next to me with the most beautiful food, a real picnic. They were from upper New York State somewhere. They gave me a piece of their chicken. Other than that, the only thing I've eaten was at the last restaurant we stopped at on the turnpike last night."

I ordered Peg some lunch.

"At one stop on the Ohio Turnpike where we ate," Peg said, "we were told that eighty-nine buses filled with people going to Washington had all come through

310

that same restaurant in the last three hours. Eighty-nine! I'll tell you another thing: all the restaurants and gas stations coming east had plainclothesmen there."

"What do you mean?" I asked. "How could you tell?"

"I don't know"—Peg shrugged—"but you could tell they were cops of some kind. I think they were counting buses so that Washington could be prepared. Where is Nixon anyway? Is he in Washington today?"

"He's at Camp David."

"Typical," Peg said. "He doesn't care one bit what's going on—Oh! And the state police? They were picking up all the hitchhikers and putting them in jail. Before we left Iowa, in fact, the Iowa police pulled our bus onto a weighing station. The sort of harassment you'd expect. When I heard about those eighty-nine buses stopping at that one restaurant in Ohio, though, well, I found that very encouraging. It meant that other people were coming, at least."

"Did you think other people wouldn't come?"

"I didn't know," she said. "There've been so many peace marches, so many protests. . . . I wasn't going to come. When the VVAW asked me, I told them I couldn't. Couldn't afford it. Couldn't take the time. But then I got to thinking. If nobody came, Nixon would feel the people didn't care anymore. That he'd gotten away with it. So I had to come. I wasn't really sure how many others felt the same way." Peg was watching the television coverage of the demonstration again. The camera was slowly panning across the huge crowds. "I guess there must be a lot, though." Peg smiled.

The march organizers reported half a million protesters had come to Washington to take part in the demonstration that day. Police and government officials estimated the figure was closer to 200,000. How could anyone tell? I know only that every road leading into the city was clogged with bumper-to-bumper traffic and that the bus, train and airline terminals were jammed with people from all over the nation who had

311

felt the need to come to Washington to show their opposition, in spite of the fact that by this time no sizable portion of the country, or even Congress, needed further convincing that the war was wrong. I know, too, that when I entered the line of march at the corner of Fourteenth Street and Pennsylvania Avenue about noon, the head of the line had not only reached the Capitol a mile and a half away but was beginning to fan out and curl backward from the Capitol steps. By the time I reached the intersection of Constitution and Pennsylvania avenues, where the avenues became nine traffic lanes wide, the Capitol was still a half mile beyond me and the crowds had become so thick it was difficult to move. What's more, an enormous mass of people stretched for a mile or so behind me, and thousands upon thousands of others were simultaneously proceeding to the Capitol by different routes.

Peg's hamburger arrived, and her hand trembled when she picked it up. I looked at the exhaustion in Peg's eyes, the way she drooped in the chair, and asked when her bus left for Iowa that night.

"We're supposed to be at the bus around six thirty," she said, "but I know it won't leave much before eight."

I looked at my wristwatch. "That's about five hours from now. Wouldn't you like a few hours' sleep? A chance to relax?"

"Well, sure," she said, "but——" And Peg suddenly gave so huge a yawn it took even her by surprise.

I was able to get Peg a room at the hotel. We said good-bye at the elevator and my heart went out to her, she was so relieved at being able to sleep.

A weekly newsmagazine later described the April 24 Peace March as "the kind that the cops could have brought their children to." People everywhere were smiling and talking, making room for others to sit or pass through. Bottles of wine and Coke and beer were handed back and forth along with sandwiches and hard-boiled eggs. The speeches continued, interrupted by an occasional entertainer; the protesters listened, or didn't listen, their expressions gentle and kind. Even the elderly had the faces of children. Gone was that anger one had seen at all those marches of the years before—the anguish, tenseness and frustration felt at defying a government that wouldn't respond. Gone, too, was that curious sense of unself, the deliberate submergence of one's entire being into the symbolic, the presentation of oneself as one less hole in the crowd. The mood of this day's march resembled not so much the protest marches of the late sixties and early seventies as it did the "love-ins" of the mid-sixties. Families were enjoying private jokes; friends were smiling. Members of a bakers' union were laughing at a troop of young Maoists curled up beside a large red flag. There were smiles on the young women, the young men perched atop statues or on branches of trees. An old man was laughing with a little boy whose shoelaces had come undone. A young woman passed her boyfriend a Coke bottle, and when he wiped the top, she playfully punched him in the ribs.

I thought a lot about those faces. Their expressions reflected more than the reassurance and comfort gained from one another's company. If this many people cared this much to travel that far to Washington, then we Americans were not so selfish and indifferent after all. And the people's faces expressed a pride in an America they had loved all along, but which they feared might have been lost: an America of the people. The government would have to end the war.

It didn't, of course. Not for another year. At that, the government ended only the overt participation of American troops.

"Look, I don't like what's happening any more than you do," one of my Senators said. "But we've got over seven and a half percent unemployment in our state. We depend heavily upon defense contracts. How can you expect me to vote against the war?" His attitude was typical. One year after that peace march, twelve states, of which mine was but one, each received prime military contract awards totaling more than $1 billion, twenty-four states received between $100 million and one billion, only fourteen states received less than $100 million.

313

Three days after the Washington march Peg wrote thanking me for putting her up at the hotel. She had slept, the trip back had been uneventful, Gene and the children were well, and bit by bit the farm seemed to be returning to normal. That would have been around the end of April.

On Sunday, June 13, the New York *Times* printed the first installment of the "Pentagon Papers" containing narrative history, appended memoranda, classified cables, and position papers excerpted from the forty-seven-volume highly classified study ordered by then-Secretary of Defense Robert S. McNamara on American involvement in Indochina from World War II through May, 1968, the date on which the Paris peace talks began. One of the most telling documents was Assistant Secretary of Defense for International Security Affairs John T. McNaughton's first draft of "Annex—Plan for Action for South Vietnam," written March 24, 1965, which articulated the priorities of the United States' aims:

70%—To avoid a humiliating U.S. defeat (to our reputation as a guarantor).
20%—To keep South Vietnam (and the adjacent) territory from Chinese hands.
10%—To permit the people of South Vietnam to enjoy a better, freer way of life.
ALSO—To emerge from crisis without unacceptable taint from methods used.
NOT—to "help a friend" although it would be hard to stay in if asked out.

Publication of these records provided the American people with a rare and disquieting glimpse into the decision-making processes of high government officials, decisions which affected the lives of millions of Americans and the lives of the people of a dozen other nations as well. What was so troubling about the Pentagon Papers was not so much the disclosures of deceitful and ill-chosen policies, but the obvious contempt with which one presidential administration after another viewed Congress and the American people. As one newsmagazine wrote concerning these papers: "The most instructive revelation may be how little faith the leaders had in those they led—a classic case of the arrogance of the powerful."

In early July the Senate rejected (55 to 42) the Hatfield-McGovern 609 amendment calling for the withdrawal of all American troops by the end of the year, and two days later I received a long letter from Peg in response to a large list of questions I had sent. I did not hear again from the Mullens until one afternoon in late July, when Gene telephoned me and excitedly said, "Listen, I've got an ending for your book!"

"Where are you?" I asked.

"We're in Washington again. At the American Friends Office. We're driving up your way tomorrow. May we stop by and see you?"

"Of course," I said, "but what's up?"

"I've gotta run. Peg's got us a cab so I can't say much yet except that I've found him! I've found the man who killed my boy! I located Schwarzkopf," Gene crowed. "We're going to see him this afternoon!"

Chapter Twenty-Two

Two mornings later I met the Mullens at their motel, then drove them out to my house. Several times at breakfast and during the drive they had started to tell me about their meeting with Lieutenant Colonel Schwarzkopf, and each time I begged them to hold off until we could be isolated from interruptions and I could take proper notes. When we finally did begin, I discovered that by having made them wait I had unwittingly created an artificial atmosphere in which they seemed to feel themselves "testifying" before some judge. Peg took notes from her pocketbook and spread them out on the low table before her as if she were playing solitaire. Gene, his hands clasped together, fingers intertwined, sat across from her and leaned forward, eager to speak.

Colonel Alan Thompson, the Pentagon officer who had helped the Mullens get Larry Phelps out of Vietnam, had located Schwarzkopf for the family, too. Peg had returned to the Pentagon on June 14 to see if she could obtain a copy of Charlie Company's morning report for the day Michael was killed. The report would have listed every man in Michael's platoon. Colonel Thompson found Schwarzkopf was assigned to Fort Myer, Virginia. The Mullens had not had time to visit Schwarzkopf then, but when they had returned to Washington in late July, they went directly to Fort Myer. There they learned Schwarzkopf had been transferred to Fort McNair, and at Fort McNair they were told Schwarzkopf was at the Walter Reed Army Medical Center on a year's convalescent leave.

"I called the hospital," Gene said, "and they told me that Colonel Schwarzkopf had been moved to Ward One, Orthopedic. I called there, and Colonel Schwarzkopf answered the phone. I said, 'This is Mr. Mullen. I'm calling about an incident that happened to your battalion, the One-over-Sixth of the Hundred and Ninety-eighth in Corps One on February 18 at two thirty in the morning.'

"Colonel Schwarzkopf said, 'Do you mean that artillery incident?'

"I said, 'Yes, that artillery incident.'

" 'Mr. Mullen,' he said, 'I can tell you about that artillery incident.'

"I said, 'Colonel, I know more about that artillery incident than you think I do. I've been looking for you for a year and a half. I consider you the man who killed my son. I am going to take you to federal court.' "

Gene paused to take a sip of coffee, then continued.

"The colonel said, 'I wish you would take me to federal court. It would prove me innocent. I would like to talk to you.'

" 'Colonel,' I said, 'I would like to talk to you, too, but how can I?'

" 'Is your time pressing?' he asked. 'Why don't you come out to the hospital to visit me? I want to talk to you.' He repeated approximately four times, 'I want to talk to you.' So we made an appointment to see him at about five o'clock at his wish—very much his wish," Gene added. "And that's when we telephoned you. We took a cab out to Walter Reed and found Ward One very easily. There were six other patients in the ward, all officers. As I stood in the doorway and looked into the room, I noticed an officer in uniform sitting on the left side of Colonel Schwarzkopf's bed and on the right side, an empty chair. I walked in, and I said, 'Lieutenant Colonel Schwarzkopf?'

"He said, 'Yes.'

"I had expected a tall, thin man with the appearance of a West Point officer," Gene said, "but I was amazed at what I saw. I saw a round-faced, blond, overgrown, boyish-looking man of about thirty-five years of age. He had a cast on, a full body cast. He was not in pain. But he was in discomfort. All during our conversation he was very restless due to the cast.

"I said, 'I'm Mr. Mullen.'

"He said, 'I am pleased to meet you.'

"I did not shake his hand.

"Schwarzkopf acknowledged me and my wife, and then he introduced us to this Major Knap. Now he never told us who this Major Knap was or what his business was there. But from the way he had positioned his chair at the opposite side of the bed, it was obvious it had been prearranged."

"Gene," I interrupted, "could you tell Knap's branch of the service?"

"I don't know," Gene said. "Frankly, I wasn't interested. He was Army, that's all I know." He looked over at Peg, but she didn't know either. "Anyway, we were introduced, and I said, 'Colonel, I would like to talk to you.'

" 'I would like to talk to you, too,' the colonel said. 'We could go to a private room if you like. I can be moved.'

" 'No, that isn't necessary.' I said. I went over to the wall and brought another chair for Peg, and we sat down. I was approximately a foot and a half from Schwarzkopf's face at all times, so I could hear and see his expression as we talked. Peg's and my chair were on the right side of the bed. This Major Knap was on the left in a position to view both Colonel Schwarzkopf and ourselves and to hear us. We sat down and I said. 'Now, Colonel, you can tell your story of what happened.' "

Gene wiped his mouth with the back of his hand. "He proceeded to tell us that on the night Michael was killed he, Schwarzkopf, was not with Charlie Company; he was instead on Hill Four Ten, the same hill as the supporting artillery. He told us, 'When the incident happened, I was notified by Captain Tom Cameron, Charlie Company's commander. I immediately ran down to the artillery unit and told them to stop firing, to lock their guns. I wanted those guns locked because this was the second incident that had happened to my battalion in thirty days! The first time it happened, the colonel in charge of the artillery unit said it was a once-in-a-lifetime fluke and—' "

"That was the Bravo Company incident," Peg interrupted. It was the first time she had spoken since Gene had started telling their story. Gene looked at Peg as if waiting for her to say something more, but when she remained silent, he continued.

"We don't know how many were wounded then, but the boys told us to ask Schwarzkopf about the time thirty-two men in Bravo Company got hurt. . . . Anyway, after Schwarzkopf ordered the guns locked, he said, he went to Michael's hill the next morning. I said. 'Yes, about ten minutes to eight.'

"Schwarzkopf turned and looked at me. He said, 'I went down with another officer—'

"I interrupted him again," Gene said. " 'Colonel,' I said, 'there were four of you. You and three other officers were at the scene at that time.'

"He looked me in the eye and said, 'Yes, Mr. Mullen, you are correct. There were three other officers, but,' Schwarzkopf said, 'I want you to know I was not part of the investigating committee.'

"I said, 'No, we know that,' " Gene continued. " 'They came out at approximately twelve o'clock noon in a big Sloop helicopter, and they consisted of the artillery, plus some liaison officers between the infantry and the artillery, plus the investigating artillery team from 'Eye' Corps artillery.'

"And Schwarzkopf said, 'Yes, you are correct.'

"I then said, 'The rumors tell us, sir, that three things could have happened: the men were drinking, or the guns were off target, or the wrong coordinates were called in. Now,' I said, 'what did you find when you got there?' And, Peg, you tell—"

"Well, he replied that the guns were perfect," Peg said. "They had told Schwarzkopf after the Bravo Company incident that they blamed it on the gun. That is why he demanded the guns be locked. He told us, 'I could have killed Colonel Kuprin when he stepped off that helicopter because this was the second incident his artillery outfit had perpetrated on my battalion.' Kuprin was the artillery commander," Peg explained. "And, see, the boys told us it was the same gun that had done it before and the gun had not been repaired. Schwarzkopf, however, insisted the guns were okay. So I said,

'Colonel, I'm just going to ask you one thing: *Were the men drinking?*' And he looked me right in the eye and said, 'Yes, Mrs. Mullen, the men had been drinking. Were drinking beer.' "

"See?" Gene said.

I asked Peg if the colonel had stated or implied that the men were drunk.

"No, only that they had been drinking beer. He seemed to want me to know that. I was kind of surprised he said yes because I don't think they should have been drinking. And then," Peg said, looking down at her notes, "Colonel Schwarzkopf told us, 'I think you should talk to Colonel Valentin Kuprin. He was the artillery battalion commander. He's in the Washington area and assigned to the Pentagon.' So that night, when we went back to the motel we called Kuprin. I told him who I was and said, 'Your name was given us by Lieutenant Colonel Schwarzkopf, and I would like you to identify the artillery officer who was reprimanded.' "

Kuprin did not remember the young lieutenant's name. According to Peg, the former artillery battalion commander said, "The gunnery officer neglected to take into account the height of the trees. He failed to use his judgment and he was reprimanded. The procedure was corrected the next day." Kuprin also told the Mullens that he did not believe Lieutenant Rocamora, the forward observer, had called in the artillery. Rocamora's radio operator had been on duty at the time; Rocamora was asleep.

"Okay," Peg said, referring again to her notes, "I then asked Kuprin about the rumors that the artillery officers had been drinking beer. He denied it. I told him that's what Colonel Schwarzkopf had said. Kuprin said, 'I'll take care of Norman.' I told him Schwarzkopf had said it was about time corrections were made because he 'had had it.' And Kuprin asked, 'Do you think the artillery just runs around with pistols shooting at people?' He said, 'Artillery isn't one hundred percent accurate. When we shoot four hundred rounds a night, we're going to kill a few people we shouldn't.' Kuprin said he had offered to remove Rocamora from Charlie Company after this incident, but Rocamora elected to stay with his assignment. He liked Charlie Company, and they liked him. And, well, my feeling is that if Rocamora *had* called in that artillery and *hadn't* alerted the boys, he wouldn't have been allowed to stay there. For his sake. That's why the boys were so upset: they didn't have a chance! When I told Kuprin Webb's comment about thinking it was an attack and sweeping people into their foxholes, Kuprin said, 'Well, if you call a six-inch sleeping trench a foxhole, then it's no wonder they died!'"

"Peg," I said, "the boys wrote they had dug foxholes, didn't they?"

"Everybody dug a foxhole that night," she said. "A foxhole and a sleeping position. But they were in their sleeping positions when the shell hit."

"Can I use one of your pieces of paper?" Gene asked. He started to draw as he spoke: "Now, there was a group here, one, two, three, four, with a guard. And then there was Michael . . . Polk . . . Hamilton . . . another one here and a guard. The First Platoon was here,

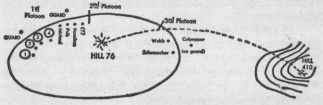

Second Platoon in the middle, the Third Platoon was over here. Webb and Culpepper were Third Platoon . . . Culpepper had just got off guard at two o'clock and he was changing positions with Schumacher. Schumacher was saying, 'The artillery's coming in closer,' and then, all of a sudden he says to Culpepper, 'My God, they're walking them right in on us! They're trying to kill us!'" Gene drew an asterisk with little lines radiating out from its center. "Right here was a high knoll. There was a tree here. This is Hill Seventy-six*—known as

---

*Although Gene correctly identified "Hill 76" as the hill mentioned in Polk's court-martial, it was not the hill upon which Michael was killed. Michael's hill had no designation other than the six digit coordinates for its peak.

'Seventy-six' because in the court-martial of Private Polk that's how it's referred to. And Hill Four Ten was back over here." Gene drew a series of elevation lines on the other side of his drawing. "The shell came right over this way"—Gene's finger followed the arc from the top of Hill 410 to the asterisk he had drawn before "—hit the tree here and"—Gene gestured as if flicking water from his fingers—"came down. It killed Michael, Leroy Hamilton and wounded six or seven others."

Gene and Peg both fell silent. I suggested we break for lunch.

If during our morning session Gene had spoken in the short, chopped phrases of a witness giving testimony, after lunch he assumed the more expansive role of a hard-charging prosecuting attorney. In turn, the conciliatory and beleaguered "Schwarzkopf," a man who had seemingly agreed with and confirmed everything Gene Mullen had said, became, in the afternoon version, a pathetic and defensive invalid crushed by the overwhelming evidence the Mullens had accumulated against him.

"I said, 'Colonel, what did you accomplish during your second tour in Vietnam? Did you do any good?'

"'I don't know,' he said. 'What I did was try to save boys' lives by enacting discipline, by teaching them to wear their helmets, their flak jackets, by teaching them to protect themselves...'

"And I said, 'Of the one-hundred-twenty men you lost in your battalion in ninety days, or in Bravo Company from which you lost thirty-two men because of your own stupidity of marching them through a minefield—'

"'Did you know I was wounded?' he asked and I said, 'Yes, Colonel, and I know *how* you were wounded. A young man who served under you told me all about it. Did you know you were suckered down out of your helicopter into that minefield by an officer?'

"'What officer?' he said.

"I said, 'I do not want to repeat this man's name. But when you got out of your helicopter, you walked approximately fifteen feet and tripped a mine, and that was how you were wounded. You were directed onto that mine and you know that!'" Gene paused for a moment and picked up one of my pens. He tapped its base against the yellow pad as though he were tamping down a cigarette. "He looked at me. I can see Schwarzkopf lying there in that bed. The expression in his eyes was that of a man thinking back on what had happened to him. 'No,' he said. 'I didn't know that.'" Gene let the pen drop. "He didn't believe me. I could tell." He leaned back in his chair. "I feel that Lieutenant Colonel H. Norman Schwarzkopf lying in the hospital, looking back on his career in Vietnam, has suddenly had a change of attitude about the military. Two things have given me this opinion. First," Gene said, holding up one finger, "his straightforward words telling us what had happened because we could either correct him—we had the information, the *signed information*. And second," Gene said, holding up a second finger, "his wanting to get the blame off himself. When he named Kuprin, he went against the book. No officer ever places the blame on another officer unless it's the truth under oath, or the man is truthful unto himself because he knows what has happened. . . . The more I think about Schwarzkopf," Gene said, "the more I think he went back that second time to Vietnam to get his rank. His colonelcy. But now he knows he's over the hill with that back injury. He sees the handwriting on the wall and realizes he will never get any higher, that he's accomplished nothing."

We spoke for quite a while that afternoon about what had happened that night on the hill where Michael died. Had the artillery been firing all night long or not? Why was it senior noncommissioned officers did not go out into the field? Why had a plea of temporary insanity never been entered in Willard Polk's case? Mightn't the explosion that night have been considered "mitigating circumstances" especially since the men on either side of Polk had been killed? But over and over again the conversation would return to Lieutenant Colonel Schwarzkopf, and finally, I asked the Mullens if their own attitude toward him had changed.

They were both silent until Peg, very hesitatingly,

said, "Yes, my attitude has changed. . . . I mean, finding him there in that body cast, I thought, 'Well, the Lord has taken care of you. . . .' " She paused again, then blurted, "I guess I really don't know how I feel about him. I'd learned to hate him after hearing the boys talk. But he told us he was hated because he insisted on discipline, on taking the proper precautions. And I couldn't help thinking, if only Michael had had his flak jacket on that night, he wouldn't have died. . . . Schwarzkopf, you know, repeatedly told us what a fine man Michael was. He said over and over again did we realize what a tremendous soldier our son had been, the rapport he had had with his men and so forth. He kept saying this to me as I was leaving. . . ."

"And, too, Mother," Gene said, "the letter he wrote us about Michael's death was very sympathetic. At the time, we thought he was laying it on a bit thick. The only thing he didn't tell us was that Rocamora was asleep. He told us as much as the investigation could have, and well, he didn't think we'd look any further."

"Who would?" Peg asked.

"What are you going to do now?" I asked.

"We'll find Rocamora. We think now he's in Hawaii," Gene said. "You see I have an undying faith. Everything we've looked for we've found out. It only takes time. Can you imagine all the information we've picked up? Just two people? And it's all authentic! It can be documented. Where in the world could two people like us do what we've done? It's not only through our efforts. At times, at certain moments we've been led some place and the story opens up. We move somewhere else, and something more opens up. The last thing we need to do is find Rocamora and," Gene said, slapping his knees, "I think we're going to find him."

"Say you do find him, Gene," I said, "what do you hope to learn?"

"How Michael died," Peg answered.

"Who . . . killed . . . our . . . son!" Gene said.

Why? What good would it do? I like the Mullens very much. I felt terribly sorry for them—it was impossible not to. But no matter how much affection and sympathy I felt for them, I could not accept that their confrontation with Lieutenant Colonel H. Norman Schwarzkopf had, as recounted by them, really taken place. I did not doubt that they had located the colonel, spoken to him face-to-face, or that he had answered their questions as best he could. I suspected only that Peg and Gene had become, like the United States government which so enraged them, no longer able to listen to what they didn't want to hear.

I was especially disturbed by the realization that their attitude was partly my fault. Gene himself had indicated as much just two days before when he had telephoned and said, "I've got an ending for your book!" That anticipated sweet revenge must have seemed the perfect ending indeed, one which the Mullens could almost set in type themselves: GOLD STAR PARENTS BRING SON'S MURDERER TO HIS KNEES.

But of course, Schwarzkopf *hadn't* killed their son. And I worried about to what awful lengths the Mullens might drive themselves to achieve their next "perfect ending" for me. The Mullens had already demonstrated a surprisingly sophisticated awareness of the impact media exposure might have. The enormous attention they had received as a result of their first antiwar advertisement could not help having seemed heady stuff indeed. National prominence once achieved—no matter how momentary and elusive—creates a craving for ever more attention. Inevitably the different media, television especially, not only report news but inspire, influence, feed upon and demand ever more news. The temptation to create "perfect endings" was the corruption I wanted the Mullens spared. The only way I could achieve this was by finding out for them exactly what had happened to their son. I believed I already knew. I believed, also, that they knew, too. Colonel Valentin Kuprin, the artillery battalion commander, had told them. It had not, however, been what they had wanted to hear.

The Mullens left late that afternoon. Peg was on her way up to Boston to be a guest on a radio show. On their way back to Iowa they were to stop at Leroy

325

Hamilton's family in Kentucky and later with the Arthur S. Krause family in Pittsburgh whose daughter, Allison, had been one of the four students killed by the Ohio National Guard at Kent State. Peg asked me what I was going to do. I told her I would go talk with Lieutenant Colonel Schwarzkopf myself.

She said, "I'll bet you ten dollars he won't even see you."

Chapter Twenty-Three

Schwarzkopf was born on August 22, 1934, in Trenton, New Jersey. Two years earlier, his father, Colonel H. Norman Schwarzkopf, superintendent of the quasi-military New Jersey State Police, had directed the Lindbergh kidnapping investigation. Young Norm Schwarzkopf grew up in the Lawrenceville-Princeton area while his father returned to active duty in the Army during World War II. After the war, he joined his father at his postings in Iran (1946), Switzerland (1947), Germany (1948–1949) and Italy (1950–1951). He left Italy in the fall of 1951 to attend Valley Forge Military Academy on a football scholarship and in 1952 won a competitive scholarship to the United States Military Academy at West Point. Schwarzkopf played football at the Academy, was a cadet captain and in June, 1956, was graduated forty-second in his class of 485. He received a Regular Army commission as a Second Lieutenant, Infantry.

Schwarzkopf's early career followed a predictable Army pattern: infantry and airborne schools at Fort Benning, Georgia, followed by two years with the 101st Airborne, the new Strategic Army Corps (STRAC) division formed at Fort Campbell, Kentucky. He was next assigned to Berlin for two years, then returned to Benning for the career officer course. In 1963 Schwarzkopf was sent to the University of Southern California to pick up a master's degree in mechanical and aerospace engineering, and in 1965 he was ordered back to West Point to begin a three-year teaching appointment. However, he remained at the Academy for only one year.

Several of Schwarzkopf's good friends had already died in Vietnam. Eight American advisers had been killed that February in their compound at Pleiku; twenty-three more Americans lost their lives several days later in an attack on their barracks at Qui Nhon. That same month President Lyndon B. Johnson ordered Operation Rolling Thunder, the sustained air bombardment of North Vietnam. In March, U.S. Marines waded ashore at Danang and raised the total U.S. troop strength in Vietnam to 27,000 men. In May there were 46,000, by June 75,000

Schwarzkopf was an infantryman. He chafed sitting at West Point and felt obligated to go to Vietnam. The Department of the Army agreed to grant him his transfer request on the condition that upon completion of his one-year duty tour he return to the Military Academy to fulfill the remaining two years of his teaching obligation. Schwarzkopf reached Vietnam early in the summer of 1965 and was assigned to the Vietnamese Airborne Division as a task force adviser. Shortly after his arrival he spent ten days surrounded at the Dak To Special Forces camp. A month later he was promoted to major. In July, 1965, President Johnson authorized the increase of U.S. forces in Vietnam from 75,000 to 125,000 men.

Schwarzkopf returned to West Point in 1966 as an associate professor in the Department of Engineering Mechanics. In August, 1968, he was promoted to lieutenant colonel ahead of the majority of his contemporaries. He had just turned thirty-four years old and was sent to the Command and General Staff College.

In March, 1969, U.S. military forces reached peak strength in Vietnam with 541,500 men. December, that same year, Schwarzkopf returned to Vietnam for his second tour. Ten weeks after he assumed command of the 1st Battalion, 6th Infantry, 198th Infantry Brigade of the Americal Division, Michael Eugene Mullen, of Schwarzkopf's 1st Battalion's Charlie Company, was dead.

I spent two days with Lieutenant Colonel Schwarzkopf during the first week of October. He had been released from the Walter Reed Army Medical Center and was recuperating at his home in Annandale, Virginia, with his wife, Brenda, a former TWA stewardess, and their then two-year-old daughter, Cindy. I had written the colonel asking if I might speak with him, and he had promptly urged me to come. I rang his doorbell, and as I waited, I recalled Gene's description of Schwarzkopf as a "round-faced, blond, overgrown, boyish-looking man." There was nothing boyish about the man who answered the door. Schwarzkopf is big, solid, over six feet tall, and weighs maybe 220 pounds. He still wore a cast starting at his hips which rode high over his shoulders like football shoulder pads. His brown-blond hair was short, but not crew-cut, and his expression—like his handshake and greeting—was open and friendly.

Schwarzkopf's two-bedroom apartment was in a new brick building identical to a row of other new brick apartment buildings in the development. Annandale is one of those rapidly expanding bedroom communities that lie within the Belt Parkway around suburban Washington, D.C. An expensive stereo-phonograph set was mounted in a bookcase against the right-hand wall; a couch and pair of Danish modern chairs were by the back wall to the left. Beyond the stereo and to the right of the living room was the small efficiency kitchen, and beyond that the master bedroom, bath and small bedroom for their daughter, Cindy. Some brass, mother-of-pearl and ebony souvenirs of the Orient were placed about, but on the whole, the apartment reflected the transient status of the Schwarzkopfs. The colonel gestured toward the dining-room table and suggested we might be more comfortable if we sat there.

I asked him if he would mind my using a tape recorder, and he replied he wouldn't mind at all; in fact, he added, he intended to use one himself. He explained he had called the Pentagon to make sure the interview would be all right, and the Pentagon had placed no restrictions on him whatsoever. They had suggested, however, he use his own tape recorder to ensure that his answers would not be distorted or lifted out of context.

As we took our places on opposite sides of the dining-room table, I explained that I had heard the Mullens' version of their conversation, and I was inter-

ested in hearing his. I asked, to begin with, how Gene
Mullen had introduced himself on the telephone.

"Okay," Schwarzkopf said, tilting back in his
chair, "I'll recite it to you exactly: I was notified I had a
phone call, and they had to bring the phone to my bed.
I was then in a body cast that went all the way down to
my knees, so I couldn't move. I picked up the telephone, and this voice at the other end said, 'Is this
Colonel Schwarzkopf?'

"I said, 'Yes.'

"He said, 'Were you the commanding officer of the
First Battalion of the Sixth Infantry in February,
1970?'

"I said, 'Yes, I was.'

"The voice on the other end said, 'Does the name
Michael Mullen mean anything to you?'

" 'I recall the name,' I said, 'but right now I can't
specifically place it. . . .' See," Schwarzkopf explained,
"it had been almost two years since the occurrence of
this thing. Mr. Mullen then said, 'Does an incident that
took place on the eighteenth of February—'and he went
into so many miles north of Quang Ni at such-and-
such—'mean anything to you?'

"I said, 'No, I'm sorry, but based on what you've
given me I can't recall exactly—wait, are you talking
about an incident where some men were killed by
friendly artillery fire?'

"He said, 'Yes, I am.'

"I said, 'Yes, I recall that.'

"And he said, 'Well, I want to inform you that we
are bringing charges against you in federal district court
for suppressing the facts of the investigation into the
death of my son.' "

The colonel's chair legs banged forward on the
floor. " 'Mr. Mullen,' I said, 'look, I think there's a
misunderstanding here. I was in no way responsible for
the investigation into the death of your son.' Mr. Mullen
was very emotional, and I said, 'But I don't think we're
going to get anything accomplished talking to each other
over the phone. Can you come out to Walter Reed and
see me?' He said he could, and I said, 'Fine. Come on

out. Let's sit down and talk about this thing. You look at me, and I'll look at you and we'll talk this thing through.' "

"Colonel Schwarzkopf," I said, "did Gene Mullen ever accuse you of having killed his son? Did he say, 'I've been looking for you for a year and a half. I consider you the man who killed my son, and I'm taking you to federal court.'?"

"No." Colonel Schwarzkopf shook his head. "Nothing like that. What I told you is almost verbatim. I remember it because it came as such a shot out of the blue: 'I want to tell you that we are taking you to federal court—' He didn't say 'for killing my son.' He said, 'for covering up the facts of the investigation.' First of all, let me tell you a couple of things." Lieutenant Colonel Schwarzkopf spoke for a while about the Americal Division's reputation, the incidents involving Lieutenant Calley, Captain Medina, Colonel Henderson and My Lai. General Donaldson was at that time under investigation for allegedly shooting civilians from his helicopter. Several of Schwarzkopf's friends, knowing he had served in the Americal Division, had made the bad joke "It looks like everybody in the division at one time or another is going to be investigated, when is your time coming?" Schwarzkopf's first reaction after Gene's phone call had been: "Here it is. It's my turn now."

"I knew I wanted to talk to the Mullens," Schwarzkopf said, "but I also knew I wanted a witness there. I didn't want to get off in a closed room someplace, talk with them, and then have them turn around and say, 'He told us this or that.' I wanted somebody there to know what I said. I also wanted some advice on whether I'd be out of line talking to them at all. So I called up the JAG [Judge Advocate General, the legal branch of the Army] section at Walter Reed and asked them to send somebody down. I just wanted to ask a few questions about what I should do. Major Knap came down. We had just about decided that sure, I could talk to them, I could tell them anything they wanted to know when the Mullens walked in through the door. At that time I thought only Mr. Mullen was coming. I had no idea Mrs. Mullen was along. I think they were rather surprised by my condition, my cast. I reached out to shake hands with them, to introduce myself when they came up to my bed, and it was very apparent that Gene Mullen was very reluctant to even shake my hand. I was concerned because I wasn't sure what their emotional state was. I was lying in bed. There was a bed on my right, five beds on my left with guys in traction, and I wasn't sure if because of the Mullens' emotional state it was going to degenerate into them shouting and screaming at me or what. So I asked if they would like to go to a private room, and they said, 'No, we'll talk to you right here.' In fact, Gene Mullen said, 'We want to talk to you, and we want you to have a witness here to hear what is being said, too.'

"I said, 'Fine, Major Knap is present.' I asked Knap to stay. I wanted to talk to them because, well, I felt I could help. Here was a family obviously very upset about their son's death, who obviously had some false information, false ideas about how and why their son had died. I felt if I could give them the circumstances of their son's death, tell them exactly what happened right down the line, if they could look me in the eye and see that I was telling them the truth, then they would feel they had finally gotten the straight story about the entire thing and that this would somehow set their minds at ease. That was *why* I wanted to talk to the Mullens. Now, *how* did I approach the interview? First of all," Lieutenant Colonel Schwarzkopf said leaning back in his chair again, "although I was shocked by Gene Mullen's opening comment about federal district court, I wasn't really concerned because I had nothing to hide and there was nothing I could be taken to court for. But more than that I felt here, coming to see me, is going to be a family whose son had been killed, was killed in an unfortunate incident in an unfortunate war, and they were obviously going to be upset. I felt what I had to do was tell them everything that happened. I didn't want to get into big arguments. I wanted to treat them with compassion, set their minds at ease. Frankly, my attitude toward them was conciliatory. I wanted to show them that their son's battalion commander wasn't a Nazi, wasn't an arch-right-wing military conservative. That I was a human being who felt like they felt, who had cared about their son. I wanted to make it very clear to them that nobody was more upset about Michael's death than I was. I was furious when it happened!" Schwarzkopf said: "Particularly since I'd had another friendly artillery incident from the same artillery battalion only a month before. I was so damned mad when the brigade commander landed with the artillery battalion commander at my position the following morning I couldn't even speak to the guy."

"Was this the artillery battalion commander Colonel Kuprin?" I asked.

"Right."

"Could you have told the Mullens, 'I could have killed Colonel Kuprin'?"

"I may have," Schwarzkopf admitted. "Like I said, I was furious! But don't get me wrong," he quickly added. "It wasn't because I blamed Kuprin directly as the man responsible, but it was as if my unit had done something terrible, caused casualties in someone else's unit. The unit commander is responsible for everything his unit does or fails to do. I was tremendously emotionally upset about that whole incident, and as I told the Mullens, nobody was more upset than I was."

"What was the Mullens' response to that?" I asked.

"The whole conversation had started off in a rather accusatory fashion," Schwarzkopf replied. "Questions like: 'Why did you do this?' 'Why did you do that?' 'Why did you cover up the circumstances of my son's death in your investigation?' I proceeded to explain that, first," he said, tapping his cast, "I did not, in fact, conduct the investigation. Any time there is a friendly artillery incident, the friendly artillery investigates it. And second, it's all disinterested parties who are involved in the investigation. Therefore, I had nothing to do with the investigation whatsoever! Still, when I tried to explain how upset I was by Michael's death, Mrs.

333

Mullen then asked me, 'Well, when you flew out in your little helicopter, wasn't your first statement, "Gee, it looks like the Vietcong did this!"?' I explained again I didn't conduct the investigation, that the artillery investigators were, in fact, the ones who flew in in the small helicopter. What happened was this: Colonel Clemens, the brigade commander, picked me up in his big helicopter as soon as he could get to my position. Kuprin was with him at the time. We next flew to Charlie Company's position—that would have been at about eight in the morning. Charlie Company had had to cut a landing zone large enough for our big helicopter to come in. We then flew back out prior to the artillery investigators' arrival." Schwarzkopf paused. "As I was explaining all this to the Mullens, the more we talked, the more I recalled the circumstances of the entire thing. I remembered then that someone later in Charlie Company had said that in fact, one of the artillery investigators had gotten out of the small helicopter and his first reaction was that it hadn't been done by American artillery at all, but by the VC. The point is, however, the lieutenant colonel Mrs. Mullen was referring to, the one who flew in the small helicopter, wasn't me at all. It was the lieutenant colonel in charge of the investigation. He had been assigned by the division."

"About what time do you think they arrived?"

"About ten in the morning would be my rough guess."

I asked Lieutenant Colonel Schwarzkopf how far he had been from Charlie Company when the shell hit. About two or three kilometers, he said. Why then if the artillery round had killed the two men and wounded six others at nearly three in the morning, had he then not been able to come to Charlie Company until five hours later?

"I couldn't," he said. "No helicopters were available. Generally I never had a helicopter at night. No one had a helicopter at night. No battalion commander, no brigade commander, no anyone—Med-evac got to them. Med-evac will fly in all weather conditions any time, any place, anywhere, under any circumstances. But that night the med-evac pilot had a tremendously difficult time even finding them. There was a thick fog, Charlie Company was down in the valley firing all sorts of flares and everything else." He took a sheet of yellow paper. "You had huge mountains on one side, very high mountains on the other"—Schwarzkopf drew two ellipses—"it was almost a river valley. A very narrow one." He penciled in a thin line meandering between the two ellipses. "But seated on the left, on the south side of the river, was another piece of high ground that rose in the middle of the valley. Charlie Company was on the top of that." He put an X on top of the small hill. "I was sitting on the mountain over here. It was Hill Four Ten."

"And that was where the artillery had been placed?"

"That's right," he said. "But let me explain this because it's one of the ironies of these things happening."

The maximum range of a 105mm artillery piece, the colonel told me, was approximately 12,500 meters. The artillery which would normally have supported Charlie Company was located at "Fat City" (the division artillery base camp over Chu Lai), and for this operation the guns would have been firing at their extreme range. The greater the range, the less accurate the artillery. Schwarzkopf, wanting to ensure that Charlie Company would be covered adequately, asked that the supporting artillery be moved forward. Colonel Joseph Clemons, the brigade commander, approved Schwarzkopf's request, and ordered Colonel Valentin Kuprin, the artillery battalion commander, to displace a battery (minus) of 105mm howitzers to a position from which Charlie Company's operation would be well within range. Kuprin had the responsibility to select that spot from which the artillery would be fired, and he chose to place the guns on Hill 410.

"Frankly, I would have picked Hill Four Ten too," Schwarzkopf said. "Hill Four Ten was the only location that far out where the guns could have been placed. There was another hill, Hill Seven Oh Seven but we're talking in meters now, and that would have placed the guns over twenty-three hundred feet high."

Was it essential the guns be placed in a position from which they would have to fire over Charlie Company's heads?

Nobody at that time could have predicted the artillery either would or would not have had to fire over Charlie Company's position, the colonel explained. If Charlie Company had set up on the north slope of the hill or on the southern side, rather than the crest, it would not have happened. But where the company commander establishes his night defensive perimeter is totally that commander's responsibility and prerogative. "In any case," Schwarzkopf added, "it's even more significant that Hill Four Ten had been used many, many times in the past for similar operations, and there had never been any incident whatsoever or any unsafeness involved. Therefore, I think it was not only the logical choice to put the artillery there, but the *only* choice."

Why, if the defensive targets had been called in earlier and if the artillery had announced its intention to commence firing Charlie Company's DTs at about eight that evening, had they then not fired but instead rescheduled the DTs for almost three the following morning?

"All artillery firing is done on priorities," he said. "Obviously a contact mission takes first priority. Say an infantry company over here is calling for DTs and the artillery unit is firing them when suddenly another unit over there is involved in a big fire fight. The priority of all the artillery units is going to shift to that unit that's under fire, in contact with the enemy. Here's how this thing works. . . ."

336

Schwarzkopf explained how a company commander, upon moving into a defensive position, attempts to determine the most likely routes an enemy might use to attack him. He and his artillery forward observer select targets that would place artillery fire upon those most likely spots. Each unit might select as many as twenty DTs, and with any given number of units requesting DTs and other units engaged in fire fights which took priority, a unit's DTs would not be fired until firing time was available. "Sometimes," he said, "this is very late. In Charlie Company's case it was very, very late. The night Michael Mullen was killed the artillery firing was interrupted and not resumed until five hours later."

Why did the round that killed Michael fall short?

"This is. . . . It was. . . ." Lieutenant Colonel Schwarzkopf shook his head. "It was fate. As I said, Charlie Company was sitting on a ridge between two mountains in what amounted to a valley. The artillery was to their north side on top of a hill and the defensive target the guns at this particular time were firing was a DT to the south side of the ridge Charlie Company was sitting on. The artillery fired the first round—the white phosphorous (WP), marking round that is supposed to burst fifty meters above the spot you want the high explosive (HE) round to hit. The WP round did, in fact, burst fifty meters above that spot. Then, naturally, to make the HE round land in the right spot, you would have to depress the tube of the gun to make the round land lower. The calculations of what data to be placed on the gun to lower the tube to account for this fifty meters of airspace are all done back at the fire direction center [FDC]. The FDC is supposed to take into account the mask clearance of the hill along the line of fire and the tree heights on top of the land. In other words, you've got to make sure you're not only going to clear the ground but where the trees stick up from the ground, too. Well, evidently"—the colonel paused—"in this case, this was not done. When the next HE round was fired, as it passed over the ridge to land on the other side, it hit a tree quite a ways up. A tree right over Charlie Company's position. . . ." Lieutenant Colonel Schwarzkopf let his breath out slowly. "Michael's death was a terrible, terrible tragedy. A tragedy typical of a profane thing called war—maybe 'typical' isn't the word—it isn't a daily occurrence. It's a unique thing that happens on a very occasional basis. But it happens! I'm not an expert on artillery procedures; this is why I referred the Mullens to Colonel Kuprin. I know the results of the investigation, but I don't know all the nomenclature, the details involved. Still, what I wanted to try to tell the Mullens was that I . . . feel that. . . ." Schwarzkopf paused again and rubbed his brow, "I don't know how to express this, but try to think of it this way: Michael was killed due to an error. It was a tragedy that Michael was killed. But I don't think it was an error of . . . of deliberate negligence. The error was made because of the unique set of circumstances surrounding this particular mission. All right, yes, it was an error committed by some individual and," he hastened to add, "I don't know the name of that individual. But I don't believe it's the kind of situation where whoever made the error can be pulled in and sent to jail for it or anything like that. I know one officer in the FDC was given a letter of reprimand, but what the guns had had set on them was what the FDC had sent. The location of where the DT was to hit was, in fact, the target location sent from the field. It was just this weird, tragic set of circumstances of the guns being located just exactly where they were, the line of flight being what it was, the fact that the DTs were bursting on the south side of the ridge and had to pass directly over Charlie Company's position. . . ." His voice trailed off.

And that's how Michael Mullen was killed. Just as Colonel Kuprin had told the Mullens, just as had been hinted at in correspondence with members of Charlie Company: someone back at the fire direction center had failed to take into account the height of the trees on Charlie Company's hilltop night defensive perimeter.

Two details remained to be cleared up: Who called in the artillery round? Were the men drinking?

Lieutenant Colonel Schwarzkopf wasn't sure who had requested the artillery. The forward observer team consists of three men: a forward observer, his recon-

338

naissance sergeant and a radio operator. Each of them is qualified to call in artillery and make corrections. Schwarzkopf believed the DTs had been radioed in late that afternoon by Lieutenant Rocamora. It was clear, however, that it didn't matter who had requested the artillery since whoever it was, he had provided the correct target coordinates. That the artillery had not fired its DTs until three that morning had nothing to do with the forward observer team; the delay was solely the responsibility of the artillery. They had fired only when firing time had come available. As for the drinking:

"General Ramsey, the commanding general of the Americal Division, had a policy when I first got to the division that there could be beer on fire bases and in the field," Schwarzkopf said, "but he had a serious incident in the Hundred and Ninety-sixth Brigade. I think it was in one of their stand-down areas that a man got drunk. General Ramsey then put out the policy that there was no more beer to be in the field period. I assume it was enforced by everyone. I enforced it in my battalion. And on this particular mission the artillery came out and set up in position on Hill Four Ten, and the next morning—not at the time, but the morning following Michael's death—when I went down to the guns to try to conduct my own semiformal investigation into what had happened, I looked down and there was a whole bunch of fresh beer cans. As I told the Mullens, it was obvious that they had been drinking beer. I doubt, however, that this fact is even contained in the investigation. Why? *Because the error was not on the guns*. Again, the error that caused Michael's death was made back at the fire direction center. So it was not a question of anybody on the guns drinking or anything else. The aiming of the guns was in no way a contributing factor to Michael's death. I'll say this again because it's important: everything that was set on the guns was, in fact, exactly what had been relayed to the guns over the radio by the FDC. The target coordinates radioed by the forward observer with Charlie Company were the correct coordinates. Now, I'm sure the reason why there was no mention in the investigation about the drinking was because it wasn't drunkenness. The division commander's policy was no beer in the field, so don't mention the beer and don't make waves. But waves were made. Colonel Clemons was out there, he knew they had been drinking beer, and he raised holy hell with Kuprin about it. Heads were chopped. Corrective action was taken but not through the investigation simply because the beer was in no way a contributing factor to Michael Mullen's death."

"You mentioned an artillery incident a month before in which artillery fire from an American unit landed on, I believe, Bravo Company?"

"That was in a different place," Schwarzkopf said. "It was Bravo Company. They were in a place called Dragon Valley, and there had been a great deal of contact out there. I can't recall if DTs were being fired or whether it was an enemy probe, but in any case the rounds fell short—incidently, no one was killed in the Bravo Company incident. There were some wounded. They conducted an investigation and found that on one of the guns there was a faulty elevating mechanism. It's a screw-type device, a bunch of teeth and a screw that turned to raise or lower the tube, and there had been a slippage in the teeth. As a result, the tube had dropped down to a lower angle than it should have been, and this is why the rounds fell short. Frankly, as an infantry battalion commander, I couldn't care less what caused it. My primary concern was to insure that it didn't happen again! And that is why, naturally, when the same guns that had an artillery firing incident on one of my units exactly one month later has another, I'm furious!"

"When you said, just now, 'the same guns,' did you mean—"

"It wasn't the same gun." Schwarzkopf quickly corrected me. "What I meant was that they were guns from the same unit, DivArty. Division artillery."

We spoke for a while about Michael's letters home and the sort of operations he had been involved in, and then Schwarzkopf talked about the Batangan Peninsula, the area his battalion was shifted into following Michael's death.

340

"The Mullens told me that from Michael's death through the next three months—from February, 1970, through that April—your battalion lost about one hundred twenty out of your nine hundred men. Does that sound right?" I asked.

"Killed? No. . . ." He thought for a while. "We could probably have had that many wounded from February through July, during that next six months. But prior to that move south, during that period while Michael was still with us, I'd say we had less casualties than any other battalion in the division. In that second AO, the Batangan Peninsula, our casualties were slightly above average—I don't think we were the highest because some of the battalions of the One Hundred Ninety-sixth brigade were having tremendous battles with North Vietnamese regiments and were taking sustained heavy casualties. The point is, however, that in our first AO, where Michael was, we very rarely had contact with the enemy. We had contact only when the enemy wanted to kill us. But that second AO, the Batangan Peninsula, was, as far as I'm concerned, the worst thing I've ever been through in my life."

The colonel paused for a moment, then said, "Look, to digress for a moment, the whole reason why I volunteered for Vietnam the second time was because I honestly felt I could be a better battalion commander, could accomplish the mission with less loss of life, than a lot of the people who were going over there. I felt this because of the tremendous experience I had had fighting with the Vietnamese Airborne in 1965 and 1966. After my first tour I came home with probably the greatest feeling of satisfaction I've ever had in anything I've ever done. I slept in the mud, ate rice and Vietnamese food with chopsticks for one solid year. Everywhere the Vietnamese went, I went. I was one of them. And I felt, I really felt, that I was honestly helping people. I met some fantastic people in that outfit, Vietnamese for whom I have the greatest respect in the world. These people were desperate. Many of them were from North Vietnam and had fled the Communists in 1954. They were true patriots fighting for their country, for their lives! I came home from that year feeling I had been fighting for freedom and democracy. Now, wait," he said, holding up his hand in anticipation of an interruption. "When I volunteered for Vietnam in 1965, it was for 'God, Country, and Mom's Homemade Apple Pie.' I got to Vietnam, and we were surrounded at Dak To. Well, when you get surrounded and the sun goes down with you sitting there thinking you may not see it come up again the next morning, it takes a helluva lot more than God, Country and Mom's Apple Pie— those words emblazoned across the sky—to keep you going."

Lieutenant Colonel Schwarzkopf pushed himself up from his chair and stood facing me. "I think we went to Vietnam in the first place for the principle of democracy. I'm not saying that that's what it all turned out to be, and I'm not saying that that was the end result. I'm saying only that this is the principle we went to Vietnam for. Well, what kept me going while we were surrounded was by that time I had honestly met enough truly fine, dedicated South Vietnamese officers in the Vietnamese Airborne Division who sincerely and honestly believed that we were fighting for their country, for their freedom and that I—as an American taught from the time I was knee-high to a grasshopper that one stands up and fights for democracy—that I was over there to help. Look, to go back over this whole business of why I volunteered a second time for Vietnam. . . . I know Mr. Mullen says the only reason why I went back was to make my colonelcy. Well, that's . . . that's hogwash! I didn't need to go to Vietnam a second time, you know? I didn't need to get a ticket punched. I didn't need any medals.* I'd already been promoted

---

*Following his second tour, the colonel's decorations included the Combat Infantryman's Badge, the Command Parachutist Medal, three Silver Stars, the Legion of Merit, the Distinguished Flying Cross, three Bronze Stars (one with "V"), nine Air Medals, four Army Commendation Ribbons (one with "V"), two Purple Hearts, the Vietnamese Gallantry Cross (with two palms and two gold stars), the Armed Forces Honor Medal, the Vietnamese Campaign Medal, the Vietnamese Service Medal, the German Occupation Ribbon and the National Defense Medal.

ahead of my contemporaries by about a year. And by being promoted that year, I just happened to fall into the cycle where I would be a lieutenant colonel in Vietnam. Also, I went to Vietnam sooner than most of my classmates. I went first as a captain/major and then again as a lieutenant colonel. Most of them, or many of them, had only been in Vietnam as majors."

"And majors don't get battalions?" I asked.

Schwarzkopf nodded. "Majors are generally staff positions." He sat back down at the table. "A captain was a company commander, a lieutenant colonel commanded a battalion. Commanding a battalion for an infantryman, a battalion anywhere, is, uh, 'career-enhancing.'" He winced at the phrase. "I've also explained that most of my friends didn't get commands at any time, and what is really important is to show that you can command—and not so much where you do the commanding. I would be foolish if I said I was unaware that commanding a battalion in Vietnam would help my career. Of course it would! But there were other things to consider."

He mentioned that following his first tour he returned to West Point and a year later was assigned to Fort Leavenworth in Kansas. Schwarzkopf had been scheduled next for an Army staff level job in the Office of the Chief of Research and Development at the Pentagon. He would more than likely be sent back to Vietnam after that. He and Brenda had, at that time, been married only one year and had no children. "Frankly I had to face the fact that if I got killed in Vietnam this time," he said, "Brenda was still young and beautiful and had a good job. She wouldn't be hurting for money or anything of that sort. However, if after three years at the Pentagon they sent me to Vietnam, by then we might well have a family, Brenda would have lost her job, and if I got killed then, it would be so much harder for her to adjust. So naturally I considered this. But my first and foremost reason, as I have said, was that based upon my experience, that first tour with the Vietnamese Airborne, I felt I definitely had something I could contribute as a battalion commander. I felt I could accomplish the mission with the minimum loss of life—none, if possible, which is what it's all about really. After all, this is what I had been trained for, what the Army kept me around to do and I felt it was my obligation to do so . . . and all right, *yes,* commanding a battalion successfully in Vietnam has enhanced my career. But if I turn around and make a mistake in my next assignment or get a bad efficiency report, my career will suffer just as much as it would have otherwise. The only difference between an officer and anybody else is that that officer has got the responsibility and you get into terrifying situations because you flat have got that responsibility. . . ."

Schwarzkopf sat looking down at his mug of coffee. "You know," he said after a while, "out at Walter Reed when the Mullens came to see me, and he's still there right now, is my former artillery liaison officer. Bob Trabbert. He's just had another operation on his head. He's missing his left arm above the elbow. His left leg above the knee. He's got a great big hole in his head. Bob always went with me. Everywhere a battalion commander went his artillery liaison officer had to go. The day this happened to Bob was the day Bravo Company got trapped in a minefield. . . ."

Schwarzkopf told me the story about the men of Bravo Company on the edge of panic, feeling their way out, his own terror at having to cross the minefield to quiet the young private whose leg had broken when a mine exploded beneath him and how Trabbert had been horribly wounded when a man beside him had, at Schwarzkopf's request, moved to cut a limb from a small tree to use as a splint.

"When I threw Bob on that helicopter, I didn't think he'd live. But he did. And the only reason why I wasn't killed or maimed was that I was over taking care of this other kid. And for that they gave me my third Silver Star. But as far as I'm concerned, I had no other choice. It was my responsibility. I had to do it. By being there where I was taking care of that kid, it saved my life. But you live with these things. You become terribly fatalistic in combat."

344

"When did this happen?" I asked.

"It was the twenty-eighth of May, 1970. Almost a year and a half ago."

"And Trabbert's still in the hospital?"

Schwarzkopf nodded. "And his wife has divorced him."

"Jesus."

"She was nineteen when they married and, well, I guess. . . ." Schwarzkopf shook his head sadly. "But to go back to the point I was making when you asked about the casualties after Michael's death, I want to emphasize that this Bravo minefield incident was in the Batangan Peninsula, an entirely different area of operations from where Michael Mullen got it. The mines and booby traps there were unbelievable. It was terrifying to me, and I know it was terrifying to the men. It wasn't easy being a battalion commander in Vietnam. It was hard going into the hospitals and looking at those kids that were wounded—terrible wounds from mines and booby traps. It's hard even to convey to you what an awful thing it was to go into a young man who had lost a leg or two legs and has just woken up. What do you say to that kid? You have to say something."

"What did you say?"

"Normally not much," Schwarzkopf answered. "Ninety-nine percent of the time these kids would carry the conversation, start talking first. The first thing they'd say—or close to the first thing—would be, 'Sir, I'm sorry. . . .' " Schwarzkopf looked up at me. "Here's this kid in bed who's lost his legs and he wakes up and apologizes to you!" He shook his head in wonder. "Generally they would ask, 'Did I hurt anybody else? Was anyone hurt?' The kid who had stepped on the mine felt guilty that he'd tripped it, because he thought he should have picked up the trip wire and avoided it. But here would be this kid lying there terribly maimed, and his first words are, 'Sir, I'm sorry. . . .'

" 'God,' I'd say, 'don't *you* be sorry!' " Schwarzkopf continued. "And I'd do what I could, find out if he'd notified his parents, get a phone call through so that he'd be able to talk directly to his folks if possible

345

so they'd know he was all right. You'd do whatever you could. Always, as soon as I had a man wounded, I would get to the hospital as rapidly as I could to see the guy . . . but it was hard seeing those kids. . . . It was even harder when somebody would give you the impression that they felt you were deliberately sending these kids to their deaths."

"Who made you feel this?" I asked.

"Well, number one, the Mullens," Lieutenant Colonel Schwarzkopf said. "The Mullens told me that in so many words. And number two, the whole public seems to give the impression the military deliberately wastes people. That we're a bunch of callous bastards to whom human lives don't mean a thing. Well, when people feel this way and then you have to see these young men with such terrible wounds, it's tough to take.

"The public seems to have lost faith in the military because of the war in Vietnam," Schwarzkopf continued. "After all, we're only an arm of policy of the United States government. We're public servants. If the public no longer has confidence in us, then what good are we? I think right now in the officer corps there an awful lot of people who feel confused about the public's attitude. I came into the Army because I wanted to serve my country. I took an oath saying that I'd protect this country from all enemies foreign and domestic—I didn't say *I'd* determine who the enemies were! I said I'd merely protect the country after somebody else made that determination. So this war comes around in Vietnam; the duly elected government officials send us, the Army, to fight the war. We go to Vietnam and fight the best way we know how—not needlessly wasting lives for the most part. We did the best we could, and it dragged on and on and on. Many of us were sent back a second time. A lot of young officers have been sent back a third time. I'm talking about the kid who went over first as a platoon leader, returned as a captain and commanded an infantry company and then, a third time, went over as a major. Three times he's gone off not knowing whether he was going to come back alive. He's got ten years in the service and in that ten years has been separated from his wife and family for three of them. He didn't go off to Vietnam because he wanted to. He was sent by his country. Now, suddenly, public opinion is violently antimilitary as though it had all been this kid's idea! So here he is, a young Army major with ten years' service and he's going to sit down and think, 'All of a sudden I'm being blamed for all this,' and he hurts. He's hurt! He doesn't understand why he's bearing the brunt of this animosity when the guys who sent him to Vietnam seven years ago are now back on college campuses writing articles about how terrible it is that he's there in Vietnam!"

"Colonel, Gene Mullen told me you had said we should never have been in Vietnam. Is that right?"

Schwarzkopf took time to pour us both fresh coffee before answering, "No, I don't think I could have told him that because I don't believe that. My feeling now is that we should get out. What we're gaining by being over there is no longer significant, and of course, we are getting out.* We're withdrawing much faster than I ever thought we could. But I think this is an important point: the government sends you off to fight its war—again, it's not *your* war; it's the government's war. You go off and fight not only once, but twice, okay? And suddenly a decision is made, 'Well, look, you guys were all wrong. You're a bunch of dirty bastards. You never should have been there!' Now this is going to make me think long and hard before I go off to war again. This is me, Norm Schwarzkopf, personally. I don't think there will ever be another major confrontation where huge armies line up on both sides. If that happens, it's inevitably going to be nuclear weapons and the whole thing. So I think all wars of the future are going to be—and again, God forbid, I hope we don't have any. War

---

*By the end of October, 1971, the month Lieutenant Colonel Schwarzkopf and I met, U.S. troop strength in Vietnam was 196,700 men, the lowest figure since January, 1966. With the exception of the week ending September 25, in which there had been twenty-nine combat deaths, the casualty figure had not surpassed twenty in the eleven weeks previous to that date. On October 6, the day I first met with Lieutenant Colonel Schwarzkopf, the United States suffered five killed, the lowest figure since the first week of August, 1965.

347

is a profanity. It really is. It's terrifying. Nobody is more antiwar than an intelligent person who's been to war. Probably the most antiwar people I know are Army officers—but if we do have a war, I think it's going to be similar in nature to Vietnam and Korea. Limited in scope. And when they get ready to send me again, I'm going to have to stop and ask myself, 'Is it worth it?' That's a very dangerous place for the nation to be when your own army is going to stop and question."

We carried our coffee back to the table. He sat cradling the mug between his palms. "I *hate* what Vietnam has done to our country! I *hate* what Vietnam has done to our Army! But to go back to your original question, could I have told Mr. Mullen that we should never have gone to Vietnam? No, I don't think I could have told him that because I don't believe that. We went to Vietnam for the same reason we went into South Korea. For the same reason we went into Germany during the Second World War. For the same reason we went to Europe during World War One."

I noticed that Lieutenant Colonel Schwarzkopf's voice was getting hoarse. We had been talking nonstop since ten that morning, and it was now nearly five o'clock. I asked him if he wouldn't like to take a break, and at that moment the apartment door opened, and his wife, Brenda, and their daughter, Cindy, returned. The little girl rushed to her father, and he swept her into his arms. Cindy laughed and chattered, and Brenda, who was very pretty with dark hair and a pale Irish complexion, said hello and excused herself to unload the groceries. The colonel asked me to stay for dinner, made us each a drink, placed a record on the phonograph, and when we sat down again, it was all very relaxed and easy. We spoke about our children, about living in Washington, about his father and the Lindbergh kidnapping and the Hopewell-Pennington-Princeton-Lawrenceville part of New Jersey. I don't think we deliberately avoided speaking about the war since occasionally the subject would naturally come up. I believe, simply, we both preferred to talk about something else. Once though, toward the end of dinner, I remember asking him how soon he felt we should get out of Vietnam. Schwarzkopf answered, "As fast as possible." He looked across the table at his wife. "I don't ever want to go back there again."

After dinner we slipped into the sort of long political discussion that doesn't change either party's mind and then, at about nine thirty, I told the colonel I felt I had taken up too much of his time, and if he wouldn't mind, I'd like to give him a break and then come back the next morning. There were many more things, he said, that he wanted to talk about, too.

Lieutenant Colonel Schwarzkopf insisted on driving me back into Washington where I had reserved a hotel room. He said he needed the air, and maybe it would help him sleep. Because of his cast, he said, he was never able to sleep more than a few hours at a time. I asked him about his wound. He was in a cast, it turned out, not because of anything that had happened in Vietnam but rather the accumulated strain and pounding his back had taken over the years had been aggravated by parachute landings.

The Army decided an operation might alleviate some of the pressure on his lower spine. He would be free of the cast, he told me, in another couple of months.

During the drive I asked him about his correspondence with the Mullens and whether Peg had sent him Michael's letters.

"The only letter I ever got was from *Mrs.* Mullen. It arrived in May, as I recall, shortly after I was wounded. She told me she had taken his gratuity pay and spent it to buy a newspaper advertisement. I think she sent me a copy of the ad and excerpts from his letters and that was about it. . . ." He thought for a moment, then said, "I was very upset by the tone of her letter. I wanted to write an answer. I contacted Division and was told I shouldn't, that I should forward the letter to Division instead, and they would handle it from there. And so, of course, that was my guide."

"You mean the two letters the Mullens received from you weren't written by you at all? Why wouldn't the Division want you to answer?"

"I don't think it was a question of not wanting me

349

to answer," he said. "I think it was because it involved friendly fire casualties—in fact, any casualties at all."

He explained how it was the Division's policy in situations involving casualties to have the Headquarters write and coordinate all letters sent to next of kin. The purpose for this policy was to ensure that no conflicting details were given, thereby sparing families the sort of anguish varying versions might cause.

The result, in the Mullens' case, however, was clearly the opposite. It was precisely the conflicting evidence, plus an implicit policy of information control, that started the Mullens out on their search to learn what had happened to their son.

I asked the colonel what he would have written the Mullens had the Division not intervened.

"Oh, God, I don't know," he said. "I probably would have tried to give them as much detail on what exactly happened as I could. And I probably would have tried to convey to them my personal feeling of . . . of, I guess, horror that this did happen. . . ."

We were both silent. The colonel was busy navigating the access route to Key Bridge across the Potomac River, and I was playing back our conversation in my mind. I could not reconcile the discrepancies between what the Mullens had told me Schwarzkopf had said and his version of what he had said. I tried to picture that conversation out at Walter Reed, tried to imagine Gene leaning over the colonel, their faces inches apart: "Colonel, now you can tell me your story . . ." and later, "Do you know you were suckered down out of your helicopter into that minefield?" I tried to imagine how Schwarzkopf would have reacted to Gene's constant correcting him on details and Gene's comment about his having "lost thirty-two men from your stupidity of marching them through a minefield."

We were across Key Bridge and in the old Georgetown part of Washington when I turned to the colonel and asked, "When the Mullens visited you in the hospital, who did most of the talking?"

"Mrs. Mullen did," he said.

"She did? Peg did?"

"As a matter of fact, I was very concerned for Mr.

350

Mullen. At times he was . . . well, he was very emotional and would become so choked up he was almost incoherent. Why? You sound surprised."

"I am. That isn't the impression I got at all."

"What did they tell you?" he asked.

"I guess it wasn't so much what they said as how they said it. The 'Colonel Schwarzkopf' they told me about just doesn't seem like you at all. Maybe tomorrow we can go over that meeting in more detail?"

"Sure," he said. "We'll cover it all."

Chapter Twenty-Four

That evening at the hotel I read through my notes of Lieutenant Colonel Schwarzkopf's and my conversation. One of his statements particularly intrigued me. Referring to the demoralizing effect of the Vietnam War upon the career soldier, he had said, "This is going to make me think long and hard before I go off to war again. When they get ready to send me, I'm going to have to stop and ask myself, 'Is it worth it?' " It was an extraordinary comment for a young West Point officer with three Silver Stars to have made.

The next morning when I returned to Schwarz-kopf's apartment, it was clear he had been thinking about that statement, too. It was one of the first things he mentioned after we had sat down.

"Let me clarify that," he said. "It sounds like I'm going to stay in the Army, continue to rise in rank or stabilize or whatever, but then someday in the future when there's a confrontation and the Army gives me a set of orders I'm going to say, 'Hell no, I won't go!' That's not what I'm implying. What I really mean is at twenty years I'm going to make a decision as to whether to pursue my military career or not. If I decide to remain in the service and the government orders me to go, I will go. I don't see how I can refuse unless I felt so strongly about it that my only alternative was to resign from the Army. I'd go because it was my duty. It's like being a fireman. You don't join up and say, 'I'll only fight chemical fires and not wood fires.' You become a fireman and say, 'I'll fight fires.' " Schwarzkopf leaned back in his chair. "We can get into a very subtle discussion here of conscience and duty, the Nuremberg Trials, the Japanese war criminals, et cetera. This is a very valid question the government is going to have to face—obviously, it's a question the public is already facing. . . ." He let his chair drop back forward. "What is moral? What is immoral? Where does duty stop and morality begin? Are we now saying that the military is supposed to question the morality of our government's commitment to a war? I don't know. . . ." He shook his head. "I really don't know. If we allow the military to question whether or not to go then," he said, "it seems to me we also have to look at the other side of the coin. What if the government decides *not* to go? Do we allow the military the right to criticize this decision? To decide whether it was correct or not? And perhaps go to war in spite of the fact that the government decides we shouldn't? See, the military is required to follow the orders given it by the government. How they pursue it is another question—and here is where you get into civilian casualties, war crimes, atrocities, ovens and all that business. If you're a member of the military, you don't really have much choice as far as pursuing the war or not. If it ever came to a choice between compromising my moral principles and the performance of my duties, I know I'd go with my moral principles. At the same time, however, I would also cease being an Army officer. I would have to resign my commission. But even at that I could be accomplishing my duty as I see it."

A few minutes later when we were discussing his conversation with the Mullens, how emotional it had been for the Mullens, as well as himself, I asked if the mood had seemed tense all the way through.

"No, not at all," he answered. "The interview started off rather hostile but became more and more cordial as time went on. Frankly it became so cordial that along about three-quarters of the way through Knap got up and indicated he felt there was no need whatsoever for a witness to remain since everybody seemed to be getting along so well. So he left."

We spoke about the sequence of questions during their conversation and under what circumstances Colonel Kuprin's name had arisen and whether or not Rocamora had been asleep. "Gene Mullen," I said, "felt you had had a change of attitude toward the military

353

because of two things: first, and I'm quoting Gene Mullen here, 'his straightforward words telling us what had happened because we could either correct him, and his wanting to get the blame off himself when it actually wasn't him.'"

"I don't think I've had any great changes in my attitude toward the military one way or the other," Schwarzkopf said, "but when he mentions those two things that have given him that opinion, my 'straightforward words' and so on, that's ludicrous!" He shook his head in dismay. "Is it . . . is it so *difficult* for the Mullens to believe that I sincerely wanted them to come out to see me so that I could honestly tell them what had happened to their son?"

Colonel Schwarzkopf pushed his chair back and stood up. "Is it impossible for them to believe I was really *concerned* for them?" he asked, "Or do they believe my only concern was for myself? I accomplished nothing for myself by talking to the Mullens other than from the standpoint of trying to clear the air for them. I felt sorry for them. Compassion for them. . . . I still frankly feel very sorry for them, but his line about my 'wanting to get the blame off' myself. . . . Blame for what? For Michael's death? I never felt I was to blame. The only letter I got from Mrs. Mullen in no way accused *me* of being responsible. It was a blanket condemnation of everything military, yes, but it did not specifically accuse me of Michael's death. So I never felt I was to blame. . . . Look, one of the important things I want to clear up here is this." He began to pace back and forth across the room. "Where Gene Mullen says my 'straightforward words'—how did that go?"

I read Gene's comment back to the colonel, who stood listening with his hands on his hips. "All right," Schwarzkopf said, "he's alluded to this a couple of times. He seems to feel the reason I was honest with him was because he had so many facts. This," he said, beginning to pace again, "this is ridiculous! The Mullens have information, yes," he said, then shrugged. "I don't know what they have, frankly. But they have some information from a few individuals in the company,

354

each of whom saw a specific incident from his specific viewpoint. None of these people were privy to the investigation that went on afterward. None of these people knew the complete facts of what went on. None of these people were, in fact, familiar with the big picture. . . . Frankly, I found the Mullens about one-quarter armed with facts. With one-fourth of the big picture. A great deal of what they feel is based, I believe, on conclusions they wanted to reach rather than what they could have reached had they learned the facts. They didn't have any straightforward, down-to-earth picture of what went on, and frankly, I'm beginning to wonder if it is possible for them to. If they ever will."

Schwarzkopf moved back to our table and stood leaning over his chair. "You know, this is one of the reasons I constantly referred them to Captain Tom Cameron, who was Michael's company commander. Cameron was there! He could probably tell you right away who called in the artillery, why the company was set up where it was. He knew everything that went on from all sides. But evidently," Schwarzkopf said, slapping the chairback, "the Mullens don't want to know. Don't want to talk to Cameron. . . . I don't know why, I really don't. As I said before, I wanted the Mullens to have a true and honest picture. I was in no way intimidated by them, and I certainly, I certainly wasn't intimidated by the information they had. . . . I find it extremely difficult to believe that the Mullens were not willing to accept that people just wanted to talk to them, to be *honest* with them. Evidently they feel anyone who wants to talk to them must have an ulterior motive. And frankly I resent the implication!" He pulled his chair out and sat down. "I'm afraid I'm getting a little emotional about this, but it's disturbing."

We spoke for a while about the peace movement; Lieutenant Colonel Schwarzkopf was convinced that the war would have ended a long time before had it not been for the peace demonstrations but added that one of his sisters was a peace marcher. "I know the intentions behind her doing it," he said, "and I don't resent her for it in the least. Based upon what the peace marchers read and what they have been exposed to, if I were them I would probably be marching in the streets, too." And then we began to talk about the court-martial of Private Willard Polk.

"According to Peg Mullen," I told him, "you had signed all the papers that had sealed his court-martial and you didn't know him at all."

"Again," Schwarzkopf said wearily, "this is a complete misstatement of fact. The minute she brought up the Polk case and told me who he was I recalled the case. The part I wasn't exactly aware of were the details. When she told me that Polk had been asleep next to Michael, that he went temporarily insane et cetera and asked why this wasn't brought out at his trial, I told her I was not familiar with that information, that as the battalion commander I was not there when Polk went berserk or whatever. I was on Hill Four Ten with the artillery. I received a report of the incident in which Private Polk shot at some civilians—that incident took place several days after Michael was killed—I then received the preferred charges from the company commander and statements from the witnesses, each of whom backed up the fact that charges should, in fact, be prepared against Polk. From the facts it was apparent that some investigation should be pursued. I therefore signed and forwarded the charges. General court-martials are not handled at the battalion or even brigade level. They're handled at division level or higher. The term 'general' implies that. The minute charges were forwarded, Polk's case was out of my hands. The court-martial took place after I had departed Vietnam."

Several questions later I said, "You know, one of the things that keeps bothering me about the Mullens' version of their conversation with you is that according to Gene, he said he had accused you of killing his son. And you, of course, have told me he accused you only of covering up the details of the investigation." I was leafing through the transcript of the Mullens' conversation with me in my house and found the place I wanted. "But here Gene has you saying, and this is his version of your quote, 'I want you to know I was not the investigating committee.' And Gene replies, 'No, we

356

know that.' It doesn't make sense. If he knew that, then why would he accuse you of covering up the details?"

"All right, this is either another deliberate misrepresentation or there's been some confusion," the colonel said. "At the time the Mullens came to see me they thought I was the person who had suppressed the facts of the investigation into their son's death. This was his allegation over the telephone, and this was his statement when he first got out to Walter Reed. This discussion where he says, 'No, we know that,' never transpired. Perhaps after they had discussed it with me, with Kuprin later on, they realized I'd had nothing to do with the investigation and they—no." He paused. "I really don't understand. The point I'm trying to make is that this conversation didn't occur because when they came to see me they were still under the impression I'd covered up the investigation, and I think this is kind of curious and worth commenting on."

Schwarzkopf picked up our coffee mugs and carried them into the kitchen. He continued to talk while he poured us fresh coffee. "For eighteen months, evidently, the Mullens thought I was guilty of killing their son. How they thought I was guilty, I'm not sure. The only conceivable reason was either, one, I had ordered the artillery to be fired without anyone's knowledge. Or, two, I had specifically covered up the investigation because of my own negligence or something of this sort. Now they are suddenly saying I had nothing to do with the investigation, and so I don't understand why they felt I was responsible for killing Michael. I don't believe they still think I'm responsible, do you? Because, as I said, our conversation became so cordial that three-quarters of the way through Knap flat got up and left. By that time we had finished the specific discussion of the artillery incident and the facts surrounding it, and the Mullens were just asking me a kind of specific shotgun question here and there. And I was answering them. . . ."

He carried our coffee back and sat down again. "I vividly recall, as a matter of fact, that at the end Gene Mullen said—and I think these are his exact words—'For a year and a half I have carried hate for

357

you in my heart. I want you to know I no longer feel that way anymore.' And then he added to that, 'Frankly, Michael liked you. In one of his letters he called you the Old Man.' . . . Now that's an exact quote! And when the Mullens left the hospital, about a week later I got a note from them saying—Mrs. Mullen knew the initial determination was going to be made the following Wednesday, they were going to cut off my cast and take X rays, then put me back in another cast—Mrs. Mullen wrote me and said, 'I hope the X rays prove that you are recovering sufficiently and that everything's going well. I hope that you'll be up and around and on your feet again soon. We had a pleasant journey and arrived home safely,' that sort of thing. There was no return address, and therefore, I couldn't answer it. But it was on this note of cordiality that everything terminated."

"Well. . . ."

"Well, what?"

I shook my head. "It didn't sound all that cordial when they talked to me." I stood up and began gathering together my notes and papers. It was time for me to catch my plane. "What I'd like to do, Colonel, is type up a transcript for you of our conversation so you can check over what you said. There may be things I misunderstood or placed the wrong emphasis on, and if you'll just pencil in your corrections or comments, I won't bother you by coming down to Washington again."

"It wasn't a bother," he said. "Look, it was nice just being able to talk to someone about all this."

A couple of weeks later I telephoned Lieutenant Colonel Schwarzkopf and said I was sending him the transcript of our conversation. I also told him I would be enclosing a transcript of the Mullens' talk with me, adding that I wasn't doing him any favor by doing so. I explained, however, with his help I hoped somehow to reconstruct the conversation he had had with them at Walter Reed and write it as it had occurred.

About a week later—this would have been around the beginning of November—Lieutenant Colonel Schwarzkopf mailed me two cassette tapes. On them he explained it was difficult for him to write because of the cast and, if I didn't mind, he would rather speak into the tape as though we were together again. The first long section answered specific questions I had added to the margin of our transcript or enlarged upon areas he felt needed clarification or qualified statements which, in print, he felt might have carried too strong an emphasis. Wherever applicable, I simply inserted these comments in the text. He next turned his attention to the Mullen transcript, saying, "You were absolutely right when you said you weren't doing me any favors by sending me this interview.

"Frankly, my immediate reaction was one of anger and shock—even after many days of reading and rereading it, of trying to assume a dispassionate viewpoint on this entire thing, I still find myself somewhat disturbed when I see their comments here. I am going to try to approach this as best I can from an unemotional standpoint, but this sheds an entirely different light on the Mullens from what I had before.

"They have quoted liberally out of context, extracted certain words I said and ignored the meaning of everything else I've said in my discussions with them. They've made assumptions that I felt or thought a certain way when I said something. Then somehow turned this into words I supposedly stated.

"Obviously they have taken my interview and twisted it to substantiate or justify whatever strange idea it is that they have—and, frankly, what their idea is I really don't know—but it upsets me that I did not accomplish what I set out to do by talking to them in the first place. I wanted to tell them the straight story of what happened to their son, to somehow set their minds at ease. Instead, all I've evidently accomplished is added fuel to their fire."

Schwarzkopf, as best he could, discussed the sequence of topics raised during their conversation. He apologized for occasional vagueness but explained he had had no idea at the time he met with the Mullens that he would be later asked to reconstruct the conversation in detail. "It was particularly difficult," he added, "because it was an emotional moment for me, and like I said, it was obviously an emotional moment for the

Mullens." Then, directly referring to the transcript, he said, "All right, where Gene Mullen said, 'Now he never told us who Major Knap was or what his business was there, but from the way he had positioned his chair at the opposite side of the bed, it was obvious it had been prearranged,' well, this is absolutely ridiculous! I explained to you before who Knap was and what he was doing there. I guess what I'm trying to point out is . . . is . . . the intent. That attitude with which the Mullens approached this interview is what has upset me more than anything else. The obvious looking for trouble, for something not the truth but which would substantiate their feelings. That statement, 'it was obvious it had been prearranged,' is typical of their evident approach to the whole thing."

The colonel paused, and I could hear a page turn. "Okay, another thing," he said. "This comment of Gene Mullen's about the minefield. Well, you know me well enough, I think, to realize that a comment such as 'You lost thirty-two men from your stupidity of marching them through a minefield' is a little bit of bravado on his part. I wouldn't have tolerated that for one minute from anyone no matter how conciliatory I was trying to be toward them. The subject was brought up, and we discussed it, but he certainly didn't approach it in that fashion. They also said that an 'officer suckered [me] down' into that area. In the first place, nobody called me in. Nobody on the ground ever calls his battalion commander and says, 'You must come down here and land.' A battalion commander does what he wants to do. It's his battalion! And secondly, no officer could have suckered me down because when I landed, there were *no officers there*. That was one of the big reasons why I went into that area to take care of Bravo Company. The one officer who was with them—a real fine young man—had been wounded and had to be evac'd out. The first sergeant had also been wounded, which upset me very much because he, too, was a fine man. So without, with this lack of real leaders I had confidence in, I felt I had to get in there and get things squared away.

"And here where he says, 'The company first sergeant was out there that night, and it was the first time he was out in the field in I don't know how long.' And she says, 'They have to go out.' 'By the book,' he says. And she says, 'Every three months or so.'

"Well, this thing about the first sergeant was ridiculous," Schwarzkopf said. "You're aware of the administrative duties that a first sergeant has in a company, the paperwork that goes with the job. But Colonel Joe Clemons decided that because first sergeants had had so much valuable experience and because we were so short of experienced NCOs, their place was in the field. He put out a directive stating that the first sergeant of every rifle company spend a minimum of fifty percent of their time in the field with their unit. It was just that simple. I concurred wholeheartedly and enforced it in my battalion. Frankly, in Charlie Company's case, there was a personality clash between the first sergeant and the executive officer. So, any time the XO was back in the rear, the first sergeant intentionally went out to the field—and one of the reasons was to get away from Charlie Company's executive officer. . . ."

The colonel paused, and I could hear him turning more pages of the transcript. "Okay," he said, "where Mrs. Mullen makes the comment 'All the boys said it was the only time they remember all the officers being there. And even Schwarzkopf—it was the first time he was in action with them on the ground.' Again, that's incorrect.

"I made it a point to be with every single one of my units every single day. I was constantly in and out. One of the reasons, as I explained to you before, why I didn't stay with one company all the time was that I didn't want to harass that one company commander. But secondly, I had a responsibility for four rifle companies on the ground, a mortar company, a reconnaissance platoon, and my rear, any one of which was or might have been in a dangerous area. Therefore, I went everywhere. And, all right, as I also explained, I wasn't even with Charlie Company on the ground that night. I was back on Hill Four Ten with the artillery because I had two rifle companies out there . . . but why am I going into such detail on this?

361

"For a very simple reason," Schwarzkopf said. "The Mullens just don't have the facts! Or if they do have the facts, they choose to ignore them. What really bothers me is that they are so convinced that they are so right. And they're so loaded with wrong information.

"I'm not sure any of this has any bearing on your book—I don't know whether it does or not. It's just that I'm sure every time the Mullens get up and issue public statements, nobody can get up and rebut them. . . ."

There was quite a long pause on the tape; then the colonel said, "God, I don't know. Maybe it just helps me to say these things to somebody who will *listen*. Look, sure Vietnam's a terrible, horrible war, and we've lost a helluva lot of good men over there, but . . . but everything is not black about Vietnam and everybody who participated is not a . . . a double-headed ogre! It's misconceptions, distortions, blanket condemnations of anyone and everyone involved with Vietnam that I disagree with so vehemently. These statements Mrs. Mullen has made about me are completely and totally untrue, and I resent them!

"I felt a—I still feel a great deal of compassion for the Mullens. I do. It's a terrible tragedy that they lost their son—it's a terrible tragedy that so many women have lost sons—but although I feel sorry for the Mullens, I think the biggest tragedy is their mental state at this time.

"I now feel the Mullens have been told over and over again exactly what happened to Michael, but unfortunately, they're not willing to believe it. They're not willing to accept it. They still apparently think everyone is wrong except them. Somehow they have adopted the very role they are condemning in the rest of us.

"I said I'd try to be dispassionate about this whole thing, but I haven't been able to. I find this entire business very distressing—not because I have anything to hide, not because I've done anything wrong, not because my battalion did anything wrong or, for that matter, because there were any irregularities throughout this entire affair. It's just that . . . it's just that. . . ."

The tape ran silent for about ten seconds. When

the colonel spoke again, his voice was discouraged, tired, a little sad.

"I find the distortions, the twisting, the accusations to be a *dirty* business. It's highly upsetting to me and so I haven't been able to remain unemotional. . . .

"I'll just finish off by saying it's a terrible thing that happened to Michael Mullen . . . a terrible, *terrible* tragedy. He was a very fine noncommissioned officer. Very well thought of by the men in his company. He was intelligent. He had brains and common sense. Michael was a leader. And that's why his death had such an impact on Charlie Company. Michael was one of those individuals who stand out. He was a very fine young man, and his death was a tremendous loss. It's terrible that any young man should lose his life in such a violent way. And I guess that is what your book is about.

"But it's an even more terrible thing that has happened to the Mullens themselves."

Chapter Twenty-Five

+++++++++++++++++++++++++++++

Almost exactly a year after I had first met Gene and
Peg Mullen at their Black Hawk County, Iowa, farm I
drove back through La Porte City to talk to them again.
I had not seen the Mullens for nine months, not since
the day we spent discussing their meeting with Lieutenant Colonel H. Norman Schwarzkopf.

Through Schwarzkopf I was able to locate Michael
Mullen's former company commander, Tom Cameron.
Captain Cameron, though still in the Army, was then
attending the University of Alabama in Tuscaloosa
working toward a master's degree in business administration. We spent three days together in mid-January,
1972.

Cameron was able to help me find Abe Aikins,
the former senior medic with Charlie Company's headquarters section. Aikins was newly married and living
in a Long Island suburb of New York City, where he
worked as an assistant manager in a Household Finance
office while attending night courses to complete his
college degree. I met with Aikins in mid-February.

During the first week in March I spoke with
Martin Culpepper, the young former assistant machine
gunner in Charlie Company's 3rd Platoon. Culpepper
had been the first of Michael's friends to correspond
with the Mullens. He, too, had married soon after his
return from Vietnam and was back now at his old job
with the Rath Packing Company in Waterloo.

The following week I received permission to visit
Willard Polk at the Federal Penitentiary in Terre Haute,
Indiana. Polk had between three and nine months of
his prison sentence left to serve. The incidents for
which Polk had been court-martialed had not, as the
Mullens had thought, occurred the night Michael had

been killed but eight days later, when Charlie Company had returned from that operation and were resting and reassembling at Hill 76, the mortar base camp. Polk had been found guilty of striking his superior officer and a noncommissioned officer and two counts of "wrongfully and willfully discharging" an M-16 rifle and M-79 grenade launcher "under circumstances such as to endanger human life." Lieutenant Colonel Kenneth A. Howard, the presiding judge at Polk's court-martial, would, a year later, preside over the trial of Captain Ernest L. Medina of My Lai. Polk's trial lasted a day and a half.

On April 12, I was finally able to locate and speak with the "Prince," the young rifleman who had lost his left leg below the knee when the same shell that killed Michael hit. Everyone I had spoken with in Charlie Company liked the Prince and praised his courage that night. His real name is Gary Samuels, and when I met him, he was living with his mother and stepfather in Caldwell, New Jersey.

Samuels, Polk, Culpepper, Aikins, Cameron. Each separately confirmed the details of the incident which had brought about Michael's death. Each of them had been on that hill that night; each of them furthered my conviction that Schwarzkopf had told the Mullens the truth.

I felt, therefore, that I had come to the end of the story. Inasmuch as any man can know another's death, I now knew Michael's. That is why, as I approached the last gentle, rolling hill on Route 218 south of the Mullens' hometown, I felt a sense of relief. It was a relief born out of the naïve anticipation that at last I could offer the Mullens some comfort. I could relieve their anguish, bestow on them a kind of peace. I still believed that the truth, inevitably, would set them free.

On either side of me were the rich black farmlands, the cedar fence posts with the tacked-up tin Felco Feed and Vinton Hybrid placards. I passed the sign on the edge of town, LA PORTE CITY: PROGRESSING WITH AMERICA, and saw it still needed paint.

Mom's Café had moved across Main Street closer

365

to Big Creek. The Tastee Freeze was abandoned and boarded up. Otherwise the town looked the same. I checked into La Porte's one motel and called the Mullens. Peg said come out right away.

Peg hugged me the moment I climbed their back stairs. Gene warmly, tightly gripped my hand. We stood by their kitchen table, smiling, happy to see each other again. Peg wanted to feed me lunch, complained I was looking thin, asked about my family, while Gene stood with his fists pushed deep inside his overall pockets, shifting his weight from foot to foot. Suddenly, almost shyly, he blurted, "We've got a real treat for you tonight!"

"Oh?" I asked, surprised. "What's that?"

"A pork tenderloin," he said. "Just about the best cut you can get from a hog. It's from one of our own."

"For heaven's sake, sit down! Sit down!" Peg said, pushing me over to the kitchen table and pulling out a chair. "Tell me now, how was your trip?"

"Did you see many trucks?" Gene asked.

"Come to think of it, I didn't," I said. "Why do you ask?"

"Well, at this truck stop down here on the road to Waterloo, I always ask how are the truckers," Gene explained. "And I talk to the truckers when they come in. They tell me they're deadheading too much. No full loads. No return loads. These are guys coming from all over the U.S."

"It's an indicator of the economy," Peg added.

The Mullens spoke about what was happening around them. Collins Radio, an aerospace communications and electronics company in Cedar Rapids, which used to have 11,000 employees, was down to 5,000. General Mills in Cedar Rapids had laid off half their work force. Rath Packing was working a twenty-nine-to thirty-two-hour week; normally the men had a forty-hour week. Gene himself was on a two-month layoff from John Deere.

"For the last six years," Gene said, "I've known exactly how many tractors John Deere sells because I was the final release inspector. I used to take down the serial numbers of every tractor. We used to hit between fifty-two and fifty-three thousand tractors a year. Last year we didn't do thirty thousand!"

The cost of running their farm had risen sharply, too. Fertilizer prices had gone up 8 percent; corn seed which used to cost $6 an acre now was $10. The cost of gas for farm operations had increased accordingly.

"Do you know what our Secretary of Agriculture, Earl Butz, told them at the Des Moines Farm Institute a couple of weeks ago?" Peg asked acidly. "He said there wasn't much they could do for the farmer, but we 'should just keep in mind how patriotic it is to feed the rest of the world.' Isn't that something!"

"You know," Gene said, "when that Another Mother for Peace film was shown over the television here—the one in which we took part?—well, the next morning, when I went to work, people came up to me and said, 'I saw you on television, Oscar!' They wouldn't say anything more. But a year ago, last year they would've said, 'You sonuvabitchin' Communist! You traitor!' and they don't say that anymore."

"The change in a year is unbelievable," Peg said.

"We went to this funeral of Cecil Joens'," Gene said.

"I told you about him," Peg said to me. "He was here when we moved here. Lived in that gray house across on the corner there. The one with the big stone in the field; they used to light fires on top of it to guide settlers home."

"He was our neighbor and friend," Gene said.

"Well, when we came back here after the war and"—Peg laughed—"of course we were the jokes of the community. We knew nothing about farming and Cec, well, he was a saint, he was so good to us." Peg was standing at the kitchen window looking out at the fields. "This was all mud around here, and every time I'd get stuck Cec would pull me out. I bet I got stuck a million times. And if I got into a situation here alone when Gene was working, well, it was Cec who came over day or night. He was that way with the kids, too. Cec adored them. He was so good to them! He did our custom work for us—"

"Picked our corn," Gene explained.

367

"And he was always so fair in his prices. I always felt he did it a little cheaper for us. Maybe instead of six dollars an acre, he'd charge us five."

"He was the kind of person everybody liked," Gene said. "I don't care where it is there's somebody like—"

"Everybody liked him," Peg agreed, nodding sadly.

"—Cec wherever you go. He's not going to set the world on fire by any spectacular thing, but every day it's little things that just keep blossoming out."

"I think I kind of worshiped Cec for all the kind things he did for us when we were struggling without a dime and Gene was working nights. That's why the funeral got to us and all the townspeople, too. Everybody was a mess because they loved him so."

"Let me tell you about that funeral," Gene said. "We were talking about the change this past year. Well, at Cecil's funeral there were people who know how we stand who came up to talk to me—I never opened the conversation myself, but these people walked up to me with smiles on their faces and they said hello. And I returned the cordiality, and when I spoke to them and they spoke to me, it sort of broke the ice. People who beforehand would see me on the street and turn their heads, a number of those people at that funeral even wanted to stand and talk to me. . . ." Gene thought for a moment, then added, "I shouldn't say I enjoyed the funeral. I didn't 'enjoy' the funeral. But it did two good things for me. It helped me pay respect to a man I had great respect for, who was a very, very good friend of mine. Mikey spent part of his last day with Cecil, you know. And okay, I paid my respects to him along with all the rest of his friends. But I had a number of people who even wanted to talk to me! The change is unbelievable."

"Let me tell you something else," Peg said. "People were thinking about us because it's been almost two years since we buried Michael. And a lot of the concern at that funeral was for us. There's a couple who publish an advertising sheet here, and they walked over to me in the dining room and said, 'We've thought about you constantly today. We've thought about you for two years continually. We think about you all the time.' But they'd never approached me on this subject before. . . . Another thing is that Cec wasn't able to come here when Michael died. He was beginning to have some heart trouble then and—'

"He couldn't even call and talk to us," Gene said.

"Anyway," Peg continued, "after he died, John wrote a letter to Cecil's mother, who was all alone. And I was over there the other day, and she showed me the letter. It was beautiful. I really couldn't believe John had written it! He said something about how his love for Cec had begun when Mary took him over to play there the first time when he, John, was three. And he went on about all the basketball games Cec had taken him to, the football games, the state fairs—Michael, too—and John said, 'Somehow I knew the war was getting to Michael those last days—' "

"We all knew it," Gene said. "Before that, see, Mikey could. . . ." Gene took a sudden gulp of air and swallowed. "Before that the house could be burning down and Mikey would never. . . ." Gene could not finish. He covered his eyes with his hands, Peg started to move toward him and paused, not certain whether he needed comforting or not. She looked at Gene and then at me, trying to remember what she had been saying.

"You were telling me about John's letter to Cecil Joens' mother," I said.

"Yes, well, John wrote that. . . ." She glanced over at Gene again, and then, with her own voice quavering slightly, she continued, "John wrote that Cecil couldn't—ohh!" Peg leaned back against the kitchen counter and gripped the edge tightly. *"I'm not going to cry today!* I'm not!" she said. "You do that to me," she said accusingly, "and I don't cry very often anymore." She turned back to pour herself a glass of tap water.

Gene was sitting quietly at the table. He had taken his hands away from his face, but his eyes remained averted, his head lowered.

Peg took a sip of water and turned to face us again. "In his letter John said that Cecil had to die because of the pain. That he couldn't live with the pain

369

any longer and that Michael, too, couldn't have lived six more months with the pain of the war. And it reminded me of how, when I had read Michael's letters, I knew the war was getting to him. Those letters and postcards that last month were disturbed."

"And Mikey wasn't that way." Gene pushed his chair away from the table and stood up. "Mikey wasn't the kind to get disturbed about things, and yet in those last letters he was!"

"He couldn't take any more," Peg said.

Gene walked over to the window looking out on the barns, and then he turned, facing me, and said, "You know, I could say something violent—I will! I will say it! GOD DAMN what's causing this!" He walked back to the table and stood gripping the back of his chair. "We have boys all around here who are basket cases in this area—"

"That story in the Des Moines *Register*," Peg said, "how many legless boys did it say are in Iowa?"

"I don't know," Gene said. "Twenty-six, I think."

"*Twenty-six!*" Peg said.

"There are two right over here about ten miles in Hudson, Iowa. One has both legs off, the other just one. . . . Well, God damn it! I—we—I can tell you, people, well-to-do people up here? They get on the telephone and call us, 'How do we get our boy out of the service? Please help us get our boy out!' And now their boy is out and they—if—I—this war!" Speechless with frustration, Gene abruptly sat down.

Peg suddenly asked, "Was Michael, or was he not, the platoon sergeant? Now this you've learned."

"He was not," I said.

"Why not?"

"Because a new sergeant came into Charlie Company who had a higher rank. He was with the company one or two days the night Michael was killed, and he was wounded, too."

"Who was he?" Peg asked.

"His name was Wetsel. He was a staff sergeant. Michael was an acting platoon sergeant, but it was only temporary."

"We know that," Gene said curtly.

"Because Michael didn't want to be platoon sergeant," Peg said. "Why was Michael made a platoon sergeant to begin with?"

I explained that Michael's previous platoon sergeant had rotated home. While Charlie Company was awaiting the replacement, Michael, as ranking sergeant in the 1st Platoon, was appointed acting platoon sergeant. Michael was a sergeant (E-5) with three stripes. When Wetsel, a staff sergeant (E-6) with three stripes and one rocker, arrived in the company, he became the 1st Platoon's platoon sergeant. "Look, I don't know whether this is the proper time for this or not," I said. "It's up to you. But if you'd like, I can cover with you all the information I've been able to learn and—"

"Oh, I don't know whether that's necessary or not," Peg said, looking distressed.

"It's up to you," I said.

"Michael was hit between the shoulder blades, wasn't he?" she asked.

"Yes, a piece of shrapnel entered his back and pierced his heart. He died right away. In his sleep. There's no question about that."

"Yes," Peg said. "They all told us that."

"But what I meant, Peg," I said, "is that I can give you the background of the operation he was involved in, what their mission was if you want to know any of this, what it was like. . . ."

"There's something I want to know," Gene said. "Something that has always bugged me: *why was it covered up?*"

"That was the thing," Peg said. "Why wasn't it ever in the news?"

"In our telegram from that general," Gene said, turning to Peg, "you have that telegram, don't you? The general told us that the incident had been investigated and the investigation was on record at the Logistics Center at . . . at. . . ."

"Long Binh," Peg said.

"Long Binh, that's right," Gene continued. "And he said it would be released to us immediately. But it never was!"

"First of all, Gene," I said, "I don't believe the

incident was deliberately covered up. I don't believe that there was ever a conspiracy to prevent you from learning what had happened to Michael. The details given you in that first letter from the battalion commander dated March second which you received the day after Michael's funeral were, in fact, correct. The reason why you were never sent the results of the investigation was that the report was classified 'For Official Use Only,' a very minor security classification, but one which would nevertheless prevent it from being released to civilians without a 'Need-to-Know.' It doesn't matter that you are Michael's parents. Secondly, the investigation would obviously contain hypotheses on what might have happened, and these hypotheses might be open to misinterpretation, depending on the point of view of the reader. If, for example, the report mentioned that a lieutenant back at Hill Four Ten with the guns was asleep at the time of the incident but that his being asleep had nothing to do with the incident, you might still believe that if he had been awake, Michael would have been spared. I don't know if I've made myself clear, but the reason why the report was not sent was to spare you more anguish."

"I don't buy that," Gene said flatly. "No, I don't buy that. The simple reason why the report was not sent was because this was the second artillery incident to have happened in twenty-one days."

"Did Schwarzkopf mention that to you?" Peg asked me.

"Yes, we talked about it."

"Schwarzkopf did tell you about that?" Gene asked, clearly surprised. "It was actually the third incident that had happened in a little over a month with this same unit. That's why they tried to hush it up."

"There wasn't a third incident," I said. "The previous incident, the one in which some men from Bravo Company were wounded—none, incidentally, were killed—the cause of that accident was a faulty artillery piece. There were teeth missing on the elevating gear, and when the tube was raised, the mechanism indicated a higher elevation than was actually on the guns because of the slippage caused by the missing teeth. As a result, when the artillery piece was fired, the round fell short. In Michael's case, however, the guns were fine. The round fell short because a lieutenant back at the fire direction center had failed to take into account the height of the trees on top of the hill where Charlie Company had set up."

"What happened to that lieutenant?" Peg asked.

"He was given an official reprimand."

"Yeah, see, Schwarzkopf said he would have had him court-martialed," Gene said.

"What about the boys who were drinking?" Peg asked.

I explained how the drinking had not made any difference because the error was not on the guns. The men at the guns had done exactly what they were told to do. The investigation confirmed that the target information shown on the guns was exactly what had been forwarded to them from the fire direction center.

"Okay now," Gene said. "Who called in the DTs?"

For the next couple of hours I answered the Mullens' questions as best I could: Who asked for the DTs at that time of night? Who adjusted the artillery? How could someone correct the artillery if he couldn't see where the shell hit? Why were the DTs postponed? If the artillery wasn't firing for Charlie Company, then why did the boys write they heard artillery firing all night long? I explained how Charlie Company was not the only infantry company operating in that area that night, that Delta Company was to their northwest and had requested DTs as well. I told them about the artillery's priorities which would cause fire to be shifted if a unit made contact. And Peg asked me why the boys who wrote were threatened with court-martials.

I tried to explain that if the boys had written, they would have directly disobeyed the order from American Division Headquarters stating that all communication with next of kin was to emanate from Division to ensure that parents were not given conflicting facts and accusations.

"We didn't get any facts!" Peg protested.

"In other words," Gene said, "they only give out

the facts they want the parents to know. To fit the story."

"But there wasn't any story," I said.

"So that's why the platoon wasn't allowed to write us," Peg said. "I see now. It has to be covered up."

"It wasn't covered up, Peg," I said. "What you were told was true." I went back through my notes until I found a copy of that first letter sent over Schwarzkopf's signature. I read the second paragraph to them. "Michael's unit was in their night defensive position where the letter says they were. The unit was 'adjusting artillery to provide a predetermined range of fire in the event of enemy contact.' Michael did receive 'a fatal missile wound when an artillery round fell short of its intended target and detonated near his position.' Admittedly you were told the barest minimum, but what you were told was the truth."

"Well," Gene said, "Schwarzkopf has destined his life for the Regular Army. But he's all through because of—"

"Because of his back," Peg said.

"His back has healed," I said. "He's out of the cast now, and he's all right."

"Listen, this so-called event they went out on," Gene said, and he began rapping the kitchen table top for emphasis, "was Schwarzkopf's [bam!] own [bam!] planned (bam!) adventure! He thought there were some Vietcong out there and this was the first [bam!] time [bam!] that Schwarzkopf had ever been out on a search and destroy mission. The first time the chaplain had been out. That the company clerk had been out. The first sergeant. Did Schwarzkopf tell you that?"

"Gene, it wasn't the first time Schwarzkopf had been out. Or the chaplain. I don't think the company clerk was with them that night, but I'm not sure. I do know that the first sergeant went out any time the executive officer came in. There was a conflict betw—"

"Schwarzkopf used to come out in his helicopter," Gene interrupted.

"He'd never stayed out all night on a mission with them, had he?" Peg asked.

"He wasn't on the hill with Charlie Company," I
374

said. "He was on another hill, Hill Four Ten, with the artillery unit."

"When I told Schwarzkopf, when he sat there in that hospital bed with that other colonel, Colonel Knap, who was sitting there with him. . . ." Gene paused, then asked, "Did he tell you about Knap?"

"Yes, he was a major in the Judge Advocate General," I said. "He was a lawyer."

"Why'd he want a lawyer there?" Gene asked.

"For a witness," I said. "He had first asked Knap to come so that he, Schwarzkopf, could ask him some questions. But when you said you wanted a witness there, too, he asked Knap to stay."

"In other words," Gene said, "he was afraid I was going to get a little bit violent?"

"I think he was concerned for your sake and his own, as well as the other men in the ward."

"Why was he concerned for my sake?" Gene asked indignantly.

"Because it was so obviously an emotional situation," I said. "He wasn't sure how you were going to react and he had asked Knap down initially to advise him. You had said you were bringing charges against him in federal court, remember, so Schwarzkopf asked Knap what it all meant and was it all right for him to talk to you."

When Gene started to tell me again how Schwarzkopf had been suckered down into the minefield, it was clear he had begun to confuse some of the details of Schwarzkopf's flight out to Charlie Company the morning after Michael was killed with his flight into Bravo's minefield area. I told him I had questioned and requestioned Schwarzkopf about the minefield incident and spoken to others about it as well. The colonel had not been suckered down, I explained. He had landed to free his helicopter for the evacuation of the wounded. Around and around we went. I read him the colonel's transcript, how the company commander had had to be med-evac'd out, how terrified Schwarzkopf had been crossing the minefield to the wounded private, and Gene said, "Now listen, I'm going to tell you something. You're hearing my side now. You've already heard his side. Schwarzkopf has had plenty of time to think of his own self, his story, his 'I.' I said to Schwarzkopf, 'Colonel, I—' "

"The thing is that it's over with," Peg said. "Schwarzkopf has had time to take care of his story."

"He's had time to plan," Gene said. "When I looked at him out at Walter Reed, I saw a defeated officer of the United States Army. I don't care what *any*body says, he's got a guilt complex."

"But, Gene, he didn't kill Michael. You know that. What should he feel guilty about?"

"Because he was hungry!" Gene answered angrily. "He wanted to be a brigadier general at thirty-five. He made that brag, and we can get the boys to prove it to you!"

"Oh-h," Peg said uncertainly, "I'm not sure whether we can or not." She pushed herself away from the sink and sat down with us at the kitchen table. "One thing I want to know," she said. "What was the company out there for? There wasn't anything in that area, was there?"

"They went out for two reasons," I said. "Their primary mission was to provide security against rocket attacks on the Americal Division Headquarters at Chu Lai. On this particular mission, however, Division intelligence had had some 'unidentified radio intercepts.' They had picked up Vietnamese talking on radios where there weren't supposed to be any Vietnamese operating. So Charlie and Delta companies from Schwarzkopf's battalion were sent in to make contact. But they didn't find any."

"You know damn well they couldn't find any Vietnamese radio!" Gene said.

"They were looking for the North Vietnamese troops using the radios," I explained.

"The whole incident was Schwarzkopf's stairway to a brigadier general." Gene shrugged.

"No, Gene, let me try to correct you on this because you've mentioned it again and again. Schwarzkopf was a lieutenant colonel. He still had to be promoted to full colonel before he could make brigadier general and—"

"He could make that in sixty days!" Gene scoffed.

"Gene, no one has made colonel in sixty days since the Army Air Corps days of World War II," I said. "We can talk about this some more if you'd like, but we'll just keep going around in circles and end up with my having to defend the military, the government, the system or whatever, and this is not what I came back out here to Iowa to do." I sat there for a moment looking at them. Gene was angry with me; Peg was clearly upset. "I thought if I could find out the truth for you," I said, "if I could learn what had happened to Michael, how he had died, what had caused the shell to explode over his position. . . ."

The Mullens' expression did not change.

"I guess," I said, "I guess I don't really know what you want from me anymore."

"What we want from *you?*" Gene said indignantly. "The whole thing is this: when you came out here, you wanted something from *us!*"

"What do you mean?" I asked, surprised. "What do you think I wanted from you?"

"You wanted a story," Peg said.

"You wanted the story, and you wanted the truth," Gene said.

They were right, of course.

I never wanted to be in this book. I had intended only to be a journalist: unbiased, dispassionate, receptive to all sides. I knew my only chance for articulating the tragedy of this war, the only way I could explain, as I had set out to do, the people's estrangement from their government, their increasing paranoia and distrust, lay in limiting my focus.

By concentrating on one specific incident, the death of Michael Mullen, but restricting myself to this one isolated Iowa farm family's story, I had hoped somehow to encompass the whole. This technique, I later came to recognize, was not a journalist's but a novelist's; and it led inevitably not only to my own participation and inclusion in the Mullens' story but also to that awful sadness and disappointment I now felt. I knew because I thought them wrong about

Schwarzkopf, they believed I had passed judgment against everything they had done. I knew they were wondering whether they could trust me, or had I, too, become a part of the conspiracy to hide the truth? Vietnam did that to us. It dragged us all in, made us choose sides. Had not Peg herself said, "There's only one side when you lose your son"?

That I disagreeed with them about Schwarzkopf was beside the point. I did agree with them on principle: Michael's death was an unforgivable tragedy—as Schwarzkopf, too, would have been and was among the first to agree. The colonel further recognized, however, that their opinion of him was a symptom and consequence of the injuries they had received. He was the one who said, "But it's an even more terrible thing that has happened to the Mullens themselves." They, like their son, like the nation itself, had become casualties of the war. And my sadness lay in knowing nothing I could say or write could change that, just as nothing they could say or do could bring back their son.

Gene had said, "You wanted the story, and you wanted the truth."

"Well, that's what he's getting," Peg then said.

"Now I'm not going to like the truth if it isn't in my favor—"

"Oh, Gene!" Peg laughed.

"You can understand that," he said, ignoring Peg.

"Yes, but I also understand that the truth is neither in your favor or their favor," I said. "It's somewhere in between."

"The truth is in *their* favor?" Gene asked, beginning to get angry all over again.

"Gene, of course, doesn't want the military ever to look good," Peg said. "We have a very slanted bias. A hatred for the military. And there's nothing that will change that, I suppose."

"I can understand that, too," I said, "but I think it's important for you to know that both Schwarzkopf and Captain Tom Cameron, your son's company commander, were fine officers. Fine men."

"Well, I don't buy it," Gene said. "I don't
378

buy Schwarzkopf, and I don't buy the military."

"Here's the whole thing," Peg said. "The military didn't want us to think our son had died simply because somebody, his own men, had shot a gun at him. How do you explain this? They don't want to admit how many boys were killed by their own troops. And thousands of them died, you know, not just Michael.

"There was a picture in *Time* magazine about three weeks ago showing the First Air Cav being combat assaulted. The photograph showed three boys being airlifted into battle. I cut it out and sent it to Mr. Nixon, saying, 'Maybe you'd be interested in the faces of these three young men. What strikes me most,' I wrote, 'is that none of these young men has a father who is a President or a Senator or a Congressman. . . .' But"—Peg shrugged—"of course I get no response to any of this mail anymore because I'm a 'crackpot.' I still wonder about those boys. They lost two or three boys a week out of that outfit for the past two months, and I worry about those three boys. I really do."

"We know we're not getting the right casualty count even now," Gene said.

"That first week a little while ago when they had a casualty count of only two?" Peg said. "Well, we had three deaths in Iowa alone. I wrote Jerry Friedheim*— they were all listed as nonbattle, see—and I said, 'Well, you'll just have to do a little better job on your homework. Three bodies returned to Iowa, but only two died nationwide.' I had a two-page letter from him saying the news media had goofed in Saigon."

Gene started in on Schwarzkopf again: the colonel had had time to change his story to suit himself; he was interested only in making general; he had spoken with the Mullens because he was "scared." Nothing good had been accomplished in Vietnam. We were being whitewashed by the Army. Schwarzkopf had been pulled out of Vietnam. He was finished because of his back injury. Finally, Peg said, "You two have been at it long enough."

---

*Jerry W. Friedheim, Principal Deputy Assistant Secretary, Department of Defense.

During dinner we talked about the upcoming presidential election. The Mullens would support the Democratic candidate, George McGovern. Nixon would carry Black Hawk County with 31,926 to McGovern's 21,721 votes. We talked about farming and the price freeze ("Gas went up, fuel went up, telephone rates went up . . . oh, what a freeze!" Peg laughed sardonically). And, of course, we talked about the war. There were still 139,000 U.S. troops in Vietnam. Several days earlier, on February 25, the 3rd Brigade of the 1st Air Cavalry Division was ambushed during a sweep through Long Khanh Province east of Saigon. The battle lasted from dusk until noon the following day and ended only when U.S. bombers, gunships and artillery came to their aid. The 3rd Brigade suffered the heaviest casualties received by U.S. ground forces throughout the previous ten months. As we covered the same ground again and again, I thought I detected a pessimism, a cynicism that hadn't been present in the Mullens before. Gene began talking about the fox hunters who came out to the farm.

"Why do they want to kill a fox?" he asked. "Foxes have been on this earth for years and will continue to be. They haven't done any real harm. If they were going to do irrevocable damage, they would have done it by now. But that's the way man is: destructive. He'll destroy himself."

I was surprised to hear Gene speak that way. "What hope do you have if you believe that?" I asked.

"Well, I hope we can learn to live together," he said. "Here you are. We talk. You have your thoughts. I have mine. You haven't imposed your thoughts on me, and I've tried not to impose my thoughts on you. Tonight we had pork tenderloin and biscuits and you enjoyed it. . . . Why can't we get along with the other people in the world?"

The following morning, March 1, 1972, was the second anniversary of Michael Mullen's burial. A gentle rain had fallen during the night, and before dawn the temperature had suddenly dropped to fifteen degrees below zero. The roads were covered with a thin sheet of ice.

380

"Jee-zoos!" swore one of the men at the breakfast counter of Mom's Café that morning. "How do you like this weather?"

His companion swiveled his stool to look out the window. "Liked yesterday a whole lot better."

The usual five-minute trip from La Porte City to the Mullens' took twenty minutes that morning. On John Dobshire's dirt road leading up to the farm I was worried that the weight of the car would simply slide me off the crown and into the ditch. On either side the barren fields had been glazed with ice, and as I passed the little patch of woods which remained from the stand of timber once containing "The Old Eagle Tree," I saw that the bare limbs were covered with crystal sleeves.

Gene was asleep when I arrived, but Peg was up and gave me a mug of coffee. "Here, read this," she added. "I found this letter last night and thought it might interest you."

The letter, written on inexpensive stationery in a rough, unschooled hand, had been mailed from a small town in Iowa a few days before.

Dear Mrs. Mullen:

They say my son gave his life for his country, that is not true. He was murdered by his country.

The book written by Robert Scheer, *How the U.S. Got Involved in Vietnam* should be required reading by all Americans; but Norman Mailer says the people in this country like war. Thank you for telling it like it is.

My wife died when Roy was five years old. I cooked, sewed on buttons, worked and farmed 240 acres. Roy was Salutarian of his High School class. Six feet tall and 180 lbs. After 2½ years of college he was drafted. After five months with the Air Cavalry he became a machine gunner on a chopper.

The way the world is going I should think of him as being safe, but I can't get over it.

Thanks again,
P_____ M_____

381

"That poor guy," Peg said when she saw I had finished reading. "He doesn't say how his son was killed, does he?"

I put the letter aside. "Peg," I said, "I don't think there is an appropriate time to ask this question, but I want to get it over with. Yesterday you mentioned being asked to speak by a women's club and someone else asked you to help organize the peace vigil here in La Porte—"

"They almost had to drag people off the street to get enough people in this town to maintain a twenty-four-hour vigil," Peg said. "I found that very difficult to understand."

"I want to continue with this question for a moment," I said. "You're known now by the newspapers, the local television stations. You're often asked to comment on the news. Presidential candidates call from Washington asking your endorsement. Has achieving this 'celebrity' status in any way disturbed you?"

Peg paused for a moment. "Well, yes. It does disturb me, I think. I mean it disturbs me because of why it happened. It came about because Michael died."

"Do people think you're cashing in on Michael's death?"

"Well," Peg said, rubbing her brow, "you wonder about it. I suppose many people do think this way, and I guess you can't help it. I have this fear of being used by groups—except groups like the American Friends. They're the one group I have faith in in the whole country. Oh, look who's up!"

Gene lumbered sleepily into the kitchen. "Some weather, isn't it? I heard on my radio this morning that it's eight degrees."

A few minutes later, when Peg started talking about the shootings at Kent and Jackson State universities, Gene said, "There've been a lot of bloody incidents in this country lately in the name of democracy, haven't there?"

"But, Gene," I said, "can you think of any other country in which you'd rather live?"

Gene thought for a moment. "No-o-o, but I'm losing my country."

382

"Our country is losing *us!*" Peg corrected. "But what can you do about it?"

"Nothing." Gene shrugged. "There's nothing you can do about it."

"If you really believe that," I said, "why have you done all the things you've done so far?"

"Well . . ." Peg said and shrugged, too. The telephone rang, and she pushed away from the kitchen table to answer.

Gene sipped his coffee, then asked me, "Are you going with me to visit Michael's grave this morning?"

"I'd like to very much."

We could hear Peg trying to comfort whoever it was on the telephone.

"Listen to her," Gene said. "That's the kind of phone call we get all the time."

Peg was reading off a list of telephone numbers the caller should try: Senator Harold Hughes' office, the Senator's military liaison adviser, a lawyer who specialized in military cases. Peg was saying don't worry, don't cry, everything was going to be all right. A few minutes later she lowered the telephone onto its receiver and slumped down at the kitchen table.

"Who was it?" Gene asked.

"A widow with six children," Peg sighed. "Her oldest son was a helicopter gunner in Vietnam. God knows how, but he survived. He's back at Fort Hood now, and this is the third time this year he's gone AWOL to come home. He was worried because his mother hasn't been real well. She telephoned to ask what she could do to help him, so he wouldn't have to go back into the stockade. Then when she got to crying, I thought, *Oh, God, that poor woman.* She told me, 'They got my one boy, but they'll never get the other.'" Peg rubbed her eyes wearily. "Here's the thing, here's what really gets me: How can I do anything for these people? How can I help them?"

"You already have," I answered. "You gave her the names and phone numbers of people to call. That's all she wanted. There was nothing but quicksand beneath her feet when she telephoned, and all of a sudden, Peg, there you were: solid as a rock."

Peg looked over at her husband. He had buried his face in his hands. "No, Gene!" she scolded. "Don't you start!"

Gene could not help himself. He was crying, and the tears coursed down his cheeks. He turned to me, his eyes glistening, "Are we crazy?" he asked. *"Are we?"*

I shook my head, not sure of my voice.

"How *long* can we do this?" he asked.

"A lady came out here who had lost her son fifteen years ago!" Peg said. "She sat there and talked about him for four, for four . . . hours. . . ." Her voice faltered, and she, too, began to cry, "And I thought to myself, *My God, am I going to be doing this for the rest of my life?"*

"I *love* my country," Gene said. "It hurts me to see what's happening. I don't understand it."

"The thing that gets me is that I'm still angry!" Peg said. "How in the hell can you live a lifetime of being angry? How can you?" She was struggling for self-control. "I just think I have to be mad about Michael's death because . . . because it was *obscene!* I have to be angry, but how . . . how do—oh, God!" Peg cried, burying her face in her arms. Gene walked around the kitchen table to comfort her, placed a gentle hand on Peg's shoulder. He stood there crying also, uncertain what to say or do. Peg rubbed her eyes against her sleeve, then, looking up, patted Gene's hand and forced herself to smile.

"Why don't both of you get out of here?" she asked. "I'll clean up the breakfast dishes while you two visit Michael's grave."

MAP
OF THE
MISSION

Map showing flight path of Charlie Company
from pickup zone at base of Hill 76 (BT451038)
to landing zone below objective (LZ at BT-
370012) the hill with unconfirmed benchmark
x156. Also shown is Hill 410, the mountain upon
which the artillery was placed. (BT389034)

Map Data: AMS Vietnam 1:50,000 scale
             "Tra Bong"
             Sheet 6739 IV
             Series L7014
             map updated to 1967

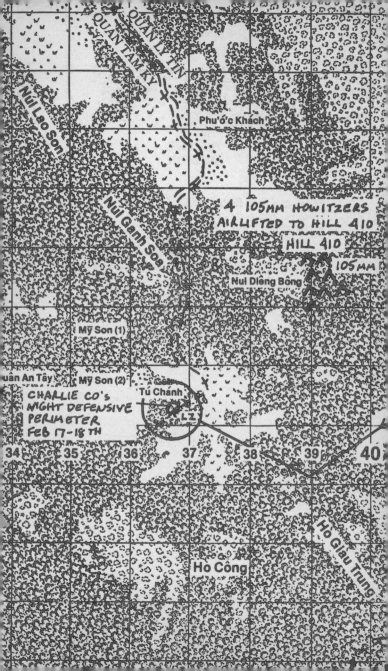

QUAN LY TIN
QUAN TAM KY

Phu'ớc Khách

Núi Lao Son

Núi Ganh Soa

4 105MM HOWITZERS
AIRLIFTED TO HILL 410

HILL 410

105MM

Núi Dieng Bông

Mỹ Son (1)

uân An Tây   Mỹ Son (2)

Tú Chánh

CHARLIE CO's
NIGHT DEFENSIVE
PERIMETER
FEB 17-18 TH

LZ

34   35   36   37   38   39   40

Ho Giau Trung

Ho Công

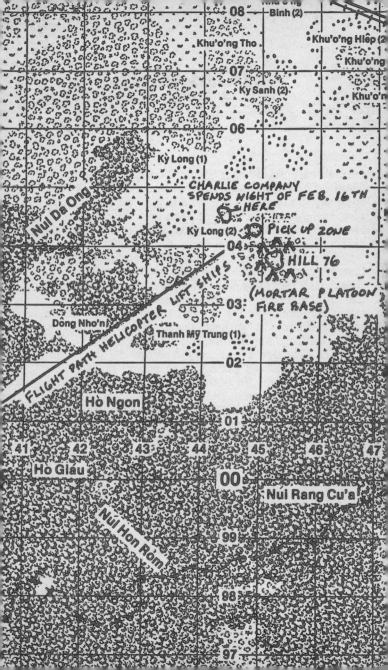

The Mission

On February 16, 1970, Captain Tom Owen Cameron, Charlie Company's twenty-five-year-old Arkansas-born company commander, briefed his platoon leaders and platoon sergeants on their mission and what to expect. He explained again how Intelligence had come to suspect a North Vietnamese Army rocket battalion command group had moved into the valley and that Charlie Company, along with other units of the 1st Battalion, would take part in a five-day operation to locate and destroy the enemy. Cameron stressed that because battalion command groups did not travel without sizable security forces to protect them, Charlie Company should anticipate being attacked.

On February 17, the night before the operation, Cameron briefed his platoon leaders and platoon sergeants once more. He unfolded his map, spread it on the ground before them and reviewed the plan in detail. Charlie Company, along with Echo Company's reconnaissance platoon, would take part in a coordinated helicopter-borne combat assault into the east end of the valley in which the North Vietnamese rocket battalion command group was suspected to be located. Delta Company was to be combat-assaulted into the valley's west end to serve as a blocking force. Four 105mm howitzers from the division artillery's base camp at "Fat City" were to be airlifted to the top of Hill 410, which overlooked the valley in which the 1st Battalion would be operating. From that hilltop position any fire support mission the battalion's rifle companies might call for would fall easily within the airlifted howitzers' 12,500-meter maximum range. Captain Cameron specified who would be in the first helicopter lift and who would be in the second. He explained what his position would be in relation to the platoons during the combat assault. He pointed out their objective: a small, steep, wooded hilltop in the middle of the valley surrounded by tall mountains a few hundred meters south of the abandoned village of Tu Chanh. In his soft Southern accent he again warned them that Charlie Company should expect to make contact with the enemy and that this would be the most dangerous mission the unit had been sent on. One man asked if the landing zone would be "hot." Would they be fired on? Cameron responded, "Expect the worst."

There were no other questions. The men were too tired and wet and muddy to talk. The operation had already got off to a bad start.

Charlie Company was to have set up that night on Hill 76, the mortar platoon fire base overlooking the pickup zone. Late that afternoon, however, when Charlie Company reached the hill, they discovered Delta Company was already on top. There wasn't room enough on Hill 76 for both rifle companies, so Cameron ordered his men to a smaller hilltop across the rice paddies 1,000 meters to the north. By dusk, when the rifle company moved out, the temperature had dropped to the sixties, cold for Vietnam. The monsoon season had just ended, so the rice paddies were still flooded. The dikes to be traversed which were not underwater were wet and slick with mud. In the fading light the men kept slipping off the dikes into the chest-high water. Over and over again the column would halt as the men stopped to pull each other out. They knew, too, it would be worse the next morning when they would have to recross the paddies in total darkness in order to reach the pickup zone at first light.

Because the men in the mortar platoon would be carrying their 81mm mortar tubes, bipods and heavy baseplates, men from other platoons were needed to carry the additional mortar ammunition the extended operation would require. The 1st Platoon had the least experienced platoon leader; Second Lieutenant Fletcher B. Joslin had been with the company but a few days.

Cameron therefore decided the 1st Platoon should fly in last during the combat assault. The mortar platoon's extra ammunition was assigned to the 1st Platoon's men. Michael Mullen, Gary ("The Prince") Samuels and Willard Polk were among those receiving 81mm mortar rounds.

Willard Polk was not a big man, but he was no weakling either. He was twenty-one years old, had light-brown skin and finely chiseled features. Polk had joined Charlie Company two days before and swiftly earned a reputation for being sullen and uncooperative. Many of Charlie Company believed Polk was simply scared; Samuels thought Polk a "dud."

Samuels was twenty-three years old, a college grad-uate, and had been in Vietnam for three and a half months. When Charlie Company arrived at Hill 76 and found Delta Company there, Samuels took advantage of the confusion to look for a Delta Company friend with whom he had gone through basic and advanced infantry training. The friend was not there, and no one knew where he had gone until someone said, "Oh, yeah, he must have been the guy that got his this morning. Booby trap. Hit him in both legs." Samuels was badly shaken. That night, after Charlie Company had re-crossed the paddies and were making their final prepa-rations for the next day's combat assault, Samuels checked over his equipment. He threw out whatever he felt he might not need to keep his pack light, and when the mortar rounds were passed out, he made certain he received an HE round instead of an illuminating. The high explosive mortar shells weighed less.

The next morning, February 17, at 0500 the men were ordered to move out. It was cool, dark; the rice paddies were shrouded in mist. The men again began slipping and falling off the slick dikes into the water. The thick mud clinging to their boots became an addi-tional crushing weight. Cold and wet, the men would be hauled cursing out of the paddies. Willard Polk, carry-ing a full thirty-five-pound rucksack, an eighteen-pound mortar round, his M-79 grenade launcher and ammunition, twice fell in over his head. Michael Mullen helped him out. None of the other men offered any assistance. The first time Polk slipped Mullen told him to unblouse his trousers, that there was no point in carrying the extra weight around. Polk let his fatigues hang free and the water poured out. When he straightened up, Michael readjusted his pack.

Captain Cameron, who was moving up and down the dike to check on the progress of his men, passed Polk and Mullen and told them to catch up. Polk struggled forward but, unused to the weight, could not keep his balance. Over and over he slipped and fell into the water or down to his knees. When he at last reached hard ground, he was so frustrated and angry he hit the emergency release on his rucksack and let his ruck, his grenade launcher and the mortar round crash to the ground. "Goddamn this fuckin' stuff! I ain't carrying *none* of it!"

Cameron, unknown to Polk, was standing right there. The company commander picked up the grenade launcher and shoved it at the private's chest. "Now pick up that mortar round, put on your ruck, and *move out!*"

"No, sir," Polk said. "I ain't in the mortar platoon, and I ain't carrying no mortar round! You can have this fuckin' rucksack and the whole fuckin' works! I ain't carrying none of it!"

"Polk, I'm giving you a direct order," the captain warned. "Pick up that round and your equipment, and move out!"

"Sir, I can't. It's too heavy."

Private Willie Johnson, another black from the 1st Platoon, picked up the mortar round and handed it to Polk. Polk let it drop again.

"I'll see you get an Article Fifteen."* Cameron told Polk. "Pick up your equipment, and move out. That's an order!"

"Sir, I'll carry it," Willie Johnson said. He lifted Polk's mortar round a second time.

---

*Punishment administered at company level.

391

"No, Polk's going to carry it," Cameron said. "Everybody else in his platoon is carrying their rounds."

"I can't help that, sir," Polk said. "Every time I walk or step on a rock or something I keep falling down. It's too heavy."

At that moment Staff Sergeant Wetsel reached the hard ground. "I'll take care of this, sir," he told Captain Cameron. "Polk's in my platoon."

Cameron, eager to complete his head count of the men and to get them in position to board the helicopters, was relieved to see the new platoon sergeant take command. As Cameron turned away, he saw Michael Mullen join Wetsel. The two of them spoke to Polk and calmed him down. Willie Johnson kept Polk's mortar round. "Here," Johnson said, "you take my Claymore. It's lighter."

At the pickup zone there was time for one final head count. Squad leaders passed among their men, checking and readjusting the men's equipment. Platoon sergeants positioned the squads according to where they would board their lift. The rising sun silhouetted the distant ridge line upon which Bayonet stood, and, for the first time, the deep, resonant beating of the approaching helicopters could be heard.

Ten camouflaged helicopters appeared above the mist in a staggered formation. Each helicopter was capable of carrying from six to eight men in addition to its crew. The thirty men of Echo Company's reconnaissance platoon would be loaded into the first five helicopters. Captain Cameron, his headquarters section and a portion of the 2nd and 3rd platoons would fill the rest.

Michael Mullen, Gary Samuels, Willard Polk, the other members of the 1st Platoon and those remaining of the 2nd and 3rd platoons would be in the second lift.

"Hey, Prince," someone yelled to Samuels, "here comes your royal chariot!"

The whole "Prince" business had started when Gary Samuels and Don Montuori, Jr., were waiting together their last day at Fort Lewis, Washington, to be shipped to Vietnam. Samuels had been in a strange mood that day—not really down, but certainly not up either. He had been sitting on his bunk, quietly thinking about Vietnam. Suddenly he had wrapped his poncho about himself like a cape and announced, "Montuori? I've got divine powers. I'm Prince Lovely. That's my new name."

"You must be kidding." Montuori smiled.

"The Prince does not kid," Samuels replied.

From that moment on, Montuori called Samuels the Prince.

When they arrived in Vietnam and were both assigned to Charlie Company—Samuels went to Mullen's squad in the 1st Platoon, Montuori to the Mortar Platoon—the nickname stuck. Even Captain Cameron called Samuels the Prince and, like the rest, would smile good-naturedly when Samuels would announce, "The Prince does not patrol." Eventually, as replacements arrived and others rotated home, fewer and fewer men in Charlie Company remembered the Prince's real name.

The approaching helicopters' engines changed pitch as each lift ship hovered over the pickup zone and set down. The men ran forward, ducking beneath the swishing rotor blades to board. The last man on each ship would barely be inside before the engines would increase speed, the pitch would again change, the nose would dip into the mushrooming dust, and the helicopter was off.

While the first lift headed down the Song Trau river valley to the mountain pass, the artillery preparation of Charlie Company's landing zone was continued. A light helicopter carrying Lieutenant Colonel Schwarzkopf with his artillery liaison officer and helicopter flight commander was hovering east of the landing zone. They were radioing any corrections necessary to ensure that the artillery fire was striking the proper place. Through his helicopter flight commander Schwarzkopf was also in touch with the lift ships, and as the first helicopter carrying men from Echo's reconnaissance platoon appeared, Schwarzkopf's artillery liaison officer called for the artillery fire to cease. Two white phosphorous rounds were exploded over the landing zone to mark the "all clear," and Lieutenant Colonel Schwarzkopf's pilot swooped down, made a low, flat pass over the LZ, and Schwarzkopf dropped a colored smoke grenade to mark where the lead lift ship was to touch down. Schwarzkopf wanted to designate exactly where the first helicopter was to land to avoid mistakes. There was no point in having a sustained artillery preparation devastate the area if the helicopters were then to unload their men in the wrong spot. The pilot of the lead helicopter acknowledged that he had the smoke in view, and Schwarzkopf's helicopter flared up and out of the way. The lift ship door gunners opened fire.

The flight from the pickup zone at the base of Hill 76 to the landing zone took about fifteen minutes. The helicopters flew at a few thousand feet, and Cameron, looking out of the open doors at the sunrise, watching the fog lift from the rice paddies, felt uncomfortably warm. Still, there he was with thirty-five pounds of gear on his back about to lead his rifle company into an area where North Vietnamese regulars were presumably operating, and it could have been twenty below zero and Cameron knew he would feel the heat.

Abraham Aikins, the senior medic attached to Cameron's headquarters section, was in the same helicopter with the captain, Cameron's radio operators, and Lieutenant Rocamora's artillery forward observer team. Aikins didn't even notice the sound of the engines or the coolness of the morning air. He was worrying how he would react if Charlie Company became involved in a fire fight. He had treated injured men before, but he had never been in a situation where men had suffered massive injuries. What if a lot of guys got badly hurt and he really had to run around? "You'll be okay," he told himself. "You won't choke up. You'll be okay." But what if—"Don't sweat it. You'll be fine."

Cameron heard rather than felt the helicopter

change direction. They had crossed the mountain pass and were heading up the valley to the LZ. The door gunners suddenly opened fire, raking the tall grasses on either side of the landing zone with M-60 machine-gun fire. Martin Culpepper, in a helicopter at the rear of the lift, wore close to 300 rounds of machine-gun ammunition crisscrossed over his shoulders and chest like a Mexican bandit's bandoliers. He also carried a Claymore mine, a machete, fifteen magazines of ammunition for his M-16 rifle, his canteens and his rucksack loaded with C rations and supplies. All that weight was pushing him down; the straps were cutting into his shoulders. He wanted only for the flight to end so he could get comfortable. He could hear the lead pilots talking back and forth over the intercom. Were they drawing any fire? No, not yet. No contact. The wash of the rotor blades sucked the engine and gun noises into the helicopter.

Ahead, Cameron was covering his ears. Suddenly the noise let up, and Cameron saw the left outboard door gunner struggling to clear his machine gun. Cameron could lip-read the gunner's "It's jammed!"

"Use your rifle!" Cameron shouted back.

The gunner grinned, grabbed his rifle, put it on full automatic and sprayed shots all around. Cameron didn't like being in a partially unarmed helicopter. It made too good a target, and the VC loved shooting down helicopters. The helicopter swiftly dropped, and Cameron, watching the hills and rice paddies rush up at him, had the sensation of being in a glass elevator. Seemingly at the last moment, the helicopter leveled, and the door gunner was slapping Cameron's men on their shoulders, "Go! Go! Go!"

The pilot had misjudged the height of the grass. Aikins leaped and kept falling, wondering where the ground was. He dropped eight feet before his boots sank into the mud.

Men were jumping from both doors of the helicopters, ducking down then scrambling for cover at the sides of the landing zone. Immediately, the helicopters lifted off and darted back down the valley to the mountain pass on their way to pick up the second lift. Schwarzkopf's helicopter now moved off, too. He would need to supervise the artillery preparation over Delta Company's landing zone at the west end of the valley. Two Cobra gunships, fast and sleek, darted in and began spraying the hillsides off Charlie Company's flanks.

Charlie Company's landing zone was flat, not very wide, thirty by eighty yards at the most. The grass was six feet tall where Aikins and Cameron's helicopter had landed; twenty yards north of their LZ there was no grass at all, just small bushes and trees. The LZ was a river valley among what had been a system of rice paddies long ago. The paddies now were overgrown.

Echo's recon platoon moved forward and secured the forward edge of the LZ. The first lift's men from the 2nd and 3rd platoons fanned out to cover the edges. There was a creek bank which would provide some safety and concealment in case of contact. It would also be possible to cover the second lift from that creek bank when it landed. Cameron was telling his platoon leaders where to move their men. The only sound was the Cobra gunships racing back and forth. The sky was overcast, humid still from the fog. The cool humidity, however, would become hot humidity as soon as the fog burned off. It was about seven fifteen in the morning. Cameron and his command group had taken a position at the southeastern edge of the egg-shaped LZ. He was huddled next to one of his radio operators and was trying to contact Schwarzkopf. "Black Smoke One, this is Black Smoke Six," Cameron said, giving his own and Schwarzkopf's call signs. "Do you read me? Over."

"—ack Smoke Six, this is Black Smoke One," Schwarzkopf replied.

"Black Smoke One, this is Black Smoke Six. We have no contact. Repeat, no contact. Our LZ is cold."

"Uh, roger, Black Smoke Six. This is Black Smoke One. Out."

Schwarzkopf now knew Charlie Company had landed without resistance. He ordered the second lift in.

There was a sudden burst of rifle fire to Culpepper's left, and he burrowed into the creek bank.

"Jesus Christ!" someone yelled. "Did you see the *size* of that deer?"

"Yeah, he took off across the paddy right in front of me," another answered. "I got off a couple of shots at him."

Culpepper sat up again. The surge of panic was replaced by relief, then anger. Finally, like the others, he laughed.

Willard Polk, in the second lift with Michael Mullen and the Prince, was too cold and wet and angry to be scared. He sat huddled up on the metal deck of the helicopter daydreaming about John Wayne. He liked to think of himself as John Wayne: tough, flinty-eyed, tight-lipped, strong, quick to fight. Somehow it helped make the situation into which he was flying seem less threatening and real.

The Prince wasn't worried either. He knew the first lift had not made contact. The LZ was quiet. He had been on other combat assaults and knew what to expect. He found himself thinking about the patrol he had been on the week before. They had passed a hootch in front of which two small boys had been carving statues. "Hey, GI!" one of the boys had called out. "You giva me some money, I show you where VC put booby trap." The boy took them to one side of the trail where the Vietcong had rigged a dud 155mm artillery round to explode when the patrol passed by. The men attached a five-minute fuse to it, cleared the area and detonated the shell. The explosion dug a crater six feet across and five feet deep. When Samuels returned to look, he saw jagged chunks of white hot shrapnel still steaming on the ground. *Jesus,* he thought to himself, *what would it feel like to be hit by that?* Now, sitting in the helicopter with the weight pushing him down, he decided it would feel like whatever his Delta Company friend had suffered when the booby trap on Hill 76 had torn apart his legs.

The helicopter door gunners commenced firing again as soon as the second lift approached the LZ. Culpepper, hearing the shooting, couldn't tell where the firing was coming from. He crouched low and looked around to see if anyone was hit. The helicopters came in fast and in trail, flared, then hovered. The second lift jumped out and ran for cover. Culpepper could hear the platoon sergeants calling back and forth: "Second Platoon this way!" "First Platoon over here!" "Everybody all right?" "Platoon leaders to the CP!" "It ain't no CP, it's just a hole in the mud."

Hank Webb, the platoon sergeant of the 3rd Platoon, told Culpepper and the others of the machine-gun team to move forward. Culpepper pushed himself up. He could hear Webb continuing down the line, "You guys, Razzle-Dazzle, Cocoanut, more to your left. The rest of you guys spread out to the right."

Captain Cameron was waiting for his platoon leaders to complete their head counts. He wanted to be sure no one had been left behind on the pickup zone or had fallen out of a helicopter on the way. When his platoon leaders assembled, he compared their maps with the LZ and discussed the best route up the hill. Culpepper had been in position fifteen minutes before he noticed the leeches. The ground was damp, the grass still wet. Everywhere Culpepper looked he saw leeches oozing along the ground.

"All right," Cameron shouted, "move out!"

At that moment the lift ships carrying Delta Company passed overhead on their way to the west end of the valley. The door gunners were firing at the hillsides, and their hot brass expended cartridges fell on Charlie Company below. The men moved cautiously forward. Mullen placed himself directly behind Willard Polk so he could keep an eye on him going up the hill.

Although the straight line map distance from their LZ to the top of their initial objective, the hill, was less than 500 meters, Charlie Company took almost six hours reaching the crest. The moment the lead elements crossed the creek bed they entered jungle, and the hill, which had not looked so steep on the 1:50,000 scale Army map, seemingly shot straight up. The ground was muddy, slick. The men climbed single file, chopping their way through the dense growth. It was not the sort of jungle that war movies had prepared them for—the usual Hollywood broadleaf plants. It wasn't woods either. There was heavy foliage, an undergrowth and overgrowth. Hanging vines snagged packs and equipment. Brush gave way to trees; trees gave way to brush. The triple canopy jungle made it impossible for the ground to dry. As each man followed the man in front, the trail became muddier, more slippery, steeper. Over and over again a man would lose his balance, slide backward, claw at the vines to catch himself and fall. Repeatedly the column had to stop.

Polk welcomed every opportunity to rest. He had sweated his fatigues wet. The thick mud clung to his boots. Again and again he would slip, the heavy pack would pull him backward, and he would start to flail. Mullen would catch him from behind.

"Mulligan," Polk said. "I'm whipped."

"We all are," Michael said. "Don't think we're not."

Ahead in the column, Culpepper could hear the men talking in low, excited voices and pushed forward to hear.

"Look," Razzle-Dazzle said, pointing at tracks on the ground.

"Jesus!" Culpepper said. "A tiger! It must weigh three, four hundred pounds!"

The tracks, at least eight inches across, were clearly defined in the soft mud. More than anything in his life Culpepper wanted to see that tiger. He had always wanted a tiger skin. Now, seeing that the tracks were fresh and wet and huge, he began to hope for a chance to shoot one. But farther on, when Charlie Company continued up the hill, the tracks veered off, and Culpepper saw no trace of the tiger again.

Whenever the men stopped, the silence closed in about them. That silence was what had always struck Abe Aikins as so strange. There were no sounds in the jungle at all—except, of course, for the heavy breathing of the men. There were no birds. In the lowlands one might hear a frog. Higher up an occasional cricket. Nevertheless, to Aikins, the eerie thing about the jungles

399

of Vietnam was that quiet. He attributed it to the bombing.

The entire time Aikins was in Vietnam he saw only one bird. It had been huge. Bigger than an eagle. Yellow with a black head. He had no idea what it was, but he had seen that same bird twice. The first time he had been in a night logger position when the bird flew overhead, making a sound like an incoming rocket, and Aikins dived for cover. The next morning the bird returned and, to Aikins' astonishment, flew smack into the brush. There was a tremendous crash, and Aikins had lain there, thinking, "Oh, my God, what if the bird decides to attack me?" The column began to move forward up the hill again.

Abe Aikins was six feet four inches. He had been a basketball player at Hofstra College and later at Fort Dix. His height had always been an advantage until now. The point man never chopped a hole large enough through the cover. Aikins would continually become tangled in the dense growth and would have to crouch and duckwalk. With forty-five pounds on his back, he found that duckwalking took little time to get to his legs.

"This fuckin' hill is too fuckin' much!" a rifleman behind Aikins swore.

"Save your breath," Aikins told him.

"Haven't fuckin' got any."

The lead elements of Charlie Company discovered an old path and started following it. Captain Cameron, fearful of booby traps, ordered them off the trail. "Stay to the left where you belong!"

"That's easy for you to say," a rifleman called back. "You ain't up here chopping!"

By now Delta Company had been combat-assaulted into its LZ and the four 105mm howitzers from Fat City had been airlifted to the top of Hill 410. A portion of Alpha Company had been placed on Hill 410, too, to provide security for the guns. Lieutenant Colonel Schwarzkopf, whose CP had been set up to one side, was in radio contact with his company commanders and knew the progress each had made. He was

400

not worried about Charlie Company's slowness in reaching its objective. But he, too, was surprised their hill was so steep.

If one were to clear off the brush and trees and look at Charlie Company's objective from above, the hill looked somewhat like one of those old profile drawings of Mickey Mouse. Mickey's dinner-plate ears were fully exposed, his nose was pointing north. It was as though Mickey were resting his head on the ground. His near ear, the "left" ear, had a higher elevation than his "right" ear. A little after three o'clock Echo's recon platoon reached the top of this near end and, as planned, separated from Charlie Company to take up its selected position along the forward edge of Mickey's "right" ear. Charlie Company continued west at this junction and moved single file across the narrow ridge toward Mickey's "head." When they reached the other side, Cameron discovered that the north face of the hilltop was a cliff that dropped nearly eighty feet straight down.

"Captain? Captain Cameron?" someone called. "You'd better come up here and take a look at what we've found."

The men were gathered around an abandoned defensive position containing foxholes, a machine-gun pit and wooden structures to dry clothes and fish. At first the men thought it might be a Vietcong rest camp. Cameron called for the Vietnamese scout and asked what he thought it was. The scout, too, thought it VC, but something wasn't right. The foxholes were too shallow, the machine-gun emplacement too sloppily dug. Cameron radioed Lieutenant Colonel Schwarzkopf and reported what he had found. He told his battalion commander that the structures did not appear to have been occupied in recent years. The drying racks had collapsed; the foxholes were overgrown. Still, as Cameron told Schwarzkopf, Charlie Company would need to check it out.

Cameron sent a patrol back down the narrow finger to ensure that Charlie Company had not been trailed. He next sent patrols off both sides and forward to the clearing to make certain no one was waiting for them to bed down for the night.

Abe Aikins was looking at the abandoned machine-gun position. Sergeant MacPhearson of the 2nd Platoon pointed out that it directly overlooked the valley in which Charlie Company's lift ships had landed. "I'll tell you one thing," MacPhearson said. "If they'd been up here with any sort of fire power at all, they could have wiped us out on our LZ."

"MacPhearson!" Lieutenant Miller yelled. David Miller was MacPhearson's platoon leader.

"Coming, sir," MacPhearson said.

Lieutenant Miller wanted MacPhearson with him when Captain Cameron assigned the platoons their defensive perimeter positions for the night.

Cameron initially assigned the 3rd Platoon the south slope of the hilltop with the 1st Platoon at the north slope overlooking the cliff, but before the men dug in, he switched the platoons around. The right flank of the 3rd Platoon and the left flank of the 1st Platoon were tucked together. The 2nd Platoon was assigned the approach from the west. All three platoons were pulled in tight to form a close perimeter. Within that perimeter were Cameron's command post, Lieutenant Rocamora's artillery forward observer post and the mortar platoon.

The most vulnerable position was the 2nd Platoon's. There the men would be facing a clearing, the only open space around with the exception of a small hole in the trees above the mortar platoon. That break in the jungle canopy provided the mortars overhead clearance to fire.

The 3rd Platoon dug in at the edge of the cliff. Although visibility was limited because of the heavy foliage, Cameron thought it unlikely that an attacking force would attempt to scale the cliff.

On the south side of the hill, where the 1st Platoon had been placed, the land was heavy virgin jungle. Some of the trees whose trunks were two feet thick rose fifty feet in the air. The jungle was so thick and the hillside dropped off so sharply that the men of the 1st Platoon could see only twenty yards or so ahead of them. Nevertheless, the Vietcong or North Vietnamese would have as difficult a time scaling that slick, steep hill as had Charlie Company. And in spite of Cameron's respect for the Vietcong's ability to sneak around, he doubted they could climb the hill without making some sound.

From its position on the south side, the 1st Platoon would be able to provide security for the rears of the

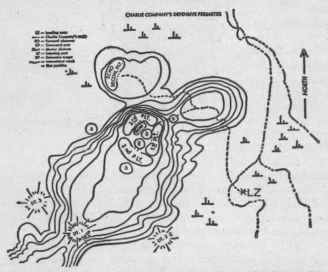

CHARLIE COMPANY'S DEFENSIVE PERIMETER

2nd and 3rd platoons and the CP. The only alternative would have been to place them farther down the slope. Had they dug in there, however, they would have been out of sight over the brow of the hilltop with little security for their flanks. Additionally, such a position would have exposed the 2nd and 3rd platoon rears.

Captain Cameron discussed the placement of the mortar platoon with Lieutenant Roderick Bayliss, its black platoon leader. Bayliss and Cameron were both satisfied with its position behind the 3rd Platoon. From there it could fire support missions not only for Charlie Company but for the Echo rconnaissance platoon as well. Cameron made one last tour of his company's defensive perimeter with his platoon leaders. He was confident he had placed his men properly and that they were digging in well.

The men dug foxholes and sleeping positions. Each man carried in his pack twelve olive-drab plastic bags which, as he dug his foxhole, he would fill with dirt for sandbags. The fox holes were large enough to provide a fighting position for from three to four men. Behind the foxhole would be the men's sleeping position. These were dug 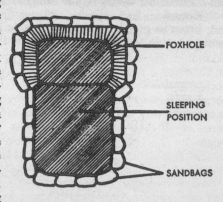 just below ground level so that anyone shooting low could not strike the men within them. The olive-drab plastic sandbags would be placed around the fox hole and sleeping position on all four sides. The men would then camouflage the sandbags so that the positions would blend with the ground.

While his men were digging in, Captain Cameron selected and positioned three listening posts along the most likely routes of attack. He placed the first LP on the narrow finger the company had had to cross single file approximately fifty meters east of the linked flanks of the 1st and 3rd Platoons. The second LP was fifty meters west of the 2nd platoon's front at the edge of that clearing. Cameron situated his third LP over the lip of the hill in front of the 3rd Platoon, where the jungle was so thick the men did not have an adequate field of fire. Each listening post was occupied by three men equipped with a radio. Once the LPs were set, Cameron met with his forward observer, First Lieutenant Albert S. Rocamora, to select the defensive targets (DTs).

Lieutenant Rocamora was small and thin, like a racetrack exercise boy. Although he had been born in the Phillipines, he had been reared and attended schools in California. He and Cameron were very close, and it was understood that if Cameron became a casualty and someone was needed to immediately take command, that commander would be Lieutenant Rocamora.

Rocamora had attended Officers Candidate School and, upon receiving his commission as a second Lieutenant, was ordered to the artillery school at Fort Sill, Oklahoma. He was immediately sent to Vietnam. (After Cameron's tour in Vietnam was completed, Rocamora was due for a job at the rear. He instead volunteered to remain in the field to help break in Charlie Company's new company commander. He then volunteered to stay an additional month in the field to alleviate the shortage of qualified forward observers.) As soon as Rocamora saw that Cameron had his platoons in position, he approached with his maps.

Cameron and Rocamora used to compete with each other to see who could come closest to locating their exact position on the map. The maps in Vietnam were often erratic, and an infantry company, deep within a jungle hilltop, was rarely able to see far enough to locate cross-references to pinpoint its position. Both Rocamora and Cameron, however, agreed on their exact position that night.

"Okay," Cameron said, "I think their most likely approach will be through that clearing toward the Second Platoon. It's relatively flat in relation to everything else around us. It's a natural attack and escape route."

"You've put a listening post somewhere out there, haven't you?"

"Right here," Cameron said, pointing to his map.

"And how close do you want those DTs?"

"Another two hundred meters out from that LP max," Cameron said. "If someone comes at me and I hit back, they'll have to stop and face me or take their chances escaping through our DTs."

Cameron and Rocamora agreed upon the need for two additional DTs to be placed on either side of the hill, and Rocamora left to radio their coordinates in. His forward observer post was being dug behind the 2nd Platoon, but the radio link between himself and the artillery on top of Hill 410 was already established. A few minutes later he walked back to Cameron and said, "Your number one DT is too close. They won't fire them two hundred meters out. For safety reasons, they said, the DT has to be at least four hundred meters away."

"That won't do us much good if someone's firing at us from fifty meters," Cameron complained. "Oh, well, tell them four hundred meters is okay. We can always adjust if we need to. Get them to drop." He followed Rocamora back to his radio. A few minutes later Rocamora told him, "They'll fire them at four hundred meters. They said to tell you, 'No sweat.' "

By twilight Charlie Company's defensive perimeter was set. The men's foxholes and sleeping positions had been dug, the machine-gun emplacements finished. The men were able to relax, eat their C rations, talk and move quietly around. Over on the north side of the hill in the 3rd Platoon's area, Culpepper had waited for the light to fade, then strung his hammock five inches above the ground. He could not sleep where the leeches could reach him. He would rather take his chances on waking up if trouble arose and having time to get into his foxhole. He stood now looking from his machine-gun pit out over the cliff. Abe Aikins wandered over and, looking down, said, "Jesus, Pep, you'd better not do any walking in the middle of the night. That must be a hundred feet straight down!"

"Straight up, too." Culpepper smiled. "Nobody's climbing that. Tonight I'm gonna get me some sleep!"

Willard Polk was sitting with Michael Mullen on the lip of the foxhole they had dug. Michael had finished the fruit in his C ration can of peaches and, with great pleasure, was drinking the syrup. Polk liked Michael, called him Mulligan. Mullen never hassled him. He was like a chaplain in some ways, Polk felt, because he was always so concerned with other people's problems. Polk had been telling Michael about the trouble he had been in in Detroit. "I'd been locked up for misdemeanors, trespassing on Ford property, simple larceny, things like that. I was with some dudes who knocked out a store window and got busted for carrying a concealed weapon, assault on a police officer. . . ."

Michael looked at him with surprise.

"I was drunk at the time," Polk explained. "And besides, he was hassling me. I got drafted just after I got out of jail. I'd been in for sixty days on account of violation of parole, you know. And the only reason why my mother paid to get me out was because I had this draft notice waiting, see. She knew they'd put me in the Army—she didn't know they'd send me here, though. But I'll tell you, Mulligan, I'm gonna get me outta here. One way or another I'll get out." Polk slapped at some mosquitoes. "Hey, you got a cigarette?"

"Don't smoke," Michael said.

Polk shrugged and took a pack of Salems from his fatigue shirt pocket and lit one. "What're you gonna do when you get out?"

"I'll have to see. There's a girl I like. I've been thinking I'd like to get me something like a VW bus and drive around the country, see all the different states. Just take it easy for a while."

"You're getting 'short,' aren't you?"

"If I get my early drop, it'll be about a hundred days."

Polk picked up his can of bug spray and sprayed his fatigue pants. "Fuckin' mosquitoes, fuckin' leeches, there ain't *nothing* good about this place."

"Sergeant Mullen?"

Polk and Michael looked up. It was their platoon leader, Second Lieutenant Joslin. Michael rose to his feet. "Sir?"

"Tell your squad to put on their steel pots and to get in their foxholes. The artillery is going to fire the DTs."

"All right, sir." Michael went to the members of his squad but could not find the Prince. He knew Samuels shared a foxhole with Leroy Hamilton, so Michael asked Hamilton if he'd seen the Prince.

"He was talking to the chaplain," Hamilton said.

"Where's he?"

"By the CP, I think," Hamilton said.

Michael met the Prince walking back to his foxhole. "They're going to fire the DTs," Michael warned him.

"I heard," Samuels said. "You know what the chaplain's name is? It's Do-Good, can you believe it? It's spelled D-U-I-good."

"What's he doing here?" Michael asked.

The Prince shrugged. "Don't know. He just said he thought he ought to be here." He slipped into the foxhole and squatted down. Mullen's foxhole was just to the right.

Over in the 3rd Platoon area, Sergeant Webb was telling Martin Culpepper and Russell Schumacher to put their helmets on.

"What good do they do?" Schumacher asked.

"Won't stop nothing," Culpepper grumbled.

"Put 'em on," Webb said wearily. "Lieutenant Rocamora said they were going to fire the DTs now."

It was eight thirty and almost dark. The men sat in their foxholes, talking quietly. They were all tired after having had to chop their way up the hill, dig their foxholes and carry the extra heavy load the five-day operation required. After an hour had passed and the DTs had still not been fired, some of the men left their foxholes, stretched out in their sleeping positions and dozed off.

Two other men shared the foxhole with Michael Mullen and Willard Polk. Their nicknames were Cactus and Dead-Eye. Cactus had guard duty first, Polk second, Michael third and Dead-Eye last. Polk, however, wanted to switch with Michael, and Michael said, "Okay, I'll pull guard next after Cactus."

Later on that night, when Cactus came off duty, Michael moved forward to take his place. Michael sat at the edge of the foxhole, his M-16 across his knees, and swatted the mosquitoes away from his face. He tried wrapping himself in his poncho—as much for protection against the bugs as the heavy dew. The fog, which had descended at dusk into the valley, was now

408

rolling back up the hill. There was a noise to his left, and Michael's hand dropped to the M-16's trigger guard. It was only Leroy Hamilton, shifting in his sleep.

Everybody like Leroy Hamilton. He was a big, strong blond-haired country boy. The men had come to realize he was very brave. Cameron himself on several occasions had watched Hamilton search through dense jungle growths that he knew he would have hesitated entering. Hamilton did it without being asked and did it thoroughly, uncomplainingly and seemingly unmindful of the risks.

When it was time to change guard again, Michael reached back to the sleeping position and awoke Polk. Polk had been sleeping on the right side of the position, so Michael simply took his place. He knelt down in the space vacated by Polk, stretched his poncho beneath him on the ground and lay down. Polk was settling himself into the foxhole when Michael looked over at him and whispered, "Stay awake!"

"Don't you worry none about that," Polk replied. "Ol' John Wayne's on duty now. Nothing can go wrong." There was a cruh-*whump!* cruh-*whump!* in the distance, and Polk, startled, whispered, "Hey, Mulligan, what's that?"

"The arty on Four Ten. They must be firing over Delta's position."

"You think they're under attack?"

"No, probably just their DTs." Michael yawned. "Maybe it's H&I, harassment and interdiction fire. I don't know." He yawned again. "It's going to feel good to get some sleep."

Over to the left someone whispered, "Hey, Prince, it's after midnight! How come they got you pulling guard?"

"The Prince does not pull guard," Samuels answered. "The Prince protects his friends."

Polk sat on the edge of the foxhole, straining to see into the darkness. He tried to remember what was out in front of him, the exact location of the nearest bushes and trees. He'd been told to memorize the layout because at night the bushes would seem to move. New men would empty their magazines at nothing whatsoever, and the noise and muzzle flash would give their positions away. Polk sat in the dark wishing to God his guard duty would end.

Culpepper, too, was on guard. He could hear the artillery on Hill 410 firing and was trying to judge its distance by the sound. Rocamora, Culpepper knew, was the best at that. The young artillery officer could tell where the round had impacted within fifty feet. In the jungle, in double and triple canopy cover, that was very, very good. Still, Culpepper told himself, Rocamora had been trained for it.

Culpepper and Polk came off guard a little after two-thirty, just about the same time that Rocamora's radio operator shook Abe Aikins.

Aikins came awake immediately. "Yeah? What is it?"

"Your radio watch."

"Right," Aikins said. "Thanks." He relieved the headquarters section radio operator and climbed into the foxhole. Rocamora's radio operator was in his foxhole a few yards away.

Samuels, hearing Aikins move, saw that it was time for him to be relieved, too. He woke up Leroy Hamilton, who stretched, yawned and said, "Okay, I'm awake." Hamilton picked up his helmet and M-16, then reached behind himself for his flak jacket. He moved to the foxhole, placed his flak jacket as a cushion beneath him and sat on the rear lip of the foxhole with his legs dangling down into the pit.

Polk had already awakened Dead-Eye. He now squeezed himself between Cactus and Michael Mullen in the sleeping position and stretched out in Dead-Eye's former place.

Culpepper laid his rifle beneath his hammock, watched Schumacher settle into the foxhole and fell asleep.

Samuels, like Culpepper, could not stand the leeches. He had filled sandbags and spread them out as a mattress so he wouldn't touch the ground. He began wrapping himself in his poncho. Starting with his legs, he wound the poncho about them like a mummy's covering and continued up his body to his shoulders. He

410

straightened himself out, lay back and pulled the final bit of poncho over his head so nothing could crawl over his face.

The artillery radio crackled, and the reconnaissance sergeant leaned closer to it. Aikins, in the nearby foxhole, could barely hear what was said. The recon sergeant woke Lieutenant Rocamora. "Sir? They're going to fire our DTs now. Do you want me to wake the men?"

Rocamora looked at the luminous dial of his watch. It was a quarter to three. There had already been one false alarm. The DTs were being fired 400 meters out, more than 1,300 feet from the closest man. "Let them sleep," Rocamora told his sergeant. "You'd better inform the captain, though."

"I'll do it," Aikins said.

Captain Cameron, asleep in his flak jacket, wearing both his helmet and glasses, awoke quickly. Aikins explained that the DTs were to be fired. Cameron waved his hand to show he had heard and lay back, still half asleep. "Roger. W.P. Airburst. Fifty meters," the recon sergeant was saying.

Moments later Cameron heard the white phosphorous marking round chuff overhead. There was a loud, hollow, *Whaing!* and the shell exploded 400 meters southwest of their position 50 feet in the air. The recon sergeant looked over at Rocamora. Rocamora nodded back. The round had exploded exactly where they wanted it. No corrections were needed.

The next round would automatically be the high explosive, the HE.

Lying there in the dark, Cameron heard the HE round coming and for some reason he just *knew*. He could tell. His brain clicked, *That sonuvabitch isn't going to make it!*

The pitch was different. It was a strange, flat rumbling noise, the sound of a shell pushing the air in front of it rather than away and over his head. Cameron heard the shell coming, there was an instantaneous awareness. He didn't have time to speak, to shout any warning, to take any evasive action. There was nothing Cameron could do but listen to that terrible, low, flat,

411

terrifying rumbling coming closer and closer and closer until it hit.

There was a sudden blinding light, the bright incandescence of thousands of flashbulbs popping all about, then a sharp, immediate, echoless, explosive CRACK! followed by a hurricane of shrapnel, dirt, stones, tree limbs, loose equipment. Small limbs hit Cameron's head and shoulders, the explosion pushed him into the ground, and he couldn't see. His first thought was, *God, stop them before they fire again!* He knew it had been one of their own rounds. There was no question in his mind whatsoever. "CEASE FIRE!" he shouted to the radio operators. "CEASE FIRE!"

Cameron could hear Rocamora shouting over the artillery radio, and he yelled at Rocamora, "TELL THEM NOT TO FIRE AGAIN!"

Cameron heard people running, could smell the cordite in the air. His eyes began to clear, and he was able to see wisps of smoke in the trees and dust drifting down to the ground.

Aikins heard Cameron and Rocamora shouting and then silence. He didn't feel any pain, but he was dazed and unsure of what had happened, Instinctively he put his hands up to his face and brought them back down to look for blood. His head hurt, but he could not see any blood. He shook his head to clear it.

Samuels, too, had been dazed by the explosion. He felt it had happened directly overhead. Specialist Fourth Class Rodriguez ran by shouting, "Prince! Grab your rifle! We're being overrun!" Samuels sat up, reached for his rifle and instantly knew something was wrong. His hand, brushing his leg to grasp his rifle had come up wet, covered with blood. There was blood all over his fatigue pants, but he couldn't feel any pain. He couldn't feel a thing! Cautiously, Samuels looked down and saw that his left leg was flipped crazily to one side midway down from the knee. There was no way his leg could be lying like that and still be . . . and still be attached! Rodriguez, too, had stopped suddenly, turned back in midstride to stare in horror at the Prince's leg. And Samuels, seeing confirmed in Rodriguez' expression

412

what he himself had dared not believe, let out a high, keening, animal cry of terrible bewilderment and pain.

"Get the medic over here!" Rodriguez shouted. "Get a medic to the Prince!"

Someone else was yelling, "A light! I need a light! Get me a light!"

The Prince was screaming, "Doc! DOC! Oh, God, help me, DOC!" Aikins, who had had to run back to the sleeping area for his medical kit, was hurrying back. Cameron's senior radio operator was calling Schwarzkopf, "Black Smoke One, Black Smoke One? This is Black Smoke Six. Do you read me?"

"This is Black Smoke One," Schwarzkopf answered.

"This is Black Smoke Six. We need an immediate dust-off. An urgent dust-off."

Schwarzkopf had monitored Charlie Company's call for a cease-fire, but he had no means of knowing how bad things were. "Are you sure you need a dust-off? Let me talk to your company commander." It was pitch-black. Foggy. Schwarzkopf knew how difficult it would be for the med-evac helicopter to find them.

Cameron took the hand mike from the radio operator, "Black Smoke One? This is Black Smoke Six. We took a short round. We need an immediate dust-off. We may even need a jungle penetrator. I don't know yet."

The jungle penetrator is a basket device lowered by winch from a helicopter hovering overhead. The helicopter must hold its position and guide the basket through the openings in the jungle canopy. The procedure is dangerous and difficult and utilized only when absolutely necessary. Cameron had mentioned the jungle penetrator because he could not yet determine whether or not he would be able to get a landing zone with enough clearance for the medical evacuation helicopter to put down.

When the shell hit, Culpepper found himself lying on the ground clutching his rifle. He did not even remember how he got there. "Jesus, Schumacher! What was that?"

"An arty round!"

413

"What?"

"Those stupid sons of bitches!" Schumacher yelled. "They're supposed to be shooting out there, but they're shooting at us! If we'd given ourselves as a target, they couldn't have done any better."

Polk didn't know what had happened either. He had heard and felt the shell explode, awoke to find Cactus screaming to his left, the scream a thin, metallic ringing in Polk's ears. He saw blood on Cactus' face, felt the terror hot, like fire, surge from his stomach to his chest. Polk sat up, patted his body searching for blood, then rolled toward Michael Mullen, asking "Mulligan? Mulligan, you all right?"

Michael didn't move. Polk heard only the hiss of escaping air.

"MULLIGAN!" Polk wailed, the panic rising heavier, hotter, higher through him. He saw the blood, heard the screaming and jerked himself like a puppet to his feet. Polk, babbling in terror, ran past the new 1st Platoon sergeant, Wetsel, and saw that he, too, was wounded. Polk didn't stop. He ran over the lip of his foxhole, fell to his knees and vomited over and over and over again.

As soon as Cameron finished speaking with his battalion commander, he could hear someone else calling for a medic and some light. The young company commander grabbed his flashlight and headed for the voice. He almost tripped over Staff Sergeant Wetsel. Wetsel was lying on his back, his knees tucked up to his chest, holding his bleeding left hand in his right. He was rocking back and forth moaning softly.

"Wetsel, this is Captain Cameron. Where are you hit?"

"Stomach, sir. My hand and my stomach."

"Let me take a look." Gently, Cameron pulled Wetsel's hands away from his stomach and was relieved to see his platoon sergeant had been wearing a flak vest. He must have been sleeping on his back with his hand across his abdomen when the shell hit. A piece of shrapnel had passed through his left hand and embedded itself in the flak vest. The shrapnel had not passed through, but it had punched his stomach with such force that Wetsel believed he had been hurt badly. Cameron started to break out a bandage, but was interrupted by Lieutenant Bayliss. "I'll take care of this one, sir," Bayliss said.

Bayliss, the mortar platoon leader, had been trained as a medic before going through Officers Candidate School.

"Fine, Bayliss," Cameron said and straightened up. He could hear Samuels screaming, and never in his life had Cameron ever heard anyone cry out like that before.

Abe Aikins was leaning over Samuels. The Prince's face had turned a ghostly white; his lips were curled back with pain. The moment Aikins had seen the Prince he recognized he would be dealing with a traumatic amputation. The whole lower part of Samuels' left leg was out to one side and connected to the rest of his leg by only a few nerves and muscle. Aikins wasn't prepared for a traumatic amputation, he wasn't sure he could cope with something like that. He desperately tried to recall what he'd been taught about traumatic amputations at the medics' school. He knew he would have to clamp the leg, put a tourniquet on it, straighten the leg and tape and bandage it in place. He also knew how painful that would be for the Prince, who was already in unbearable pain.

Typical of a traumatic amputation, Samuels' leg practically bled not at all. The hot shrapnel had "cauterized" the wound, and the shock had made the veins retract. Aikins filled a syringe with morphine. He knelt down and began to talk gently to the Prince, tried to soothe him, explain what he would have to do. At the same time he was thinking that the doctors would have to operate and did not like to do so if the man was under morphine. Aikins knew if he gave the Prince the shot now, it wouldn't take hold for another half hour or forty-five minutes. The dust-off helicopter would have evacuated the Prince and had him in the hospital by then. But Samuels was in such pain; he was screaming so terribly. Aikins gave him the shot.

The men over in the 3rd Platoon's area still did not know what had happened. Sergeant Webb had run through, pushing the men into their foxholes. They had remained still for a while, but now they wanted to know what had happened. Culpepper, cradling his M-16 in his arms, had crawled to the machine-gun pit and dropped down inside.

"Be quiet!" the men were told. "Hold it down!"

Culpepper heard for the first time the strange noise and did not know what it was. It wasn't screaming, exactly. It sounded more like a laugh. A very high-pitched laugh, and he asked, "What's going on?"

No one answered. They were all hearing it, too. It wasn't a scream of pain—at least, it didn't sound like any scream of pain anyone had ever heard. It was too high. Like a horror movie, Culpepper thought, except worse. He wondered whether somebody was kidding around. Perhaps the shell had hit so close the men in the 1st Platoon were making jokes. But the laugh suddenly changed pitch, and Culpepper, able now to identify the different sounds, could hear the men calling for medics, the groans of the wounded, and even before their 3rd Platoon's leader came to tell them, knew that the company had been hit and men hurt bad.

Aikins was kneeling on either side of the Prince's leg. The 1st Platoon's medic ran up. He had been directly under the shell and dazed, too. Each platoon had its own medic. Aikins was the medic for the headquarters section, and counting Lieutenant Bayliss, Charlie Company had five trained medics in all. "I'll work on the Prince," Aikins told the 1st Platoon medic. "You go check on the others, and when you're through, come on back."

Captain Cameron was relieved to see that his men had responded properly as soon as the shell hit. The platoon leaders and platoon sergeants had seen that the men had taken cover in their foxholes. The only people in the open, other than the medics, were the young lieutenants who were moving among their men, calming them down, assuring them it wasn't an attack, that they had taken a short round and the artillery had ceased firing. Cameron moved to Samuels to see if he could help.

Cameron hated seeing the Prince wounded. It could be pouring down rain, the company had not received any hot meals or mail for three or four days, Samuels would have been assigned some dirty detail, and still he would smile and tell Cameron, "Fetch my chariot! The Prince must be off!" When a company had someone who could make light of the worst in Vietnam, Cameron believed that man worth his weight in gold. Cameron knelt beside Samuels and spoke to him, tried to comfort him. Aikins said, "Goddamn it, hold him down!"

Samuels was trying to push himself up to see his leg, and Aikins didn't want him to look. He had not known it was Captain Cameron who had knelt beside him. Cameron took Samuels' shoulders and gently eased him back.

Aikins couldn't tell whether the blackness of Samuels' leg was dirt, dried blood or burn. He had clamped the upper thigh, and there was nothing left to do but straighten out the leg. Slowly, carefully, the medic slid his fingers underneath the Prince's calf and gently moved the leg forward.

Samuels screamed again.

"I know it hurts, Prince," Aikins said. "It can't be helped. Don't you worry. You'll be all right. I've just got to straighten out your leg. It's almost there . . . just a little more. . . . *There!*" Aikins reached inside his bag for some tape.

"Anything I can do, Doc?" Kleeman asked. He was one of Samuels' friends from the 1st Platoon.

"Yeah, Kleeman, good," Aikins said. "You hold the tourniquet, and keep it tight."

"Right," Kleeman said, "Howya doing, Prince?" he asked, giving the tourniquet a twist.

Samuels howled with pain, "Goddamn you, Kleeman! Not so tight!"

"Got to," Kleeman said. "The Prince must not bleed."

Samuels' head fell back. He felt himself slipping into shock and, opening his eyes to fight it, found himself focusing on the 1st Platoon medic working on Leroy Hamilton less than a foot away. *"Hamilton?"* the Prince whispered.

"Don't worry about him," Cameron said. "I'm going to see how he is, myself." As Cameron rose, his place was taken by Chaplain Duigood.

Cameron came to Specialist Fourth Class Ivy, the 1st Platoon leader's radio operator. Ivy had suffered a massive wound in his back and lesser wounds on each hip. A medic had already stripped Ivy down and rolled him over onto his stomach. "Ivy," Cameron asked, "are you all right?"

"Yes, sir," Ivy said. "I'm okay."

Cameron looked at him in disbelief. The hole in Ivy's back was large enough for Cameron to have pushed his fist through. Ivy's rib cage showed, a portion of his spine and intestine had been bared, and yet Ivy was absolutely coherent. He wasn't moaning, crying at all. "I'll be all right, sir," Ivy said, twisting slightly to see the captain's face. "You go ahead, and take care of everybody else."

Leroy Hamilton had suffered the worst wound of all. He had been torn open from his left armpit down to his hip. He was alive, but unconscious, and a medic was trying hard to bring him around. The shell must have exploded just behind Hamilton. The impact had blown him out of the foxhole and left his legs completely untouched. As the medic attempted to cover Hamilton's wound with a dressing, part of his intestine spilled out onto the ground.

Samuels was asking Aikins how bad his wound was. "Will I be able to walk?"

"Sure, Prince. You'll be okay," Aikins said. "I won't kid you, it's bad. But you'll be able to walk again." Aikins knew Samuels would lose his leg, but he lied to prevent him from going into shock.

418

Samuels was biting his lip to keep from screaming while Aikins taped his leg. "There's just one more thing, Doc," he said.

"Yeah? What's that?" Aikins had done everything he could for Samuels, and he straightened up.

"Will I be able to waltz?"

"Waltz?" Aikins laughed. "Sure, Prince, you'll be up and around in time for the coronation ball."

"Hey, Doc?"

Aikins felt a hand on his shoulder and looked up. Captain Cameron was leaning over him. "You'd better take a look at Leroy Hamilton. He's hurt real bad."

Samuels twisted to look. The medics were still hard at work on Hamilton, and the awfulness of Hamilton's wound and the realization that if the shell had hit five minutes earlier instead of Hamilton in the foxhole it would have been himself combined to cause Samuels such terrible anguish and grief that he had to look away.

Hamilton was now on his back. His eyes were open, but when Aikins touched his arm, he felt that Hamilton's body was already cold. Aikins didn't understand how that could happen so fast. Shock? Loss of blood?

"Abe," the 1st Platoon medic was saying, "I think I'm still getting a slight pulse."

Aikins moved his fingertips to Leroy Hamilton's neck. He tried to find a pulse, too. If there was one, it was too faint for Aikins to detect. "Well, try mouth-to-mouth on him again," Aikins told the medic. He didn't think there was much that anyone could do. As the medic tried breathing air into Hamilton's lungs, Aikins placed more bandages on the wound. But the wound was so huge, he didn't see how Hamilton could survive. "Keep working on him," Aikins said. "Maybe you can bring him around."

"Doc," someone else said. "Mullen's been hurt, too."

At first no one had known about Michael. Only Polk had realized Michael had been wounded, but Polk had been too sick to talk. The others had thought Mi-

chael was sleeping since he hadn't moved. Aikins
grabbed his flashlight and hurried over to Michael Mullen's sleeping position. Another medic had already
pulled up Michael's shirt to expose the wound. Aikins
could see where a tiny crescent-shaped piece of shrapnel had cut through Michael's back and entered his
heart. His body was still warm, and Aikins wasn't sure,
but in the dim glow of his flashlight, it appeared Michael might still be breathing. He laid a clean dressing
across Michael's wound and rolled him over onto his
back. There was no exit wound, and Aikins tried giving
Michael mouth-to-mouth resuscitation. He kept working over Michael for a few minutes, then straightened
up and felt for a pulse. There was none.

Aikins applied mouth-to-mouth resuscitation
again and kept at it. Michael wouldn't breathe, and
Aikins still couldn't find any pulse. He saw that the 1st
Platoon medic was still working on Hamilton, heard
the medic tell Captain Cameron, "I don't think he's
going to make it. I'm not getting a pulse anymore."

"Keep working on him," Cameron said. "He's
strong, and he's young."

It was no use. Samuels, eight inches away from
Hamilton's boots, flinched when the medic covered
Hamilton's body with a tarp. "Aw, for chrissake." Samuels sighed. "Poor Hamilton. He was such a nice,
straightforward guy, you know?"

"I know, Prince," Kleeman said.

"I mean, Jesus, what did he ever do to deserve
that garbage, huh? What did he do to deserve getting
killed?"

"Take it easy, Prince," Kleeman said. "Don't you
worry yourself about Hamilton now."

Samuels grimaced. "These goddamn leeches are
gonna eat good tonight."

Aikins saw the medic cover Hamilton's body and
knew that Michael Mullen, too, was dead. There was
nothing more he could do but see who else had been
hurt. He crossed to where the medics were working on
Ivy.

"Hello, Doc." Ivy smiled up at him. Ivy was still on his stomach and had had to raise himself slightly to see Aikins' face.

"You're looking good," Aikins said. "You're gonna be all right."

"I know that," Ivy said. "How are the rest?"

Aikins shook his head, "We got some hurt pretty bad." He patted Ivy's shoulder. "You take it easy, okay? I'm going to check the others."

"Sure, Doc," Ivy said. "Don't worry about me."

Aikins looked at Ivy for a moment. "You're a good man, Ivy. Take care." He started away and passed Captain Cameron, who was moving toward Mullen. Aikins grabbed the captain's shoulder and held him back. "Sir, Mullen is dead."

"Oh, son of a bitch!" Cameron swore. He crossed to Michael anyway and shone his flashlight down. Michael looked so peaceful, so untouched, Cameron couldn't believe he was dead. He knelt and felt Michael's chest, then slapped him to get a reflex, a flinch, a response of any kind. He was going to slap Michael again when someone took his arm. "We already tried that on him, sir," a medic said. "It's no use. Sergeant Mullen is dead."

"Okay," Cameron said softly, sadly. "You'd better cover him up."

Michael Mullen and Leroy Hamilton were the first men Captain Cameron had seen killed since he had been out in the field. It disgusted him that they had had to die in such a way—that they had died at all, but particularly the manner of the deaths struck him as such a terrible waste. They had been such good men. Cameron glanced at his wristwatch and, astonished, took a long look at it again. Only fifteen minutes had passed since the shell had hit. Because of the killed and wounded, there were now gaps in his company's defensive perimeter. He sent for Lieutenant Steven Boeri, the 3rd Platoon's platoon leader, and told him to take a squad and secure the 1st Platoon's portion where the men had been hit. He next told Lieutenant David Miller

421

of the 2nd Platoon, "I need to secure a LZ for the med-evac. Get some people down on the other side of the clearing, and see what you can find."

"Right, sir," Miller said and started off.

"MacPhearson?" Cameron called.

"Here, sir," the 2nd Platoon's platoon sergeant said.

"Mac, get me a litter detail, will you? Take some men from your platoon and the Third Platoon. We'll need to move the wounded down to the pickup zone." Cameron returned to the radio again. "Black Smoke One? This is Black Smoke Six. . . ."

Culpepper knew that two men had been killed, but not until MacPhearson picked him for a litter detail did he learn that Michael Mullen had been one of them. Culpepper felt himself sink. Never before had he felt so totally depressed so fast. Michael had always been such a calm person, so quiet. Nothing had ever seemed to rattle him. That's what seemed so utterly strange to Culpepper: Michael had been so normal. How could he now be dead?

Lieutenant Colonel Schwarzkopf was clearly upset. He told Cameron not to leave the radio again. Schwarzkopf needed to know what was going on. "Are you sure you need a jungle penetrator? You know they're risky even in the daylight."

"Sir," Cameron answered, "the only thing I can tell you is that two of my people have bought the farm, and if I don't get it, two more will."

"Okay," Schwarzkopf said. "That's what I needed to know."

"How long before we get the dust-off? We—wait one," Cameron said. Lieutenant Miller had returned from the clearing and was saying, "Sir, we've got you an LZ."

"Are you sure?" Cameron asked.

"Yes, sir," Miller insisted. "All we've got to do is chop down one or two trees."

Cameron clapped the young lieutenant on the

back. "Good enough! Get some men with axes and machetes and get to it." He picked up the handmike again, "Black Smoke One? This is Black Smoke Six. Send the dust-off. We can bring him in close enough to the ground to get everybody on board. I repeat, send the dust-off. We have an LZ."

"This is Black Smoke One," Schwarzkopf said. "Good work. Dust-off's on the way. Stay in touch."

"Roger, this is Black Smoke Six. Out." Cameron handed the microphone to the radio operator. "Stay with me," he told him. "We'll go down to check the LZ."

Aikins caught up with Cameron and reported on the wounded. Samuels and Ivy would need litters. So would Sergeant Gonzales, who had been wounded in the foot and arm. Staff Sergeant Wetsel could walk, but the shrapnel wound in his hand necessitated his being evacuated. Cactus, who had been sleeping next to Polk, was more sick and scared than hurt. He had been hit in the brow by a rock and said it impaired his vision. "So, you might as well let Cactus go, too," Aikins said.

"Samuels, Ivy, Gonzales, Wetsel and Cactus. Five," Cameron counted. "Is that all?"

"I think you ought to take a look at Lieutenant Joslin, too."

"Joslin?" Cameron asked, surprised. "Was he hurt, too?"

"He was right under the blast and was pretty shaken up," Aikins said. "I think he was hit hard by a rock or a tree limb. He's sitting over there by that tree."

Cameron shone the light in his young 1st Platoon leader's face. Joslin's features were black with dirt.

"How do you feel?" Cameron asked him.

"I'm okay," Joslin said, wincing at the bright light.

"You sure? The medic says you got hit pretty hard."

"No, I'm all right. I only got a lot of dirt in my eyes."

"I can have you med-evac'd out," Cameron said.

"No, please. Don't do that, sir," Joslin said. "I'm fine. I don't want to go."

"Are your eyes still bothering you?"

"I just feel a little dizzy still. A little sick to my stomach from the concussion. It'll pass, sir."

Cameron looked at Joslin closely. "It's a helluva thing to have happen your first night in the field."

"They were good men," Joslin said. "I wish I'd had time to know them better."

Aikins was helping to load Samuels onto a litter made by threading two six-poles through some ponchos. The morphine had barely started to take hold, so any movement caused Samuels excruciating pain.

"Try to relax and lie still," Aikins told him. "We'll slide this litter under you and get you out of here."

"Doc," Samuels said, "are you sure I'm going to walk again?"

"Yeah, man, no problem. . . . Okay," Aikins said, turning away from the Prince, "I need someone to hold his leg steady."

"I'll do it," Kleeman said.

"*You*, Kleeman?" Samuels groaned. "For chrissake, don't you do it! You won't take two steps without tripping!"

"Yeah, well, Prince," Kleeman said, "there are trips and then there are 'trips,' you know?"

"I know. And this one's a real bummer."

Willard Polk had pulled himself together and was standing beside Samuels when they slid him on the litter. "Polk," Aikins said, "you take that end by his head." The medic stationed one man at each corner of the litter, then reconsidered and told Polk, "You'd better give Gonzales a hand. They need another man on that litter there."

"I can carry the Prince," Polk insisted.

"I don't want to risk having you fall," Aikins said.

Polk shrugged and looked down at Samuels. "Don't sweat it none, man, you dig? You're gonna be *all* right."

424

Aikins had removed his belt and was using it to strap Samuels to his litter. "Doc, hey, I'm really serious now," Samuels said. "Please, please don't let them cut my leg off."

Polk answered instead. "Man, there ain't *nothing* wrong with your leg!"

"Go on, Polk," Aikins said, "give them a hand with Gonzales."

"Just trying to help," Polk said.

A man was stationed at each end of Samuels' litter poles, and Kleeman was by his leg. "Okay now," Aikins said, "when I count to three, lift together. Don't jerk. Just lift him slow and easy. . . . You all set, Prince?"

Samuels, looking at Leroy Hamilton's tarp-covered body next to him, gritted his teeth and nodded yes.

"One," Aikins counted, "two . . . *three*—not too fast, take your time. Kleeman, keep that leg in tight." The poncho was not long enough to support Samuels' entire body; Kleeman was needed to keep Samuels' wounded leg from dropping. They gently began to move across the perimeter through the brush toward the clearing. "Keep it easy," Aikins warned. "The more you move around, the more pain the Prince will be in."

Willard Polk on one end of Sergeant Gonzales' litter, heard the sergeant, halfway to the clearing mutter, "Fuck it! I'd rather walk." Gonzales got off the litter, threw one arm over Polk's shoulder, his other arm over another man's, and hopped on his good foot the rest of the way.

Captain Cameron had finished pacing off the clearing by the time Samuels and his litter bearers reached the edge. He was kneeling with his radio operator, watching two Cobra gunships circling high overhead. They were dropping flares, and as the sky lit up, the men ducked and worked their way back to the edge of the clearing. It was eerie watching the slowly descending flare. Each man realized the enemy now knew exactly where they were. The sharp, brightly burning flares, swaying gently back and forth in their parachutes, illuminated the clearing and etched the lines in the men's upturned faces. The moment one flare would start to fade, a fresh one would pop.

"Black Smoke One? This is Black Smoke Six," Cameron was saying into the radio. "We have flareships, but where in God's name is the med-evac?"

Aikins kneeled down beside his company commander in the grass. "What's the problem, sir? It shouldn't be taking this long."

"Black Smoke Six? This is Black Smoke One. . . ." Lieutenant Colonel Schwarzkopf explained that the helicopter had had a radio malfunction and had returned to Chu Lai. "They'll slide it out and slap in a new one," Schwarzkopf said. "Your med-evac will be airborne again in a few minutes."

"Roger, Black Smoke One. I hope to God he hurries." Cameron handed the microphone back to his radio operator and turned to his senior medic. "Stick with the Prince, Abe. Tell him dust-off will be here soon."

Cameron then positioned four men with red-lens flashlights at each corner of the landing zone and placed Lieutenant Bayliss with the pocket strobe in the center of the clearing to mark where he wanted the helicopter to put down. "Don't turn that thing on until I tell you," Cameron said. Bayliss waved to show he had heard.

Aikins, again with Samuels, saw that the Prince wasn't joking anymore. Chaplain Duigood was squatting beside the litter, and the morphine was at last taking hold. Aikins drew a big *M* with his grease pencil on Samuels' forehead. The *M* for "morphine" was there so the doctors back at the hospital would know what the wounded men had been given. In the harsh light of the flares the *M* looked the color of fresh blood.

"Where's the dust-off?" Samuels asked.

"It's coming," Aikins said. "How do you feel?"

"It still hurts, Doc," he said. "But I'll be okay."

"You want a cigarette?"

"Sure."

As Aikins tapped one out, Polk asked for a cigarette, too. "The Prince said he was thirsty," Polk added. "Is it okay if I give him some water?"

"Water?" Kleeman scoffed. "The Prince drinks only wine."

"This Prince would settle for a beer," Samuels said.

"We could all use one," Chaplain Duigood agreed.

Aikins checked on Ivy, who was lying facedown in his litter. He would try to roll over and sit up and Schumacher and Culpepper would press Ivy back down. Ivy was moaning slightly, his head to one side. Culpepper, seeing Ivy's eyes becoming opaque and unfocused, was sure he was dying. Culpepper turned to Abe Aikins, who was marking an *M* on Ivy's forehead, "Doc," he whispered, "Can't you do something? Look at his eyes."

"That's the morphine," Aikins answered. "That and shock. . . . How you doing, Ivy?"

Ivy tried to speak, but nothing intelligible came out.

"Keep talking to him, Pep," Aikins told Culpepper. "Make Ivy listen to you. He's going to be all right."

"Sure, Doc," Culpepper said, not believing Aikins at all. "Where the hell's that med-evac? They always tells us, 'You guys get wounded, you'll be outta there in fifteen minutes.' It's been three-quarters of an hour since the shell hit!"

"It'll be here any second," Aikins said. "Just keep talking to Ivy. Stick with him. I've got to see about the Prince again."

Russell Schumacher leaned back on his elbows and stared up at the circling Cobras. "What are they doing up there? They going to wait until everybody dies?"

"Those are gunships," Culpepper said. Ivy's eyes cleared for a moment, and Culpepper recognized his look; it meant, "Am I going to die?"

"You're going to be fine, Ivy," Culpepper said, but he still didn't believe it. Culpepper felt so empty, so lonely and useless. He wanted to help Ivy, was trying to help him, but there was absolutely nothing

427

he could do. He patted Ivy's shoulder. "Just hang on. Dust-off will be here any second."

Cameron had made radio contact with the Cobra gunships, and from them he learned the medical evacuation helicopter was at last inbound.

"Bayliss! Make sure that as soon as dust-off gets close you turn off that strobe light or you'll blind the pilot."

"Right, sir," Bayliss called back. "Shall I turn it on now?"

"Turn it on!"

The gunships were still dropping flares. Every now and then they would call down to Cameron to ask if he had had any enemy contact. Cameron would answer, "Not yet." Lieutenant Bayliss, in the middle of the cleared landing zone, turned on the strobe. The light began to pulse, shooting an intense beam visible for miles. Cameron soon heard the dust-off approaching. Its engine made a different sound from the gunships; the med-evac noise was more a piston beat than turbine, and there was something strange about its pitch.

"He's really beating the air!" Cameron's radio operator said.

"Yeah," Cameron said, realizing why the engine's pitch had seemed odd. "He must be coming in at max speed." He had given the med-evac a vector off Hill 410, a compass direction to follow. He knew the med-evac would be familiar with Hill 410; they were out there every day flying around. The men with the red-lensed flashlights were properly stationed at the corners of the LZ; Bayliss was holding the strobe light up as high as he could. Cameron believed the med-evac might even be able to see the strobe from 410. He took the hand mike from the radio operator and began talking to the med-evac, telling the pilot where Charlie Company was, what the LZ was like, and waited for confirmation. There was no response.

"For chrissake! Dust-off doesn't answer!" Cameron swore. He called the Cobra gunships. "I can't talk to dust-off."

There was an electronic crackle; then the pilot of

428

one of the gunships identified himself and explained that the med-evac's UHF radio had malfunctioned again. The helicopters could talk to each other over VHF, but the dust-off couldn't talk to the ground. "Tell me the details," the Cobra pilot said. "I can relay."

"Roger," Cameron replied. "I have four corners marked with red lights, strobe marks my center. I've got five packs: three ambulatory, two litter." Cameron was still describing the LZ when the medical evacuation helicopter came screaming in, low and fast. Bayliss wasn't able to extinguish the strobe, and the helicopter suddenly banked sharply, dropped down over the side of the hill and disappeared.

"Oh my GOD!" Cameron said and waited for the crash.

"I can't get the strobe off!" Lieutenant Bayliss shouted. He was shaking it and banging it against his palm.

"Put the goddamn thing in your pocket!"

The helicopter shot up in the air on the other side of the hill and swung back around to the LZ. Cameron positioned himself in the center of the LZ and held his arms out horizontally to show the pilot he would be the one to guide him down.

The pilot headed directly toward Cameron, then hovered while Cameron, waist-high in the tall grass, slowly lowered his arms to put the helicopter on the ground. The instant the skids settled, the litter detail hurried forward, and the pilot motioned Cameron closer.

"How many you got?" the pilot asked.

Cameron was surprised to see the pilot was an Oriental. "I've got five," he said. "And listen, tell the doctors two of the men have been given morphine."

"Right," the pilot acknowledged. "Let me know when everyone's on board."

Cameron walked around to the side. Samuels had been loaded headfirst, the litter pushed as far back as possible to make certain his leg was completely inside. "Well, Prince," Polk said, "at least you're getting out of here." Samuels nodded and gave a little wave.

Ivy's litter was loaded next. Culpepper helped

Schumacher push the litter in and stepped back. "Hey, Pep," Schumacher said. He was pointing at the nickname painted on the helicopter's nose. "Did you notice what it's called?" The nickname was Tired Angel.

Sergeant Gonzales was helped inside the helicopter; Cactus and Staff Sergeant Wetsel were able to board by themselves. Cameron checked with Abe Aikins. "Is that everybody?"

"Everybody who's going," Aikins replied.

Cameron went to the pilot's side and held his thumbs up. The helicopter jumped up into the air, fell off to one side down the hill, picked up momentum and was gone. As soon as the helicopter disappeared, Cameron returned to his radio to report that the medical evacuation was completed. The Cobra gunship pilot called back to ask if he needed anything else. "No," Cameron told him. "I appreciate what you've done."

"Uh-roger," the gunship pilot acknowledged, and before the last flare had sputtered out, the Cobra gunships, too, were gone.

The litter details and the other men at the clearing slowly made their way through the jungle back to their night defensive position. They moved wearily, heads down, depressed. No one felt like talking.

Captain Cameron gathered his platoon leaders around him to reorganize his defenses and to make certain his rifle company was secure for the night. Lieutenant Joslin was still shaky, so Cameron told him he would set up the 1st Platoon's defense for him but wanted Joslin to come along.

Cameron appointed the 1st Platoon's single remaining sergeant platoon sergeant. He next repositioned some of the 1st Platoon's men and shifted three men from the 3rd Platoon to cover the positions previously occupied by Hamilton, Ivy and Michael Mullen. Leroy Hamilton's foxhole had been so flooded by blood the men shied from going in it. Cameron had the men dig a fresh foxhole nearby.

Culpepper and Schumacher sat on the lip of their foxhole. For a long time they did not speak; then

Schumacher sighed, saying, "What a way to die, you know? You go through all this and then you turn around and your own men kill you. . . ." He shook his head bitterly.

"A guy gets killed by rifle fire or an ambush, you expect that," Culpepper said. "But by your own artillery?"

Schumacher picked up a clod of dirt and tossed it over the edge of the cliff.

"It isn't the way we're supposed to die," Culpepper said.

Willard Polk came over and dropped to the ground beside them. "Man, I was sleeping right between them!" he said.

Culpepper looked at him coldly.

"I heard a big noise," Polk was saying, "I woke up, and all Mullen did was sigh one time, 'ahh-h-h-h' . . . but Hamilton? He didn't die that quick. He died a little hard. He made a lot of noise before he died."

Culpepper noticed that Polk's hands were shaking badly.

"Man, I don't know how it happened," Polk continued. "I was sleeping right dead between them, and I didn't even get hurt!"

Culpepper rolled back a little to look Polk in the face. "It's just God's will," he said. "Leave it at that."

"I'll tell you one thing," Polk said. "After I helped load Prince in the helicopter, the only thing in the world I wanted to do was get in there with him. Get on that bird, get out of here and be gone!"

Schumacher finally spoke: "It's no different for the rest of us, Polk. We're here just like you. The only difference is we've been here longer, and you'll still be here when we're gone."

"Hey, Pep," Polk said, looking first at Schumacher and then at Culpepper. "Who's your honky frien'?" He got up and went to find someone more sympathetic to be with.

Captain Cameron walked among the survivors from the 1st Platoon speaking gently and quietly with each of the men. When he was satisfied they all were all right, he moved to the 2nd Platoon and asked Sergeant MacPhearson to have some people from his platoon take care of Hamilton and Mullen.

MacPhearson chose three men and had them gather ponchos. MacPhearson had them wrap Leroy Hamilton's and Michael Mullen's bodies carefully and moved them up to the CP area. MacPhearson made certain that the ponchos were neat, that the bodies were wrapped tightly and were well covered. They were left there for the night.

Cameron found Aikins sitting on the side of his foxhole with his head lowered. He thought Aikins was probably upset, but asked, "What's wrong?"

"I'm a little sick."

"How? In what way?"

Aikins held up his right hand; it was covered with blood. "I took a piece of shrapnel," Aikins explained.

"Why in the hell didn't you say something about it before?" Cameron asked. "I could have had you evac'd out!"

"More important things needed to be done."

"I'll get you out first thing in the morning. Is it bothering you enough to take a shot of morphine?"

"Naw," Aikins said. "Anyway, we don't have any morphine left. I'm all right, sir. I'm just going to sit up here for a while. You get some rest."

Cameron nodded and went back to his radio. He and Lieutenant Colonel Schwarzkopf spoke for a while, and the battalion commander said, "I'll have a chopper out there at first light to get your killed-in-actions out."

Cameron returned to his sleeping position and sat down. He was suddenly terribly thirsty. He drank and drank and drank, then lay back and attempted to get some sleep.

Abe Aikins remained sitting. He was trying to calm himself down, mindful of the two dead men close by. The instant the dust-off had lifted Aikins had felt his first rush of panic. Ever since the shell had exploded Aikins had operated on spontaneous, instinctive reaction. Only when the wounded had been evacuated did he suddenly realize how close he himself had come to being killed.

Willard Polk was too nervous to sleep. He was speaking with Razzle-Dazzle, a black in the 3rd Platoon. Razzle had just said that Lieutenant Rocamora had been the man who had called in the shot.

"He called it in?" Polk said. "I'm gonna kill that mother. I'm gonna lay my M-79 upside his head!"

Razzle smiled lazily. "Aw, no, you ain't."

The next morning, a little after seven o'clock, the sun had risen hot enough to burn off the morning fog. A light utility helicopter from the 176th Aviation Company, the unit which normally flew resupply and utility missions for Schwarzkopf's battalion, approached Charlie Company's hilltop clearing and set down on the LZ. Michael Mullen's and Leroy Hamilton's bodies were gently loaded on board, their rucksacks and equipment slid in next to them. Aikins had awakened with his finger too swollen to move, and at Cameron's insistence, he, too, was placed in the helicopter to have the wound looked after at the rear. No supplies were brought in this trip; only Aikins and the dead men were taken out. The 176th Aviation Company's resupply and utility missions were known as Hash & Trash.

A few moments after that helicopter departed, Lieutenant Colonel Schwarzkopf, Lieutenant Colonel Valentin Kuprin, the artillery battalion commander, and Colonel Joseph Clemons, the brigade commander, landed at Charlie Company's position. Clemons asked to see the company's defensive perimeter. The men had filled in their foxholes in preparation for moving out and were standing on the hilltop with their gear packed, awaiting orders. Schwarzkopf told Cameron his company was to remain on the hill a second night. The artillery investigators would be coming soon and would need time to complete their survey.

Following his tour of Charlie Company's position, Colonel Clemons asked Cameron to report on what had happened the night before. Cameron told his brigade commander that Charlie Company had taken a short round. The shell had exploded in a tree directly above the 1st Platoon. "Two men were killed and six wounded," Cameron said and explained the sort of wounds received. Colonel Clemons next asked the forward observer, Lieutenant Rocamora, a few questions, then announced he had seen what he had come to see. Schwarzkopf, Clemons and Kuprin climbed back into their helicopter and left.

The artillery investigators landed next. They surveyed Charlie Company's position, measured the trees, searched for pieces of shrapnel, asked a lot of questions and took a lot of notes.

The men of Charlie Company watched the investigators warily. When one of the artillerymen asked, "Are you sure it wasn't the VC shooting at you? That it wasn't a VC mortar?" a man in Charlie Company answered, "It wasn't no mortar."

"Are you *sure?*"

"You fuckin' well know what it was!" the enlisted man answered. "You know goddamn well who fired it and where it hit!"

"All right, take it easy," the man's platoon leader said. "They're only trying to do their job."

"We have to look at all the possibilities," the investigating officer explained. "Maybe it wasn't an error. It might have been the enemy."

Everyone in Charlie Company knew it had been their own gun.

That same morning, in the middle of the operation on his leg, Samuels awoke from the anesthetic and asked, "Is it off yet?"

He was put back to sleep.

On February 20, two days after the shell had hit, Samuels awoke to discover Lieutenant Colonel Schwarzkopf standing beside his bed. Schwarzkopf explained he had been able to put a telephone call through to Samuels' mother in Caldwell, New Jersey,

434

and he would be able to speak with her soon. Thirty minutes later Samuels was on the phone with his mother. He told her that he was all right and that he was going to Japan. He did not tell her his leg had been amputated. She later received a telegram from the Army to that effect.

On February 23 Charlie Company was walking back out of the mountains toward their bunker line. No trace had been found of any North Vietnamese rocket battalion command, nor had Charlie Company made any contact with the enemy. Their secondary mission was now to search out rocket caches. Late that morning the men were hot and tired and were given a chance to bathe, cool off and rest at a stream. When they started to move out again, Willard Polk slipped and accidently discharged his M-79 grenade launcher. There was a hollow *toop!* as the round was fired. "GRENADE!" Cameron shouted, and the men hit the ground. Fortunately the grenade exploded out of range, but a sergeant in the mortar platoon dislocated his shoulder diving for cover and had to be med-evac'd out.

On February 24, when Polk became mired down in some mud and two men taunted and laughed at him, he loaded his M-79 and aimed it at them. Twice Polk disobeyed his platoon leader's direct order to put his weapon down. The third time Polk reluctantly handed Lieutenant Joslin the M-79.

On February 25, when the 1st Platoon's medic accused Polk of shamming an injury to his foot, Polk slugged him. He then pointed his M-79 at the medic, who said, "You'd better plan on using it." Polk was disarmed by his squad leader, but not until they, too, had exchanged blows.

On February 26, when Charlie Company returned to Hill 76, the mortar platoon fire base, Polk fired first an M-16 rifle at some Vietnamese civilians working in a rice paddy and then his grenade launcher. Polk again struck his squad leader, who was attempting to disarm him, and later punched Lieutenant Roderick Bayliss, the black platoon leader of the mortar platoon.

On February 28, 1970, charges were brought against Polk, and he was placed in confinement at Bayonet. Two weeks later he was moved to an Army stockade, and a month after that he was confined at the III Marine Amphibious Force Brig (IIIMAF) at Danang. He remained there until his trial on May 29.

When I spoke with Willard Polk at the federal penitentiary at Terre Haute, I asked why he had fired on the Vietnamese civilians working in the rice paddies.

"I like the Vietnamese," Polk told me. "I had nothing against them. When I went into their villages, they'd always treat me right. I wouldn't have wanted to hit them. I like them! . . . I'd like to go back there someday as a civilian."

"Then why did you do it?"

"Look," Polk said, "all I wanted was to get-*out*-of-the-field! That's why."

"You mean out of combat?" I asked.

"Combat!" Polk snorted. "I hadn't seen no combat. All I seen was guys getting *killed!*"

On March 29, 1973, the last American troops left Vietnam, formally terminating the United States' direct military involvement. The Defense Department's official casualty report for the Vietnam War lists 45,958 combat deaths and 10,303 nonhostile deaths for the period between January 1, 1961, and March 31, 1973. Of the 10,303 nonhostile deaths, 3,060 died in aircraft crashes and 1,075 in motor vehicle crashes. There were 1,172 deaths by suicide or accidental self-destruction, 1,163 homicides and 102 deaths from drug abuse. And 3,731 men, Michael Mullen among them, died of other causes.

On April 30, 1975, South Vietnam surrendered to the Communists.

A SILENT message to fathers and mothers of Iowa.

We have been dying for nine, long, miserable years in Vietnam in an undeclared war ... how many more lives do you wish to sacrifice because of your

SILENCE?

Sgt Michael E Mullen — killed by friendly fire

In memory of Vietnam War Dead whom our son joined on February 17, 1970....and to those awaiting the acceptable sacrifice in 1970...

From an advertisement in the Des Moines Register April 12, sponsored by Mr. and Mrs. Gene Mullen, La Porte City, Iowa.

*These 714 crosses represent the 714 Iowans who have died in Vietnam.

ABOUT THE AUTHOR

C.D.B. BRYAN is the author of two novels, *P.S. Wilkinson,* which won a Harper Prize for fiction, and *The Great Dethriffe.*